MADRAS, MYSORE, AND THE SOUTH OF INDIA

MADRAS, MYSORE, AND THE SOUTH OF INDIA:

OR,

A PERSONAL NARRATIVE

OF

A MISSION TO THOSE COUNTRIES:

FROM 1820 TO 1828

BY ELIJAH HOOLE.

GYAN

Published by

Gyan Publishing House
5, Ansari Road
Daryaganj, New Delhi-110002
Phone: 011-47034999, 9811692060
E-mail: books@gyanbooks.com

Distribution Network
gyanbooks.com
India, USA, Canada, UK, Australia

ISBN: 978-81-212-5699-5 (PB)
First Published, 1829

2nd Impression 2024

Printed at: Gyan Press, Delhi.

MADRAS, MYSORE, AND THE SOUTH OF INDIA
Author: ELIJAH HOOLE

Printed in Oil Colours by G. BAXTER, Patentee, 11 Northampton Square

DESTRUCTION OF THE "TANJORE" BY LIGHTNING OFF CEYLON.

MADRAS, MYSORE, AND THE SOUTH OF INDIA:

OR,

A PERSONAL NARRATIVE

OF

A MISSION TO THOSE COUNTRIES:

FROM MDCCCXX. TO MDCCCXXVIII.

BY ELIJAH HOOLE.

SECOND EDITION.

WITH ENGRAVINGS ON WOOD BY BAXTER.

MISSIONARY PREACHING IN INDIA.—*See page* 48.

LONDON:
PUBLISHED AND SOLD BY LONGMAN, BROWN, GREEN, AND LONGMANS;
SOLD ALSO BY JOHN MASON, 66, PATERNOSTER-ROW.

1844.

MADRAS, MYSORE, AND THE SOUTH OF INDIA:

OR,

A PERSONAL NARRATIVE

OF

A MISSION TO THOSE COUNTRIES:

FROM MDCCCXX. TO MDCCCXXVIII.

SECOND EDITION:

WITH

SOME ACCOUNT OF THE JESUIT MISSION IN MADURA;

BRIEF HISTORICAL NOTICES OF MADRAS, AND OTHER IMPORTANT PLACES WITHIN THE PRESENT RANGE OF THE WESLEYAN MISSIONS IN INDIA;

REMARKS ON TAMUL LITERATURE, AND ON THE RELIGION AND RELIGIOUS STATE OF THE HINDOOS;

AND A HISTORY OF THE ROMISH PERSECUTIONS OF THE NESTORIANS, OR SYRIAN CHRISTIANS OF TRAVANCORE.

BY ELIJAH HOOLE.

LONDON:
PUBLISHED AND SOLD BY LONGMAN, BROWN, GREEN, AND LONGMANS;
SOLD ALSO BY JOHN MASON, 66, PATERNOSTER-ROW.

1844.

CONTENTS.

CHAPTER I.

NOVEMBER, 1819, TO SEPTEMBER, 1820.

CHAPTER II.

SEPTEMBER 6TH, 1820.

CHAPTER III.

SEPTEMBER, 1820.

CHAPTER IV.

SEPTEMBER, 1820.

CHAPTER V.

SEPTEMBER, OCTOBER, 1820.

CHAPTER VI.

OCTOBER, 1820.

CHAPTER VII.

NOVEMBER, 1820.

CHAPTER VIII.

CHAPTER IX.

OCTOBER, 1820, TO FEBRUARY, 1821.

CHAPTER X.

MARCH, 1821.

CHAPTER XI.

APRIL, 1821.

CHAPTER XII.

APRIL, 1821.

CHAPTER XIII.

MAY, 1821, TO FEBRUARY, 1822.

CHAPTER XIV.

FEBRUARY AND MARCH, 1822.

CHAPTER XV.

APRIL TO DECEMBER, 1822.

CHAPTER XVIII.

JULY TO SEPTEMBER, 1823.

CHAPTER XIX.

SEPTEMBER, 1823, TO MARCH, 1824.

CHAPTER XX.

CHAPTER XXI.

1824.

CHAPTER XXII.

1825.

CHAPTER XXIII.

1826.

CHAPTER XXIV.

1827 AND 1828.

CHAPTER XXV.

CHAPTER XXVI.

1828.

ESSAY ON THE RELIGION AND RELIGIOUS STATE OF THE HINDOOS.

INDEX TO THE ILLUSTRATIONS.

PREFACE TO THE PERSONAL NARRATIVE

ON ITS FIRST PUBLICATION.

INDIA, by its political and commercial relations to Great Britain, has justly become the object of anxious inquiry and speculation, both as regards its own interests, and as connected with the interests of our native country.

But the solicitude with which India is viewed by the British public, in reference to its commercial and political importance, must yield, in the mind of the Christian philanthropist, to the deep feeling with which he contemplates the religious condition of so large and fair a portion of the British empire.

That there is a connexion between the political circumstances of a people and their religious interests, is as clear as is the fact that the God of providence is the God of all grace. And that India has been allotted to England in the distribution of power by Him who is the sole arbiter of human events, with the design that it might become a field as open as it is extensive for the propagation of the Gospel—cannot, for a moment, be doubted, by the enlightened and pious observer of the operations of Providence.

The design of the Narrative now offered to the public, is to afford some information on the religious state of the people of the south of India, and to illustrate the difficulties and facilities experienced by those who are labouring for their conversion to Christianity—with a view to animate the religious public to increased exertions in behalf of the Hindoos, and thus to serve the cause in which it has been the Narrator's honour to be engaged, and which, he trusts, will ever be nearest his heart. Many facts, however, are incidentally stated, which cannot fail to interest the public, by their bearing upon the commerce and policy of that highly peopled region.

The journal of the author, kept as a matter of official duty, for the purpose of transmitting to the Society at home periodical information of the progress of the Mission, and without any ulterior view, has been the source from which the Narrative has been chiefly compiled. Had he ever contemplated a work like the present, his journal might have been written with more copiousness of detail and particularity of description.

The author does not profess to give a general account of the Wesleyan Mission to Continental India; but his work will, at least, form a record of some of the earliest efforts of Wesleyan Missionaries in that country, where, it may be confidently hoped, they are destined to share largely in the spiritual conquests which Christianity must ultimately achieve over Hindoo superstition and Mahommedan delusion.

The names of several highly respected individuals resident in India, are introduced in the following pages; if necessarily without their express permission, it is hoped in a manner to which they will not feel any objection.

An observation of Govinda Moodely, the Tamul

teacher at Bangalore, affords the author the best form of an apology for the style of his composition. When pressed to learn the English language, as the best means of gratifying his thirst for general knowledge, he used to say, that he never knew a man who paid attention to many languages, excel in any of them; and he therefore preferred to perfect his acquaintance with his own, rather than attempt the acquisition of any other. It is not intended to defend the general application of this remark; but it may, perhaps, be admitted as an apology for the deficiencies of one who has passed some of the best years of his life in studying the peculiarities and idioms of foreign languages, rather than the powers and elegancies of his own.

PENDLETON, *near* MANCHESTER,
April 10*th*, 1829.

PREFACE.

In the year 1829, soon after my return from India, I took advantage of the leisure kindly afforded me by the Wesleyan Missionary Committee for the recovery of my health, to prepare and publish a "Narrative" of my Mission; in the hope that, by affording a comparatively minute detail of my journeys and labours for nearly eight years, the public at large, and especially the supporters of our Missions, might be satisfied that the Missionaries in that remote country, although encountering obstacles of a most formidable character, both physical and moral, were yet diligent and faithful in the prosecution of their work. I had the satisfaction of knowing that to some very considerable extent this object was accomplished. I soon discovered, however, that there was a wish for some general information concerning India, and especially concerning those parts of it to which the Wesleyan Missions extend, which my "Narrative" had not anticipated, and therefore was not prepared to satisfy; and that particularly those persons who were interested in modern Missions were also curious to know something of the character and success of the Missions of former times in those eastern regions. I had also observed that, as in my own case, the average duration of Missionary service in India, chiefly through the influence of the climate, was comparatively brief; and that as the information a Missionary ought to possess concerning that field of labour, and the facilities for the prosecution of his work, being scattered through many volumes, some of them rarely to be met with, he may often have been obliged to retire from India before he had gained an adequate knowledge of its history and present state. I therefore concluded it to be my duty, should opportunity be afforded me, to offer my contribution towards supplying the desired addition to our Missionary publications. In the following work, I have retained my "Personal Narrative" as first published, with many additions, and some emendations; I have given such general historical notices of some of the more important places within the present range of the Wesleyan Missions, as will suffice for those who have no leisure for the perusal of works professedly on the history of India, and which, though brief as an outline, will be easily filled up by those whose reading has been more extensive; I have endeavoured to afford to our junior Missionaries such directions as shall make it easy for them to select a suitable course of Tamul reading and study; and have compressed into a small compass such information concerning the older Romish and Protestant Missions, as appeared necessary for every Missionary, and which could not fail to be interesting to every reader.

In collecting this information I have availed myself chiefly, in Tamul, of Walther's *Historia Ecclesiastica*, of which an account will be found, pages 60—63, of Churchill's "Collection of Voyages," Lock's "Travels of the Jesuits," Thornton's "History of British India," Hough's "History of Christianity in India," and other works of minor importance.

It is with great diffidence that I submit my little

work in its present form to the Christian Church and to the public at large. Its execution might have been more perfect could I have commanded more leisure to re-compose and revise. I trust, however, that it will be received as the result of a good intention, and dealt with as leniently as the demands of just criticism will allow. There is one notice of my former publication upon which I now consider it my duty to offer some remarks.

The Rev. Dr. Wiseman, Romish Bishop of Melipotamos, in a note to the Sixth of his "Lectures on the Catholic Church," vol. i. p. 187, says, "It is evident from later writers, that little or no improvement has taken place in the Indian Mission since the date of the documents I have quoted. Consult, for instance, Hoole's 'Personal Narrative of a Tour in the South of India,' from which I could draw both negative and positive proof of the total failure of any thing like conversion among the Hindoos." The title of Dr. Wiseman's Sixth Lecture runs thus: "On the practical Success of the Protestant Rule of Faith in converting heathen Nations;" that of his Seventh Lecture is, "On the practical Success of the Catholic Rule of Faith in converting heathen Nations." The object of these Lectures is to draw a comparison between the successes of Protestant Missions and those of the Romish communion, and to establish the immense superiority of the latter, and thus to secure an important evidence in favour of the spiritual purity and power of the Romish Church.

Not to open too wide a subject for discussion in this preface, it may be sufficient for the purpose of refuting the Doctor's assertions, to remind him that the word *conversion* is perhaps used by him in a very different meaning to that attached to it by evangelical Protestants. We do not think a man *converted,* in the right sense of the word, unless he be "turned from darkness to light, from the power of Satan unto God, that he may receive inheritance among them which are sanctified by faith that is in Christ." Thus, if a man were a Heathen, a Hindoo, we should not reckon him *converted,* until he forsook idols, and began to worship the one true God; until his understanding were enlightened and informed as to the "exceeding sinfulness of sin," and his heart became the seat of true "repentance towards God;" until he had not merely received the word of God as true, but had "believed on the Lord Jesus Christ" "with the heart unto righteousness," or unto justification; and, according to God's gracious promise had received the Holy Ghost, to comfort him with the blessed assurance of God's favour, and to aid and sanctify him for all his duties upon earth, both towards God and man, and for the presence, and enjoyment of God in heaven for ever. Such is the meaning which we attach to *conversion* in this country, where there are many thousands of living and happy witnesses to its reality; and we attach the same meaning to it abroad, in America and the West Indies, in Africa, India, and Ceylon. If we are in error on this all-important subject, we shall be thankful to Dr. Wiseman, or any one else of any church or country, to correct our mistake, and set us right.

But probably the learned Doctor will not *totally* dissent from me on this subject. He will perhaps not deny that instruction, repentance, faith, and holiness, are inseparable from conversion. I can tell him, then, that so far from *conversion* having extended by means of the Romish Church to "one million two hundred thousand Asiatics, of whom one half or six hundred thousand are supposed to be in the Peninsula of India," (Lecture, vol. i., p. 223,) the work of *conversion* has yet to be *commenced* among them. The dupes of Romish superstition in India are without instruction in the "pure word of God, by which we are begotten again." (James i. 18.) They do not "worship God in the spirit," but reverence idols, pictures, relics, and pay adoration to saints and to the blessed mother of our Lord; and "what agreement hath the temple of God with idols?" They have not true repentance, but are still in their sins; of which their Pastors make a profitable trade. They give no evidence of that "faith which is of the operation of the Spirit of God;" and as to the Holy Ghost, "they have not so much as heard whether there be any Holy Ghost;" for the majority of native Romanists in India are ignorant of the existence, the personal character, and the gracious work of the third Person of the blessed Trinity, and neither seek nor desire his all-sufficient grace. In the proper meaning of the word, Rome has no *converts* in India. I make these assertions from extensive personal observation, and from a sincere conviction of their truth. I make them with unfeigned sorrow, and confess my disappointment; for I had been accustomed from my youth to indulge in the thought, that whatever might be the state of Romanism as exhibited in Europe, yet in Missions to heathen lands I might expect to find Ministers of that communion truly spiritual in their character, and amongst its members some knowledge and enjoyment of the salvation of God. I have found some Priests of the Romish idolatry distinguished by courage, and perseverance, and learning, and worldly wisdom; but entirely void of spiritual religion; and, with respect to their flocks, it may be said, "Like Priest, like people." I have sought among them for evidence to the contrary, by personal intercourse, but in vain. I shall still be glad to be informed, if there is any evidence to the contrary in existence.

Such being our view of "conversion," we are amply repaid for our labours and sufferings if, by the blessing of God, we can "convert one sinner from the error of his ways," and thus "save a soul from death, and hide a multitude of sins." The "converts" of the Protestant Missions in India are not numerically important, when considered in comparison with the whole amount of the population. Yet we rejoice that there are such, and will continue carefully to watch over "those few sheep in the wilderness."

But although Protestant Missionaries in India cannot present converts equal in number to the adherents of the Romish superstition, they can with thankfulness contemplate a work which has been accomplished by their instrumentality, such as Romanism has never effected. They have diffused the light of divine truth among the Hindoos, which Rome withheld from them, and have thus placed the pure doctrines and precepts of Christianity in bold contrast with the absurd dogmas and abominable practices of Hindooism. They have lifted up their testimony against all idolatry, and proclaimed that "God is a Spirit, and that they who worship him must worship him in spirit and in truth," whilst the Romish Missionaries have only removed one class of idols to introduce another, and have permitted the continuance of many ceremonies, strictly Hindoo, in the honours rendered to the "Virgin and the Saints." The Protestant Missionaries have protested against the divine origin of the system of caste, which Romanism conceded and perpetuated; and have successfully contended with the absurd and cruel consequences of that system, both to families and communities. The modern Protestant Missionaries, in short, have within thirty years brought about a change in the general intelligence and feeling of the Hindoos, acknowledged and observed by almost all old residents in India, such as the emissaries of Rome failed to effect during more than two hundred years. The Protestant church, especially the Wesleyan section of it, is encouraged by the results of its labours which it has witnessed in India, and fully intends to persevere in its exertions. The foundation has been laid; the work has commenced,—such a work as Popery must ever fail to produce; and a glorious harvest will be reaped from the vast field of India, "in due season, if we faint not."

I can safely leave to others, more immediately concerned, to confute the statements which the Doctor derives from sources which he assumes to be unexceptionable, and even favourable to Protestant Missions: among these he reckons the "Quarterly Review," the "Monthly Review," and the "British Critic;" he takes advantage also of the imperfect information contained in Bishop Heber's Journal, concerning the Missions in the South of India where the Bishop died, when he had only commenced his visitation. He adduces, as conclusive testimony against the success of the labours of Swartz and his successors, that at Tanjore the Bishop found only *fifty* candidates for confirmation, among the natives, and at Trichinopoly only *eleven;* when it is indeed a matter of surprise that there should have been so many, as the Missionaries, being Lutherans, confirmed their own catechumens; much in the same way as the Ministers among the Wesleyan Methodists receive probationers to full membership. But it could scarcely have been anticipated that the Doctor should have fallen into so palpable and absurd a mistake as that the "converts of Swartz and his followers were chiefly among the half castes, or descendants of Europeans!"

Any one who is acquainted with the Missions in the south of India, either from a perusal of the Reports of the various Societies, or from actual conversation with the Missionaries and with the native Christians in their own language, after reading the Doctor's Sixth Lecture, will know whether the conclusion of the Doctor's preface to his Lectures is consistent with the honest truth, or whether it does not, on the contrary, strongly remind one of the cant of hypocrisy. He says to the readers of his book, that "*whatever they shall read hath been written with a kind intent, and hath proceeded from a charitable spirit, and wishes to be received and pondered in hearts that love Christian meekness, and long after unity and peace.*"

INTRODUCTION.

THE revival of religion which commenced in this country more than a century ago, has perhaps had no parallel in the history of the church since the days of the Apostles. The object of the great men, who were honoured of God to be the most prominent instruments of its accomplishment, was not the conformity of the visible church to some peculiar model of ecclesiastical government which they fancied to have divine authority; nor was it the reformation of the national forms of worship and professions of faith from alleged corruption and error. Their object was the promotion of *personal religion*,—the spread of scriptural holiness throughout the land. They asked not of their crowded congregations whether they would support Episcopacy or Presbyterianism; whether they preferred a written form of devotion, or extemporary prayer; nor did they inquire into their opinions or forms of belief. They took the holy Scriptures as the acknowledged standard of the faith of Christendom; they enforced upon all men, of whatever creed, the great doctrines which they found therein, and insisted on the absolute necessity of personal repentance towards God, personal faith in the Lord Jesus Christ, and the personal reception, on the part of the individual believer, of the testimony of the Holy Spirit to the fact of his adoption into the family of God; and that he should give evidence of the reality of his faith by those fruits of the Spirit, which are "love, joy, peace, long-suffering," &c. Without this *personal religion,* they showed that all orthodoxy and outward privileges were practically vain and valueless, whilst, on the contrary, the possession of it secured peace, and comfort, and safety, even though it might have been received amid many outward disadvantages, and retained together with many errors of judgment.

This truly catholic doctrine was gratefully received by multitudes in almost every part of England, who were associated together as United Societies, for the purpose of mutual counsel and help in the spiritual life to which they had been awakened, and with a view to its maintenance and further promotion amongst mankind. There was no intention on the part of their leaders to form a separate church; but the hope was indulged that the pious of all churches would adopt a view so eminently practical, and so exactly in accordance with the Scriptures, and that thus a true reformation would be effected; that the little leaven would leaven the whole lump. This hope was disappointed; and the Wesleyan Church has been formed as a necessary result of the rejection, by the Establishment, of the Ministers and people who enjoyed and advocated the blessings thus described. It may be regarded as the gracious wish of divine Providence that truth so *vital,* should be thus rendered *conspicuous,* by a distinct and constant testimony; and that it should be maintained against all gainsayers, by the principles and affections of those who have received it, and who, by the love of the truth, have been associated in a distinct religious communion; "the church of the living God is the *pillar* and *ground* of the truth."

It might be expected, that a system which had

such an origin, and which was maintained by such principles, would be expansive; that by extension it would not weaken its power, but increase it. Accordingly, in 1747, it spread to Ireland, and in 1756 to New-York, in North America; in 1760, to Antigua, in the West Indies, where it was received as the richest boon by the despised African captives. In all these places, as well as in Western and Southern Africa, in Australasia and Polynesia, it has been made the means of salvation to many thousands. By insisting upon the possession of personal religion, and describing its nature and results, the Wesleys and their coadjutors and successors have been the instruments of an extensive spiritual awakening to the national and other churches of these countries; they have carried the ordinances and comforts of Christianity into barbarous and heathen lands; and whilst teaching personal religion to great as well as small, they have given *the faith* to whole tribes and nations, and have laid the foundation for just and equal laws, and for civil institutions amongst people the most savage and barbarous. The latest returns of the numbers now united in the churches of the Wesleyan Methodists throughout the world, including the Ministers and Missionaries, exhibit a total of one million and a half, of whom little less than half-a-million are found in Great Britain and Ireland, and more than a million in America and other parts of the world. These returns include the accredited members only, and not the children, connexions, and dependents of the members, who may, nevertheless, attend public worship, and make part of the congregations.

In the year 1813, the Rev. Dr. Coke, one of Mr. Wesley's coadjutors and successors in the ministry, obtained the sanction of the British Conference to his much-cherished project of commencing a Mission in the East. He had crossed the Atlantic eighteen times, and had exposed himself to innumerable toils and hardships, that he might plant and cherish churches of Christ in the neglected settlements of North America, and among the despised and degraded slaves of the West Indies. These objects he had successfully accomplished; the blessed fruits of his labours, and of the labours of those who were honoured to be his coadjutors and companions, are found in the Methodist Episcopal Church of North America, and in the Wesleyan Missions in British North America and the West Indies. But he considered himself "debtor" to the East as well as to the West, and was anxious to preach the Gospel on the Island of Ceylon and on the Continent of India, as well as in the West Indies and in North America. He willingly offered his fortune and his life to be expended in the undertaking, could he only obtain the sanction of those with whom he was ever anxious to co-operate. Many reasons were urged why his wish should not be acquiesced in. He was now at the advanced age of sixty-six. The projected scene of labour was at a great distance from Europe, separating those who should engage in it, to a great extent, from intercourse with their brethren at home, and from the immediate advantages of our peculiar discipline. The expense of Missions to the East, it was certain, would be very great. It was also further urged, that such was the peculiar relation in which Dr. Coke stood to the Missions in the West Indies and North America, that it would be impolitic to allow him to cease his care and oversight of them, as he necessarily must, should his intended Mission to the East be carried into effect.

But no arguments could suffice to damp the ardour of the zeal of Dr. Coke. With joy and thankfulness he received the sanction of his brethren in the ministry to his projected Mission; and at the close of 1813, he embarked for India, accompanied by six other Missionaries.

The venerable leader of this band of Christian labourers died within a few days' sail of India, on May 3d, 1814, and his body was committed to the deep by his bereaved companions, in sure and certain hope of a joyful resurrection to eternal life. The Missionaries proceeded to the Island of Ceylon, where they met with a kind reception, and a promising sphere of usefulness. Their number was speedily reinforced by new arrivals from England; so that, in 1816, one of them was spared to accept an earnest invitation from Madras, to take charge of a few pious people who had become acquainted with some of the writings of the Rev. Messrs. Wesley and Fletcher, and were anxious for a living ministry which should teach the doctrines they had learned from the books of those admirable men.

The Rev. James Lynch was very happily selected for this honourable service. He proceeded to Madras in 1817. His simple, unassuming manners, his honesty of purpose, and his untiring zeal for the salvation of sinners, in whatever class of society they might be found, commended him to the warmest affections of many, and to the just respect of all who became acquainted with him in Madras. A small society of the English inhabitants was soon formed, who acknowledged Mr. Lynch as their Pastor; a native congregation was also gathered, to whom he preached, through the medium of an interpreter, in the Tamul language. The Mission-house at Royapettah was soon after purchased, and a chapel erected on the premises. A plot of ground, with a large room upon it, sufficient to contain a congregation, was also purchased in Black-Town, within the walls of Madras; and Mr. Lynch's labours were divided, for the most part, between these two places of worship.

To assist in the good work thus commenced in Madras, the Rev. Titus Close was sent out from England early in the year 1820. In the same year, the Rev. Thomas H. Squance formed a mission at Negapatam, on the Coromandel Coast, in the kingdom of Tanjore, about one hundred and eighty miles south of Madras. Meantime, Mr. Lynch had reported to the Committee of the Wesleyan Missionary Society the facilities which existed for the establishment of a Mission at Bangalore, in the Mysore country; and it was with immediate and direct reference to that part of India, that the Rev. James Mowat and myself were appointed to that Mission in 1819, and dispatched to Madras in 1820. To what degree we were enabled to accomplish the object intrusted to us, and how we were employed in Bangalore, and in other parts of the Madras Presidency, will be seen from the following narrative.

It now only remains to give an account of the state of the Wesleyan Mission in India down to the present time. The following Summary of the Statistics of the Madras Presidency, and of the Missions established within its boundaries, and on the Island of Ceylon, compiled from the most recent returns, will furnish a ground-work for calculations on the possible extension of Missionary operations, and will serve to show how, in this most favoured part of India, with respect to Missions, the providence of God has already gone far beyond the diligence and zeal of his church.

From the subjoined Tabular Summary of the Wesleyan Missions, it will be seen, that the Society not only retain all the Stations occupied when the author was in India, but that they have also commenced several new Missions; as for instance, the Canarese Mission in BANGALORE, in MYSORE, in GOOBBEE, and COONGHUL; and that, in addition to the English and Tamul Missions in MADRAS, BANGALORE, and NEGAPATAM, they have commenced a Mission at MANARGOODY, and MELNATTAM, in the Tanjore country. In all these places our faithful Missionaries are favoured with encouraging indications of success; many thousands of the adult Hindoos have received some measure of instruction in Christianity, and perhaps an equal number of children have been made familiar with divine truth. Every year adds to the number of the converted, and the baptized; Hindooism is no longer undisturbed in its hold on the minds of the natives; by many who conform to it, it is despised, by a greater number it is doubted; the Missionaries are encouraged to persevering exertion in the propagation of the faith of Christ, and whilst they labour, preaching the Gospel in churches and schools, in the streets and bazaars, by the way-side and at the very gates of idol temples, as well as from house to house, "teaching every man and warning every man;" they ask for the *sympathy* of British Christians, but more especially do they entreat their *prayers*. "The good that is done upon earth, the Lord doeth it;" the

Spirit of the Lord must "breathe upon the slain," before they can "stand up a great army," in the "valley of vision:" under this conviction the Missionaries, during their persevering labour, continually exclaim, "Brethren, pray for us, that the word of the Lord may have free course, and be glorified, even as it is with you."

The Missions in North and South Ceylon have increased in magnitude and importance since the author visited some of them: and never were there more cheering indications in that island than at present. The Government School Commission, in the most liberal and enlightened manner, are co-operating with the Missionaries to instruct and elevate the natives by means of a more thorough education. Among the Singhalese "the fields are white unto the harvest." "More labourers" are arising from among the natives themselves; and those European Missionaries who have been long toiling in the field are anticipating that they shall personally unite in the joyful shout of "harvest home!"

The educational establishment under the direction of the Missionary in Jaffna, Mr. Percival, is said to be equal to any which may exist throughout the Eastern world. In Batticaloa, a great revival of religion has taken place among the natives; and during its progress many Hindoos have embraced Christianity, and have been baptized. Very remarkable success has attended the humane and judicious attempts which have been made to civilize and instruct the Veddahs, a tribe of native savages, whose state and character were, until lately, considered hopeless. Three villages of them are now settled, and are all under the instruction of the

Mission. Encouraged by these examples, the Government and the Mission are determined to proceed until the whole race of Veddahs are brought under the same beneficial influences. The Missionaries, and those who support them in their toil, have a rich reward in the present state of the Missions in the East,—in the successes already achieved; but the anticipations in which we have authority to indulge are glorious; the idols of India shall be "cast to the moles and to the bats;" every ancient superstition and prejudice, every civil barrier, which at present "exalt themselves against the knowledge of God," shall be removed. These Gentiles "shall come to the light" of the knowledge of God. The "Son shall have these Heathen for his inheritance, and the uttermost parts of the earth for a possession." "He shall reign from sea to sea, and from the river to the ends of the earth:" "All nations shall call Him blessed." "BLESSED BE THE LORD GOD, the GOD OF ISRAEL, who only doeth wondrous things; and BLESSED BE HIS GLORIOUS NAME FOR EVER; and let the WHOLE EARTH BE FILLED WITH HIS GLORY. AMEN, AND AMEN."

STATISTICS OF THE MADRAS PRESIDENCY.

COLLECTORATE, OR COUNTRY.	SQUARE MILES.	POPULATION.	LAND REVENUE. RUPEES.	
Madras,		630,000		Occupied as a Mission-Station by various Societies.
Chingleput,	2,253	336,219	1,482,916	No Missionary residing.
North Arcot,		506,831		Four European Missionaries of different Societies.
South Arcot,	4,500	550,239	2,416,828	One Missionary.
Salem,		905,190		Two Missionaries.
Coimbatoor,	8,392	800,275		One Missionary.
Trichinopoly,		654,780		One Missionary.
Tanjore,		1,128,730		Ten Missionaries.
Madura,		1,306,725		Two British and Seven American Missionaries.
Tinnevelly,		850,891		Eight Missisonaries.
Travancore,		1,280,664		Sixteen Missionaries.
Cochin,		288,176		Two Missionaries.
Malabar,		1,140,916		Seven Missionaries of the Basle Society.
Canara,	7,000	771,623		
Coorg,		100,000		No Missionary.
Mysore,		3,250,000		Seven Missonaries.
Bellary	12,703	1,112,839		Three Missionaries.
Cuddapah,		1,063,164	2,334,057	One Missionary.
Nellore,	12,000	846,572	1,860,553	No Missionary.
Guntoor,	12,317	267,416		No Missionary.
Masulipatam,	4,810	332,039		Two Missionaries.
Rajahmundry,	4,600	578,520		No Missionary.
Vizagapatam,		1,010,414	1,415,008	Three Missionaries.
Ganjam,	3,700	588,079	1,339,328	No Missionary.
Hydrabad,		3,351,782		No Missionary.
Nagpoor,	70,000	2,470,766		No Missionary.

"Independently of the subsidiary states of Travancore, Mysore, Hydrabad, and Nagpoor, which collectively comprise a population of about nine millions, there are in the collectorates, properly under the Madras Presidency, 263 counties, 71,135 villages, 18,814,605 persons, on an area of 171,028 square miles. The total revenue of the Madras Presidency, is 46,970,776 rupees," or £4,697,077. —*Smith's Appeal for Southern India.*

The Population of the Island of Ceylon is estimated at 1,009,008.

SUMMARY OF MISSIONS

IN

SOUTH INDIA AND CEYLON,* 1844.

WESLEYAN MISSIONARY SOCIETY.

MADRAS,	Three Missionaries, and an Assistant Missionary.
NEGAPATAM,	Two Missionaries, and an Assistant Missionary.
MANARGOODY,	Two Missionaries.
BANGALORE,	(Tamul,) One Missionary.
BANGALORE,	(Canarese,) One Missionary, and two Assistant Missionaries.
MYSORE,	Two Missionaries, and an Assistant Missionary.
GOOBEE,	Two Missionaries.
COONGHUL,	One Missionary, and an Assistant Missionary.

Total number of Hearers, about 3,390
Total number of Members or Communicants 342
Total number in the Schools. 1,900

CEYLON.

SINGHALESE DISTRICT.

(South.)

COLOMBO,	One Missionary, and an Assistant Missionary.
NEGOMBO,	One Missionary, and an Assistant Missionary.
SEEDUA,	An Assistant Missionary.
MOROTTO,	An Assistant Missionary.
PANTURA,	An Assistant Missionary.
CALTURA,	One Missionary.
GALLE AND AMBLAMGODDE,	One Missionary, and an Assistant Missionary.
MATURA,	An Assistant Missionary.
DONDRA,	An Assistant Missionary.
GODDAPITIYA,	An Assistant Missionary.

Total number of Hearers, not ascertained.
Total number of Members or Communicants 763
Total number in the schools 3,036

* For full and most interesting particulars of the early History of the Wesleyan Mission in the Island of Ceylon, see Harvard's "Narrative."

CEYLON.

TAMUL DISTRICT.

(North.)

JAFFNA, One Missionary.
POINT-PEDRO, Under the care of the Missionary in Jaffna.
TRINCOMALEE, One Missionary.
BATTICALOA AND BINTENNE, Two Missionaries, and an Assistant Missionary.

Total number of Hearers, not ascertained.
Total number of Members or Communicants 204
Total number in the Schools 1,250

Total number of Wesleyan Missionaries in South India and Ceylon 22
Assistant Missionaries 17

Total number of Hearers, not ascertained.
Total number of Members 1,309
Total number in the Schools 6,186

CHURCH MISSIONARY SOCIETY.

MADRAS,
TELOOGOO,
TINNEVELLY,
TRAVANCORE, (Cottayam,)
MAVELICARE,
ALLEPIE,
COCHIN and TRICHOOR,

} Twenty European Missionaries, and three native Assistants.

Total number of Hearers 13,995
Total number of Members or Communicants.................... 1,639
Total number in the Schools 5,090

CEYLON.

COTTA, Three Missionaries, and an Assistant Missionary.
KANDY, Two Missionaries.
BADDAGAME, Two Missionaries, and an Assistant Missionary.
NELLORE, Two Missionaries.

Total number of Hearers 4,300
Total number of Members or Communicants 111
Total number in the Schools 3,443

LONDON MISSIONARY SOCIETY.

MADRAS, Five Missionaries.
VIZAGAPATAM AND CHICACOLE, Three Missionaries and One Assistant Missionary.
CUDDAPAH, An Assistant Missionary.
BELGAUM, Two Missionaries.
BELLARY, Three Missionaries and an Assistant Missionary.
BANGALORE, Four Missionaries.
MYSORE, One Missionary.
SALEM, One Missionary.
COMBACONUM, One Missionary.
COIMBATOOR, Two Missionaries.

SOUTH TRAVANCORE.

NAGERCOIL, Three Missionaries.
NEYOOR, Two Missionaries, and an Assistant Missionary.
QUILON, Two Missionaries.
TREVANDRUM, One Missionary.

Total number of Hearers, not ascertained.
Total number of Members or Communicants 557
Total number in the Schools 7,952

BAPTIST MISSIONARY SOCIETY.

CEYLON.

COLOMBO, including Pettah and Slave Island, Three Missionaries, and seven Assistant Missionaries.
KANDY, One Missionary and an Assistant Missionary.

Total number of Hearers, not ascertained.
Total number of Members or Communicants, about 600
Total number in the Schools, upwards of........................ 1,180

AMERICAN BOARD OF MISSIONS.

MADRAS.

ROYAPOORUM, One Missionary.
CHINTADREPETTAH, One Missionary.
BLACK-TOWN, One Missionary.

Total number of Hearers, not ascertained.
Total number of Members or Communicants, not ascertained.
Total number in the Schools................... 495

MADURA.

MADURA,	One Missionary.
MADURA FORT,	One Missionary.
DINDIGUL,	Two Missionaries and an Assistant Missionary.
TERUPUVANUM,	One Missionary.
SEVAGUNGA,	One Missionary.
TERUMUNGALUM,	One Missionary.

Total number of Hearers, not ascertained.
Total number of Members or Communicants, ditto.
Total number in the Schools 3,304

CEYLON.

TILLYPALLY,	One Missionary.
BATTICOTTA,	Three Missionaries and an Assistant Missionary.
OODOOVILLE,	One Missionary.
MANEPY,	Two Missionaries.
PANDITERIPO,	One Missionary.
CHAVAGACHERRY,	Two Missionaries.

Total number of Hearers, not ascertained.
Total number of Members or Communicants, ditto.
Total number in the Schools.. 3,541

SOCIETY FOR THE PROPAGATION OF THE GOSPEL IN FOREIGN PARTS.

MADRAS,	Six Missionaries.
TANJORE, MADURA, &c.,	Sixteen Missionaries.
PULICAT, &c.,	Four Missionaries.
CEYLON,	Three Missionaries.

To this Summary must be added the Danish Mission at Tranquebar, the particulars of which have not been ascertained; and the Mission of the Basle Missionary Society in Malabar and Canara.

MISSIONS OF THE CHURCH MISSIONARY SOCIETY TO THE SYRIAN CHRISTIANS OF TRAVANCORE.

In the Summary now given, it will be observed that the Church Missionary Society has agents among the Syrian Christians of Travancore. This interesting sphere of labour appears by common consent to have been resigned to them, and our best wishes and most earnest prayers are engaged, that they may happily succeed in reviving scriptural Christianity in that remarkable remnant of a very ancient church.

According to a recent Report of the Bishop of Madras, the Church Missionary Society has five churches among the Syrian Christians, which are attended by some thousands of hearers. The beneficial results of that Mission cannot be doubted, although the difficulties and discouragements have been numerous.

In order to render as complete as possible the comparatively limited sketch of Christianity in Southern India, I have appended to this volume an outline of the History of the Syrian Christians of Travancore, from the earliest age down to the eighteenth century, and more particularly of the cruel and treacherous treatment they received from the bigoted emissaries of Rome. An attentive perusal of the history of those remote and much-injured Churches cannot fail to excite the deepest sympathy and commiseration. When shall Christian Europe repay to India the injuries she has inflicted upon the ancient Churches of India, or discharge a moderate share of her obligations to the Heathens whom she has brought into political subjection? In estimating these obligations, we may learn our unprofitableness and insufficiency. We should feel our need of divine and gracious assistance; and, encouraged by the past dealings of God with his church, and by the precious and repeated promises recorded in the word of truth, should pray, "God be merciful unto us, and bless us, and cause his face to shine upon us: that thy way may be known upon earth, and thy saving health to all nations. Let the people praise thee, O God, let all the people praise thee." Amen.

The Friends of Wesleyan Missions will be gratified to see a connected List of the Missionaries who have been sent out to the East, by their own Society; which we now present. It may afford subject of consideration to those who are curious in statistics.

DATE OF DEPARTURE FROM ENGLAND.

1813. Dec. 31st. Thomas Coke, LL.D. Died at sea, May 3d, 1814.

James Lynch. Returned to Europe in 1824. At present a Supernumerary Minister in Ireland.

George Erskine. Proceeded to Sydney in 1821, where he died April 20th, 1834.

William Ault. Died at Batticaloa, April 1st, 1815.

W. M. Harvard. Returned to England in 1819. At present Minister in Canada.

Benjamin Clough. Returned finally to England in 1838. At present Minister in England.

Thomas H. Squance. Returned to England in 1822. At present Minister in England.

1814. Dec. 23d. Samuel Broadbent. Returned in 1820. Now Minister in England.

Robert Carver. Retired from the Society in 1841.

Elijah Jackson. Returned home soon after his arrival in Ceylon.

John Callaway. Returned in 1826. Died Nov. 23d, 1841.

1816. April 29th, John M'Kenny. Returned from Ceylon in 1834, and proceeded to New South Wales, where he still resides as Missionary.

John Horner. Returned from Bombay in 1822. Since deceased.

Nov. 22d. W. B. Fox. Returned from Ceylon in 1823. Died April 9th, 1834.

Thomas Osborne. Returned from Ceylon in 1824. Died October 30th, 1836.

Robert Newstead. Returned from Ceylon in 1826. At present Minister in England.

DATE OF DEPARTURE FROM ENGLAND.

1818. May 17th, Daniel J. Gogerly. Remains as Missionary in Ceylon.

1819. March 23d, Alexander Hume. Returned from Ceylon in 1830. At present Minister in England.

Samuel Allen. Returned from Ceylon in 1832. At present Minister in England.

March 28th, Joseph Roberts. Returned from Ceylon in 1834. Appointed to Madras in 1842, where he at present resides as Missionary.

Abraham Stead. Returned from Ceylon in 1827. At present Minister in England.

Joseph Bott. Returned from Ceylon in 1825, and was dismissed from the Society.

Joseph Fletcher. Returned from Bombay in 1821. Proceeded to the West Indies. Returned thence in 1833. At present Minister in England.

1820. Titus Close. Returned from Madras in 1822. Died on June 10th, 1833.

May 19th, James Mowat. Returned from Madras in 1829. At present Minister in England.

Elijah Hoole. Returned from Madras in 1828.

1823. March 14th, J. F. England. Returned from Madras in 1833. At present Minister in England.

1824. Feb. 12th, William Bridgnell. Remains as Missionary in Ceylon.

Richard Stoup. Died in Ceylon, Oct. 5th, 1829.

1825. March 8th, Thomas J. Williamson. Died at sea on his voyage homeward in 1827.

April 9th, Robert Spence Hardy. Remains in Ceylon as Missionary.

1826. May 5th, John George. Returned from Ceylon in 1838. At present Minister in England.

DATE OF DEPARTURE FROM ENGLAND.

1826. Peter Percival. Remains as Missionary in Ceylon.

Nov. 18th, Alfred Bourne. Returned from Madras in 1834, and died May 27th, 1836.

1828. June 14th, Samuel Hardey. Remains as Missionary in Madras.

1829. Nov. 23d, William Longbottom. Quitted India in 1836. At present Missionary in Van-Diemen's-Land.

Thomas Cryer. Returned to England in 1838. Proceeded again to Madras in 1842.

Thomas Hodson. Returned from the Mysore Country in 1843.

1829. Ralph Stott. Remains as Missionary in Ceylon.

1831. March 1st, Elijah Toyne and Thomas Kilner. Returned from Ceylon in 1840, and are at present Ministers in England.

1836. April 11th, Thomas Haswell. Remains as Missionary in the Mysore Country.

George Hole. Remains as Missionary in Ceylon.

1837. Sept. 5th, Jonathan Crowther. Returned from Madras in 1843.

Joseph K. Best. Retired from the Society in 1842.

John Jenkins. Returned from the Mysore Country in 1840, and has since been Missionary in Malta.

Matthew T. Male. Remains as Missionary in the Mysore Country.

Richard D. Griffith. Remains as Missionary in Madras.

William S. Fox. Died at sea, on his voyage homeward, March 18th, 1841.

1839. April 15th, Edward G. Squarebridge. Died at Coonghul, in the Mysore Country, August 18th, 1840.

John Garrett. Remains as Missionary in the Mysore Country.

William Arthur. Returned from the Mysore Country in 1841. At present Minister in England.

DATE OF DEPARTURE FROM ENGLAND.

1839. George U. Pope. Retired from the Society in 1841.

1840. Sept. 22d, Andrew Kessen. Missionary in Ceylon.

1842. March 23d, Edward J. Hardey. Missionary in the Mysore Country.

Daniel Sanderson. Missionary in the Mysore Country.

1843. Sept. 10th, Robert Pargiter. Embarked for Ceylon.

Sept. 30th, John Gostick. Embarked for Madras.

John Pinkney. Embarked for Madras.

Joseph Little. Embarked for Madras.

Peter Batchelor, Missionary in Negapatam, was not sent out in that capacity, but was accepted by the Society as resident in India.

MADRAS, MYSORE, AND THE SOUTH OF INDIA:

OR,

A PERSONAL NARRATIVE,

&c.

CHAPTER I.

NOVEMBER, 1819, TO SEPTEMBER, 1820.

THE VOYAGE TO INDIA.

THE voyage to India, by the Cape of Good Hope, occupies about four months. Formerly it was not uncommon for vessels to be ten or twelve months on the passage; but the seas are now so thoroughly explored, and the seasons, the changes of the wind, and the courses of the currents, so well understood, that the probabilities of a voyage may be calculated with tolerable certainty. The "overland journey," as it is called, by way of Egypt and the Red Sea, by steam-vessels, may be accomplished in less than two months. In cases where dispatch is essential, the latter route has the advantage; but the voyage by the Cape of Good Hope introduces the European more gradually, and, therefore, perhaps more favourably, to the fervours of a tropical climate, and affords him the opportunity of conveying under his own care all the property he may think necessary to carry with him. Travellers by the overland route have generally to send a great part of their luggage by way of the Cape of Good Hope.

It is worthy of remark, that the route now taken by our steam-vessels to India, is the same which was pursued by the Phenicians, Egyptians, Greeks, and Arabs, for more than two thousand years. Eighteen hundred years ago, the Greeks discovered the regularity of the monsoons in the Indian Ocean, and ventured to quit the coast on their voyage to India. From Berenice, in the Red Sea, they reached Cana, in South Arabia, in thirty days; and thence, in forty days, stretched across to India, completing the voyage and return within twelve months.

Another route to India, much used for trade, in ancient times, was by the Caspian Sea, the river Oxus, which then flowed into it, and so, by the passes of the Hindoo Cush, to the river Indus. But the oldest route of all, and that by which the productions of India were brought to Egypt before the time of Moses, and were therefore known to him, and recorded in Exod. xxx. 23, as ingredients of the "oil of the sanctuary," was along the Syrian coasts, and the great rivers of Mesopotamia. Tadmor in the Wilderness was built by Solomon upon this line of road, and continued to flourish until conquered and destroyed by the Roman power, in the time of Aurelian.

By one of these routes overland, or by a tedious coasting voyage, Pythagoras, who is said to have been contemporary with the Prophet Daniel, must have proceeded to India, when he visited the sages of that country, to make himself acquainted with their science, and with the doctrines and practices of their religion; and from the Hindoos he is said to have adopted his doctrine of metempsychosis. The reader of the Essay at the end of this volume may admire his earnest pursuit of knowledge, but may also safely be left to judge whether he found any thing in that doctrine, or any other Hindoo notion or practice, to repay the labour and risk to which he subjected himself. The Black Jews of Cochin, who are supposed to have been a colony of those taken captive to Babylon, probably reached their destination by sea: it is conjectured, that the White Jews followed in their track soon after the destruction of Jerusalem; and the Syrian Christians of Malabar, if a colony from Mosul, and not, as is most probable, converted from among the Aborigines, must have voyaged direct to their present residence, and not have reached it by the tedious method of a land journey.

The discovery of the passage to India by the Cape of Good Hope, in 1486, opened the way for the Portuguese conquests in the East. They maintained their supremacy for about one hundred years, when their power was broken by the Dutch. The Dutch, in their turn, yielded to the growing influence of the English East India Company. The Portuguese and French have still a few settlements on the coast of India; the Dutch ceded what remained of theirs in 1825, in exchange for the British settlements in Sumatra.

In November, 1819, I took an affectionate leave of my dear relatives and friends in Manchester, many of whom I was never again to see; and proceeded to London, to wait a convenient opportunity of embarking for Continental India, to which country I had already been appointed a Missionary by my honoured fathers and brethren, the Wesleyan-Methodist Missionary Committee.

The kind attentions shown to myself, and to the Rev. James Mowat, my colleague, and Mrs. Mowat, by the official and private members and friends of the Society in London, during our stay, demand a grateful acknowledgment; and, in our peculiar circumstances, made an impression on our hearts never to be effaced.

After an unavoidable delay of some months, we embarked at Gravesend, on Friday, May 19th, 1820, in the ship "Tanjore;" a private trader of five hundred tons' burden, bound (on her first voyage) for Madras and Calcutta, and commanded by Captain G. H. Dacre, an able and experienced officer of the Royal Navy.

Besides my valued colleague and his wife, I had the happiness to reckon among my fellow-passengers, the pious and much-esteemed Sir Richard Otley, Chief Justice of the Island of Ceylon, and the Rev. Thomas and Mrs. Browning, of the Church Missionary Society, who were appointed to Kandy, in the same Island, whose friendship and society formed a principal part of our enjoyments on board, and rendered more tolerable the prospect of the confinement and tedium of so long a voyage.

On the evening of the following day we anchored off Deal, and gladly embraced the opportunity afforded us of passing another Christian sabbath in our native land. The Rev. W. M. Harvard, formerly Missionary in Ceylon, showed us much kindness. He introduced us to his congregations, commended us to their prayers, and when we re-embarked, on the morning of Monday, May 22d, dismissed us with some valuable advice, respecting our voyage, and the climate in which we should probably have to reside and labour for many years.

Our passage down the Channel was boisterous, and exceedingly trying to persons unaccustomed to the sea. I was the only passenger who did not suffer from sea-sickness, and was happy to have it in my power to render some assistance to my less favoured friends. The Lizard-Point, the last English land we saw, died away from our view on the evening of May 31st; we then immediately entered into fine weather, and became more settled and comfortable in our new circumstances.

Our voyage was now become pleasant; the cabins were comfortable and clean, our ship being entirely new; the cuddy, or dining-room, was commodious; our meals were regular, our food tolerable, our water good; and the party on board, on the whole, social and agreeable. By permission of the Captain, we held divine service once or twice every Sunday; on deck, if the weather permitted; if otherwise, under cover; the Church Missionary and ourselves taking it in rotation, to read and preach to the attentive congregation formed by the passengers, officers, and crew. We administered the sacrament of the Lord's supper three times during the voyage; we assembled for family worship, every morning and evening, in the cabin of our highly-respected friend, Sir Richard Otley; and those of us who were Methodists enjoyed every week the peculiar privilege of a social class-meeting. Thus our spiritual advantages during the voyage were great and consolatory; and we had reason to believe that our exertions for the benefit of others were not lost on those who sailed with us; whilst our diligent attention to reading, study, and composition, happily beguiled the time, and enhanced the pleasantness of our hours of relaxation and mutual converse.

We passed through the Bay of Biscay without experiencing the rough weather we had anticipated: we entered the Tropics, extended our sails to the trade winds, which blow there all the year round, and sailed on the vast ocean as smoothly as on a lake. We had a distant view of St. Antonio, one of the Cape de Verd Islands, the only land we saw until we made the Island of Ceylon; and were delighted by the interesting phenomena peculiar to those latitudes; such as, the thousands of flying-fish, the beautiful bonito and dolphin, the voracious shark, (of each of which we caught several,) the glories of the rising and setting sun; and, during the night, the phosphoric brightness of the waves and spray of the sea, the gradual sinking of the north polar star, and the rising of the beautiful constellations of the southern hemisphere.

Crossing the Equinoctial Line, we had the usual visit from Neptune and Amphitrite; and the ceremony of shaving with tar, and dashing about water in abundance, by the passengers and crew, was duly observed. Some of the passengers, with myself, disapproving of so ridiculous and heathenish a custom, "more honoured in the breach than in th' observance," gained exemption from any participation in it, by paying a fine of some Spanish dollars each.

Baffling and contrary winds occasioned the loss of ten or fourteen days, in doubling the Cape of Good Hope. Beyond the Cape, in about 36° south latitude, we were overtaken by a tremendous gale of wind: it was impossible to carry sail; the sea rose in awful grandeur, and the mountains and valleys it presented to our view reminded me of the scenery of some parts of Derbyshire. Our vessel was tossed about like a cork or a splinter of wood; and rolled so from side to side, that the heaviest furniture and packages, not well secured, were loosened and dashed about in a manner at once alarming and dangerous. In these seas we saw many grampuses and whales.

The gale, and the favourable breezes which succeeded it, carried us so much to the eastward, that when we re-entered the Tropics, we were in the longitude of Point de Galle, and had consequently to keep a due northern course. We rode on the wings of the monsoon, till the 3d of September, when we saw the Island of Ceylon, having been only three months and three days in making the voyage from land to land. During the whole of this period, we had only seen one sail,—a homeward-bound vessel.

Sir Richard Otley and the other passengers for Ceylon were desirous of landing at Point de Galle; but the wind blowing steadily from that quarter, made it impracticable to retrieve the few miles we had passed to the eastward of it: we therefore coasted along the south-east side of the Island, enjoying the smell of the land, which was extremely grateful, much like the scent of new hay; and admiring the many romantic views of hill and dale, cultivated land and jungle, skirted by the cocoa-nut tree and the palmyra, which every hour of our progress opened to us.

On Monday, the 4th, we were visited by many of the natives, in their homely but ingenious canoes, who brought for sale various kinds of fruit, which, though unripe, proved very acceptable to us. Adam Munhi Rathana and Alexander Dherma Rama, the two Buddhist priests who had been instructed and baptized in England, and were our fellow-passengers in the "Tanjore," proved of service here. By their interpretation we learned the news of the Island, and understood we might conveniently land our party for Ceylon, at Batticaloa, which was not far distant. The master of a large native vessel undertook to conduct us; and finding that, though under shortened sail, we went much quicker than themselves, they fastened a tow-line to their fore-ship, to enable them to keep up with us. Towards evening the wind freshened a little, and we thought to give them a fair specimen of our superiority in sailing; but they became frantic with terror, and, with violent shouting and gesticulation, begged us to loosen the line, or their vessel would soon go to pieces, for it was already giving way. We could not but be amused with their alarm, from which, however, we quickly relieved them, and, proud of our gallant ship, left them far behind.

CHAPTER II.

SEPTEMBER 6TH, 1820.

BURNING OF THE SHIP, AND ESCAPE.

THE following day we made Batticaloa, and came to anchor. Our excellent friend, Sir Richard Otley, landed the same evening, accompanied by Mr. and Mrs. Browning. The boat was too small to accommodate all the passengers, and it was too late in the evening to make more than one trip. The next day, Wednesday, September 6th, Sir Richard's Secretary, and other passengers, with Adam, one of the Singhalese, went on shore, with all the baggage belonging to the Ceylon party; and about one P.M. we weighed anchor, and stood out for sea, intending to make direct for Madras.

Although oppressively hot, it was a fine day. In the evening, however, we were neither surprised nor alarmed at a heavy storm of thunder, lightning, and rain, coming direct upon us; for we had seen much lightning every night, since we had been in the neighbourhood of land. It was dusk, and I was taking a farewell view of the tops of the mountains of the island, fast diminishing in the distance, when I observed an unusually heavy cloud hastening towards us. I pointed it out to Captain Dacre, with whom I was conversing at the time: he replied that it was of no importance; and, alluding to a luminous appearance in the centre of it, said that we might see through it. The rain soon began to descend in torrents, and drove all on deck to seek shelter in the cuddy, or below: the storm increased; and flash after flash of lightning followed each other in such quick succession, that, with little interruption, it would have been possible to read by the glare.

I sat in the cuddy, watching the storm, till past eight o'clock, when a flash which illuminated the whole hemisphere, and was accompanied with loud cracking, and a tremendous noise, struck the ship, prostrated one of the passengers who was reading by the glare, and killed upon the spot two of the seamen on the fore-castle. I ran to the door, to ascertain the effects of the stroke, and heard the second mate, who was between decks, cry out, "Fire in the hold! Fire below!" The cargo had taken fire from the electric fluid. The scene which followed exceeds all description; it was one that can never be forgotten by any who witnessed it.

In a moment all hands were on deck; buckets were supplied in abundance; the pumps were manned and leaked, that the water might be discharged on the burning cargo; passengers and crew were all on the alert; I threw off my boat-cloak, which I had procured by rushing below through the smoke into my cabin, and assisted at the pumps. When the hatches were taken off, to allow of water being poured into the hold, flames and clouds of smoke issued forth as from a furnace, increasing every instant in heat and density. It was soon found that all exertion was in vain; the vessel must perish.

From the pumps we ran to the boats: the gig hung over the larboard quarter, so as to be lowered in a moment; but we should have lost its valuable services, had not a gentleman threatened to send a bullet through the head of the carpenter, who, insane with terror, had brought a hatchet to cut the ropes, and drop it at once into the sea. The yawl, a larger boat, was our great difficulty; it was turned, keel upwards, over the long boat, to serve as a roof to the live stock kept in the latter. Many attempts were made in vain to raise it from its situation; the long boat was already on fire by the flames bursting from the main hold. I climbed into it, (without feeling that, in doing so, I broke my shins severely,) to give my assistance; and when we were just ready to despair, the yawl eased and rose, no one knew how, and was over the side, and floating in the water, more quickly, the seamen said, than they had ever before seen it.

Captain Dacre had already affirmed, in answer to my inquiries, that the two boats could not carry all the ship's company, passengers and crew; (and, under other circumstances, we should not have dared to try them;) but the trial must now be made. The two ladies, one of whom had to be hurried from her bed, where she had retired for the night, were first put safely into the yawl; some other passengers and myself, with part of the crew, followed, and our weight sank it nearly to the water's edge; the Captain and others entered the smaller boat, and sufficiently filled it, leaving the vessel with honourable reluctance, while the first Mate, Mr. Ibbetson, gallantly remained on board to the last, suggesting the best arrangements, and assisting to hand to us any article that could be secured at the moment, which might possibly be useful to us in the extreme perils we were about to encounter.

Many of the party, having retired to their hammocks before the electric fluid struck the vessel, were half naked, but were supplied with trousers and jackets by those seamen who had been on the watch, who, in consequence of the heavy rain, had cased themselves in double or treble their usual quantity of clothing. My own dress was merely a nankeen jacket and trousers, a shirt and neckcloth; I had lost my hat in assisting to get out the boat.

We happily succeeded in bringing away two compasses from the binnacle, and a few candles from the cuddy table, one of them lighted; one bottle of wine and another of porter, were handed to us, with the table-cloth and a knife, which proved very useful; but the fire raged so fiercely in the body of the vessel, that neither bread nor water could be obtained.

It was now about nine o'clock: the rain poured in torrents; the lightning continued to stream from one side of the heavens to the other, one moment dazzling us by its glare, and the next leaving us in darkness, relieved only by the red flames of the conflagration from which we were trying to escape.

Our first object was to get clear of the vessel, lest she should explode, and overwhelm us. But to our great distress we discovered, that the yawl had no rudder, and that in the two boats we had only three oars, all exertions to obtain more from the ship having proved unsuccessful. From the gig, which had a rudder, they gave us a line, to keep us in tow; and by means of a few spars, found at the bottom of the boat, we assisted in moving ourselves slowly through the water. Providentially, the sea was very still, or our boats would have swamped, and we must have perished. There was also very little wind; but it sometimes changed, and, assisted by the prevailing current, urged forward the burning ship; for the sails, being drenched with rain, did not easily take fire. Our situation, therefore, was, for some time, exceedingly perilous. The vessel neared us more than once, and seemed to threaten to involve us in its own destruction. The cargo, consisting of combustible articles, including a considerable quantity of spirits, burned with violence and rapidity, and the flames rose to an amazing height.

We succeeded in increasing the distance between us and

the vessel; directing our course towards land, by help of the compass, which we could see by the light of the candles we had with us. About ten o'clock, we saw the masts fall over the side, and the vessel seemed to be burnt down to the water's edge. The spectacle was grand, contemplated abstractedly from a recollection of our own circumstances. The destruction by fire of the animals on board, dogs, sheep, &c., at another time would have excited our deepest commiseration; but, at present, the total loss of property, the awfully sudden death of the two seamen, our own narrow escape, and the great probability, even yet, that we should never again see the light of day, or set our feet on solid ground, seemed to absorb our faculties and feelings: for some time the silence was scarcely broken, and I doubt not, that many, like myself, were engaged in thoughts most suitable to immortal beings on the brink of eternity,—in self-examination, and in prayer.

The number of persons in the two boats was forty-eight; and all, with the exception of the two ladies, who, I must observe, bore these awful circumstances with extraordinary fortitude, took it in turns to work at the oars and paddles. After some time, to our great relief, the rain ceased; the labour of baling water from the boats was considerably diminished; the occupants of the two boats hailed each other frequently during the night, and the honest tars, true "hearts of oak," occasionally gave a simultaneous "hurra," to cheer each other, and to keep up our spirits.

The "Tanjore" must have risen in the water, as it gradually consumed: we saw it burning the whole night, and at day-break could distinguish a column of smoke arising from it; which, however, soon ceased; and we saw and heard no more of our favourite ship. Some months afterwards, during my residence at Negapatam, on the Coromandel coast, about three hundred miles from the spot where the disaster occurred, a spar, partially consumed by fire, was thrown on the beach by the surf; and appeared to me to have been the fore-sail yard, or fore-top-sail yard, of the unfortunate "Tanjore."

When the sun arose, we could clearly discern land a head: the sight of it filled us with grateful joy, and nerved us with fresh vigour for our exertions in managing the boats. We then discovered, that the purser was the only person in our party decently attired: the wretched and forlorn appearance presented by the rest, in either only half clothing, or the unsuitable clothing of others, increased by exposure, want of rest, and the anxieties of the past night, could not but provoke a smile and a few good-natured remarks.

As the day advanced, we more clearly discovered the nature of the country which we were approaching. It was wild and covered with jungle, without any appearance of population: could we have got ashore therefore, our condition would have been little improved; many of us might have perished, before human habitations could have been reached, or assistance procured; but the breakers dashing upon the rocks convinced us that landing was impracticable, even had we desired it.

About seven o'clock A. M. we discovered a dhoney, or native vessel, lying at anchor at some distance; the wind just then began to favour us, and we exercised our ingenuity to avail ourselves of it. In the yawl, we managed to extend the table-cloth as a sail; and in the other boat, a blanket (which the butcher had brought away with him, being the whole of his property) was made to serve the same purpose. We were delighted with this additional help; which was the more seasonable, as the rays of the sun became intolerably hot, and greatly increased our sense of weariness. One of the officers gave Mrs. Mowat his tartan cap, to serve as some cover from the heat; and I thought myself happy in securing a hat that had been used during the night for baling water: it was soon partially dry, and screened the top of my head from the direct rays of the sun. Some of the seamen, suffering from heat and exhausted by their exertions, began to drink salt water; but the passengers abstained from it.

It was near noon before we reached the dhoney. The natives on board of it were astonished and alarmed at our appearance, and expressed some unwillingness to entertain us; but our circumstances would admit of no denial, and we scarcely waited till Alexander, the Singhalese, could interpret to them our situation and our wants, before we took possession of their vessel; assuring them, that every expense and loss sustained on our account should be amply repaid.

They treated us very kindly; gave us water sparingly, but as many cocoa-nuts as we could devour; they also boiled some rice for us, which they presented in cocoa-nut shells, with curried fish, and jaggery, a sort of coarse black sugar; and laughing at our method of eating, made for us a few rude spoons of bits of cocoa-nut shell and splinters of bamboo. They informed us that Trincomallee, which we knew to be one of our Mission Stations, was not far distant; and, agreeing to take us thither, they proceeded to weigh anchor, while we stretched our cramped and weary limbs on the pent-roof thatch, which served as a deck to the vessel.

In the evening they cast anchor for the night: the heavens were again darkened with clouds; the lightnings flashed, and the distant thunder rolled and murmured; awakening us to a more lively and awful remembrance of the dangers we had escaped.

We had some difficulty in fixing ourselves for the night: the ladies were accommodated with the master's apartment, if a small but clean division of the vessel, in which it was impossible to stand upright, may be dignified with the name; and the rest were left to choose their own quarters. The smoke of cooking deterred me from going below, till the cold and dew made me think shelter necessary. I then stooped into the interior of the vessel, and creeping over the cargo, which seemed to consist entirely of cocoa-nuts, thought myself fortunate in finding a narrow board, five or six feet in length, on which I stretched myself, putting a bundle of fire-wood under my head as a pillow. Alexander, who had attached himself closely to me since our misfortune, came and lay by me. In the night he roused me, to drink from a cup he held in his hand: it contained hot conjee or rice-water, not an unpleasant beverage at any time, but then peculiarly grateful to my parched mouth.

I slept soundly, and rose refreshed; but should have been more so, had not one of the seamen, in searching for accommodations, after I had fallen asleep, chosen my head for his pillow, which before did not rest very easily on the bundle of sticks, and now, pressed by the weight of a sailor's skull, felt, when I awoke, as though it did not belong to me: a bathe in the sea-water restored the circulation.

In the morning we again weighed anchor, and in a few hours came in sight of the flag-staff of one of the forts of the harbour of Trincomallee: the wind was unfavourable, and we could not get into the harbour; we therefore sent our smaller boat, with four of the best seamen and the purser, to give information of our circumstances. It was a good distance, and the men were weary; but within two or three hours, we discerned the beautiful boats of a man of war, then in the harbour, hastening towards us under crowded sail: next we could distinguish the naval uniform of the officers; and, as they drew nearer, could see the fine countenances of our countrymen beaming with interest and commiseration, as they gazed on us, and directed their boats alongside: it was a scene to awaken the most powerful feelings; and will, I think, ever be depicted on my memory. My heart had been stout till that moment; but I then leaned against the mast, scarcely able to stand, from the mingled emotions excited in my mind.

We soon stepped into the boats, answering the numerous and kind inquiries of the officers, and enjoying the slight refreshment of fruit, &c., they had brought with them. The men pulled hard at their oars: we soon entered the harbour, admiring its spaciousness and the beauties of its scenery; but admiring, most of all, the wondrous dealings of that gracious Providence, which had preserved us in such unusual perils, and brought us to a place of rest and safety. We landed in the dockyard of Trincomallee, about three P.M. on Friday, the 8th of September, 1820, being exactly sixteen weeks after our embarkation at Gravesend.

CHAPTER III.

SEPTEMBER, 1820.

THE ISLAND OF CEYLON.

The harbour of Trincomallee is essentially necessary to any naval power which would keep possession of the coast of Coromandel, and maintain the command of the Bay of Bengal. It is the only port, available in stormy weather, south of Bengal, and is both safe and commodious. The Dutch had held it more than one hundred and fifty years, when, in 1791, the British took and retained it for a while; but in 1795, the annexation of Holland to France gave the British the opportunity of expelling the Dutch, and taking possession not only of Trincomallee, but of the entire Island of Ceylon.

Whatever may be thought of the government or commercial policy of the Dutch, in one respect they deserved the highest praise. They showed an earnest desire for the conversion of the natives to Christianity; and a succession of learned and pious Ministers from Holland devoted themselves to this good work. If on the arrival of the Wesleyan and American Missionaries, there was little genuine fruit to be found, after all their labours, it must be remembered, that compulsion, on the part of the Government, in which the example had been set by the Portuguese, would, as a consequence, produce hypocrisy in the people; that slavery, with all its debasing effects on master and servant, prevailed throughout the Island; that Popery, together with its twin superstition, Buddhism, had obtained firm hold on the minds of the population; and that from 1795 to 1816, little care had been taken to continue the work begun by the Dutch.

Ceylon was visited and described by the Mahomedan traveller Ibn Batuta, in the fourteenth century, and by the Venetian merchant Marco Polo, in the thirteenth. It had been the resort of Arabian merchants for many centuries. About fifty years before the Christian era, an ambassador from Ceylon made his appearance at Rome, at the court of Claudius Cæsar; and it is worthy of remark, that when the foundation of the Portuguese church in the Island of Manaar was dug, by a colleague of Xavier, in 1544, there was found a Roman coin of the Emperor Claudius.* The account of Ceylon obtained by the Greeks at the court of Chandragupta, three hundred years before Christ, and that of Aristotle, one hundred years previous, are distinguished by greater accuracy than some of more recent date; as is also that of Jambolo, recorded in Diodorus Siculus.

The natural riches and capabilities of the Island of Ceylon make it worthy of the high eulogies which have been recorded by its visitors from the earliest times. Under the dominion of the British, it has been delivered from slavery, and from all compulsory religious profession. It is to be deplored, that the superstitions of

* "A discovery of great historical importance was lately made by a gentleman at Manaar. In digging under the foundation of a very old house, some Roman bricks of a flat form were found; and, in sifting the rubbish, a gold ring, marked ANN. PLOC., (our types cannot imitate the exact characters,) turned up, of ancient manufacture, quite plain, and of a shape similar to those in the British Museum, which are said to have been worn by Roman knights. Now we know, from Pliny, that the farmer of the duties in the Red Sea, Annius Plocamus, was carried by a storm to the coast of Ceylon, 50 B.C. He was of the equestrian order; and there seems little reason to doubt of the ring having belonged to him. It is much time-worn, or rather injured by the effects of damp and corrosion."—*Ceylon Herald, July 4th*, 1843.

Buddhism are yet patronized and supported by the Government; but most sincerely do we hope that this stain will soon be wiped away, and that religious and commercial prosperity may yet be the lot of this beautiful island.

On our arrival, C. Upton, Esq., His Majesty's Commissioner in the Naval Department, already informed of our circumstances, was waiting to receive us. We were taken into an apartment, where a number of small loaves of excellent bread, and several bottles of wine, were set before us, for our immediate refreshment. The tidings of our escape and necessities were soon promulgated; and the carriages of the British residents came to the door to convey us to their respective houses, each vying with the other in kindness and hospitality.

Meantime Commissioner Upton, looking at my colleague's black coat, had inquired if any of our party were Ministers; and immediately congratulated us on the circumstance of our having a Mission on that station; observing, "Mr. Carver, your Missionary, is a most respectable man, whom I have known many years; he will be happy to receive you, and to supply all your wants." A message was sent to the Mission-house, and we soon found ourselves in the company of our excellent brethren, Messrs. Carver and Stead, who received us with open arms, uniting with us in thankful acknowledgments to the God of all our mercies.

Mr. S. gave up his room to Mr. and Mrs. Mowat. He initiated me into the modes of living and acting in a tropical climate: both he and Mr. C. showed us attentions, honourable to their feelings and their hearts, and which have left an indelible impression upon ours. They have never been repaid, except in the satisfaction of their own minds: for a full recompense, they must wait till "the resurrection of the just."

One of our fellow-passengers was entertained with us,

at the Mission-house;* the other passengers, and the officers of the ship, were received by different gentlemen on the station, and the seamen found suitable accommodations on board one of the hulks in the harbour.

Notwithstanding our anxieties, our exposure to rain and sun for forty-three hours, with the total want of food and water for a considerable time, and afterwards only a scanty supply of aliment, such as we had been unaccustomed to; our passengers generally, after a day or two's rest, were in tolerable health and spirits. Some of the seamen became unwell, and two of them, very fine, strong men, were carried off by the cholera morbus, the third night after we landed.

Our kind brethren opened their stores so liberally, and used their influence with their neighbours so effectually, that we were soon supplied with several changes of clothing, suitable to the climate; and were able to walk out morning and evening, to see the town and neighbourhood.

The scenery of Trincomallee is picturesque and beauti-

* Alexander, the Singhalese, was also kindly received by Mr. Carver, at the Mission-house, and supplied with a few books, clothes, and other things immediately necessary. He had not landed with Adam at Batticaloa, from an intention of proceeding with the vessel to Calcutta, where he hoped to receive ordination from Bishop Middleton. He subsequently came to Madras, soon after we arrived there; but, within a few days, returned to Ceylon, where, I believe, he still resides.

Adam, I have been informed, is now one of the Proponents, or native Preachers, employed by the Colonial Government of Ceylon, in the southern part of the Island.

These young men received from Sir Richard Otley and ourselves every attention during the voyage, but manifested no disposition to have religious communion with us, or to engage in any department of our Mission. Any religious convictions they may have received were not strong enough to preserve them from the love of the world: like many others, of whom better things might have been expected, they risked their religion, that they might be respectable; and it is to be feared that they are now neither religious nor respectable.

ful; none more so, I am informed, in the whole Island of Ceylon. The extensive harbour, with its forts, and its islands rising high out of the water, and covered with verdure to the top, and the shipping and public buildings, give a richness to the varied prospect, truly pleasing to the eye, and which the clear atmosphere of the island enables one to enjoy to perfection.

The public buildings of Trincomallee are magnificent; the native town is extensive, but the houses are mean and small; and I thought the inhabitants had an appearance of great poverty and wretchedness: this might be owing to their comparative nakedness, and to my not being accustomed to black skins, or to seeing so much of the body exposed, as is common among the native inhabitants of hot climates. The two most respectable-looking natives I saw in Trincomallee, were at the Mission-house: one of them, a venerable old man, the schoolmaster, who presented himself every day, with his *ola,* or palmyra-leaf book, to make his report. He was a Christian, and has since died in the faith and hope of the gospel: the other was a young man, a Christian also, in the service of Government.

The cattle and animals of all kinds appeared to me very small, the pasturage poor; and the land, from the long drought that had been then experienced, presented an appearance of barrenness.

The Mission-house in Trincomallee, like most houses in Ceylon and India, is only of one story; but has rooms sufficient to accommodate a family, or two single Missionaries. I there first admired the beautiful light given by lamps of cocoa-nut oil: the lamp is of glass, in the form of a tumbler, with a foot fitting into a candlestick, and having a cotton wick on a wire, standing upright in the middle of the lamp: the doors and windows of the house being generally open during the evening, and the wind blowing strongly, a cylindrical glass shade, fifteen or eighteen inches in height and about six inches in diameter, is placed over the whole, allowing the lamp to burn with a bright and steady flame. Finding one on the table, when retiring to rest, I inquired how I must extinguish it, and was informed, that it was intended to burn the whole night. I afterwards found that it is the practice throughout India, to burn lights in the chambers, or immediately within reach, to prevent the approach of noxious insects or serpents; or to procure immediate relief and satisfaction, if annoyed with them during the night.

On Sunday, the 10th, a respectable and attentive congregation assembled in the Mission-garden; and Mr. Mowat preached. The place of worship was a bungalow, a low building with a pent roof and thatched, which served as a school-room during the week, and as a chapel on the Lord's day. We were glad to enter again the courts of the Lord's house, and were particularly gratified by the spirit and feeling exhibited by many of the congregation, to whom we were then introduced for the first time. A good chapel has since been erected, more commodious, and more suitable for the sacred purpose to which it is devoted.

Commissioner Upton having kindly offered to Captain Dacre the use of H. M. schooner "Cochin," fifty tons' burden, commanded by Lieutenant Twineham, R. N., to convey him and our party to Madras, we embarked early in the morning of Friday, September 15th, being commended by our brethren and friends to the care of Him "who gathereth the winds in his first, and the waters in the hollow of his hand."

Our accommodations on board this vessel were not very commodious. The cabin was given to the ladies: the rest of the party had hammocks slung so near together, that by every motion of the vessel they rubbed one against another. Not having been used to a bed of this kind, at my first attempt the moment I entered it at one side, I fell out at the other, alighting upon two native men, who were trying to make themselves comfortable on the cargo.

On the passage across the Straits, between the island and the continent, the wind was strong and the sea very rough, frequently washing over the vessel, and exciting some alarm in those whose nerves had not recovered the severe shock they had sustained by the conflagration of the "Tanjore," and our subsequent perils and sufferings. The voyage proved longer than had been expected, and famine might have again stared us in the face, had it not been for the liberal supply of bread, fowls, wine, &c., which had been sent on board for our private use, in addition to the public supply allowed to the vessel. The bare deck served us for chairs, tables, and couches; and after an uncomfortable passage, we anchored in the Madras roads, at half-past eight on the evening of Sunday, the 17th of September.

Our small vessel rolled and pitched violently during the night by the influence of the surf and current, though we had anchored one or two miles from shore. Early next morning several Masoola boats came off to us, which, though large and deep, and lightly laden, did not convey us through the surf without subjecting us to a copious sprinkling by the spray of the sea.

By direction of some friendly persons we met with immediately on landing, we entered three palankeens, and soon found our way to the Mission-house, beyond Royapettah, about four miles distant from our landing-place; and in the kind attentions of Messrs. Lynch and Close, and Mrs. Close, we soon forgot the inconveniences we had recently suffered.

Immediately on our arrival at Madras, a Gazette Extraordinary was published, announcing the destruction of the "Tanjore," and the escape of its crew and passengers. This document, as I afterwards found, reached England, (probably by way of Bombay,) and was published in the London newspapers, long before our letters arrived. It was a fortunate circumstance that it mentioned particulars, and contained the names of the parties, or it might have occasioned much uneasiness to our friends at home.

From the deck of our tiny vessel the "Cochin," Madras presented a line of coast several miles in extent, varied by gardens, houses, churches, minarets, waste lands, esplanades, public buildings, and fortresses, which only a panorama could depict. The most prominent object was the Fort, with the flag-staff; from which the British flag at once announced to us the protection we might expect on shore, and the safety we might enjoy at our anchorage: when the roads become unsafe from unfavourable winds, the flag is struck, and every vessel puts out to sea.

FORT ST. GEORGE, MADRAS; AND CATAMARANS.

CHAPTER IV.

SEPTEMBER, 1820.

MADRAS AND ST. THOME.

MADRAS, or Fort St. George, the seat of the Government of the British possessions in the south of India, N. Lat., 13° 5′, E. Long., 80° 25′, cannot boast of any great antiquity. Like the other great Presidencies of India, it owes its importance to the commerce and government of the English East India Company. It is, however, the oldest of the three. Calcutta was commenced in 1690, Bombay was ceded to the British in 1661, and the old fort at Madras, which forms the public offices in the centre of the present fort, was erected in 1640. This occurred forty years after the incorporation of the East India Company, their first Charter having been granted by Queen Elizabeth on the 31st of December, 1600, under the title of "The Governor and Company of Merchants of London, trading to the East Indies."

It would be somewhat difficult to decide what reasons should have induced the selection of the site of Madras for a British settlement. The land is low, and for many miles round exceedingly flat, and naturally barren, though now greatly improved. The vicinity of St. Thomè, a flourishing Portuguese settlement, four miles to the south, and of Pulicat, a Dutch settlement, thirty miles to the north, may have presented some advantages, at that time, of importance to the English adventurers; but the selection was probably made from the circumstance, that the Hindoo Rajah of Chandergherry, of the dynasty of Bijanagar, made no difficulty of ceding an unprofitable tract of land, on which the foreign traders might erect warehouses and dwellings. Devapatnam, or Fort St. David, about one hundred and thirty miles south of Madras, was purchased from Rama, the Rajah of Ginjee, in 1690, for twenty-eight thousand pagodas, about £9,300; and was in like manner fortified and made a station of some consequence.

The declaration of war between France and England in 1744 was speedily followed by an interruption of the peaceful and lucrative pursuits of the merchants of Madras. A French fleet appeared in the roads, and the town was obliged to capitulate; the Governor of Pondicherry, Dupleix, promised Madras to the Nabob of Arcot, as a reward for his breach of engagement of protection to the British; the Nabob, not trusting the promises of the French, endeavoured to possess himself of it by force of arms, but was repulsed by the French with considerable loss. The property of the English was seized, notwithstanding a treaty to the contrary, which had been concluded with the French Admiral, La Bourdonnais; and the Governor and principal inhabitants of Madras were marched to Pondicherry, as trophies of the victory of the French. The peace of Aix-la-Chapelle restored Madras to the English in 1749.

Within ten years the horrors of a siege were again experienced by Madras. In December, 1758, Count de Lally, French Governor-General in India, advanced against it with a considerable force. He took possession of Black-Town, and continued his operations against the Fort for about two months; whilst the British were reduced to the greatest straits, not being able to command sufficient money to subsidize native troops from the Rajah of Tanjore. At length, on the 16th of February, 1759, when every man capable of bearing arms was called upon duty, under the expectation that an assault would be made through the breach that night, the arrival of a fleet under Admiral Pocock, with reinforcements, relieved the anxieties of the British, and hastened the departure of the besieging army.

On the 29th of March, 1769, Hyder Ali, with a party of six thousand horse, suddenly made his appearance before Madras. His object, however, was pacific. He was anxious to put an end to a disastrous and ruinous war, which had been some time carried on between him and the British; and a Treaty was accordingly executed by the Governor and Council on the 3d of April, and by Hyder Ali on the 4th, to the satisfaction of both parties, and to the joy of the poor natives, who were almost ruined by the ravages of contending armies.

A pleasing contrast to the general low and dull appearance of the coast, is presented by the beach opposite the anchorage; to the right is a line of lofty and handsome buildings, consisting of the Custom-House, the Supreme Court, the Offices of Houses of Agency, &c., extending to a considerable distance; to the left is Fort St. George, with its public edifices, flag-staff, and glacis; beyond that, the Governor's garden-house and banquetting-room. The spacious opening, intervening between the Fort and the buildings on the beach, allows an interesting view of the outer streets of the town of Madras, overtopped here and there by lofty *pandals* or sheds, adorned with flags, on the occasion of a marriage ceremony, or to the honour of some god; or surmounted by the tops of public buildings, and the towers and spires of churches, of which there are many in Madras, Armenian and Romish, Scotch and English. The tall minarets of the Mohammedan mosques, and the towers of the Hindoo pagodas, with brasen tops, glittering in the sun, cannot fail to attract the attention of a stranger.

Madras, like the rest of the Coast of Coromandel, possesses no harbour. The communication between the shipping and the shore is carried on exclusively by Masoola boats and cátamárans. The form of the boats is exhibited in the accompanying sketch, taken from

MASOOLA BOATS.

the beach at Madras: they are here represented, as they usually appear when waiting for employment, lying high and dry on the sand; that on the left shows the manner in which they are pushed off; the men who are employed in launching, climb into the boat, with astonishing ease, as soon as it is afloat. These boats, which are from twenty to thirty feet in length, and about six feet in depth and breadth, are constructed of strong planks, bent by means of fire; stitched together, through holes drilled all round the edges, with thread or cord of *coir*, the outer fibrous covering of the cocoa-nut; inside the boat, the stitches enclose a sort of calking or wadding of straw, rendering the seams water-tight. Masoola boats are generally manned by ten hands, eight men at the oars, one at the helm, and a boy to bale out the water: they strike their oars with great regularity, keeping time by a song kept up by one voice, the whole company joining in chorus at the end of each stanza. There are usually three waves to be passed between smooth water and the shore; these waves frequently rise to the height of six feet and upwards, and, breaking with a curl, the highest part of the wave falls over first, leaving a kind of hollow underneath. Unless well managed, even a Masoola boat would be overwhelmed: any other kind of boat would perish.

The boatmen, accustomed to the surf, are very skilful in avoiding its violence: when they come towards the first wave, they rest on their oars in total silence, and the helmsman directs the boat into the most favourable position; when it begins to rise on the wave, they at once burst out singing, *Alé, alé,* "A wave, a wave," and pull away with all their might, till the wave has expended itself; while the passenger does well to cover himself from the spray with his boat cloak. They then rest, waiting for the succeeding wave, which is passed in the same manner, till the boat is thrown almost dry upon the beach, and the men jump out to secure it from being carried back.

In passing the surf, I have often noticed that the wave, before it is expended, strikes the boat so severely, as to excite some apprehension; and there have been instances of the boat having been dashed to pieces by its force, with the consequent loss of the lading, and endangering of the lives of the persons on board. The boats employed in embarking or disembarking passengers, are therefore often attended by cátamárans.

A cátamáran (in Tamul *kattamaram,* from *kattal,* "to tie or bind," and *maram,* "wood," literally *tied wood,* or timber lashed together) is a raft, from twelve to fifteen feet long, by three to five feet in breadth, composed of three spars or logs of light wood, lashed together; and managed by two or three *kareiars,* or beachmen, persons of the same caste as those employed in the Masoola boats.*

When the surf is so high that Masoola boats cannot venture, cátamárans are used to communicate with the shipping, usually anchored two to four miles from the shore: the men secure letters, or small parcels, in their conical caps, formed of the leaf of the palmyra-tree: larger packages, covered with canvass or wax-cloth, are lashed to the raft; and they fearlessly venture into the most tempestuous seas. Though sometimes washed from the raft, their dexterity in swimming and diving enables them to regain it; and the loss of a man, in this perilous occupation, is of rare occurrence.

Besides these important services, the cátamárans are generally used in conveying the mails, in stormy weather, from the coast of Coromandel to Ceylon, a passage of sixty miles. They are also used by the fishermen, all down the coast. On fishing excursions, they generally go in a party, setting out early in the morning, well supplied with nets and baskets. When outside the surf, they carry a neat three-cornered sail, and proceeding many miles to sea, do not usually return till evening.

I remember to have seen the Captain of a vessel,

* The *kareiars*, or persons thus employed on the beach at Madras, amount to many hundreds, residing chiefly at Royapooram, a village to the north of the town: they are generally Roman Catholics. A Masoola boat can make three or four trips to merchant vessels in the course of one day. The regulated charge for each trip is fifteen *fanams*, or near two shillings and four-pence sterling. Vessels of war anchor at a greater distance from the shore; consequently, a trip to them is charged double the amount, and two trips only are made in the day. When in full employ, therefore, these men do not gain more than one shilling each per day. Small as this sum appears, they have of late years contributed out of it so liberally, as to raise for themselves a large and substantial church, in Royapooram, the erection of which cost several thousand pounds.

driven by a heavy storm from her anchorage off Negapatam, while he was ashore, set out in quest of her, seated on a chair lashed on one of these cátamárans. He thus crossed the straits, which divide Ceylon from the Continent, and succeeded in finding his ship.

The town of Madras, usually called Black-Town, is about a mile in extent from north to south, and not much less from east to west; fortified to the north and west by a wall, kept in constant repair, having five gates, opening to main roads leading to the surrounding country; and to the south, lying open to the Fort, which is a sufficient protection on that side. It contains numerous public offices, markets or bazaars, shops and taverns. Many Armenians reside in it, some streets are occupied by families of the descendants of Europeans; but by far the greater part of the inhabitants are Hindoos and Mahommedans, using the Tamul, Teloogoo, and Hindostanee languages. It is worthy of remark, that although so populous and central a place, there are no Jews dwelling in it.

The low site of the town is unfavourable to its being thoroughly drained and kept clean; though considerable pains have been taken for that purpose. Foul smells, and myriads of musquitoes, abound in most parts of it, particularly during the night, and render it an unfit habitation for Europeans, especially for those who have recently arrived in the country, and are unaccustomed to its inconveniences: few Europeans therefore reside in the town. The barracks for the soldiers, and quarters for the officers, are within the walls of the Fort. But the residences of the English generally are situated in gardens, extending from the immediate neighbourhood of the Fort to beyond St. Thomè, as far as Kilpauk, nearly four miles to the west; and to the village of Royapooram, a mile to the north.

The roads intersecting this extensive neighbourhood are formed of a red earth, brought from the neighbourhood of St. Thomas's Mount, well adapted to the purpose, being easily wrought when moistened with water, but hardening in the sun. They are generally smooth, and in good repair; bounded by hedges, or garden walls, and shaded with lofty trees. Every few hundred yards a gateway, or an avenue of trees, opens to the view an elegant mansion, seldom more than two stories high, but covering a great extent of ground, and well arranged for the comfort of its inhabitants; the kitchen, stables, and other out-houses, being at a considerable distance, to allow of an uninterrupted circulation of pure air.

The roads of Madras present to the stranger a lively and interesting scene. The four-wheeled carriages and gigs of the British inhabitants and of wealthy Hindoos and Mahommedans pass quickly along; the carriages of native construction, drawn by bullocks, move at a slower rate. Palankeens of both Europeans and natives are very numerous; and throngs of well-dressed Hindoos and Mahommedans, both male and female, in all the variety of their light and graceful costumes, and the marks of their different castes or professions, pass and repass in pursuit of their occupations or amusements. Their general appearance is much superior to that of the people I saw at Trincomallee.

In the month of September, when we arrived, the hottest season of the year had passed. Refreshing showers of rain in the evening were not uncommon; in consequence, the earth had the appearance of a verdant carpet, the trees were clothed with luxuriant foliage, and the gardens were adorned with beautiful plants and flowers of the richest hues; most of them new to me. Like the generality of persons on their first arrival in India, I did not think the heat worth noticing. The clear and constant shining of the sun, the lightness and freedom of the air, together with the attentions of my friends, and the satisfaction I felt in having reached the end of my voyage, and being safely placed among the objects of my mission, produced a cheerful exhilaration of spirits, more delightful to experience than easy to describe.

Many populous native villages and crowded bazaars are included within the limits of the jurisdiction of the Supreme Court of Madras, embracing a population of, it is supposed, not less than 630,000 souls, of whom 530,000 are Hindoos, 80,000 Mahommedans, and 20,000 Europeans of various nations, and the descendants of Europeans.

Some further estimate of the importance of Madras may be obtained by referring to the statistical statement which is appended to the Introduction, and which details some particulars of the vast and populous districts which form the Madras presidency, and to which Madras is the principal entrance and key.

One of the most remarkable of the villages in the neighbourhood, is St. Thomè, in Tamul, *Mielapoor*; or, as it is sometimes written, *Meliapoor*, "the City of Peacocks." It has been generally believed, that St. Thomas the Apostle preached the gospel in India, and founded a Christian church at this place. This opinion has been thoroughly examined and successfully exploded by the Rev. James Hough, M.A., the learned and laborious author of "The History of Christianity in India." It seems more probable that a Nestorian Missionary, of the name of Thomas, had preached in India in the fifth or sixth century, and had been the instrument of extending to this part of the Coromandel Coast the Christian church, which no doubt existed in India at least so early as the second century, when India was visited by Pantænus, the President of the celebrated school in Alexandria.

It is said that St. Thomè was quite desolate when the Portuguese first visited it in 1545. Subsequent to its occupation by them, it became one of the finest cities on the coast. It was fortified with a wall of stone, strengthened by several bastions, and had under its jurisdiction three hundred villages and towns. At first it was under the ecclesiastical government of the Bishop of Cochin; but it was afterwards erected into a bishopric, subject to the Archbishop of Goa. There was also a college of Jesuits, for the instruction of youth.

In 1662 the Portuguese are said to have sold St. Thomè to the Hindoos. At all events, it ceased to be a garrison, although it does not appear that it was forsaken by the Romish Clergy and their adherents. During the wars which took place between the French and the English, its vicinity to Madras afforded its inhabitants the means of acquiring information concerning the transactions of the English; which was often employed to the disadvantage of the latter. For some time neither civil nor military authority existed within St. Thomè, and it seemed to belong to no one. Dupleix wished to claim it for the French; and the only question being, whether it should be garrisoned by them or their European rivals, Admiral Boscawen promptly determined the point in 1749, by taking possession of it on the part of the English.

The original Hindoo town of Mielapoor stands at a short distance from the beach, and was never included within the Portuguese fort. It has a large ancient temple of considerable repute; adjoining it is a deep stone-built tank, filling a very large quadrangle, where the natives bathe, and from which they supply themselves with water. The annual festival of the temple is attended by tens of thousands of worshippers; and is celebrated with barbaric splendour, and at great expense. There is no place within the same distance of

Madras where the traveller may see such an assemblage of *Yogis, San-yasis, Tabasis, Pandarams,* all the varieties of heathen priests, priestesses, and devotees, each making an exhibition of his peculiar mode of dress, worship, and penance, as in Mielapoor, on this occasion. The Brahmans and other heathen inhabitants of Mielapoor are less accessible to the exertions of the Christian Missionary than the inhabitants of the interior generally; a consequence of the long and habitual association of the Christian name with many of those whose character and actions have disgraced it. On the north side of Mielapoor there are many Mahommedan inhabitants.

There are several Romish churches within the limits which bounded the old Portuguese town or fort. The largest is the Bishop's church, or cathedral, on a line with his residence, but nearer the sea. At the eastern end of it is enclosed a small building, which has the appearance of a heathen temple. It is here that the sword was found, with which it is said that the Apostle was slain, and the cross, stained with his blood. Underneath is a deep and wide excavation, where it is said that the Apostle was buried. It is still a practice to carry away the holy earth in small quantities, to preserve voyagers from shipwreck, and to answer other purposes of superstition.

Gibbon* mentions a very remarkable corroborative testimony to the antiquity of the Christian church in Mielapoor. He says: "At the end of the ninth century the shrine of St. Thomas, perhaps in the neighbourhood of Madras, was devoutly visited by the ambassadors of Alfred; and their return with a cargo of pearls and spices rewarded the zeal of the English monarch, who entertained the largest projects of trade and discovery." At

* "Decline and Fall," vol. iv. p. 599.

the foot of the page he subjoins the following particulars: "The Indian Missionary, St. Thomas, an apostle, a Manichean, or an Armenian merchant, was famous as early as the time of Jerome. Marco Polo was informed on the spot, that he suffered martyrdom in the city of Maabar, or Meliapoor, a league only from Madras, where the Portuguese founded an episcopal church, under the name of St. Thomè, and where the saint performed an annual miracle, till he was silenced by the profane neighbourhood of the English." With reference to Alfred's embassy to Mielapoor, he adds: "Neither the author of the Saxon Chronicle, (A.D. 883,) nor William of Malmsbury, *(De Gestis Regum Angliæ,* vol. ii. c. iv. p. 44,) were capable, in the twelfth century, of inventing this extraordinary fact; they are incapable of explaining the motives and measures of Alfred; and their hasty notice serves only to provoke our curiosity. William of Malmsbury feels the difficulties of the enterprise, *quod quivis in hoc sæculo miretur;* and I almost suspect the English ambassadors collected their cargo and legend in Egypt." Whether Gibbon's surmise be well founded or not, it is still very interesting to know, that the existence of Christianity in India was reported in England at so early a period, and excited the attention of the pious and sagacious Alfred.

The Romish Church, with its usual ingenuity, has invented further local legends concerning the apostle. Whilst they profess that the sword and cross above mentioned were discovered at Mielapoor, they show the place of the martyrdom of St. Thomas at some rocks, about four miles distant in the interior, called the Little Mount. The Jesuits have built there a church and dwelling-house; the situation is salubrious, and the view extensive. It is one of the stations where they prepared themselves, by study and discipline, as *san-yasis* or devotees, for their mission in the interior. They show a fountain, made by the apostle, between two rocks, of which the visitors drink; and two crosses, cut in the hard rocks, as the workmanship of the saint. There is also a cave, where the apostle is said to have retired for prayer; on one side of which there is a small breach, which serves as a window. The tradition is, that when the Heathen came to kill him, he would transform himself into a peacock, and escape that way. There are also marks in the rocks, where it is said that the apostle stumbled and fell, at the time of his martyrdom.

About three miles further there is another eminence, still higher, called St. Thomas's Mount. The ascent is steep, and would be difficult, but for steps which have been cut or built, for the convenience of visitors, and seats and resting-places at certain distances. On the top is a small level or plain: in the middle of it is a curious old church, in which the above-mentioned cross is kept, and displayed only on particular occasions. There is also a house for the residence of the Priest. The annual festival of St. Thomas is held here in December. At night the steps leading up the mount are illuminated. It is attended by many thousands of Portuguese and native Romanists; some of whom exhibit a semblance of devotion; but the greater part appear to assemble only for pleasure and dissipation. It is not unusual to see Heathens and Mahommedans taking part at the festival, in fulfilment of vows which they have made in times of sickness or danger. In the course of my experience in India I had frequent occasions of observing, that Hindooism and Romanism, as twin superstitions, have no difficulty in reciprocating with each other; while they are both equally opposed to the clear light of scriptural truth.

CHAPTER V.

SEPTEMBER—OCTOBER, 1820.

MISSIONARY OCCUPATIONS.

It had been intended, by our Missionary Committee in London, that we should proceed to Bangalore, a town in the interior of the Mysore country, and there attempt the establishment of a Mission. Mr. Mowat and myself were desirous of following these instructions immediately; but our brethren in Madras kindly urged us to remain with them a few months, till we could replenish our wardrobes and collect a few books, towards replacing those we had lost; reminding us, that meantime we might have access to their libraries, and, whilst we applied ourselves diligently to the attainment of the Tamul language, might have the advantages of society, and occasional opportunities of addressing the congregations already formed in Madras and its neighbourhood.

Concurring, in some measure, with these representations, we agreed to remain. We were introduced to many highly respectable individuals, friendly to the promotion of Christianity in India; to the excellent Missionaries of other Societies, and their families, then resident in Madras; and to our own congregations and societies, both English and native, in Black-Town, Royapettah, and St. Thomas's Mount. From the peculiar circumstances of our voyage, we were extensively known, and in every quarter experienced much kindness and hospitality.

I was greatly interested by the first native Christian congregation I had an opportunity of seeing. It was in the Mission chapel, Royapettah, a place of worship erected by Mr. Lynch, chiefly for the accommodation of the natives, and of late devoted to them exclusively. An Assistant, of Dutch descent, commenced the service by a Tamul hymn, and by reading the Rev. Dr. Rottler's translation of the Liturgy, with the lessons of the day. The Missionary, Mr. Close, then ascended the pulpit, and prayed and preached in English; pausing at the end of each sentence, while the Assistant, who remained in the desk, interpreted in Tamul to the congregation, who were wonderfully attentive, responding aloud to questions put by the Preacher at intervals during the sermon, to ascertain whether they understood the subject of his discourse. The whole assembly, men, women, and children, sat upon mats, spread upon the ground. They stood up during singing; and at prayer, knelt with their bodies inclined forward, almost prostrate, their hands and faces resting on the ground. The men were neatly attired in white cotton cloths; the women, in red or blue cloths, of the same material, or of silk, one piece of about nine yards in length being disposed, (without the aid of pins or sewing,) into a modest covering of the whole person; one end being drawn over the head, to serve as a veil, when they assemble in a public congregation.*

* Some of the Hindoo women wear under the cloth a *ravvikei*, or body-dress, usually of fancy silk, fitting close to the person, and only long enough to cover the bosom; it has short sleeves, reaching half way to the elbow.— Many of them have gold or silver bracelets and anklets of large size on their arms and ankles, and abundance of rings and jewellery about their noses and ears, fingers and toes: they wear no shoes and no head-dress.

The men wear turbans. The rest of their dress consists of two cloths, one disposed about the loins, forming something like a pair of loose trousers; the other gracefully thrown over the shoulders. Native men, in the service of Europeans, generally wear also a close jacket, of muslin or calico, with sleeves down to the wrist.

The cloths described are of native manufacture, and in general

The class-meeting, which was held immediately after service, for the members of our society, gave me an opportunity of ascertaining, that many of these persons, who had lately been either Heathens or Romanists, now knew and valued the power of experimental religion. Seeing what the Almighty had been pleased to effect among the natives, by the instrumentality of my brethren, I could not but "thank God and take courage."

Within a few days after my arrival, I witnessed a much more numerous assembly of native Christians, on the occasion of opening the church in Black-Town, erected by the munificence of the Government of Madras, for the Missionaries of the Church Missionary Society. On that occasion, the natives connected with the different congregations in the neighbourhood of Madras, but chiefly, I believe, with the Christian Knowledge Society's Mission in Vepery, assembled so numerously as to fill the church, and presented a scene which it was impossible for the Christian or the philanthropist to gaze upon without interest and delight. The Rev. T. Barenbruck read the Liturgy, in the Tamul language; and the Rev. Dr. Rottler, a venerable Missionary, more than seventy years of age, delivered, in the same language, a sermon, which seemed to be understood and felt by all to whom it was addressed.

compose (with the turbans of the men) the entire dress of the southern Hindoos. The quantity used for a dress, by each sex, (about nine yards in length, and one yard and a quarter in width,) forms an entire piece, as it comes from the loom; the man's cloth being divisible into two parts, at a place left for the purpose. They are frequently bordered with red, and sometimes with gold thread. Specimens of these cloths are in the possession of my friends in Manchester, which, being of the better sort, a kind of strong muslin with borders of gold thread, cost me five and a half pagodas each, or about thirty-seven shillings sterling, for nine yards. For the humbler classes, the dress may generally cost ten shillings, or about thirteen-pence halfpenny per yard.

I was much interested by the native school in our Mission garden, where I saw their mode of writing with an iron style on the *ola*, or palmyra leaf, and heard both male and female native children repeat their lessons in the Tamul language, with an ease which I then could not but envy.

It was in Madras I first entered a Hindoo's house. They are generally of a quadrangular form, having a door to the front, but no windows. In the inside is a square court, open to the sky, in which their domestic concerns are usually transacted. The accompanying plate is a

INTERIOR OF A NATIVE HOUSE.

representation of the interior of a habitation of this kind, and displays the females of the family, employed in carrying, beating, and winnowing the rice grain, to free it from the husk.

The *mohorum*, an annual Mahommedan feast, continuing ten days, commenced about this time. The streets and roads of Madras were crowded by farcical masques and mummeries. Some of the parties consisted of men and boys, whitened over with chalk or chunam; one being dressed as a tiger, with an enormous tail, and held in a chain by his keeper; others had given themselves a darker hue than that which nature had bestowed, by means of oil and lamp-black, and performed a dance, keeping time and making a sort of accompaniment by striking together the small clubs they grasped in each hand. Other parties had a still more grotesque appearance, having as their principal character a man dressed to an unusual size in swathes of hay or oakum, giving him a shaggy and terrific appearance. But the most imposing scene was a splendid illumination of a large house and garden on the Mount-road, belonging to a rich Mahommedan, a relation to the Nabob. I was taken to see it, about ten o'clock at night, and introduced to the inner court of the house, where I found a large assemblage of natives, and a party of ladies and gentlemen, partaking of refreshments, and waiting for an oration about to be delivered in Hindostanee or Arabic. Whatever the intention of the feast might be, I never, on this or on any future occasion, saw any thing indicative of religious feeling connected with it.

During my short stay in Madras, at this first visit, I several times addressed the native congregations, by means of the interpreter; but more frequently preached to the English congregations, at St. Thomas's Mount, Royapettah, and Black-Town, consisting of some Europeans, but chiefly of Indo-Britons, or descendants of Europeans, born in India. We commenced a week evening English service in another crowded part of Madras, called John Pereira's, where a house full of people assembled; but the fewness of the Missionaries did not allow of its regular continuance. Our chapel in Black-Town was small, and very much crowded; liberal subscriptions towards erecting a larger one, on the same premises, since completed, were already commenced. A Missionary Auxiliary Society had been formed, and had been the means of bringing some contributions into the funds of the Parent Society in England.

I employed a Moonshee or teacher, to assist me in gaining a knowledge of the Tamul* language. Tamul is, I conceive, more extensively spoken than any other language in the south of India: it is used by the natives of the north of Ceylon; and by the population of the eastern side of Continental India, from Cape Comorin, the southern point, to some distance to the north of Madras, amounting to many millions. It is one of that peculiar family of the Indian languages, that disclaims the Sanscrit as its origin, though many terms from the latter have been introduced into it; and whilst it has many words and idioms in common with the cognate dialects of the Malayalim, Teloogoo, and Cannada, it differs from them essentially in its letters and sounds, and in its own peculiar and extensive literature, both ancient and modern. As a refined and cultivated language, used by so large a portion of the human race, its character is worthy of the attention of the linguist; the curious stores it opens to him will amply repay his toil: but to the Missionary to the natives of that part of India, its acquisition is absolutely necessary. The Old and New Testaments were translated into Tamul, more than a century ago, by Ziegenbalg and his coadjutors, of the Danish Mission of Tranquebar. Another translation was made, about fifty years since, by Fabricius and others. A still more idiomatic translation was effected by the late learned and laborious Missionary, the Rev. C. Rhenius, of Palamcottah; concerning which, I can say from my

* It is sometimes written Tamil; but the true sound of the word, is, I think, more correctly conveyed in the mode I have adopted, and which was used by Beschi, and others of equal authority. The first syllable, should be pronounced as the first syllable in the word *tamper;* and the second, as the first syllable in the word *ultra.*

own knowledge, that its style is both clear and elegant, and is perhaps not excelled by any modern translation of the Holy Scriptures.

When in London, preparing for my voyage to India, after considerable trouble, I had procured from Paris a copy of a Tamul grammar, in Latin, by Ziegenbalg. I soon made myself master of the characters, of the declensions of the nouns and conjugations of the verbs, contained in it, and of its vocabulary and phrases; but found, when I recommenced my studies in Madras, that I had formed an erroneous idea of the pronunciation of the letters, for want of a living instructor; for many of the sounds in the Tamul language are such as cannot be conveyed correctly, either by the letters of our own language, or the most elaborate description. My teacher, during my stay in Madras, was a very stout native, whose conceit and bad English afforded me no small amusement. However, he rendered me considerable assistance, and attended me regularly at six o'clock in the morning.

But I did not at this time remain long in Madras. The Rev. T. H. Squance, of the Wesleyan Mission, who had recently removed from the north of Ceylon to Negapatam, on the coast of Coromandel, one hundred and eighty miles to the south of Madras, wrote from thence, that there were considerable openings in that neighbourhood for Missionary labours, to an extent to which he was not adequate, while alone, and begged that one of the newly arrived brethren might come to his assistance. It was toward the end of the month of October; the rainy season had commenced, and there was every prospect of an uncomfortable journey; it would have been too great a risk for Mr. Mowat, with Mrs. Mowat, to have attempted it. It was determined that I should go, and within five weeks after my arrival at Madras, I was ready to leave it for Negapatam.

CHAPTER VI.

OCTOBER, 1820.

JOURNEY TO NEGAPATAM.

PALANKEEN AND BEARERS.

I DID not part with my companions in danger and suffering, nor leave my newly formed acquaintance in Madras, without regret; but the path of duty was before me, and I considered the call imperative. On Tuesday, the 24th of October, at four P.M., I set out on my journey;* having ten bearers to my palankeen, and six men to carry my baggage, cooking utensils, &c. The palankeen with which I was provided differed from those commonly used in India, being a double *tonjon,* admitting two

* On this, and on all similar occasions, the whole of the time I resided in India, I found no difficulty in obtaining the requisite passports from the proper authorities, on stating the object of my journey, and the route I wished to travel.

persons to sit face to face, and being sufficiently long for one person to recline in. The possibility of thus changing the position, on a journey, is a great advantage; the common palankeen does not admit of it, but requires a position like that of sitting up in bed, supported by pillows: easy at the first, but when long continued, very tiresome to persons unaccustomed to it.

In the first stage, I sat or reclined about two hours and a half, the poles of the palankeen supported on the shoulders of four men, who were relieved about every ten minutes by four others; those who were not actually carrying, running before or behind; the whole party talking, laughing, and singing, and moving at the rate of about five miles an hour.

When I first saw this mode of conveyance, I heartily pitied the men employed in bearing the palankeen; and could not dismiss a strong sense of self-disapprobation for allowing myself to be carried by them. But this method of travelling is often indispensable to an European, in a torrid clime like India; and in a country so extensive, where the roads are commonly little more than tracks, through swamp and jungle, where bridges are comparatively rare, and the passes of the mountains not unfrequently impracticable to any beast of burden without extreme difficulty and danger, experience has fully established its necessity. Travelling on horseback is the only alternative; and with this mode, tents are required: the stages, too, must be short, unless the traveller can bear exposure to the dews of the night and the heat of the day. Observation has convinced me, also, that there is no description of men in India better satisfied with their employment, than palankeen-bearers: they are cheerful in the performance of the journeys they undertake; and though they run thirty or even forty miles at one stretch in the course of a night, they are prepared to recommence their task on the succeeding evening. Six men once carried me thirty-two miles, between sunset and sunrise; and on another occasion, six men took up my palankeen, at the Mission-house door in Madras, with the intention of performing a journey of six hundred miles; and said they were ready to travel with me even to Kási, or Benares, (the most distant place a southern Hindoo thinks of visiting,) if I desired it.

The palankeen-bearers rarely quarrel with the people of the villages through which they pass; but at the end of a stage they often dispute violently among themselves about the veriest trifles; and when they are excited, their language and gestures are most extravagant, so as to lead a stranger to apprehend serious consequences. A friend of mine, a Danish Missionary, on his arrival in Madras, was dispatched to his station, in the interior, by palankeen. At the end of the first stage the bearers quarrelled violently: as he knew neither their language nor character, he imagined that he was the subject of their quarrel, and that they intended to murder him. His imagination was so wrought upon, that he supplicated them, in Danish, to have mercy upon him, and offered them his money and his gold watch, if they would spare his life, and conduct him safely on his journey. They gazed at him with astonishment, not comprehending either his fears or his promises; and his uneasiness continued until the next day, when he met with an European friend, who relieved him from all further apprehension, and advised the bearers to be more peaceable towards each other.

As their caste does not allow them to eat promiscuously with others, one of the party is usually occupied in carrying their pots for preparing food, and in cooking their meals, which consist chiefly of rice. Whilst at rest during the day, if they do not sleep, some amuse themselves with cards, or a sort of backgammon; the more thrifty employ themselves in spinning cord, of which their fishing-nets are made, or in weaving the nets, with which, in passing through the country, they almost every day provide a plentiful fish-curry to their rice.

I rested the first night in a choultry, or *chattram;* an edifice of one story, constructed of brick and chunam, or of granite, presenting no other accommodation than bare walls and a roof. Choultries abound in the parts of India I have traversed: they are erected from charitable motives, or as works of merit, by opulent Hindoos, for the accommodation of travellers, of whatever class, who may choose to rest in them by day or night. They usually have near them the valuable addition of a tank, or pond of water, of a square form, built up the four sides with steps of bricks or granite, and sufficiently deep to secure the continuance of water, good or bad, throughout the longest dry season; often with a small temple on the banks, containing an image of the patron's favourite object of devotion. One of these native inns, or rest-houses, is depicted in the vignette on the title-page of this volume.

One or more Peons, or native officers of police, employed by Government, are usually in attendance at these places, to maintain order among the visitants, and to assist the traveller in obtaining supplies for himself and party.

Some choultries have divisions, to accommodate different classes of travellers; others consist of one apartment only: in such I have often slept, whilst the floor around me has been covered with strangers, of all classes, and both sexes, wrapped separately in their various coloured cotton cloths, and lying side by side, like so many bundles. Sometimes it is necessary to use some degree of authority, to silence a noisy crowd of people, who have had some hours' rest before the weary traveller arrives ; and more than once I have been under the necessity of turning a large party out of their lodgings, before I could secure any rest for myself.

Choultries are generally open to the road, and, having no windows, are liable to much dust and heat, without securing the advantage of a circulation of air : they are also frequently filthy, and the haunts of bats, monkeys, and serpents. When the weather has permitted, I have generally preferred passing the day under a shady tree, or the night in the open air, to encountering the vile smells and inconveniences of a choultry.

The traveller pays nothing for his accommodation in these buildings : he remains as long as he pleases, and proceeds on his journey when it suits his convenience. As there are no inns on the roads in India, these establishments are invaluable to those who do not travel with tents. But the munificence of the Madras Government has lately been providing bungalows, buildings of a superior description, at intervals of twelve or fifteen miles on the most public roads, for the accommodation of English travellers.

Opposite the choultry where I rested for the first night was a bazaar, kept by dealers in rice, the various condiments for curry, oil, &c. : both they and their customers seemed to think a loud noise necessary to the driving of a good bargain. A native woman having left her child screaming on the floor of the choultry, while she had a little chat with the people opposite, I went to look at it by the glimmer of the lamp burning in the wall : she saw me, and came running with great alarm, snatched her child from the ground, and, hastening away, left me in quiet possession of my quarters. The Peon, or Policeman, came, as usual at these places, to inquire my name and character, whence I came, and whither I was bound; and offered his assistance to procure any thing I might need. One of my attendants, whose business it was to cook for me, kindled a fire outside the choultry, and prepared me a cup of tea. I then lay down, and slept undisturbed till three o'clock in the morning.

The moon shone beautifully clear: I roused my men, who were sleeping on the ground around me, that we might continue our journey before the heat of the day. We had not proceeded far before we came to the banks of a river, much swollen by the late rains, but which, like many on the same journey, had to be passed without either bridge or boat, in the manner which I shall now describe.

On these occasions, the palankeen-bearers take off the greater part of their clothing, and fold it on or about their heads. They advance till about knee deep in the water, bearing the palankeen in the ordinary mode; when they stand still, and, by a joint effort, raise it upon the heads of six of them; (the traveller, of course, remaining in it the whole time;) they thus proceed to the opposite bank, sometimes up to the neck in water, the hands of those who are bearing the palankeen being held and supported by their companions. This plan of crossing rivers may appear dangerous; but the men are so careful, that it is seldom any serious accident occurs: I have, however, heard of instances in which a sudden rush of water from the mountains has overwhelmed the whole party, and washed them into the sea.

I proceeded without accident to Covelong, where I dined with Mr. and Mrs. Close, and a friend from St. Thomas's Mount: they were spending a few days in the retirement of that place, to recruit their health.

Covelong was formerly a fortress belonging to the Nabob of Arcot. It had no ditch, but a strong wall, flanked by round towers, on which were mounted thirty pieces of cannon. The French obtained possession of it by stratagem in 1750. The fortress being within musket-shot of the sea, a French ship anchored in the roads, and made signals of distress. Several natives thereupon went on board, where they were told that most of the crew had died of scurvy, and that the rest must perish in like manner, if they were not permitted to land immediately, as they were unable to navigate the ship. The Nabob's Officer in command of the fort granted their request, and thirty men, apparently labouring under great infirmity, were admitted. They had arms concealed under their clothes; and, notwithstanding the alleged ravages of disease, they took the earliest opportunity of convincing their native friends, that they had not quite lost the power of using them. In the night they rose on the garrison, whom they overpowered, and added Covelong to the list of the French possessions in India. In 1752 Captain, afterwards Lord, Clive wrested this fortress and Chingleput from the hands of the French.

Covelong is now nothing more than a fishing village; and would not be so large as it is, were it not for a Romish church, and a charitable establishment connected with it, for the reception of the poor and infirm of all descriptions; the cottages originally erected for the accommodation of visitors having been appropriated to the purpose of alms-houses. The whole establishment, religious and charitable, is, I believe, supported by legacy of the late Mr. De Monte, of Madras, a gentleman whose wealth and charity have rendered his name imperishable in that neighbourhood.

The whole of this country has been traversed by Romish Missionaries, chiefly from Goa; and their churches and followers are very numerous. These Missionaries are generally native born, though of Portuguese descent; and, their mode of living not being expensive, they appear generally to be well supported by the contributions of the people, in addition to a pittance to which each of them is entitled from their respective colleges in Goa.

In the evening neither entreaties nor threats could induce my bearers to travel further than Tripatoor, though I had engaged to preach at Sadras, a small Dutch settlement about ten miles further down the coast.

Tripatoor is a large native village, with wide and clean streets, presenting an appearance of great respectability and comfort. The principal tank is on a rising ground to the west: it is built round with stone, and has a temple near it of the same substantial materials. To the north is another temple, on the top of a hill, from whence there is a beautiful and extensive prospect; the ascent is by several hundred steps of hard stone. No European resides in the neighbourhood: I walked about, without expecting to find any person with whom I could converse; and was agreeably surprised to be accosted in English by a man as dark as a native, but who said he was a Portuguese, and a Roman Catholic. He proved to be amazingly ignorant about religion; Christ's being the son of the Virgin Mary, was the sum of his knowledge of the Saviour; and as to the transgression of our first parents, he thought they did right, because they were much wiser after it than before. How great is the guilt of those who, professing to be Christian teachers, take no pains to communicate a knowledge of the truth to their flocks!

The following morning I reached Sadras, and passed a pleasant day, in the society of F. P. Regel, Esq., a Dutch gentleman at the head of that settlement. The fort of Sadras lies in ruins, having been blown up during the war; and the place altogether is too small and too poor to be of any value to the Netherlands Government. They retained it, however, and some other stations in India of a similar description, until an advantageous exchange was made by them for the beautiful island of Sumatra. I preached in the evening to a respectable congregation in Mr. Regel's hall. The people were the more glad to hear the word of God, as they had no opportunities of enjoying that privilege, except on the occasional visit of a Missionary.

My road now lay through jungle, and a flat country, intersected by the Palaur, and other rivers, and two wide inlets of the sea. Jungle is uncleared and uncultivated ground; in some parts overgrown with wild plants and shrubs, rising to the height of twelve or sixteen feet, and almost impenetrable; in other parts presenting a green sward, which serves as a pasture for sheep and cattle, which are under the care of herdsmen, and are kept together by the leaders having bells on their necks. Clumps of thicket are every where interspersed, forming a perfect wilderness; an excellent cover for game, which is found in abundance; but also the haunt of serpents and other noxious reptiles. Jungles are the resort of tigers; several of a smaller kind, called *chetas*, have been killed or taken in that which I now traversed; but I met with none.

On Saturday morning I rested in Pondicherry, under the shade of trees, not being aware that it contained some decent houses of entertainment. It is one of the few stations the French still hold in India, and is a populous and pretty town: the European part of it is regular and clean, and adorned with several churches: the native part is so thronged with inhabitants, as to remind me, in walking about, of the difficulty of pressing through an English market.

Pondicherry (or *Puthu-Cheri*, literally, "New-Town")

was ceded to a French merchant of the name of Martin, who peopled it in 1672, with the remains of an unsuccessful expedition against Trincomalee, then in the possession of the Dutch, and a number of colonists who had been expelled from St. Thomè, which they had forcibly taken possession of. To this place, in 1689, resorted the French Jesuits, who had been driven from Siam, with the famous Father Bouchet at their head. Here they erected a church of large dimensions and uncommon splendour, and planned an extension of their Mission into the interior of the country, to the west and north, in emulation of the Mission at Madura, so greatly boasted of by Romish writers. Their success appears to have equalled their expectations; for, in 1725, they reported that there were three thousand Christians in Pondicherry, and in the interior eight thousand, connected with eleven churches. These Missions are still maintained, as will appear from subsequent parts of this narrative. Some details of the operations of these Missions, and the questionable methods adopted to induce the Hindoos to prefer the Romish to the Brahmanical ceremonies, will be found below. It is worthy of remark, that the French Government admitted native Christians into their service in every department, and thus held out a substantial encouragement; whilst an opposite policy was strictly observed by the British Government, until a very recent date.

The following brief summary of the progress of the French Mission in the Carnatic, is translated from Walther's "Tamul Ecclesiastical History:"—

"The Jesuits who came from Siam formed a plan, by which the French Missionaries might extend to the north the Mission which the Portuguese Missionaries had formed in Madura. They accordingly proceeded to erect a church in Pondicherry; but their proceedings were interrupted in 1694, by the capture of Pondicherry by the Dutch.

At that time some of the French Missionaries were absent in the interior, for the purpose of acquainting themselves with the plan of the Madura Mission.

"Peace being restored between the Dutch and the French in 1697, they retarued again to Pondicherry in 1699.

"In the month of June, 1700, the Jesuit Maduit went to Conjeveram, and within three months and a half baptized one hundred and twenty persons, and built two churches.

"In October, 1700, Father Dolu wrote to Europe from Pondicherry, that the Heathen were much impressed with the Romish festivals and ceremonies; and that he therefore made it his daily study to have them celebrated with the utmost pomp and magnificence. In the same year Father de la Fontaine returned from China, and went to Aoor, where Bouchet had baptized eleven thousand persons within four years and a half.

"In 1702 these two Missionaries entered on the Carnatic Mission. Bouchet, as the Superior, conducted the Mission in Turkullam; Mauduit took charge of that in Karuvei Poondu, and de la Fontaine that in Punganoor.

"In 1708 there were five Missionaries in the interior. The Brahmans and Daseris, (heathen mendicant friars,) and other Hindoos, persecuted them; but they were protected by the Mahometan rulers.

"In 1712 Father Bouchet began to form a church in Ariancoopam.

"In 1722, at the celebration of Christmas in Veiavoor, the Heathen of Pavuni, Piratoor, and Kalamvarum, not only adorned the whole street, but requested permission to have a feast to the honour of the Queen of Angels, celebrated at their own expense.

"In 1725 there were as many as three thousand Christians in Pondicherry; in the interior, as many as eight thousand; and eleven churches. The Governors of Pondicherry admit Christians into the service of Government; a circumstance which is very favourable to their increase. The performance of a comedy in Ariancoopam, at the festival of the nativity of the Virgin Mary, in which the heathen deities were ridiculed, was the means of inducing many of the Heathen to embrace Christianity, which at that time was protected in the Carnatic by order of the Mogul."

The territory of Pondicherry is circumscribed, extending but a short distance on each side of the town, but so entirely cultivated as to resemble one large garden. If the British territory were as industriously improved as the neighbourhood of Pondicherry, it would be the richest, and perhaps the most beautiful, country in the world.

In the evening I reached Cuddalore; but not succeeding in my inquiries for the person to whom I was directed, and at whose house I was to have preached the following day, I pursued my journey during the night, and passed the Sunday at a solitary choultry; where I had an opportunity of giving tea and other refreshments to an English soldier and his wife, who had travelled on foot about five hundred miles from the Travancore country, and were now on their way to Madras.

On Tuesday morning I arrived at Tranquebar. I was hospitably received and entertained by Dr. Caemerrer, Chaplain to the Danish Government of Tranquebar, and Missionary of the Royal College of Copenhagen. He showed me the churches, the library, and the houses belonging to this Mission; which was once extensive, having no less than six Missionaries employed in it. I viewed with interest the place where the devoted Ziegenbalg, the first Protestant Missionary to India, and his companions, had lived and preached, and where their remains are deposited till they shall be raised to their reward: but the sight which most affected me, was the library, composed of the best works on biblical criticism, in various languages, and of rare and valuable books, on every subject suitable for such an establishment, falling to pieces by the influence of the climate, or partially devoured by insects, from which no book can be preserved in India without uncommon care.

This settlement was formed by the Danes in 1620. The Mission was commenced by Henry Plutscho, and Bartholomew Ziegenbalg, in 1706. These apostolic men were Germans, though sent by Frederic IV. of Denmark. From this Mission proceeded the first translation of the Old and New Testament into Tamul, and a most useful course of Christian literature, to which all modern Missions, in the south of India, and in north Ceylon, have been greatly indebted. In 1734 the number of converts in Tranquebar, and in the interior, was reckoned to be three thousand and twenty-one. The Catechists were thirty. The number now connected with this Mission is very considerable, although the native Christians have been widely scattered, in consequence of the present insignificance of Tranquebar, and the superior advantages to be enjoyed under the English Government; and our earnest wish for them is, that they may again be favoured with a supply of Missionaries, whose piety and enlightened zeal shall be blessed with a revival of the Christian life which once undoubtedly existed in this Mission, and which we hope is not yet totally extinct.

The pious founders of the Mission in Tranquebar, and their successors, have pursued their arduous work with much meekness and patience. Soon after his arrival in India, Ziegenbalg might be seen with his dress loosened at the knees, and seated on the ground with the youngest children, in a native school, repeating their lessons with them, as the only means he could command for the acquisition of the rudiments of the Tamul language, in which, as might be expected from the dispositions manifested by such a course, he soon became a proficient. These humble, self-denying men were not found deficient in sacred learning, or controversial ability, when circumstances arose to require their exhibition.

Ziegenbalg, in a letter addressed to the Society for the Promotion of Christian Knowledge, in reply, as it would appear, to certain apprehensions which had been expressed lest he should introduce among the converts from the Heathen, a knowledge of the distinctions and controversies which divide the visible church of Christ, wrote as follows: "As to what relates to party names or distinctions, the divine Wisdom, which is without partiality, has taught us to abhor them. Our scholars know not so much as the bare name of Luther, or of Calvin. When we ask our scholars what religion they are of, they answer, 'We are *Tchettiawedakarer*,' that is, 'Christians bound to observe the truly divine law;' the word 'law' being taken in that comprehensive sense, whereby it contains in it both the law and the Gospel. After all, we assure you, that we allow of no party names to be used either in the Malabarick or Portuguese pulpit; and we design to be equally cautious in the books which we shall happen to print."

This letter was written in October, 1714, eight years after the commencement of the Mission. At that time the converts were about three hundred in number, and there were eighty children in the schools.

In the course of a few additional years their churches greatly increased; their numbers were augmented, not only by converts from Heathenism, but also by the accession of many native Romanists, some of them highly respectable by descent and property. The Missionaries had also completed the publication of the entire Old and New Testament in the Tamul language, and had issued many other books which were eagerly sought after, and widely distributed. Being now in some measure relieved from the work peculiar to the study and the printing-press, the Missionaries began to take extensive journeys, and to visit those converts, at their homes, who resided in towns and villages in the interior of the country.

These vigorous and successful operations excited the jealousy, and roused the anger, of the Romish Priests, whose congregations, in the south of India, were at that time very numerous and extensive; and Constantine T. Beschi, an Italian Jesuit, residing at Elakurichi, wrote a book, in 1728 or 1729, containing a most violent attack upon the religion of Protestants, and the principles and proceedings of the first Reformers. In this work, the title of which is, *Veda Vilaccam*, or "Light of Religion," the author paid no regard to truth; the most gratuitous and often-refuted calumnies against the character and doctrines of Protestants were repeated with the most unblushing effrontery; and were detailed with a point and humour peculiarly adapted to the genius of the people to whom they were addressed.

This direct attack, and others of a similar character, disturbed the plan of happy simplicity which the Missionaries had framed for their Hindoo converts, and which Ziegenbalg stated in the above extract from his letter. It was necessary to put it within the power of the Protestant Christians to repel the attacks made upon them; and that the native teachers, and especially such as had been converted from the Romish Church, should be furnished with facts and arguments in defence of their principles and doctrines, which the opposite party would be unable to refute.

To answer this purpose, the Missionary, Christopher

Theodosius Walther, composed, in Tamul, his *Historia Ecclesiastica;* and he was remarkably qualified for the happy accomplishment of his important undertaking. He had studied under Professor Francke, of Halle, and had been strongly recommended by him, for piety and learning, to the Society for Promoting Christian Knowledge, by whom he was sent to India. He, and the two Missionaries who accompanied him, had applied themselves, on their voyage, to the study of the Tamul language with so much diligence, that, within three months after their arrival, they were able to take the full duties of their important office; and, subsequently, Walther had given evidence of his learning and industry by the composition of a work on the Hindoo chronology, entitled, *Doctrina Temporum Indica,* which, in 1738, was printed for the Academy of Sciences at St. Petersburg.

Combined with learning and diligence, (eminent qualifications for a historian,) Walther possessed the necessary and inestimable advantage of an extensive and well-selected library, which had been accumulating on the Mission since its commencement, and had been enriched by the judicious liberality of some of the most pious and learned men in Europe. His work bears throughout the clearest evidence that he possessed ample means for its accomplishment, and that he gave his utmost diligence to make the most effective use of the stores at his command.

As Walther was writing for Hindoos, it was necessary that he should treat on Indian affairs somewhat at large; and he was prepared for this department of his work by extensive Tamul reading, and an intimate acquaintance with the history of the East. He has interwoven various particulars concerning the Hindoo rulers, and the Mahometan conquerors, of the East, in a manner which does not fail deeply to interest the native reader, and which affords him a clue to unravel, and, in some measure, understand, the intricate and absurd compositions of the native historians, which better deserve the name of romance than of history; affording to the Hindoos an outline of the history of their own country, in connexion with the history of the Patriarchal, the Jewish, and the Christian dispensations, enlarging, as opportunity was presented, when he came to treat on the Papal corruptions and usurpations, the Mahometan imposture, the zeal for extending the bounds of Christendom, awakened by the Reformation, both in the Romish Church, and in those who separated from her communion and protested against her corruptions and tyranny.

In an early part of his work, he has a chapter on the subject of idolatry, in which he very ingeniously compares the idolatry described in Scripture, and that of the Greeks and Romans, with the idolatry practised among the Hindoos at the present day; establishing the identity, to a considerable degree, of their respective pantheon and mythology.*

In another chapter he traces the existence of scriptural tradition in the mythology of the Hindoos; especially instancing the creation, the first man, the fall, giants, the flood, the destruction of Sodom and Gomorrah, the sacrifice of Isaac, the history of Moses, the paschal lamb, Job, Samson, and our blessed Lord.

The style of the book is concise, yet lively; it abounds with references to the Scriptures, and to other authorities; it gives a distinct account of the principal heresies and divisions which have occurred in the church from the earliest age; and it is not its least praise, that, although it was called forth by a most violent attack from a Missionary of the Romish Church, who triumphed

* This subject has been ably treated by the Rev. Joseph Roberts, Wesleyan Missionary in Madras, in his "Oriental Illustrations of the Sacred Scriptures." Second Edition, London, Tegg, 1844.

over the disunion and distinctions existing among Protestants, it discusses the errors, corruptions, and divisions of the Romish Church in calm and dispassionate language; and affords all due praise to those exertions which that Church has made, since the Reformation, for carrying the name of Christ among the Gentiles; with reference to them, quoting the words of the Apostle of the Gentiles: "Some indeed preach Christ even of envy and strife; and some also of good will: the one preach Christ of contention, not sincerely, ...but the other of love......What then? notwithstanding, every way, whether in pretence, or in truth, Christ is preached; and I therein do rejoice, yea, and will rejoice." (Phil. i. 15—18.)

On the whole, next to the translation of the holy Scriptures, I consider Walther's "Ecclesiastical History" one of the most interesting and useful books which has been printed in the Tamul language.

Two editions of it have been issued from the Tamul press at Tranquebar; the first in 1735, when its appearance must have amazingly strengthened the infant church in India; whilst it had the effect of silencing their Romish adversaries, who did not even attempt a reply to it. Beschi is said to have read it with attention, and to have ceased from that time to revile the Protestants. The second edition was printed in 1799: the paper is good, but the type was much worn, so that in some parts the impression is indistinct, and the page difficult to read. Both editions were printed, I believe, at the expense of the Society for Promoting Christian Knowledge, whose various operations to the date of the work are detailed therein, and its liberality to the Tranquebar Mission fully and repeatedly acknowledged. I shall be happy if, by thus calling attention to this book, I should be the means of inducing that Society to direct that a third edition of the entire work, without alteration, should be printed at the Tamul press under their control in Madras. It would there be executed correctly and legibly. The edition should be large, commensurate with the wants of the widely-spread Protestant church in the south of India; and it should be sold at a price which would place it within the reach of every native who can read his own language. That Society could not confer a more valuable boon on the churches they have so long fostered; and although their Missions are transferred to the Society for the Propagation of the Gospel in Foreign Parts, yet as it is still within their province to publish such works as tend to serve the benevolent and holy object for which the Society was established, we may hope that a third edition of a work so valuable will not be called for in vain. The advantage of its re-publication would be greater, at the present day, than might appear on first consideration. The facts and details which were sufficient to silence the Romish adversary, would be equally advantageous as an antidote to the doctrines of the Oxford Tracts, which are now diligently taught to the Christian natives of Madras. The dogmas of apostolical succession, sacramental efficacy, the schismatic state of all churches not Episcopal, and other doctrines peculiar to the Tractarian school, as asserted and enforced for the benefit of the poor natives, in a Tamul "Theological Dictionary" recently published in Madras, would fail of their intended effect, if Walther's "Ecclesiastical History" were generally possessed and read by them. I will venture to add, that every Missionary to the Tamul population would find it to his advantage to make himself acquainted with it. He will find compressed within a comparatively small compass a mass of information relating to the East, which, by other methods, it would require him years of study and research to obtain.

CHAPTER VII.

NOVEMBER, 1820.

THE JESUIT MISSION IN MADURA.

The "Ecclesiastical History" by Walther, furnishes a condensed, but circumstantial and impartial, account of the Missionary efforts of the Portuguese, especially of those which they commenced in the Tamul country, where, in Madura and various other quarters, they were afterwards aided or succeeded by the Italians and French. A translation which I have made of this part of his work, together with other copious information collected from various authentic sources, are now submitted to the reader; who will thus have brought within his view the history of one of the most remarkable, as well as one of the best, Missions of the Romish Church. In none of their Missions have there been greater eminence and purity of character in their founders; or greater sacrifices of life and comfort in those who succeeded them, for more than one hundred years; and yet in this, their best and noblest Mission, the corrupt and destructive influences of Popery have so triumphed throughout, that it may fairly be questioned, whether Christianity in India has not suffered damage by it to a considerable extent, or has in any respect been advanced. It is hoped that the introduction of this account will not be considered irrelevant or unseasonable. It will accomplish the object I have in view if, on the one hand, it shall serve to excite modern Missionaries, and those who co-operate with them, to emulate the zeal and perseverance and self-sacrifice displayed by the earlier Romish Missionaries, apart from their will-worship, superstition, and guile; and if, on the other hand, the exposure of the acknowledged and even vaunted deceptions and falsehoods, by which the Mission was supposed to be advanced, shall have the effect of silencing the proud and empty boastings of modern Romanists, in their frequent comparisons of the Missions of their Church with those of the Protestants, in which they pretend the advantage to be exclusively in their favour.

The extract from Walther's work is followed by some account of Francis Xavier, and Robertus de Nobili.

"In the year 1498, the Portuguese were conducted by sea to India, by their Admiral, Vasco de Gama. They landed at Calicut in Malayala (Malabar); and because the natives of that country (the western coast) are called Malayalis, they gave the name of Malabars to the Tamul people of this part (the Coromandel coast) also. In Calicut, they baptized a Yogi,* by the name of Michael; and by his means opened a commercial intercourse with the King of Cochin.

"Pedro Covillam,† the Admiral's Chaplain, was the first to administer baptism in India, after the Portuguese had established themselves. Subsequently, Michael Vaz,‡ James Porpa, his colleague, and other Franciscans, made the baptism of the natives their special object.

"In the year 1505, the Portuguese concluded a treaty with the King of Visanagur. They built Colombo (in the island of Ceylon) in 1506, and Goa in 1510; and

* A contemplative ascetic, esteemed as a saint among the Hindoos.

† Pedro Covillam had travelled to India by land, before the passage by the Cape of Good Hope had been discovered. An account of his journey thither, and back, as far as Grand Cairo, was published in Spanish, under the title of *Relazao do Viage de Pedro Covillam de Lisboa a India, per Terra, e volta do Cairo.* 1587.

‡ Michael Vaz was appointed Vicar-General of all India.

afterwards, by means of their Missionaries, converted many of the Heathen.

"In 1512, General Albuquerque forbade the infidels to dwell any longer with the Christians, in Cochin: on that occasion, four hundred persons conformed to the faith. (Ezra x. 11.)

"In 1537, Pope Paul III. made Goa the seat of a Bishop.

"In 1541, the pious and truly diligent Missionary, Francis Xavier, came to India, by command of John III., King of Portugal.

"The Paravas (fishermen) of the south of India were greatly oppressed by the Mahometans. At that time, John de Cruz, a Tamul man, who had visited Portugal, and had been baptized in the presence of the King, persuaded them to unite with the Portuguese, and receive baptism. They consented, and sent certain of their Chiefs to Cochin. The Portuguese afforded them the desired assistance. They restored to them the pearl fishery, which had formerly belonged to them. They also baptized the inhabitants of thirty villages, to the number of twenty thousand. But, as the Portuguese Priests themselves have written, their Christianity speedily decayed, and Heathenism again prevailed amongst them, both in doctrine and practice.

"Xavier heard this report; and in 1542, proceeded from Goa, and went to the Paravas; accompanied by another Priest and two interpreters. During the year 1543, he studied Tamul, and mean time, for that year, taught diligently through the medium of his interpreters.

"He then went to the neighbourhood of Cape Comorin,* and in one month, introduced ten thousand of

* A head-land forming the most southern point of Continental India.

the Mukkuvas (another tribe of fishermen) into the church.

"He also sent his colleagues to the Island of Manaar,* who converted the inhabitants of that place; afterwards, the Governor of Jaffna persecuted them cruelly. We shall find the death of Xavier recorded below, in the history of Japan.

"A coin of the Roman Emperor Claudius was found in digging the foundation of a church in the island of Manaar.†

"The Prince of Danoor,‡ who was a Brahman, was baptized secretly by the name of John. He was confirmed in Goa, in 1549.

"In 1546, John III. sent to the above-mentioned Michael Vaz, Bishop of all India, a letter dated the 8th of March, which he had addressed to the Viceroy of Goa; in which he commanded him to care for the interests of Christianity, and to protect the Paravas and other Christians, meeting the expense out of his revenue. Vaz took counsel with Xavier, and exerted himself very diligently for the diffusion of religion.

"In 1547, the Portuguese seized upon Mielapoor, and gave it the name of St. Thomè. The Priest Gabriel Atayda beginning to demolish a temple, found a cross of stone, stained with the blood of St. Thomas, and the sword with which he was slain. It is said that this cross did sweat blood on December 18th, 1555, and ceased in 1556: whether or no, it has been adored ever since.

"In 1549, Antonio Criminal, an Italian Jesuit,§ went,

* An island adjoining the north-western coast of Ceylon.

† See page 18.

‡ A district on the Malabar coast, south of Calicut.

§ In the Tamul, *Paulist*, a term usually applied to the Jesuits in India, from the college of St. Paul in Goa, which was given to the Jesuits in the time of Francis Xavier, and continued long in their possession.

at the command of Xavier, to instruct the Paravas of Pinneykail.* At that time some Portuguese soldiers had pillaged the Brahmans of Piricandoor; and six thousand Vadugas † assembled; and, having first assaulted Ramisseram, came to take vengeance. The Portuguese fled to their ships for refuge; and the Paravas endeavoured to escape. The commander of the Portuguese, anxious for Father Anthony's safety, that his life and labours might yet be long continued, for the benefit of the Christians of that country, called him to accompany them; but he remained on shore; and when he had visited the church and engaged in prayer, after the example of our Lord he voluntarily went forth, (John xviii. 4,) with a cheerful countenance, to meet the Vadugas, with the full expectation of death. So John de Lueenas, the Jesuit, who died in 1600, has recorded in his Life of Xavier. And Mavvei has stated, that he hid himself when the Christians each one brought his boat, and earnestly besought him to escape from impending danger.

"In this, Father Anthony did not follow the advice of our Lord, when persecuted in one city to flee to another. (Matt. x. 23.) He did not give his life for his sheep; (John x. 11, 12;) but exposed himself without any necessity, from a mere desire of obtaining the reputation of a martyr. (Matt. iv. 7; Ecclus. iii. 26.)

"With the intention of falling into the hands of the atrocious Tondans, he knelt down in the way over against his enemies, joined his hands together, and looked up to heaven. The first division passed him, only taking away his hat. The second division also passed. A Mahometan in the last division struck him with a lance, and others tore off his garments.

* A town on the eastern coast, south of Tutocorin.

† Or Badugas; a powerful tribe of the interior, often at enmity with the Paravas.

His blood flowed profusely, and he tried to reach the church. They thought he fled, and pursued him; but he returned to them again, when they stabbed him, and cut off his head; which they carried away, and placed on the tower of their temple. The Portuguese who ventured on shore interred his body. In after-times many persons sought that sacred relic, but were unable to find it.

"In 1556, and the three following years, the Jesuits in Goa alone introduced eighteen thousand and ninety-eight persons into the church; independently of all that was done by the Franciscans and Dominicans.

"In 1557, Pope Paul IV. made Goa the seat of an Archbishop; to whom the Bishop of St. Thomè was to be subject.

"Cochin was made a bishopric in 1559.

"In 1570, Hidal-khan, the Nabob* of the Carnatic, laid siege to Goa: he addressed a letter to the Viceroy of Goa, alleging as a reason (for hostilities) that the children of Hindoos were taken by force, and coerced into Christianity; for some of the monks had taken arms like soldiers, and had forced the people to be baptized.

"In 1597, Nicholas Ippemenda, a Jesuit, went to Madura; and with his colleague Henry Henriquez, laboured for the conversion of the Heathen. In 1607, the Christians were reckoned at one hundred and thirty thousand.†

"At that time Robertus de Nobili, who was called Tattwapothagar, or "teacher of the attributes," assuming the character of a *San-yasi*, sought to promote Christianity in the interior of the country. Xeres, the treasurer of the Congregation *de Propaganda Fide*, writing to Pope

* Mahometan ruler, tributary to the Great Mogul.

† Probably, in the whole of India.

Innocent, in the year 1676, concerning the Romish religion throughout the world, says, that although 'he professed to be a Brahman, he did not tell an untruth. He subsisted solely on rice, and other vegetables; and died happily in Mielapoor on the 16th of January, 1656.'

"In the year 1729, he was thus celebrated by [Beschi,] a writer in Elakurichi :—

"'As though the sun which shines in the heavens should take his circuit without showing his glorious face; so Thomas, one of the twelve Apostles of our Lord Jesus, and besides him, St. Xavier, illustrious by the performance of many miracles, took a circuit round this country, without penetrating into the interior; and, notwithstanding their journeys and labours, the darkness of the interior was long continued; was it not? At length, as the sun, at the time of his rising, by discovering his face, gives out his beams, disperses the universal thick darkness of night, and creates the day; so the Lord in his mercy turned his eyes on this land, immersed in Heathenism; and was pleased, one hundred and twenty years ago, to send teachers of unperverted word in the way of truth, to enlighten the souls of men. First of all Tattwapothagar was sent by the Lord, adorned with unchanging mortification of life, with unerring science, and unfailing charity. He long shone here like the morning sun; the light has not yet set, but shines with unfading splendour, in the Kàndam, and other works on religious science which he wrote as with a sun-beam. After him has followed an unbroken series of countless sincere teachers, continued from that day to this.'

"It is to be observed, however, that when he revised the Common Prayer, and the language used on religious subjects, he adopted a refined phraseology which he had learned from the Brahmans; he did not thoroughly investigate the true meaning of some of the words which he used, and he has purposely darkened his style; a practice which is not to be commended.

"For his sake Cardinal Onopari settled certain charitable gifts from the Congregation *de Propaganda Fide* in Rome, on the Brahmans who may embrace Christianity.

"In 1620, Philip Oliver, the Portuguese Commander, overcame the Singhalese in battle: he wrested Jaffna from the King of Kandy, and erected there several Christian churches.

"In 1655, the new converts of the Mission in Madura were reckoned at nine thousand and thirty-one.

"In 1687, the Jesuit, John de Brito, or Arulèndren, went to Rome on the affairs of the Jesuits, and returned by permission of Charles II., King of Portugal.

"He quitted Goa; and, having traversed the interior for fifteen months, he returned to the Marava country, with a desire to lay down his life for the sake of the truth; as Father de la Lane, the Superior of Madura, has recorded in his account of him.

"In a disturbance which had formerly occurred in that place, Regunāthadeven had said to him openly, 'Henceforth thou shalt not teach in my kingdom, but at the peril of thy life.' Notwithstanding this threat, and fearless of the result, he returned with a cheerful heart, a high courage, and a passionate desire voluntarily to resign his life. On his way he visited Tanjore, and said to the Christians of that place, 'I go to suffer in the Marava country: pray for me.'

"Tureitadiadeven, who had been instructed in religion, himself and his Officers went out to meet him, and brought him to his residence with great pomp. Afterwards, in 1693, he caused a splendid celebration of the feast of the three Kings.* He had five Queens of royal descent. He was told that in order to become a convert he must put away four of them. On this, the youngest, who was the daughter of the elder brother of Regunāthadeven, set out to Ramnad,† as though she was going to her father's fortress. She complained to the Governor; and the Priest of the fortress also complained that God's religion levelled all distinctions, and was now spread everywhere. The Governor sent his Officers, and commanded them to arrest and imprison that sorcerer, as he called John de Brito.

"Afterwards, on the 20th of January, when he had offered sacrifice, and was indulging in intoxication to excess, certain enemies took occasion to mention some unfounded calumnies against the Priest, [John de Brito]. The Governor then drew his sword, and demanded of him, 'What is thy religion? What are thy doctrines?' In reply, he recounted to him the divine attributes, and the commandments of God. The Governor then, in his drunken rage, directed that he should be shot; but, fearing a tumult, he afterwards sent him from Ramnad to Orioor,‡ to Udeiadeven, his elder brother; and commanded that he should be slain. Arulendren, having visited the church of Pilicakudi, where he conducted the religious drama of *Pavi Nadaca*, "the Sinner's Progress," proceeded to the Marava country. When he drew near to Orioor, and was engaged in the choultry in religious meditation and prayer, the Priests of that place inquired of him what food he would take.§ Seeing he

* Epiphany; called by the Romanists the Feast of the three Kings, from the Magi who came to Jerusalem on the birth of our Lord, who, they say, were three in number, and of royal dignity.

† The chief fortress of the Marava country.

‡ Another fortress in the Marava territory.

§ From his appearance they judged him to be one of their own body.

was silent, they said, 'Who is this? He does nothing but count his beads; he is surely a man of prayer.' Having come to this conclusion, they apprised Udeiadeven of his approach.

"On the 3rd of February he wrote thus to his Superior from the prison of Orioor: 'By great exertion I arrived here on the last day of January. I now wait in prison for the death which I must suffer for my God's sake. To obtain this honour I have come twice to India; and for this very purpose I have visited the Marava country.'

"On the 4th of February he was led to the place of execution. He passed a short time in prayer, and then, without fear, stretched out his head, which the barbarians cut off. They chopped off his legs and arms, and exposed his body and head on the gibbet. They also cut off the ears and noses of his two disciples, and drove them away.

"The miracles which are said to have been wrought by John de Brito, whom the natives call Arulananden, (or Arulendren,) the heavenly Physician, are believed among the imaginative and credulous Hindoos.

"In the month of October, 1700, Sakki, the King, seized, scourged, and imprisoned many of the twelve thousand Christians of the kingdom of Tanjore. He plundered their property, and made their children slaves. The two Priests were loaded with manacles; and one of them, Father Joseph Carvalli, died on the 14th of November.

"In 1703, seven thousand, seven hundred and eighty-one persons embraced Christianity in the Madura Mission.

"In 1711, it was estimated that there were thirty thousand Christians in Madura, Tanjore, and Arialoor.

"In 1722, Tittyapillei, Subadar * of Myaveram, levied a fine upon the Christians."

* An officer of the Nabob.

FRANCIS XAVIER.

This eminent Missionary, whose memory is respected by Protestants, as well as by members of the Church of Rome, was born in April, 1506, in the province of Navarre, in Spain, at a castle which bore the family name, and which had been in their possession more than two centuries.

He is said to have been educated with care until he reached his nineteenth year, when he devoted himself to the pursuits of literature and philosophy; and proceeded to Paris, that he might profit by the advantages the University of that city then presented, which is said to have been superior to every other in Europe.

He had taken his degree, and commenced the duties of a public lecturer, when Ignatius Loyola, the founder of the Society of the Jesuits, came to Paris in 1528. Loyola was fourteen years older than Xavier: he had been a soldier, had visited Palestine and other countries, and had gained great knowledge of the world and of human nature. He had already formed the plan of a Society, whose members should vow chastity, poverty, and obedience, and whose object should be the conversion of the Saracens and other infidels. He obtained the ascendancy over the youthful and noble Spaniard, Xavier, whom he exhorted to despise the world, and to devote himself to the service of God in the edification and extension of his church.

The characteristics of Xavier's mind were simplicity and energy. He sternly disciplined himself to the contemplation of spiritual and eternal things, until he had learned to look with contempt on temporal avocations and enjoyments; and was prepared to make any sacrifice, and to brave any danger, for the good of souls. He visited Venice, where he again met with Loyola, and was ordained Priest. He exercised his ministry in several places with great zeal and devotion, continuing to macerate his body by fasting and other austerities, whilst he sought to raise and purify his heart and affections, by spiritual pursuits and conflicts.

Loyola called Xavier and his other associates to Rome in the year 1537; where Xavier distinguished himself by the powerful rebukes he administered in his preaching to the vices of the imperial city, and by the exhaustless patience and charity with which he attended the sick during the prevalence of famine and disease. From the time he had begun to listen to Loyola, he appears to have made it his chief concern by every means to mortify his natural pride and love of praise, and to inure himself to humility and self-government.

Xavier had intended to visit the Holy Land, that he might see those places which had been consecrated by the presence and sufferings of our blessed Lord. He had regarded with pleasure the possibility that he might there attain the honour of martyrdom. But he was disappointed of this intention by a war which interrupted all intercourse with Palestine. Honours of a yet higher character awaited him.

John III., King of Portugal, was desirous of sending Missionaries to his possessions in India, where some success in the conversion of the Pagans had already attended the occasional efforts of such Priests as had accompanied his fleets and armies. A Portuguese ecclesiastic, on an embassy to Rome, admired the person and character of Xavier; and strongly recommended him to the notice of the King, as suitable for his object. The King accepted the proposal; and Xavier, delighted with the prospect of the labours and sufferings for the sake of Christ, and the salvation of souls, which he had before him, at a single day's notice, patched his cassock, the only preparation he had to make, and set out from Rome to Lisbon in April, 1541, for the purpose of embarking thence for Goa, in a

Portuguese ship. The navigation to India was at that time imperfectly understood: many were the dangers and sufferings to which he was exposed; but his fortitude and patience were invincible. During the voyage he employed himself in spiritual ministrations, for the benefit of the crew and passengers, and in attending on the sick. Some months were passed in refreshment and recovery at Mosambique in Africa; and he did not arrive at Goa, the Portuguese capital in India, until May, 1542, thirteen months after his embarkation.

The ministry of Xavier produced a wonderful effect on the inhabitants of that dissolute city. His self-denial and habits of devotion reproved the luxury and ungodliness which prevailed around him. His nights were passed in prayer; four hours only being devoted to sleep. In the morning he visited the sick and poor; and in the afternoon he would walk about the town, and, by the sound of a bell, summon the heads of families to send their children and slaves to be instructed. They would gather in crowds around him, and follow him to the church, where he suited his teaching to their capacities. Old and young, master and slave, acknowledged his wisdom and superior sanctity; and it is reported that, during his stay of six months in Goa, there was an almost universal reformation among its inhabitants.

At the call of duty, Xavier left the dignified and brilliant society of the capital, and entered on a life of danger and privation, that he might publish the name of Christ to a barbarous and indigent race. He was now more than thirty-six years of age; yet he attempted the acquisition of several languages; the Tamul, the Malay, and afterwards the Japanese. He several times returned to Goa; but he was chiefly employed among the Heathen; first on the Malabar coast, and as far as Mielapoor on the eastern side of the peninsula. He also visited

Ceylon, Malacca, Amboyna, Ternate, and the Isles del Moro. After visiting a second time the churches he had planted among the Paravas, he embarked for Japan, in 1549, in company with a Christian native merchant of that country, who assisted him in the acquisition of the language, and introduced him to the inhabitants of Japan. He found that the introduction of the Gospel into China would considerably facilitate its progress among the Japanese, who had received their religion and literature from that country. He therefore returned to Goa, and prepared to visit the celestial empire. On his voyage to China, he was seized with fever, and died at the island of Sancian, Xan Choang, or St. John, in the forty-fifth year of his age.

It was a peculiarity of Xavier, in which he differed from many of his successors, that he preached the Gospel to the poor. Himself of a noble family, in a country where the nobles are proud to a proverb, he learned to value the soul independently of all distinctions of worldly rank: and "he had his reward;" for "the common people heard him gladly."

The best Romish writers deny, that miracles were performed by Xavier. He himself disavowed them; but they have been plentifully introduced into various memoirs of his life. The miraculous gift most suitable to him, would have been the gift of tongues; but we find him applying with diligent assiduity to the acquisition of the languages he had to use, and mourning over the delay thus occasioned to his ministry.

There is evidence, that his teaching was not free from the errors which are peculiar to the Church of Rome; but it appears to have been as evangelical as might possibly consist with those errors. All parties unite in admitting, that, in him, the Heathen world saw a rare exhibition of purity, zeal, and devotion; and that the conversions effected under his ministry were not produced by guile, and by the influence of secular power, as were those by many of his successors; but were the result of conviction occasioned by the truths which he enforced and exemplified.

In 1686, one hundred and thirty-four years after his death, his body was removed from its first tomb to Malacca, and thence to Goa, where it is enshrined in a monument of exquisite art, and his coffin is enchased with silver and precious stones. It is said, that his flesh has suffered no decay.

It is too evident, that the successors of Xavier have not taken pains to afford Christian instruction to the numerous congregations under their care. The Scriptures have not been translated by them, nor are the people permitted to read the translations made by Protestant Missionaries. In their place, there are most stupid and incredible legends of saints, and trifling poems equally valueless; except some works written by Robertus de Nobilibus and Constantine Beschi, for the Madura and Carnatic Missions; and even these are known to few. Indeed, the Tamul Romish Missions are generally supplied with native Priests from Goa, who take little pains to acquire the language of the people, and whose character and education are very inferior. They are supported by the people among whom they reside; and the royal grant made to each of them from an endowment by a former King of Portugal, is generally assigned by them to the relatives they have left behind in Goa. Those endowments are now said to be the chief subsistence of that city.

Father Martin, in June, 1700, tells us, that "the church of Cotate, near Cape Comorin, derives much of its importance from the spot on which it is raised; for the church and altar are built over the very place where stood the hut whither St. Francis Xavier used to retire every evening, after having preached in the day-time to the idolaters. One night they set fire to the hut, in hopes of burning St. Francis alive; but, though the hovel was consumed, the tenant of it received no hurt. I arrived at Cotate a few days before the festival of St. Francis Xavier; and was an eye-witness of the vast multitudes who come hither annually on that occasion, people flocking from all parts, within twenty or thirty leagues round. A few days after the solemnization of this saint's festival, an idolater came to his church, and there made a vow." He then relates what he considers to be a miraculous interposition of the saint, by which the Heathen votary obtained two successive prizes in a lottery: he faithfully paid his vow, but could not be persuaded to become a Christian.

ROBERTUS DE NOBILI, OR DE NOBILIBUS.

Beschi is not correct in saying, that this eminent Missionary was the first to penetrate the interior of the Tamul country. Nicolas Ippemenda, and Henry Henriquez, had occupied Madura for ten years previous. But Robertus de Nobilibus was the first to assume the character and appearance of a San-yasi: a sort of religious philosophers among the Hindoos, who retire from the world which they profess to contemn; repress all desire, (from whence their name San-yasi, that is, "without desire,") and live a life of penance and mortification. The example furnished by De Nobilibus was followed by all the Jesuit Missionaries of the interior.

The first object they had in view was to conceal the fact, that they were Europeans. The dissolute lives of the Europeans who had formed settlements on various parts of the coast of India, had made them objects of abhorrence to the natives, especially to the higher castes, many of whom are remarkable for their temperance and sobriety, and for strict observance of what they regard as essential to religion. The policy and power of the Europeans had also begun to awaken the jealousy and dread of the Chiefs of the interior. The Jesuits, therefore, endeavoured to disguise themselves; and nothing appears to have given them greater concern, than the suspicion of being Europeans with which they were occasionally met.

Another object was, that, by conforming to the customs and religious prejudices of the natives, they might the more easily win proselytes from among them. The natives of the higher castes will not slaughter the ox or cow, because they regard that animal as sacred. Their motive for abstaining from the flesh of other animals, and from taking the life even of the most destructive and noxious, is founded on their belief in the doctrine of metempsychosis, and the consequent equality of the souls of all living creatures with the soul of man. Great merit is attached by them to the abstinence from animal food. And if, in addition to these observances, a man becomes a San-yasi, and, in consequence, remains in celibacy, and lives retired from the ordinary pursuits and enjoyments of life, devoting himself to religious contemplation, he is regarded by them as a kind of deity, and is in some cases actually worshipped.

In order to support this assumed character, a knowledge of the language and manners of the people was necessary. With this view, a Missionary intended for the interior was not permitted to enter on his work until he had passed some months on the coast, where he studied the language, and inured himself to some of the practices he would have to follow, in order to fulfil his mission. He would then proceed into the interior, and before he arrived at the district where he had to labour, he would lay aside his European costume, and reach the termination of his journey clothed in the attire, and following the practices, of a San-yasi.

This was not accomplished without exposure to danger from the jealousy of the natives, and considerable suffering necessarily connected with the mode of life they adopted. Let us take the testimony of the Jesuit Missionaries themselves as to their manner of life and the character of their labours.

Father Martin, on his arrival in Pondicherry in January, 1699, wrote thus to Father de Villete: "Here, excellent father, we shall be in the neighbourhood of the Mission of Madura, the noblest, in my opinion, in the world. Seven Jesuits, most of them Portuguese, are employed there. The people of Madura have no communication with the Europeans, who, by their riotous excesses, have corrupted all the Christians in India. The Madurans spend their lives in the utmost sobriety and frugality, not concerning themselves with traffic, but contenting themselves with the food and raiment with which their native country supplies them.

"The Missionaries lead an extremely mortified life. Their only dress is a long piece of linen cloth wound round their bodies; and they wear sandals, which by their shape are exceedingly troublesome. They abstain totally from bread, wine, all sorts of meat, and even fish. They eat nothing but rice, pulse, and herbs, plain, and without seasoning of any kind: and it is with great difficulty they get a little flour to make wafers* with, and wine for the mass. They are not known to be Europeans; for were the natives to have the least notion of this, the fathers would be obliged to quit the country,

* Used by the Romanists in the sacrament of the Lord's supper.

since it would be impossible for them to do any good there. Several motives prompt the Indians to have the Europeans in so much horror. Great cruelties have been committed in their countries; they have been eye-witnesses to the most shocking examples of their vices of every kind. But that which offends them most is, their seeing the Europeans eat flesh; a practice, according to them, so very horrid, that they look upon all who make it their food as infamous.

"To this rigorous life of the Missionaries, add their continual danger of falling into the hands of thieves, who are here more numerous than among the Arabs. The fathers are almost afraid of keeping any thing under lock and key, lest they should be suspected of hoarding up riches. They are obliged to carry and preserve all their little moveables in earthen pots or vessels. They call themselves Brahmans, that is, Divines, come out of the north, to teach the law of the true God. Though they are obliged to lead a life of the greatest poverty, and require but little money for their own support, they yet are forced to expend considerable sums in maintaining their Catechists; not to mention what is extorted from them by the natives. They often suffer persecution: and not above four years since, one of our most famous and most holy Missionaries* was beheaded by a Prince of Marava for preaching Christ."

Father Bouchet, the Superior of the Mission, wrote thus from Madura, December 1st, 1700: "Our Mission at Madura is in a more flourishing state than ever. We have suffered four violent persecutions this year. One of our Missionaries had four of his teeth beat out; and I am now at the Prince's court to solicit the liberty of Father Borghese, of the family of Prince Borghese in Rome, that father having been confined forty days in the

* John de Brito, whose death is described p. 73.

prison of Ticherapali.* You have often heard that the Missionaries of Madura eat neither meat, fish, nor eggs; and that they never drink wine or other strong liquors, but live in wretched huts covered with straw, having not so much as a bed, a chair, or piece of furniture of any kind; and they are forced to take their food without either table, napkin, knife, fork, or spoon. But this is nothing to the sufferings they undergo."

In December, 1700, Father Martin, who had then joined the Mission, wrote from Aoor, the principal Station, about twelve miles south of Trichinopoly, as follows: "I had been told, and accordingly expected, before my arrival in this place, to find neither bread, meat, eggs, fish, nor wine, except what is used at mass; but I will frankly tell you that things are much worse than I imagined. Nothing is drunk here but water, which often is very muddy, and never very clear; it being drawn out of ponds wherein men and cattle wash themselves daily. Our only food is herbs, roots, and pulse, the taste of which is much more insipid and bitter than any of those in Europe. No person can eat them with any tolerable appetite, unless he has been accustomed to them from his infancy. We are allowed to use butter with them; but those who dress our victuals (which were we to do ourselves, the Indians would think we disgraced our ministerial character) cook it up so wretchedly, that it is a real mortification for us to eat any of it. Farther, as the rice which serves as bread is boiled only in water, it takes away its taste. A Missionary imagines at his first coming, that if he does but make a hearty resolution, he will soon accustom himself to this food, though so vastly insipid; however, the stomach loathes it to such a degree at last, that nothing but real necessity could force an European to touch any of it. Fruits are

* Trichinopoly.

so rarely met with here, that we think it a banquet if we get only a radish or a little cucumber in the afternoon. Father Bouchet and I have often had no more in the evening (even when it was not a fast day) than a piece of thin cake, baked on the coals, and half burnt.

"Besides the sad disquietude of our minds, on account of the persecution which our brethren frequently suffer, I may add the dreadful solitude of many of our Missions here, which commonly remove us far from all our acquaintance; we not having the least society but with an ignorant, unamiable people; not to mention our being forced to comply with their forms of ceremony, which are inexpressibly troublesome and ridiculous in every respect; our being deprived for years together of all spiritual succour, as well as of all correspondence by way of letter, this being rare, and very difficult to be carried on, for fear we should discover ourselves to be Europeans. It would raise some suspicion in the natives were they to know that we have any concerns with the Portuguese, and other Europeans of the coast; and cause us to be persecuted, as has happened more than once."

A San-yasi, when at his residence or hermitage, never goes out but for some religious purpose: he is supposed to choose retirement as favourable to religious meditation. In the morning early he must visit some sacred pond or river, and wash his entire person, in company with the Brahmans and other idolatrous devotees; and, placing a mark of ashes or of sandal-wood on his forehead and other parts of his person, make his morning ceremonies to the object of his worship. The Jesuits carried with them, on these occasions, the crucifix or an image of the virgin. He may not use the left hand in eating, or in presenting any thing to another person; and is under other restrictions equally troublesome and ridiculous.

It is not difficult to picture to oneself one of these

grave and learned men on his journey through the country. He has allowed his beard to grow long, has laid aside all his European clothing, and in the place of it wears only one cloth of cotton, about nine yards in length, disposed about his person after the native fashion. He has a turban on his head; and awkward, uneasy sandals on his feet. On his forehead there is some mark to indicate the caste to which he professes to belong; and perhaps he wears the Brahman string over his left shoulder. He grasps in his hand a book of prayers written on the ola

JESUIT MISSIONARY IN MADURA.

leaf, or a portion of the "Introduction to Theology" by Robertus de Nobilibus. He has two or three attendants; one of them bears a few earthen pots, containing all the supplies he allows himself for his journey. Perhaps another carries the deer or tiger skin, which is the only seat, couch, or bed the San-yasi allows himself, either at at home or abroad. Thus accoutred and accompanied, he penetrates deep forests, toils over lofty mountains, drags himself through plains of heavy sand, and often fords rivers and arms of the sea. He is exposed to the burning sun or heavy tropical rains, frequently without any shelter; his lodging by night is the open choultry, or the house of some hospitable native, more private, but not more commodious. On his arrival at a strange town or village, he does not dare to enter until the approach of night. The next day he is discovered, and the wondering inhabitants ask who the stranger is. His native attendants say, as they have been instructed, that he is a Brahman, or Shastri, from Rome, a teacher of the true religion. Thus introduced, and seated under a tree, by the side of a tank, or in front of some native's house, he commences his instructions; anticipating objections, and replying to them. He displays the crucifix and other figures to excite his own devotion, and to strike the attention of a people who are much impressed with outward show: and when a few proselytes were made in any place, the celebration of the mass would deepen the effect thus produced.

It is certain that, for nearly two centuries, the Jesuit Missionaries of the interior endured the fatigue, privations, sufferings, and dangers incident to this mode of life. And to this day, many of them reside among the natives with little more of the comforts and conveniences of life, than are possessed by the natives themselves among whom they labour. It is a strong testimony to the advantage of temperance, and even abstinence, in that climate, that De Nobilibus himself lived to a great age, and that many of those who have followed his example have, in this particular, equalled or exceeded him. Those whom the writer has known personally were, with one exception, tall, powerful-looking men; who had no doubt been chosen for this service on account of their robust constitution, as well as for their mental qualifications. Pere Austrey, whom he met with in the year 1825, at

Keelcheri, about forty miles in the interior from Madras, was living in a room not larger than the cabin of the poorest Irish peasant. He was dressed in a coarse cotton shirt, and drawers of the same; and he supported his steps by a staff as large, but not as neatly finished, as that of the drum-major of a regimental band. His only ailment was a slight bruise on his leg, which he had not been able to heal: he was otherwise a strong, hale man, although seventy-eight years of age. When reference was made to the insufficiency of his habitation, and the absence of many comforts, which he must have known well how to appreciate, his only reply was, *Satis est, Satis est!* He was a Frenchman, and spoke Arabic, Teloogoo, and Latin, with great fluency. In him there was an example of what the Jesuits still are in India. The *exception* above referred to was a Frenchman of rather diminutive stature, and of little mental energy, who was the successor of the famous Abbè Dubois in Mysore. He complained of his circumstances, and expressed his regret that he had not chosen to go into the army, instead of entering the service of the church.

To the adoption of this deceptive and difficult mode of life and Missionary labour, Robertus de Nobilibus led the way in 1607. According to the practice of the Jesuits, not to admit any one fully into their Society until he was thirty-three years of age, and allowing two years for his voyage and preparatory studies, he must have attained his thirty-fifth year before he entered upon it. It may be permitted us to admire the self-denial and determination necessary to adopt such a mode of life, and the perseverance which enabled him to continue it for the space of fifty years. And it is cause for still further admiration that there should have been found so many men of education and learning, who had been accustomed to the pursuits of literature, and the enjoyments of life, in

Europe, to follow his example. But here our admiration must end. Their whole life was a practical falsehood. They professed that they were not Europeans; that they were Brahmans, and San-yasis; their assumed character was frequently challenged by the natives, and had as frequently to be met by direct denial, or by evasions unworthy of the Christian character. Nor is it probable that they succeeded to any great extent, or for any considerable time, in keeping up the delusion, either amongst their converts, or the Heathen. There is evidence that they were often persecuted and maltreated on the suspicion of being Europeans. It was necessary that their secret should be intrusted to some of the native Christians; but these were not always faithful. The continual practice of deceit, on their part, furnished the most powerful sanction to their converts to indulge in deception, a crime to which the Hindoos are proverbially prone. How shocking to reflect, that, in inducing the Heathen to take upon themselves the profession of Christianity, they should use such means as must necessarily result in rendering them more the children of hell than they were in the heathen state! Besides, their adoption of the character of Brahmans and San-yasis was a practical admission of some of the main errors of Hindooism, which it should have been one of their chief objects to refute and dispel. The whole proceeding was one of mere human craft and policy, without any sanction from the word of God, or even from heathen morality; and, when rightly considered, changes our admiration into disgust and abhorrence. The publication of Walther's "Church History," in the language of the natives, must have entirely removed the cloak from them, even if they had been able to keep up the deception until that time. Some of their successors, to the present time, assume something of the character of San-yasis; but it is only by an accommodation of the term that they are allowed to be such; and by their own admissions the success of their labours is at an end.

The following are specimens of the treatment which the Jesuit Missionaries who followed the example of De Nobilibus sometimes met with, and the persecutions they endured.

Father Martin, in December, 1700, says, "I had the consolation to meet with Father Bouchet. He had been persecuted not more than three months before, and was not quite recovered of a fit of illness he had in consequence. Here follows the occasion of his being persecuted.

"Three Catechists, forgetting their duty, and the sacred character of the ministry with which they were invested, were guilty of such dissolute practices, that it was necessary to divest them of their employments. These wretches, instead of profiting by the sage admonitions which were given to them, and reforming their lives, threw off the mask, turned apostates, and resolved to ruin both the Missionaries and the Mission. To succeed in their detestable design, they brought three accusations against the Gospel Preachers: First, that they were *Pranguis*, or Europeans; an infamous set of people, who ought to be hated by the whole nation. Secondly, that though they had been long in the kingdom, and had the direction and government of a great number of converts, they yet had never paid the least thing to the King. Thirdly, that our Missionaries had assassinated a Friar of another order, which, they declared, had made them so odious to the Pope, that he had refused to canonize Father John de Brito, who fell a martyr to the faith in Marava. This was a shocking and ridiculous calumny, the Friar being then at Surat, on his return from Rome, where His Holiness had made him a Bishop. But it was greatly to be feared that the wretched apostates would succeed in getting all the Gospel labourers banished the kingdom, especially Father Bouchet, against whom they had a particular spite; as they had offered to give the Prince twenty thousand crowns, provided he would extirpate the Christians.

"That zealous Missionary had first recourse to God, to implore his protection; and then, in order to prevent those pernicious designs from taking effect, he resolved to go and salute the Prince Regent,* and implore his protection. This was so bold a step, that no Missionary had ever presumed to take it, lest the colour of his face should betray and discover him to be an European; the Prince above mentioned detesting *Pranguis* to such a degree, that, notwithstanding his being engaged in a dangerous war, he yet had dismissed from his service, not long before, some very skilful gunners, (whose assistance, one would have concluded, he absolutely wanted,) the moment he heard they were Europeans.

"But Father Bouchet, putting his whole confidence in the Almighty, prepared his presents, went to the city, and proceeded to the palace, where he desired an audience of the Prince, who governs under the Queen. This Regent's conduct is so very sagacious and equitable, that he is supposed to be the greatest Minister that ever governed Madura.

"Yet Father Bouchet imagined that it would be improper to appear before him, without observing the ceremonial of the country; that is, without making presents. Those prepared by the Missionary were of no great value; but then they were of a new kind, and all he could bestow. He had brought with him a terrestrial globe, about two feet in diameter, on which the names of the several kingdoms, provinces, coasts, and seas were written in the Tamul language; another globe of glass, about nine inches in diameter, cut within like mirrors; some

* Of Trichinopoly.

multiplying and burning glasses; several Chinese curiosities sent him from Coromandel; many bracelets of jet, adorned with silver; a cock, made with shells, very neatly and skilfully wrought; with several common looking-glasses, and such curiosities as the Missionaries had purchased, or had had presented to them. The Father also concluded, it would be necessary to obtain the favour of some of the courtiers, in order that they might speak in his behalf, and procure him a favourable audience; it being of the utmost importance, both for the honour of religion, and the good of the church of Madura, that the Doctors of the holy law should be received with distinction the first time they made their appearance at court; a circumstance which would enforce the authority of their ministry in the minds of the common people, who obey implicitly the will and inclinations of their Sovereign.

"The Father having thus taken all the prudent measures he judged necessary in order to succeed in his design, reposed the utmost confidence in God, in whose hands are the hearts of Princes, to dispose of them at pleasure. He was not mistaken; the Talavai, or Prince Regent, receiving him with greater honour and distinction than he could possibly have expected. The Prince not only rose up the moment the Father appeared, but saluted him in the same manner as disciples here salute their masters, and the common people their lords; which is performed by joining both hands, and raising them to the forehead. Father Bouchet, to maintain his character, and to return this favourable reception, saluted the Prince as masters do their disciples, by opening his hands and stretching them towards the Prince by way of receiving him. The Regent then caused the Missionary to sit down by him, on a kind of sofa, with this mark of distinction, that the sofa being too narrow for two persons to be seated conveniently upon it, the Prince straitened himself, made the Father sit by him, and even laid his knees on those of the Father.

"A man must be well acquainted, as we are, with the customs of this country, and with the natural detestation which the natives of it, especially the Brahmans, bear to the Europeans, to have a perfect idea of the very honourable reception which the Father met with on this occasion. The Father himself was astonished at it, as likewise the whole court, which was vastly numerous, there being that day upwards of five hundred persons, the greatest part of whom were Brahmans. The Father, being thus seated, made his complaints. He then declared that he was come from the north, from the mighty city of Rome, to instruct the inhabitants of this kingdom in the Supreme Being, and in his holy law; that, having been, for several years, a witness of his heroic actions, and the many victories he had gained over his enemies, he was therefore desirous of seeing so great a Prince, and imploring his protection in favour of his ministry; that, as one of the principal articles of the law inculcated by him obliged subjects to pay the strictest obedience to their sovereigns, and to be inviolably attached to them, he might be assured of his fidelity, a duty which he did not fail earnestly to recommend to all his disciples.

"The Prince replied, that the God he worshipped must be very powerful, and deserved the highest honours, since it had prompted so worthy a person to take so long a voyage, solely in the view of making him known to a people who had never heard of his name; that his (the Missionary's) pale cheeks plainly proved him to lead a very mortified life; and that the presents he brought with him showed, that necessity had not forced him to quit his native country. That he had already heard the most advantageous particulars concerning his learning and good sense. That as the multiplicity of his affairs would not give him leisure to understand, in the manner he could wish, the explanation of the figures drawn so artfully on the globe he had brought, he therefore had sent for the most famous astrologer in the kingdom to discourse with him upon it, in order that he might learn the uses of this wonderful machine. That, perceiving among his presents some things which could not fail of pleasing the Queen, he therefore would leave him for a moment, and go and present them to her Majesty with his own hand. The Prince then rose up, and ordered some of the courtiers to take the Father into the garden, and keep him company until his return.

"As Father Bouchet had vanished from court, as it were, and been led into the garden, a report prevailed in the palace, and in the city, that he was seized and thrown into prison. This news proved subject of triumph for some little time to the enemies of our holy religion; and threw the Christians into the utmost consternation, who waited with great uneasiness to hear the success of this visit. However, their sorrow was soon changed into joy; for the Prince, at his return from the Queen's apartment, received the Father, in the presence of the whole court, with the same honours as are paid to Ambassadors; he put upon his head, in the form of a veil, a piece of gold brocade, about eight feet long, and shed on him some sweet-smelling waters; after which he declared he was expressly ordered by the Queen to grant him every thing he desired.

"Had the Father then thought proper to insinuate a word or two concerning the catechist apostates, who for so many months had occasioned such disturbances, and given so much scandal to his church, the Prince would certainly have punished them severely, and perhaps banished them the kingdom; but the Missionary, animated with the spirit of his Lord and Master, and calling to mind that he was a Father, would not destroy his children, though they had been so ungrateful and treacherous with regard to Christ and his church. He therefore contented himself with preventing, by his visitation, their doing any further prejudice to the church, or imposing on the people by calumnies or horrid accusations. For this reason, after assuring the Prince that he retained the deepest sense of his favours, he again begged his protection for himself and his disciples; assuring him, that they, in return for all his goodness, would daily implore the Lord of heaven and earth, whom they worshipped, to shower down upon him his choicest blessings, and give him the victory over his enemies. The Prince promised not to forget him; when, after saluting him in the same manner as at first, he withdrew, commanding his officers to let the Father be carried through every part of the city in the first court-palankeen, to show the world that he honoured this foreign doctor, and indulged him with his protection.

"The modesty of Father Bouchet was put to a great trial on this occasion. He combated with himself, whether it were not incumbent on him to refuse the public honour now offered him; but, after pouring forth his heart before the Lord, he imagined that it was necessary for his glory, and the honour of the Christian religion, that all the inhabitants of that capital should plainly see that the Prince esteemed the religion he taught, and that it would find a protector in him, when necessary. He therefore got into the palankeen, and permitted the Indians to carry him through every part of the city, with music playing before him. This pomp soon drew numberless people into the streets, through which he passed, who all saluted him in the most respectful manner. The Christians, who till now were afraid that the religion they professed would be despised and censured by the Prince, crowded after the Missionary with acclamations, and the highest demonstrations of joy; publishing aloud, that they were Christians, and disciples of the foreign doctor. The success of this kind of triumph strengthened the proselytes in their faith, and prompted a great number of idolaters to beg to be baptized. Not satisfied with carrying Father Bouchet through the whole city of Trichinopoly, they likewise conveyed him in this manner to the place of his abode, which is about four leagues from the capital. The moment he arrived there, he assembled the Christians in the church, dedicated to the blessed virgin, that they might all return thanks to God for this signal blessing.

"Though this affair ended happily, yet the fatigues Father Bouchet had undergone on this occasion threw him into a fit of sickness, from which he was not well recovered when I found him in Serhinne. We stayed there but one day; and the next went to Aoor, which is but a short day's journey from thence. When Father Bouchet first came into the Mission of Madura, about twelve years ago, the Missionaries were under such fears, that they never entered the villages except at night; but, Heaven be praised! things are much altered for the better since that time; for we not only went to Aoor in open day, but the Christians of the neighbouring towns, assembling together, received us with music and acclamations; a circumstance which drew tears of joy from my eyes.

"Aoor is certainly the most considerable Mission now in Madura, not only on account of its neighbourhood to the capital of the kingdom, but also because there are twenty-nine churches dependent on it, in which are computed upwards of thirty thousand Christians, converted by the Father Visitor."

Another instance of persecution, which ended tragically, is mentioned by Father Santiago, in a letter addressed to the provincial of Goa. He writes from Capinaghat, on August 8th, 1711. He says,—

"Father Dacunha was the first Missionary your reverence sent into the Mission of Mysore since you governed the province. The old church Father Dacunha had in the dominions of the King of Cagonti, having been burnt by the Mahometans, he designed to build one much larger. He obtained leave of the chief of the town; and, having found a convenient place, began to erect the structure.

"Having as yet no house to live in, he took up his lodgings in a wood, under a tree, where the Christians had made him a small hut of the boughs of trees, in which he might reside with some decency and comfort. A multitude of Gentiles resorted thither to visit the Missionary; attracted partly by the good account they had heard of him, and partly because they were charmed with his discourses concerning religion. Many of them were sensibly touched, and promised to embrace Christianity; and some allowed their children to be baptized.

"Several Dasseris, disciples to the Gooroo, who is chief in religious matters with the King of Cagonti, came from him to the Missionary. The argument turned upon two points: they denied the unity of God, and maintained that God has a body.

"It was no difficult matter for the Missionary to confound them; and their confusion gave pleasure to several Gentiles of other sects who were present: most of them were moved, and desired the Missionary to instruct them. But the Dasseris, who had been so haughty before the dispute, had not a word to say for themselves, and went away, threatening the Father, that they would soon revenge the affront done to them and their deities.

"The Christians being careful for the safety of their Pastor, conjured him to pass the night in his old church; though there were only the walls half burnt down remaining, because, being within the town, he would be in less danger; but he valued not those threats, but relied on the favourable reception he had from the General of the King's forces, and the assurances he had given him of protection.

"His new church being finished, he prepared to celebrate the Feast of the Ascension in it, not regarding the plots the Dasseris were contriving against him. The Christians being assembled, he said mass, which was the first and last he said in that church.

"During the time of mass there came forty Dasseris with banners and music. The Magistrate of the place, who had given leave to open the church, sent for one of the Christians, and dispatched him to the court, to inform the General, and receive his orders. The Father, after the mass, made a short exhortation to the Christians, encouraging them to suffer to the last in the cause of Christ.

"By this time some of the Dasseris had placed themselves at the window, lest the Father should make his escape. But the danger being equal, whether he went or stayed, he chose to remain in the church, waiting the General's answer.

"Before that could arrive, above sixty Dasseris, followed by a great number of Brahmans, appeared before the church-door; and, meeting with no opposition, ran at him. One of the Brahmans struck the Father across the reins, which blow was followed by many others; some striking him with staves, others with butts of spears, and others with swords. Had it not been for a Brahman, who had been present at the dispute about the unity of God, and who took the Father's part, he had been killed at the foot of the altar. That Brahman was not of the sect of the Dasseris, and perhaps had been convinced of the truth.

"At last the Father was dragged before the Gooroo, all wounded and bloody. That infidel was sitting on a carpet, and showed as much pride and passion, as the Missionary did constancy and humility. The Gooroo first gave the Father some language of contempt, then asked him who he was, whence he came, what language he spoke, and what race he came of. The Father gave him no answer; and the Gooroo, attributing his silence to his weakness, questioned the Catechist who stood by the Father. He answered, that the Father was a Kshatri, of the race of the Kshatris, or Rajahs, the second in India.* Then the Gooroo proceeded to questions concerning religion, asking the Catechist, 'What is God?' 'He is a Sovereign of infinite power,' answered the Catechist. 'What do you mean by those words?' added the Gooroo. The Catechist endeavoured to satisfy him. They spent some time in these reciprocal questions and answers; and, at length, the Catechist said, that God was Lord of all things. 'What is that Lord of all things? I say again,' added the Gooroo; then the Father took upon himself to answer, and said, 'He is a being of himself, independent,—a pure spirit, and most perfect.' The Gooroo laughed aloud at these words, and rejoined, 'Yes, yes, I will soon send you to see whether your God is nothing but a pure spirit!' The Father answered, he would be willing to demonstrate it to him, if he had a mind to learn. The Gooroo was not ignorant of the success of the former disputes, and feared to engage in another, which would infallibly have turned to his confusion; and, therefore, satisfied himself with asking whether Perumal of Tripetti was a god; (that is an idol much

* A specimen of the falsehoods the Jesuits taught their disciples to utter, and by which they disgraced their character, and rendered abortive the success for which they laboured and suffered with such admirable constancy. He might with as much truth have affirmed, that Father Dacunha was the Grand Seignior, or the Emperor of Russia.

honoured in this country). The Father answered in the negative. Therefore the Gooroo flew into a passion, and called the Magistrate of the town to witness. He had certainly put the Father to death on the spot, but that some Gentiles, being moved to compassion, conjured him with tears to spare what little life remained in the Missionary, and not to imbrue his hands in the small quantity of blood still remaining in his veins.

"One of his converts, and two ancient Christians, stood by him undaunted, and his Catechist received the stroke of a scimitar. The chief of the Dasseris perceiving that the Brahmans, and the people who were not of his sect, pitied the Missionary, commanded him immediately to quit the country; and no entreaties could prevail, but he must be gone that night, and guards were appointed to see him out of the kingdom. He lay that night in a weak condition, in a village where there were some Christians; and was thence, with much difficulty, removed to Capinaghat, the principal place of his residence.

"The Christians there sent an express to give me notice of his condition. I repaired thither, and assisted him; but he died the eighteenth day after he had received all that ill usage from the Brahmans, and the Dasseris of Cagonti."

Dr. Buchanan visited one of the principal Stations of the Madura Mission, ("Christian Researches," pp. 147, 148,) and makes some very appropriate remarks; and from his own observation confirms the view which it has been felt a duty to give of its character and effects. He says, "At the present time we see Popery in Europe without dominion; and hence it is viewed by the mere philosopher with indifference or contempt. He is pleased to see, that the 'seven heads and ten horns' are taken away; and thinks nothing of the 'names of blasphemy.' But, in the following pages, the author will have to show what Rome is, as *having* dominion; and possessing it, too, within the boundaries of the British empire.

"In passing through the Romish provinces in the East, though the author had before heard much of the Papal corruptions, he did not expect to see Christianity in the degraded state in which he found it. Of the Priests it may truly be said, that they are, in general, better acquainted with the Veda of Brahma, than with the Gospel of Christ. In some places, the doctrines of both are blended. At Aughoor, (Aoor, the chief Station of the Madura Mission,) situated between Trichinopoly and Madura, he visited a Christian church, and saw near it, in October, 1806, a tower of Juggernaut, (a ponderous car in imitation of those used at heathen temples,) which is employed in solemnizing the Christian festivals. The old Priest Josephus accompanied him to the spot, and while he surveyed the idolatrous car and its painted figures, the Priest gave him a particular account of the various ceremonies which are performed, seemingly unconscious himself of any impropriety in them. The author went with him afterwards into the church, and seeing a book lying on the altar, opened it; but the reader may judge of his surprise, when he found it was a Syriac volume, and was informed, that the Priest himself was a descendant of the Syrian Christians, and belonged to what is now called the Syro-Roman Church, the whole service of which is in Syriac. Thus, by the intervention of Papal power, are the ceremonies of Moloch consecrated, in a manner, by the sacred Syriac language. What a heavy responsibility lies on Rome for having thus corrupted and degraded that pure and ancient Church!"

The conformity to heathen practices which Dr. Buchanan found at Aoor, may be seen throughout the worship of the Church of Rome in India. At the principal Romish Mission Stations, it is usual for them to have a car, in imitation of those used by the Hindoos, on which the image is placed, and taken in procession on festival occasions. In the intervals it stands near the church, under shelter of a thatched roof, which is removed when it is required; and then the car is adorned with drapery, banners, garlands of flowers, &c.; and the attendance on the image is with a pomp as nearly like that of Heathenism as circumstances will allow. The procession is accompanied with the discharge of rockets and crackers; a practice which is also borrowed from the Heathen, but in the frequent use of which the Romanists now exceed them. And their worship is rendered the more imposing and attractive to the poor natives, by dramatic exhibitions, in which also they have imitated the Hindoos.

Father Martin says, "The persecutions which broke out against the Christians of Cootoor detained me in Coonampettah, as I observed in my former letter.

"On Saturday evening I got ready a small triumphant chariot, which we adorned with pieces of silk, flowers, and fruit. On it was placed an image representing our Saviour risen from the dead; and the chariot was thrice drawn in triumph round the church, several instruments playing at the same time. The festival was greatly heightened by illuminations, lustres, sky-rockets, and several other fire-works, in which the Indians excel. Then verses were spoken or chanted by the Christians, in honour of our Saviour's triumphing over death and hell.

"Such multitudes, both of Christians and Heathen, crowded on this occasion, that the yard round the church was scarce able to contain them. They were seen, by the lights, sitting on the boughs of trees, planted in the above-mentioned yard; and seemed like so many Zaccheuses, whose curiosity prompted them to ascend over the heads of their brethren, in order to view the image of Him whom that happy publican was worthy of receiving personally into his house. The chief personage of the settlement, his whole family, and the rest of the Heathen who assisted in the procession, fell prostrate thrice before the image of our Saviour risen from the dead; and worshipped him in such a manner as, very happily, blended them indiscriminately with the most fervent Christians."

Such were the miserable triumphs for which the Jesuits laboured and suffered. And such were the first impressions of Christianity given to the natives of India. It is no wonder that they learned habitually to despise its teachers and professors, and that the difficulty of bringing them to a knowledge of the truth is greatly increased.

Father Martin continues his narrative: "But now the reservoir of Coonampettah being entirely drained, I resolved to retire to Elacoorichi; but thought to travel first to Aoor, in order to confer with the Missionaries on certain particulars which gave me uneasiness. I there met with Fathers Bouchet and Carvalho, almost exhausted by the toils which had oppressed them during a month. The festival of Easter had never been solemnized with so much magnificence, nor with so vast a concourse of people. The Indians are extremely fond of poetry. Father Bouchet had caused to be represented in verse, David's triumph over Goliath; this piece being a continual allegory of the victory which Christ gained, in his resurrection, over the powers of hell. The whole was instructive, and strongly affected the spectators."

At this celebration, however, it appears that the Fathers forgot their usual caution. Goliath was represented by Perumal, the elephant-headed god of the Hindoos. Some who were in attendance were greatly scandalized to see Perumal lose his head by the hand of a youth, and complained to the native Prince. "Is it not a shame," said they, "that you should entertain in your dominions a stranger, who makes it his only business to destroy the worship of our gods? He spares neither labour, nor expense, nor festivals, to raise his religion on the ruin of ours. He seems by the multitude of his disciples to give laws to you in your own territories; the very Gentiles are devoted to him; more people resorted to his last festival than were requisite to subdue a whole kingdom. Besides, that foreign doctor has publicly affronted our gods. What can be more insulting than to represent to an innumerable multitude of people, a young lad cutting off the head of our god Perumal? Even those who profess our religion are so infatuated by that stranger, that they applaud him, and clap their hands, when they see our gods dishonoured. If you are so mean-spirited as to permit him any longer on your lands, we have resolved to expel him ourselves by force."

In consequence of this representation, they were commanded to quit the territory within three days. But by the promise of certain presents, and on the condition that they abstained from such exhibitions in future, they were allowed to remain.

The intelligent reader will require no additional particulars to enable him to judge of the character and value of the much-boasted Jesuit Mission in Madura, proclaimed by the Romish Church as the noblest in the world.

CHAPTER VIII.

HINDERANCES TO THE SPREAD OF CHRISTIANITY.

The journey down the coast from Madras to Negapatam has given us the opportunity of becoming acquainted to some extent with the Missionary operations of the Portuguese and French, the Danes and the Dutch. The details, though brief, are important; and demand serious reflection and inquiry. The speedy, and numerically large, result of these older Missions, Protestant as well as Romish, is a most striking fact. It must be granted, that the Missionaries were earnest, laborious, and persevering men. Different motives may have entered into the elements of their zeal. Some may have persevered with the earnestness of men who have devoted their lives to the accomplishment of an object. Others may have had in view the wider acknowledgment of the Pope's supremacy, or the advance of their own reputation by the increase of the church. Others, no doubt, were impelled by the love of Christ their Saviour, and pity for the perishing souls of men, and accounted no sacrifice too great, no exertion too laborious, which should rescue the Heathen from their abominable idolatries, and acquaint them with the great and saving truths of the Gospel. This we know to have been the case with many of the Protestant Missionaries; their lives, as witnessed by their colleagues and converts, and the writings they have left behind them, testify to this fact. Various also were the means which were used by the Missionaries to increase the number of their followers. The Portuguese used their power and political influence in behalf of the Church of Rome. The French Missionaries dazzled and won the hearts of the people by gaudy pageants, processions, fireworks, and dramas on sacred subjects. The Protestant Missionaries directed the attention of the people to the word of God. They addressed the conscience and the understanding, and with prayers and tears besought them to be reconciled to God. But whatever the means which were used, it is a fact, that in the early Missions, both Romish and Protestant, there was a proportionately greater number of the Hindoos who yielded to the persuasives against their own religion and in favour of another, than is found to be the case in either the Romish or Protestant Missions of the present day. Tens of thousands of Hindoos, of all ranks, from the Brahman down to the lowest caste, embraced the profession of Christianity; and it is not too much perhaps to conclude, that, had no interruption been given to the process, the whole of the south of India would by this time have been at least nominally Christian. In no Heathen country did the Missionaries find more willing converts, or experience greater success, than in India. It is true, we may search in vain for spiritual religion among the Romish converts; and it may be granted also, that some of the Protestant converts were only babes in religion, and, with all their sincerity, were little acquainted with the work of divine grace in the heart, and would hardly have been considered suitable members of the church, according to the standard at present maintained by the evangelical denominations of this country: still they were separated from the mass of Heathenism, and estranged from its worship and many of its worst practices, and they acknowledged the name and the authority of Christ. They were thus, to a great extent, equal to a majority of the inhabitants of Christian Europe.

To what, then, is the subsequent tardy progress of Christianity in India to be attributed?

In the first place, it must be borne in mind, that the Protestant Missionaries of the present day are very careful not to add to the number of natives who merely *profess* Christianity. Whilst they "plant" infant churches, and exercise their spiritual husbandry with all the zeal and ability they can command, they are resolved to have only as "increase" that which "God giveth." They determine to use no methods of conversion, but the word of God and prayer, which, as the divinely appointed means, they know will be accompanied by the blessing of God; they receive none as converts without scrutinizing the motives of their profession, and inquiring into the state of their consciences and hearts. The American Missionaries, when I conversed with them, would not admit any adult to baptism, whom they would not have considered eligible to Christian communion, at the Lord's table, on the same day. The Wesleyans do not baptize a candidate unless he afford proof of a work of divine grace upon his heart by amendment of life, repentance towards God, and an earnest desire for the blessings of redemption in Christ, and whom they would, therefore, admit or continue as a probationer for membership in the church. The Missionaries of the Church of England, and of the London Missionary Society, whom I have known, have been equally strict; and thus have modern Missionaries guarded the entrance to the church, and shown their respect for its spiritual character and purity: they have, by their ministry and writings, published the Gospel more widely among the Hindoos than any of their predecessors; they have proclaimed the willingness and power of Christ to receive and to save all men; but they have also been careful that none should practise a deception upon themselves or others by a profession of Christianity, without a knowledge of its principles, and some experience of its spiritual and vital energy. It may be easily imagined how the adoption of such a standard for the reception of candidates would deter many from making application for baptism, and would reduce the number of those who should finally be received. On this system there can be no large accession to the church except as God may be pleased to pour out his Holy Spirit to awaken the idolatrous natives to a sense of their spiritual wretchedness and danger, and "to convince them of sin, of righteousness, and of judgment." And it is better for the world and the church that it should be so, rather than that whole classes and tribes of men, as in the times of the Portuguese power, should be coerced into Christianity, or should assume the profession of it for the sake of civil protection or worldly advantage, and continue in the state of darkness and spiritual death in which they were before they were baptized. There is a danger concerning such men, that "their last state should be worse than the first."

Another cause of the slow progress of Christianity among the Hindoos may be found in the deceptions formerly practised among them, under the name of Christianity, as already described in the account of the Jesuit Mission in Madura, and the disgrace it has continually to bear by the introduction of the idolatries and corruptions of Rome, and by the open profligacy and immorality of many upon whom the name of Christ has been called. The Hindoos plead Romish idolatry as an excuse for their own; and can with justice argue, that their morals are as good as those of many who are called Christians.

But it cannot be doubted, that the progress of Christianity in India has been mainly retarded by the manner in which all matters connected with religion have been administered by the English Government. As a nation, the British have failed of their duty to their Hindoo fellow-subjects.

Other European powers encouraged Missionary operations for the conversion of the Hindoos on the part of their respective churches, and to the full extent of their influence among the people; they preferred to employ men who professed Christianity, in offices of honour and responsibility; they gave no encouragement to Hindooism, showed no respect to its festivals or Priests, and took no interest in the appointment of its officers, and the management of its revenues. If, in some cases, they cared little for Christianity, they cared less for the mummeries and abominations of Hindoo idolatry. In consequence, in those parts of the country which were governed by Europeans, Heathenism was abashed, and the profession of Christianity was considered honourable. The policy of the British Government has been very different. They wisely, perhaps, banished some of the Romish Priests from their territory; neither they nor their followers could be safely trusted by the English, from their known adhesion to the Portuguese or French interests. But it is difficult to decide whether folly or wickedness had the greater part in the enactment which provided, that no natives (except Hindoo idolaters and Mahommedans) were eligible for employment in any office of trust or responsibility; and one can scarcely imagine any mode of proceeding more directly calculated to bind for ever the chains of superstition and idolatry on their subjects than that which the British Government adopted. They have had settlements in India more than two hundred years; and yet they practically, if not literally, forbade any English Missionary to visit them until a period within our own recollection. They discouraged the communication of Christian knowledge to the Hindoos; they refused to native Christians admission to the ranks of the army, or to employment in any civil capacity; they attended Hindoo festivals, and contributed largely to make them more splendid and imposing; they managed the appointment and promotion of the officers of Hindoo temples, and economized and enlarged their revenues. In short, they frowned on Christianity, and cherished and abetted Hindoo institutions and idolatries. These principles they carried out in organizing the most extensive armies in the world, in the administration of law throughout every town and village in the land, in their systems of revenue and police which permeate the entire of their vast empire, and in the thousand undefinable methods by which a despotic government can act upon a sensitive and submissive people. The consequence is, that Hindooism, which a century ago was easily shaken off, either in part or entirely, for the profession of another religion, has, by the sanction and support of the British Government, deepened its hold on the minds and habits of the people. To this deplorable cause, combined with others already suggested, may be attributed much of the callous indifference and hatred to Christianity manifested by the present race of Hindoos; and the task of the Missionary is rendered more difficult. If these proceedings were not sanctioned by the British nation, they were at least permitted and connived at; and the consequences are not the less disastrous to the spiritual interests of the Hindoos, than if they had resulted from direct legislation. How great, then, is our national responsibility; how urgent the obligation to do more for India than for any other heathen country! There is much mischief to be undone, as well as much good to be accomplished. It is impossible for Englishmen to be too liberal, too laborious, too zealous, for the conversion of the Hindoos, injured as they have been by our criminal patronage of idolatry and superstition.

CHAPTER IX.

OCTOBER, 1820, TO FEBRUARY, 1821.

NEGAPATAM.

I REACHED Negapatam on Wednesday, the 1st of November, having been eight days in travelling one hundred and eighty miles, and was glad to quit my palankeen. Mr. Squance received me with every demonstration of affection: in his society, and that of his family and other residents in Negapatam, I found some recompence for the journey, and for my separation from my friends in Madras; and could require no other relaxation from my studies and labours while resident there.

The first European occupants of Negapatam (in Tamul, *Naga patnam*, or "Serpent-Town") were the Portuguese. They erected the fort; and the number of Romish churches in and about Negapatam attest the assiduity with which they propagated their faith among the natives. According to an official return obtained in 1840, it appears that, in the district of Tanjore, about seventy miles from east to west, and about the same from north to south, of which Negapatam is the chief European station, there are one hundred and forty-six Roman churches, and twenty thousand eight hundred and eighty-two professors of the Romish faith; of whom eleven hundred and forty-two are Mirasdars, or principal renters of land, and two thousand five hundred and eighty-seven small farmers under them.

The Dutch took forcible possession of Negapatam in 1658, and in 1690 removed hither the seat of their

Indian Government from Pulicat. In 1758 the British applied to the Dutch in Negapatam for a loan of money to assist them in raising the siege of Madras; but as they would make no advance except on terms which implied a loss of twenty-five per cent., their assistance was dispensed with.

The famous Dutch Missionary, Philip Baldæus, visited Negapatam in July, 1660; and, preaching in the Portuguese and Dutch languages, attempted a reformation both of religion and manners. In this good work he was aided by another Minister, whose name was Frontinius. Among those who succeeded Baldæus was Nathanael de Pape, or Baup, who, having made himself acquainted with the Tamul and Portuguese languages, laboured diligently for the propagation of Christianity. Until within a few years of my residence in Negapatam, a venerable Dutch Minister was in the habit of making an annual visit, to preach and administer the sacraments, and to confirm the catechumens.

The town of Negapatam is large and populous. The fort, which was extensive, has been destroyed, and the materials sold and shipped away: the ditch, the mound, and the glacis remain, and, when I last saw them, they were nearly covered with the indigo plant. The burial-ground, within the bounds of the fort, though neglected, presents some curious and affecting monuments to worth and talent, both ancient and modern. Among the present inhabitants of Negapatam are many families of English, French, Dutch, and Portuguese descent; but the bulk of the population consists of Hindoos and Mahommedans. The principal streets are broad and airy; but others are so narrow, that three persons can scarcely walk abreast. Heathen temples abound in it. It contains some remains of the former prevailing system of Buddhu: in one of the streets is a well-executed sculpture of Buddhu, full size, and seated as though in meditation. Outside the town is a high tower, usually called the *Tzina*, or "Silver Pagoda," concerning which the traditions are many and contradictory: that which attributes its erection to the Chinese, appears to favour the notion of its having formed part of a Buddhist temple. It is constructed of red bricks, quite smooth, and of a small size; with so little cement, that it has been disputed whether any at all had been used: an intelligent native of the place, who was with me when I examined this building, said that a cement had been used, consisting entirely of the earth thrown up by the white ants in forming their mounds and cells; that this earth had been ground into a fine paste, and used as a cement between each brick. The tower is so lofty, as to be the first object visible at sea, and was used by the Dutch for their flag-staff. I have been concerned to hear a report, which I hope is untrue, that preparations were making to take it down. The old Dutch church is one of the chief indications that remain of the former importance of the place: the English residents assemble in it for divine service, conducted by our Missionary, every Sunday morning; but the tones of the organ, which must at one time have been a fine instrument, are now too broken to be awakened for the purposes of devotion.

The amount of the population of Negapatam has been variously computed, and, as is the case throughout India, is difficult to be ascertained; the lowest calculation I remember to have heard was, that it contained thirty thousand inhabitants. The English residents of Negapatam, chiefly in the service of Government, civil or military, occupy houses of a good size and construction, opposite the Fort, and in gardens a mile or two distant to the north-west. The best road out of the town is that leading towards Tanjore, the capital of the ancient kingdom of which Negapatam forms a part; but the favourite morning's walk and evening's drive is round the Fort, and along the sea-beach.

A few days sufficed to introduce me to the objects of our labours, and the circle of our acquaintance of all classes. The English congregations, both morning and afternoon, were respectable and attentive. The Portuguese services, on Sunday and Thursday evenings, held by Mr. Squance in our own house, were well attended; and gave promise of results which have been fully realized. Among the Heathens and Mahommedans, little had been accomplished: it would have been vain to expect them to assemble for instruction in places of Christian worship; and, until a spirit of inquiry could be excited amongst them, we could not expect them to visit us in our own houses, for conversation on the subject of religion.

My zealous fellow-labourer, Mr. Squance, adopted a plan for the excitement of inquiry, and the diffusion of Christian knowledge, among the natives, in which I was happy to join him. In Negapatam are several choultries; and there is scarcely a village among those which abound on every side that does not possess one of these buildings. He determined to make trial of these choultries, as places of preaching or conversation with the natives. We proceeded to one of them; and, after a crowd had been drawn together by our singing a verse in Tamul, Mr. Squance addressed them in that language, and read portions of the New Testament. The attention of the people encouraged us to try other places on subsequent evenings; and at length we selected seven of the most promising choultries, to be visited in rotation on each successive evening of the week. I myself occasionally addressed these crowds, by means of a young native Christian, who acted as interpreter; and have witnessed among them a seriousness and attention corresponding with the importance of the subjects of my discourse, and the solemnity of the feelings of my own mind. Tracts were inquired for, and distributed by us, with portions of the Scriptures. On this plan, we found no difficulty in assembling native congregations; and I was never more satisfied that I was in my proper work, than when engaged in choultry-preaching.

The Wesleyan Mission in Negapatam has led to the establishment of other Stations in the Tanjore country. The Rev. Thomas Cryer has charge of a Mission at Manaargoody and Melnattam, to the south-west of Negapatam, and pays a visit every three months to Trichinopoly, where there is a society and congregation. At Trivoloor also, fifteen miles west of Negapatam, a commencement has been made under circumstances of considerable promise.

The chief part of my time in Negapatam was occupied in the study of Tamul. In this I was assisted by the young man just alluded to, and another who attended when required: the opportunity of referring to my colleague in any case of difficulty was of great service and encouragement to me. The Grammar I was tolerably master of; the sounds, and idioms, and a ready supply of suitable words, were what I required. To obtain these, I devoted several hours of each day to study: I read much aloud, sentence by sentence, after my Teacher, imitating his method of pronunciation and accent; and then required him to listen and correct me whilst I read alone. I continued for some months to form a vocabulary of the new words I met with in reading; and which I made use of in my attempts to speak or to write. As my studies suffered little interruption, I soon understood the translation of the New Testament, and could read easy compositions. Within seven months after my arrival in

India, I had composed, with the assistance and corrections of my Teacher, two sermons in Tamul.

In our evening excursions we several times visited Nagore, a town on the coast, about four miles to the north of Negapatam, chiefly famous for its commerce and its mosques. Native vessels of a large size, from the opposite coasts of Malacca, Acheen, and Pegu, were often to be seen in the roads. Arab ships sometimes visit it; and I was told that constant communication is maintained with Mecca. The trade appeared to be entirely in the hands of the Mahommedan natives. Nagore being the burial-place of a Mahommedan saint of great celebrity, whose tomb is visited by pilgrims, and to whose honour an annual feast is held, is regarded as a holy place in this part of India; so much so, that the late Nabob of Arcot made a pilgrimage to it from Madras. Its mosques are extensive, and its minarets are the highest and most beautiful I ever saw: one of them is twelve stories high. We saw there a fine cassawary, kept in one of the mosques as a curiosity: it had probably been brought from Java: the natives assured us that it would eat fire. After we had several times visited this place, our assistant, a native of Ceylon, ventured to go alone to address the people. He returned in a dreadful fright, having been rudely used by the inhabitants, and narrowly escaped being stoned: he had sustained no injury; but his alarm made him unwell for some days.

At Christmas, and the commencement of the year, Mr. Squance and his family were quite troubled by the number of natives who appeared with small presents to offer the compliments of the season.

In the month of January, I witnessed, for the first time, the annual Hindoo festival of *Mauttoo Pungul*, or boiling of rice, &c., to the honour of cattle. At this season, bullocks for draught or carriage, though not generally treated with kind consideration, have their horns fancifully painted and adorned with garlands. I saw a large herd of them collected into a circle, standing quite unconscious of the respect paid to them by a number of men who marched round them to the sound of the *tarei*, a long trumpet, and at intervals prostrated themselves on the ground, as though praying for remission of the guilt of their cruelties and ill usage at other times. It appeared to me, on this and similar occasions, that the people attach little or no meaning to their observances, but practise them chiefly because they are ancient and established usages. In the multiplicity of their ceremonies and objects of worship, they are "without God" so far as the heart and judgment are concerned.

Towards the close of the month of February, I had again the pleasure of seeing my colleague and companion in misfortune, Mr. Mowat. Mr. Lynch and he travelled by land from Madras to Negapatam,* on their way to Jaffna, in Ceylon, where the annual meeting of the Wesleyan Missionaries of the Tamul District was to be held. Mr. Squance and myself joined the party; and, having engaged a small vessel to convey us to Jaffna, we embarked on Wednesday, February 21st. The vessel was too small to allow of much comfort: my only accommodation was the deck, on which I slept during the night, wrapped up in a boat-cloak; or, if awake, enjoyed the clear moonlight, and was soothed and amused by the song of the helmsman, by which, in the softest tones of the Tamul language, he seemed to woo the wind. On Friday, the 23d, we landed at Kaites; and on the evening

* They performed the journey to Negapatam on horseback: the exposure to heavy dews, to wet feet and legs from fording the rivers, and to the direct rays of the sun, with the other inconveniences and fatigues of such a journey, proved very detrimental to Mr. Mowat, who did not recover from the ill effects for several months.

of the same day, proceeded in two small boats up the shallow strait of the sea which divides the province of Jaffna from the rest of the Island of Ceylon; and arrived late at night in Jaffnapatam.

That regulation of Methodism, which requires the annual assembling of its Ministers from different points of the same District, is of especial advantage in foreign lands. On most Stations, the members of our societies are comparatively few; and the number of those who can enter into the feelings of a Missionary, assist his counsels, and solve his difficulties, is fewer still. If he were entirely debarred from personal intercourse with others of the same views and pursuits, he must be superior to the common infirmities of human nature, if his sympathies be not deadened, and the lively interest wherewith he commenced his labours considerably weakened. The interchange of thoughts and counsels, therefore, and the opportunities of mutual addresses and prayers, on these occasions, which have their results in the freshness and vigour with which each Missionary returns to his Station and his work, are advantages, in my estimation, as valuable as the professed object of a District-Meeting,—the transaction of public business.

We were affectionately received by the Rev. Joseph Roberts, and our other brethren in Jaffna, and by those from Point Pedro and Trincomallee. Mr. Mooyaart, one of the Magistrates, hospitably entertained Mr. Mowat and myself during our stay of more than a fortnight.

CHAPTER X.

MARCH, 1821.

JAFFNA.

In the Island of Ceylon, and particularly in the northern part of it, the Portuguese Missionaries appear to have had few obstacles to contend with in carrying out their plans. Little short of the whole population embraced the profession of Christianity; and on every hand to this day are to be seen the remains of large and substantial stone-built churches, and in some cases so near to each other as to excite astonishment that there could have been a population to render them necessary. The Dutch Survey of 1784 lays down about sixty churches in the province of Jaffna; thirty-seven of which were built by the Portuguese, and were afterwards repaired or re-erected by the Dutch. Several of these churches have since been restored and occupied by the American and Wesleyan Missionaries. It is said that the converts made by Francis Xavier's Missionaries about 1650, had to endure severe persecution from the native Governor of Jaffna.

It would appear, however, that the Romish Missionaries were satisfied with something less than a consistent profession of Christianity: as in other Missions in India, and other parts of the world, they allowed or connived at the continuance and practice of Heathen rites; the distinction of caste was permitted and even encouraged; so that at the moment the outward motives for the profession of Christianity were withdrawn, the converts were prepared to relapse into Heathenism. It is to be feared that few of them were made sensible of the sin and peril of idolatry, or had any adequate knowledge of the blessings of redemption in the Lord Jesus, to be received through faith in his blood. The story of Donna Caterina, Queen of Kandy, affords ground for hope that there may have been some whom the blessed Spirit of God led to the exercise of saving faith in Christ. For the particulars of her story, as for many other of the facts and details introduced in this edition, I am indebted to Walther's Tamul *Historia Ecclesiastica*, published in Tranquebar in 1735. Walther's account is as follows :—

"In 1612, the Dutch sent one Bouchaver as ambassador to the King of Kandy, and a treaty was agreed on between them on the 11th of April. The King, however, would not permit Bouchaver to depart, but detained him as one of his Ministers. In the following year, on the 20th of July, the Queen, Donna Caterina, died. She was of royal descent, and had been baptized in her infancy, and educated in the knowledge of Christianity by the Portuguese, who were at that time very powerful in Ceylon. She had, however, relapsed into Heathenism when elevated to the royal dignity. As she lay sick, she sent for Bouchaver, and said to him, 'It is a great affliction to me now, that, though a Christian and well-instructed, I have worshipped idols, and offered sacrifice to devils : many fiends are now prepared to destroy me !' Bouchaver encouraged her; he said, 'You must pray to God to have mercy upon your soul, for the sake of the Lord Jesus.' She replied, 'I am a Christian : I will pray, I will repeat after you !' He then pronounced the Lord's Prayer and the Apostles' Creed, which she repeated after him; she then exclaimed, 'O Christ, save me! I come, O Lord; graciously preserve my soul!' And thus she died in the thirty-fifth year of her age."

The Dutch took the Island of Manaar, and the province of Jaffna, from the Portuguese, in 1658. Baldæus, the Missionary, immediately commenced his labours among the people. He found them wretchedly ignorant, though professing Christianity. Vast numbers had been baptized on their repeating certain formulas, without having, in any respect, been instructed in their meaning, or in any of the doctrines of Christianity. The Dutch appear to have entered heartily upon the work of teaching these nominal Christians. In 1688 they had five Ministers in Jaffna, who had one hundred and thirty thousand three hundred and ninety-four persons under their care. In 1729 it was reported, that, in the Districts of Colombo, Colpetty, and Negombo, there were thirty-nine thousand nine hundred and fifty-five Christians; in Galle and Matura, seventy-four thousand and thirty-four, Singhalese and Tamul; in Jaffna, Trincomallee, Batticaloa, and Manaar, one hundred and eighty-seven thousand one hundred and thirty-three; in Ternati, Makkia, and Vakkia, islands of the Moluccas, seven hundred and eighteen; and in the Celebes, eighteen thousand five hundred and fifty. The Dutch East-India Company supported teachers of religion in all these places, at an annual expense exceeding thirty thousand pagodas, or more than ten thousand pounds sterling.

From the year 1796, when the British took possession of Ceylon, for nearly twenty years there appears to have been little attention paid to the religious state of the natives. The Chaplains limited their attention to the British inhabitants; and one or two Dutch Ministers, who traversed the island with commendable zeal, found sufficient employment for their energies among those who spoke the Dutch and Portuguese languages. The poor natives were as sheep having no shepherd. The consequence was, that they rapidly relapsed into heathen idolatry. A generation grew up unbaptized and uninstructed, in the place of those who had been at least nominally Christian. The churches erected by the Portuguese, which had been occupied and kept in repair by the Dutch, now fell into ruin; and, in the country parts of the province of Jaffna, the work of conversion of the natives from Heathenism had to be recommenced. In 1814 the Rev. Messrs. Lynch and Squance began their Tamul studies and labours in the town of Jaffna; and in 1816 the American Missionaries arrived, and were directed to those parts of the District where the population and the ruined churches were most numerous.

After our District-Meeting had closed, I passed an interesting day in visiting the Stations of the American Missionaries. I found them industriously engaged in repairing some of the old Portuguese churches and houses, and in calling the attention of the natives about them to the great truths of Christianity.

Their discipline is Congregational: they place themselves at a Station with no intention ever to remove; distant from any other society, they devote their time and attention exclusively to the natives; take as many children as they can support, into their own houses, to be educated in Christian principles, and general knowledge; and, when I saw them, they expressed hopes of success, which have since been, in some measure, realized. Their characters and operations commanded my respect; and I heartily wished them "good luck in the name of the Lord."

Our own Missionaries in Jaffna have been laborious; and God has blessed their exertions. When I was there, a society had been formed for some years; the congregations were numerous and respectable; and so great was the change that had taken place in the general character of the town since their arrival, that a gay visitor complained, that formerly there was music and dancing in every street; but now, wherever he went, there was singing and prayer. Subscriptions were then on foot towards the erection of a new chapel, which has since been completed. An extensive establishment of schools is connected with this Mission.

The Rev. Peter Percival, who succeeded Mr. Roberts in the Jaffna Mission, and is still (in 1844) its Superintendent, has been very successful in the organization, on the Mission premises, of a connected range of schools for the education of natives, both male and female, from early childhood until they are prepared for the active duties of life. Several valuable Agents and Assistants in the Mission have been prepared and instructed in these establishments; and a still greater number, who have been thus educated, are filling respectable and useful stations in their several spheres of life. The influence of these schools, and of those of the other Missions in Jaffna, on the native population is very observable, in the higher degree of intelligence and courtesy which they manifest. The publication of a newspaper in the Tamul language, for the diffusion of general knowledge among native readers, and of a monthly magazine, are indications of progress of a very pleasing character. The vigorous prosecution of this Mission cannot fail, by the blessing of God, to be rewarded with the early extension of Christianity throughout the whole province.

The prejudices of the heathen natives of Jaffna and its neighbourhood are said to be weaker than those of the natives of Continental India; though their religion and ceremonies in this northern part of Ceylon are substantially the same,* their regard for the distinctions of caste

* Brahmanical; in other parts of Ceylon, the system of Buddhu prevails.

is trifling. The climate is good, the town neat and pleasing in appearance, and the people very affectionate.

But I was glad to leave it for my own scene of labour. We returned down the shallow arm of the sea, and embarked in the evening of March 12th, to re-cross the straits, in a *kalla-dhoney*, an open boat of about twenty feet long, and eight feet in breadth, over part of which a shed of palmyra leaves was constructed, to screen us from the heat of the day, and the dews of the night.

The following morning, about two o'clock, I was aroused from sleep by the roaring of the wind and sea, and the violent motion of our little bark: the sky gathered blackness; the stars, our only guide, became obscured; the lightning flashed every two or three seconds; and there were strong indications of a fearful storm. The native passengers seemed apprehensive of danger, and I heard them praying to their gods; but the seamen, natives also, kept their presence of mind, and managed the boat exceedingly well. In a short time it was necessary to take down one of our two sails: the sea rolled tremendously, often threatening to overwhelm us. We got several slight sprinklings of it, till, at length, a wave actually broke in upon us. The natives shrieked with terror; my mattress and clothes were entirely drenched, and my companions were not in much better circumstances. The seamen, however, attended to their duty; the wind moderated, and by sunrise the storm subsided, leaving us a favourable breeze, which enabled us to make Negapatam at seven in the evening, when we landed, thankful for our preservation, and alive to the importance of the work before us.

Mr. Lynch proceeded immediately to Madras; but Mr. Mowat, whose delicate state of health required rest and medical advice, remained with me a fortnight.

CHAPTER XI.

APRIL, 1821.

TANJORE AND TRICHINOPOLY.

SOME doubts having been expressed in our District-Meeting as to the preferableness of Bangalore to some other places of importance, in the same direction, equally unoccupied by us, it was decided, that one of the brethren in Madras, and myself, should take a journey for the purpose of ascertaining what place was most suitable as a residence, and most promising as a Mission Station. I was advised from Madras, that Mr. Close would proceed from thence to Bangalore, and that I might meet him there at the end of April.

Mr. Squance being detained in Jaffna, I thought it best to wait his arrival before I left Negapatam, and to endeavour, meantime, to supply his place. In the Portuguese congregation, and in addressing the natives, I still used an interpreter; an inferior method, certainly, of conveying instruction, but which may be used by a Missionary advantageously until he acquires the ability of expressing his thoughts, and choosing his own phraseology, in the language of his congregations. My interpreter being a zealous Christian, who has since been received as an Assistant Missionary, I could rely on his faithfulness; and even when I had gained enough of the languages to understand his interpretation, I found preaching by his assistance a profitable exercise, which brought to my notice words and phrases that could not have occurred to me had I been confined to my own composition.

On the last opportunity I supposed I should have in Negapatam of thus preaching to the Heathen, a large crowd assembled at one of the choultries, and appeared to listen with great interest and amazement to a discourse on the day of judgment, a subject to them entirely new. My own heart was affected, and I thought the hearts of my hearers also; the event I leave with God who alone "giveth the increase."

Among the natives who about this time waited upon me, for the purpose of compliment or inquiry, were two Brahmans; one of them who was acquainted with music had come from Tanjore, to tune a piano-forte for a lady resident in Negapatam: he surprised me by opening Mrs. Squance's piano and playing a hymn-tune called "Frodsham," to which I was always partial, but had not heard it since leaving England. He was not the only native I have met with able to play on European instruments. Although the musical instruments, and the style of singing of the natives, differ very much from ours, their music is evidently on the same principles, and is a matter of science and study.

When Mr. Squance returned from Jaffna, I made my arrangements for leaving Negapatam. No palankeen could be purchased; I had lent my own to Mr. Mowat; I therefore prepared to go by way of Madras, by sea; but John Cotton, Esq., then principal Collector of Tanjore, and at present the Chairman of the Court of Directors of the East India Company, a gentleman who had already rendered me many kind and valuable services, strongly recommended a journey through the country, and generously begged my acceptance of an excellent palankeen for the purpose.

I thankfully accepted his offer; and, supplied by him with a route and passport, commenced my journey at four o'clock in the morning of Monday, the 16th of April.

When I arrived at Trivoloor, the first stage, I found that Mr. Cotton had sent one of his peons to prepare a comfortable part of the Rajah's bungalow for my reception; and, what was of still more importance, had given an order for the attendance of a *taleiari*, or guide, from stage to stage. This proved of great service in the various districts I had to pass through before I reached Bangalore.

At Trivoloor the view from my resting-place was peculiarly Indian, and very beautiful. It presented an immense tank, or pool, perfectly square, each side several hundred yards in extent, and regularly built in steps the whole length, affording an easy descent to the water in every part. In the centre of the tank arose a large *Mandabam*, or elevated platform of stone, open on all sides, its roof being supported by pillars, and surmounted by a heavy tower; the entrance to it ornamented by two large figures of elephants. To the right of the tank stood a superb temple, whose tower, several stories in height, was covered to the top with figures of gods; on every side were magnificent buildings; forming altogether, with the cheerful appearance of the surrounding well-cultivated country, scenery worthy of the ablest pencil, or the best talents of description.

Leaving Trivoloor at eight in the evening, I proceeded on my journey; and the next morning, at sunrise, found myself in Neddiamungulum, a large native village, the appearance of whose houses and inhabitants indicates a considerable degree of wealth and comfort. A feast was holding to Rama, one of the incarnations of Vishnu; a deification of one of their ancient monarchs. The firing of crackers, beating of tomtoms, and shouting of the people, almost stunned me. Great crowds had assembled to witness the procession, or to assist in drawing the car. I went to look at the car, which was now on the road: I found it of a pyramidal form, as the cars of the Hindoo gods, and the towers of their temples, usually are. It was about fifty feet in height, of a heavy black wood, not unlike ebony, and exquisitely carved with very disgusting figures, illustrative of the history of the god. The idol was seated at a great height, and accompanied by a number of Brahmans, (of whom some rode in the car,) who directed and animated the multitudes by their shouts: the whole was surmounted by a canopy of fine cloth of different colours, and adorned with flags. Its weight was so great, that several hundred men, employed at the cables fastened to it, assisted by others who worked with levers at the wheels, could not move it many feet in an hour; and I was told it required nine days' exertion to drag it round the temple. The vast expense of constructing such a machine, and the labour and privations of many who assist at these festivals, are proofs either of the great attachment of the people to their superstitions, or of the extraordinary influence of the Brahmans, under whose direction they are celebrated. The result of my inquiries and observations is, that the latter has more to do with it than the former, as the people not unfrequently complain of the labour exacted from them on these occasions.

In the evening, setting out on my journey, I again passed the car, and found it had not been moved for six hours, but was leaning much to one side, one of the wheels having imbedded itself in a soft part of the road. Such detentions are not of rare occurrence, and are remedied by propping the body of the car, and by digging under the wheel, and forming, of logs and planks, a level track to firmer ground. I thought the people looked on me with suspicion, as though my presence had obstructed the progress of their god; and, sincerely pitying their mistaken views and fruitless devotion, I pursued my way.

I walked along the road, before my palankeen, a full hour. It was a beautiful evening; the sky was without a cloud; the full moon shed a silvery splendour on the scenery; and every creature, even the plants and shrubs, seemed to enjoy the cessation of the burning heat of the day, and the refreshing rest to which a cooler atmosphere invited.

Before midnight I reached Tanjore, and entered the garden of the Rev. Mr. Kolhoff, Missionary of the Society for Promoting Christian Knowledge. The deep silence of all in the house and garden, bespoke a rest I was unwilling to disturb; so directing my palankeen to be placed under a tree, I lay down in it, and slept soundly till five o'clock in the morning.

Mr. Kolhoff, who is the son and successor of the late Mr. Kolhoff, the immediate disciple of Mr. Swartz, received me with truly Christian hospitality, and, after breakfast, carried me to wait on the British Resident of the Court of the Rajah of Tanjore, Lieutenant-Colonel Blackburne, and Sir T. Sevestre. His Highness, the Rajah, was absent on a pilgrimage to Benares, more than a thousand miles distant, the avowed object of which was, to wash away his sins in the waters of Gunga,—the river Ganges; but the true reason was said to be something else: it was perhaps a slanderous report, that the Brahmans, having prophesied that he would die within two years, he had left the country to deprive them of the opportunity of accomplishing the fulfilment of their own prediction.

Though this personage continues a Hindoo, he has a high regard for Europeans; and having himself been educated by the venerable Swartz, he maintains an European instructer for his own son. He has made extensive grants to the Mission; and, by his manner towards the Missionaries, evinces the high estimation he has for them,

In the church within the walls of the Fort he has erected an exquisite monument of marble, to the memory of Swartz, representing his dying scene, himself grasping the hand of his instructer, and appearing to take an affectionate farewell. In a smaller church in the suburbs Swartz was interred; and it was not without emotion that I visited the grave of this eminently successful Missionary.

The school and work-shops connected with the Mission were neat and commodious. The children, besides being taught the rudiments of learning in Tamul, Portuguese, or English, are instructed how to gain a livelihood. Some attend on silk-worms; others dress the silk, and make it ready for market: some are taught to bind books, others to weave mats: but what most interested me was a room occupied by girls, who are taught to read and write, and to spin cotton. Such was the state of society among the natives, and the systematic neglect of female education, that Mr. Kolhoff assured me, that it was with much difficulty they could raise a female school, even from among the children of the Christian natives, who are numbered by thousands.

I saw also the Rev. G. S., a junior Missionary, but a man of considerable talent and general information. He attended the party in the evening, and, at family worship, accompanied our Tamul hymn by his performance on the piano-forte. Mr. Kolhoff prayed in Tamul, and I in English, and thus we commended each other to God. Being furnished by my kind host with additional supplies of bread, wine, and medicine, for my journey, I took leave of Tanjore at ten o'clock at night, much refreshed in body, and greatly interested by what I had seen.

The choultry of Kellycotta, in which I passed the

following day, was a miserable building, hemmed in on every side by houses, and, in consequence, insufferably hot. A native Hindoo visited me, and entreated my acceptance of a number of eggs, though he seemed too poor to have any thing to spare. I have often received presents of this kind, and even a good dinner or supper has been prepared and brought to me, when travelling in India, by persons of whom I had no knowledge, and whose kindness I never had any opportunity to requite.

THE ROCK OF TRICHINOPOLY.

In the evening we approached Trichinopoly, The first view of it was striking: the rays of the setting sun were glancing on the rock, which rises from the level plain to an astonishing height, in the centre of the Fort; the buildings on the rock, having an appearance of strength and impregnability, reminded me of the scenery presented to my mind by the romances of early youth, or seemed a realization of the rocks and castles I have fancied in the evening clouds. Close to the rock, I found something better than imaginary gratification, in the kind welcome of the Rev. Mr. Rosen, and in the refreshing sleep I enjoyed during the night, in a bungalow or shed of bamboos and palmira-leaves, erected on the roof of his house for the advantage of cool air.

Rising early, Mr. Rosen accompanied me to the top of the rock. The ascent is by steps of stone, built or cut in the rock, and is partially covered in: about mid-way is a large Hindoo temple, whose endowments are said to yield a monthly income of many thousand rupees; and on the summit, which is rather narrow, is a smaller temple, on the top of which the British flag was hoisted. The view afforded from this eminence was

INTERIOR OF THE TEMPLE ON THE ROCK OF TRICHINOPOLY.

varied and extensive. Enclosing the rock is the Fort, built in the form of an oblong square, adorned with tanks and public buildings, and entirely filled up with regular streets, containing, I was told, thirty-five thousand inhabitants: to the east, the sun was rising on the fertile plains of Tanjore; to the south the cantonment, and the garden-houses of Europeans, extended a few miles beyond the Fort; to the north was the river Cauvery, on an island of which we could see the great temple of Seringham and the groves surrounding it; and the horizon to the north-west was bounded by hills of a bold and rugged appearance, through which the Cauvery winds its fertilizing course, and where lay my road to Bangalore.

It being Good-Friday, I attended service in the church connected with the Mission erected by Swartz.* The Lutheran service, and a sermon, in the Tamul language, were read with distinctness and propriety by a native Catechist. Mr. Rosen then administered the sacrament of the Lord's supper; the communicants, chiefly natives, were so numerous as to fill the table four or five times.

The heat throughout the whole day was excessive, and occasioned an exhaustion of strength and spirits I had not hitherto experienced: I thought the rock gathered the heat, which, with the reflection of the sun's rays from its surface, rarefied the air so as to render it inadequate to the purposes of respiration.

The kingdoms of Tanjore and Trichinopoly continued in the hands of native Hindoo Sovereigns after the establishment of the Mogul or Mahommedan empire in India. Tanjore was seized about 1650 by Venkajee, brother of Sivajee, the founder of the Mahratta empire, which was also Hindoo: his descendants still occupy the throne. In 1736 Trichinopoly was treacherously wrested from the widowed mother of the rightful Hindoo Sovereign, by Chunda Sahib, the Finance Minister of the Nabob of the Carnatic; the latter being Provincial Governor under the Nizam, or Viceroy of the Deccan, whose appointment proceeded direct from the Mahommedan Emperor of Delhi, or Great Mogul. The unfortunate Princess died in prison; and Dost Ali, the Nabob, confirmed Chunda Sahib, who was his son-in-law, in the possession of Trichinopoly. He was soon dispossessed by an army of Mahrattas; but in the course of the constant wars

* It was in this church that the late much-lamented Bishop Heber officiated on the morning of his death.

which at that time were waged in the Carnatic, Trichinopoly once more fell into the hands of a Mahommedan governor, Mahommed Ali. It is no part of the design of this narrative to enter upon the details of the ruinous wars which revolutionized the Carnatic. The French and English continued in open hostility with each other, even when their respective Governments in Europe were at peace. In the broils which arose among the native Princes themselves, or between them and the Mahommedans, or the contest for the Nabobship among the latter, the French and English were always found taking part, and always arrayed against each other. The result was briefly this, that Mahommed Ali, having been acknowledged by the British, Nabob of the Carnatic, and his right having been maintained by them against all competitors, showed some tardiness in complying with the wishes of his brave allies; the consequence of which was, that the British took the administration of the affairs of the Carnatic into their own hands, and have continued to maintain the Nabob and his descendants in idle state and useless pageantry to the present day. With little interruption, the country now included in the Presidency of Madras continued to be afflicted with the horrors of war until the death of Tippoo Sultan, and the capture of Seringapatam in 1799.

Meantime, in the gracious providence of God, the way was opened for the extension of Christianity in this part of India. In 1750 the apostolic Swartz arrived at Tranquebar, with two other Missionaries, to reinforce the Danish Mission. After labouring here with great success for several years, in 1764 he took a journey on foot, in company with another Missionary, to Tanjore and Trichinopoly, preaching on the way both to Christians and Heathens. In the latter place, he was received with great kindness by the British; and aid was afforded him to erect a small place of worship. In Tanjore he preached not merely in the city, but in the palace, within hearing of the King: he returned to Trichinopoly in September. The promise of success being so favourable, in 1767 Mr. Swartz transferred his services from the Danish Mission to that of the Society for the Promotion of Christian Knowledge, and resumed his labours in Trichinopoly. Here he acted as Chaplain to the Forces, whilst he also pursued his vocation as Missionary to the Heathen. In both capacities, he met with encouraging success. In 1779 he removed to Tanjore, where he acted in similar capacities, receiving from the Government of Madras, at both places, for fulfilling the office of Chaplain to the Garrison, one hundred pounds per annum. At Tanjore he remained until his death, in 1798.

The times in which this venerated Missionary lived seemed to give him a prominence from which he would otherwise have shrunk. Such was his character for honesty and truth, that more than once his word procured supplies for a famishing army, which supplies neither the influence of the British, nor the interference of the native authorities, could command. And when the Government of Madras required a confidential messenger to Hyder Ali, they dispatched Mr. Swartz to Seringapatam, where he was received by the warrior Chief with great respect. He was subsequently engaged by the British as interpreter, in negotiating a peace with Tippoo Sultan, in 1784. Thus was this good man honoured by earthly authorities; but he had the greater honour from God, of being the founder of the prosperous Mission at Tanjore, and that in Trichinopoly, and of seeing many thousands of the Hindoos converted to Christianity.*

* One of the best Missionary biographies I am acquainted with, is the "Memoirs of Swartz," by Dr. Pearson, the venerable Dean of Salisbury, who is also the author of the Memoirs of Dr. Buchanan.

CHAPTER XII.

APRIL, 1821.

JOURNEY FROM TRICHINOPOLY TO BANGALORE.

In the evening I was glad to leave the neighbourhood, and to resume my journey to Bangalore. I travelled through a woody and well-watered country, along a road shaded by venerable trees, and about midnight reached Musallee, a large native town, where I rested the remainder of the night, and passed the following day.

An extract from my journal will familiarly introduce the reader to the next stage of my journey.

"Namcul, Easter-Sunday, April 22d.—Intending to give myself and my bearers a full day's rest, I left Musallee last evening at sunset, with the expectation of reaching Namcul by midnight; but we lost our way amongst the hills, and the sun had risen upon us before we entered the town. The light of the moon, but little past full, made it easy to discern the character of the country through which we passed: the valleys were covered with jungle, with the exception of here and there a well-cultivated spot in the neighbourhood of the villages; the hills were rugged, steep, and many of them peaked, some entirely barren, but others clothed with trees to the top; the scenery of a deep valley in which we rested for an hour at midnight was of surpassing grandeur and beauty.

"This town appears to be of some importance, being the residence of a *Tasildar*, a native Magistrate, several of whose peons have waited on me. There are no large temples here, and I see very few Brahmans; the people seem to be poorer and simpler than those on the Coast, and I think would more readily embrace the Gospel, were a few self-denying men, willing to forego the comforts of European society, to take up their residence among them, and attempt its introduction.

"The choultry in which I rest, and now stand to write, (on the roof of my palankeen,) has a *sanctum sanctorum*, into which I have no access; and, besides a number of mythological sculptures, has the figures of a man and a woman on two opposite pillars, in a posture of devotion, intended, probably, to represent the wealthy devotees who erected it. At a short distance is a large, irregularly built tank, which washes the foot of a bare rock of considerable height and magnitude, whose top is fortified, and probably has a temple also; for a procession of Hindoos, principally well-dressed females, attended with music of a sweet and simple character, descends from its summit towards the tank. O that they were engaged in Christian worship; and that on this great and holy day, in this distant, but populous, part of the world, I had no reason to be so sensible of loneliness and singularity in my meditations and sympathies!"

Both myself and bearers gained fresh energy by a day of entire rest; our observance of the Sabbath occasioned no real loss of time, and greatly increased the pleasantness of our journey. At Moonoochoudy, where I passed the middle of the day on Monday, I found little accommodation,—the larger choultry being in ruins; the smaller one contained many idols. I was amused by observing the great quantity of food (entirely of boiled rice, seasoned with a little vegetable curry) taken by a native man on the banks of a rivulet near my resting-place; he finished his repast by taking up water from the rivulet, with his two hands, and drinking. I was the more struck with his heartiness from my own want of appetite, arising from so much exposure to the sun, and a want of such food as I had been accustomed to. Nothing but rice and the ingredients for curry are to be purchased in the village bazaars; fowls are generally to be met with amongst the country people, but mutton cannot usually be had without buying a whole sheep. I have since often purchased a sheep for myself and my men: the animal is brought to be looked at and bargained for; the usual price is a rupee, about two shillings sterling, and the man who kills it takes the skin for his trouble. But, at this time, I was too young a traveller in India to manage sufficiently well for my own comfort; and though suffering from thirst and fatigue, I was afraid of taking any thing more stimulative or invigorating, than very weak wine and water.

My stomach had lost its tone, and my health might have been seriously injured before reaching the end of my journey, but for the advice and refreshment I received the following day, under the hospitable roof of M. D. Cockburn, Esq., Collector, of Salem.

My bearers put down the palankeen in Salem soon after sunrise, opposite a choultry quite filled by natives. I was soon surrounded by a crowd, whose curiosity was of a more bold and obtrusive character than I had observed in those places where no Europeans reside: I therefore, at once, desired to be conducted to the house of Mr. Cockburn, who received me with that open hospitality peculiar to India, though I had no previous acquaintance with him, nor any letter of introduction.

A remark made by this gentleman in conversation is worthy of being recorded, as containing a fact perhaps not generally known, and on which a volume might be written, without conveying the idea more correctly. It was, "That the Hindoos, allowing them their own religion, are the most religious people in the world." No one who has resided in India, and has taken pains to observe the manners and character of the people, can doubt the correctness of this assertion.

It was with difficulty, at night, I could tear myself from the company of my entertaining host and his friends to pursue my journey. I found my palankeen stored with beer, and other refreshments, to enable me to follow the advice Mr. Cockburn had given me as to my mode of living. My regret at the necessity of hastening away was moderated by a hope, afterwards realized, of paying a longer visit to this part of the country, which, I believe, had never before been traversed by a Protestant Missionary. Romish Missionaries there are; for whilst I was with Mr. Cockburn, a petition from one of them was presented to him, complaining of some interruption to a procession connected with the late festival, in the course of which the image of the Virgin had been despoiled of its crown.

The sun had risen, and the day was hot, when we arrived at the choultry, at the bottom of the Tapoor pass. A heavy shower of rain fell in the course of the day, which not only allayed the oppressive heat of the atmosphere, but relieved us from some anxiety, by enabling us to ascend the pass by daylight. Even with this advantage we found it both difficult and dangerous: by night it would have been almost impracticable; the more so as my bearers had neglected to purchase oil for their torch at Salem, and none was to be procured in this neighbourhood.

About three P.M. we began to ascend the pass, which extends, with various degrees of steepness, about five miles. A further run of an hour and a half, through a beautiful and well-cultivated country, brought us to

Adamancottah, where we procured oil, and rested till three in the morning. We then pursued our way to Pallicode, a large native town, with a fort in ruins, situated amidst hills and rocks. The country maintained the same character the whole of the next stage, to Ryacottah, where I arrived on the evening of Thursday, the 26th of April.

It was nine o'clock at night when I entered the house of Dr. Thomas, a fellow-passenger from England, attached to the troops of the Honourable Company at this station. Mrs. Thomas had not recovered the effects of the shock occasioned by the burning of the "Tanjore." My arrival brought the circumstances fresh to her memory; nor was it surprising that when, an hour or two after my arrival, a tremendous thunder storm expended itself over us, it should occasion more than ordinary alarm, and raise a suspicion that I was the person whom it followed. But whatever might have been the fears of the moment, they had no effect on the hospitalities of the following day. At night I again resumed my journey, over some of the highest land in this part of India, and where the temperature of the air is moderate during the day, and the nights are cold and sharp.

On Saturday, the 28th, I rested at Oosoor, in a bungalow to which I had been directed by Mr. Cockburn, of Salem, delightfully situated on an eminence, from which there is a view of several miles in extent. The town is large and well built: the houses are roofed with black tiles, the colour of which is owing, I believe, to some peculiarity of the clay. Water guglets and other ware made of the same earth, and quite black, are used in Bangalore, and have a neat appearance. In most other parts of the country the earthenware is red.

The inhabitants of Oosoor were busily engaged in their various occupations, and appeared to want nothing to complete their happiness but that certain knowledge of God and of futurity which the Gospel alone can impart.

Whilst looking about me in this neighbourhood, I could not but reflect on the extent and importance of the work a Missionary to India has before him, and realize some of those feelings by which he should be actuated.

The next stage brought me to the end of my journey, and to the house of the Rev. W. Malkin, A.M., the Chaplain of Bangalore.

The reader will observe that, during this journey, my colloquial acquaintance with the language was not sufficient to enable me to converse freely with the natives: my communications with them were consequently brief, and elicited no particulars of interest.

Considerable difference of character might be observed in the population of the different districts through which I had passed. The beautifully rich country of Tanjore, remarkable for its entire cultivation, is peopled by a gentle, and comparatively a polished, race: if the inhabitants of Trichinopoly and its neighbourhood differ from them, it is in being of a darker hue and of a bolder demeanour. The more scattered population of the Collectorate of Salem, and the kingdom of Mysore, had an appearance of greater hardihood and rusticity; and did not seem to include so large a proportion of Brahmans, or of others who subsisted independently of the labour of their hands.

The Hindoos have the character of indolence very freely attributed to them, and it may perhaps be merited by many of those who enter the service of Europeans; but the appearance of neatness and comfort about many of the habitations of the merchant, the manufacturer, and the farmer; their successful vigilance in observing the seasons for ploughing, sowing, &c.; the instances of skill and labour observable on every hand, in their tanks and conduits for water; and their great personal exertions, day and night, for the irrigation of their land, when the season requires it; are sufficient to convince an impartial observer, that they deserve the character of an ingenious and industrious people; especially when it is considered that the climate, and the circumstances of the country, neither require, nor generally allow them to possess, the robust vigour of body enjoyed by Europeans.

Their good breeding appears in the collectedness and ease with which they converse with strangers; and though rarely indulging in boisterous mirth, they are generally good humoured and cheerful.

My palankeen bearers performed nothing extraordinary on this journey. They were thirteen in number, twelve to the palankeen, and one for their cooking utensils, rice, &c. In thirteen days they travelled three hundred miles; and for that service, according to regulations fixed by the Government, had each to receive ninety fanams, about fourteen shillings sterling, which would be about sevenpence farthing per mile for the whole set; their maintenance, all the while, being at their own charge. I added a small present in acknowledgment of their good behaviour. The honesty of this class of men is almost proverbial, and gives a feeling of confidence to the solitary stranger who commits himself to their guidance. In all my journeys, though often obliged to trust much to their care, I do not recollect ever having sustained the least loss from them.

It was early on Sunday morning when I arrived in Bangalore; the services of the church, and the excellent sermon delivered by Mr. Malkin, were refreshing to my spirit. The day was delightfully passed in the society of Mr. Malkin and his family, and in that of Mr. Close, my brother Missionary from Madras, who had arrived to meet me the evening before.

CHAPTER XIII.

MYSORE, BANGALORE, AND SERINGAPATAM.

THE MYSORE COUNTRY.

MAY, 1821, TO FEBRUARY, 1822.

ONE of the most remarkable passages in the history of the British empire in India is that which relates to the kingdom of Mysore. Early in the eighteenth century, the Hindoo occupant of the throne of Mysore was deaf and dumb. The affairs of government were therefore of necessity intrusted to Ministers, and its duties discharged by them; the Rajah, or King, only supplied a name, under the authority of which armies were commanded and revenues collected. The mental weakness of successive heirs to the throne favoured the continuance of this mode of government. Meantime, Hyder Ali, a Mahommedan, the orphan son of a murdered Fouzdar, or provincial Chief, made himself remarkable, first, in the regular military service of Mysore, by his extraordinary courage, and his admirable coolness and self-possession; and afterwards, as commander of a body of freebooters, whose singular success, in the acquisition of booty and territory, is scarcely to be paralleled. His services in the suppression of a mutiny in the Mysorean army, and in the overthrow of an opulent Chief, who was charged with disloyalty and defection, were rewarded with a grant of the district of Bangalore, as a personal *jaghire;* that is, all the revenue he could raise upon that district would be for his sole use and benefit. He appears to have attained the highest honours, by satisfying the demands of the Mahrattas against the Mysorean Court. Nothing now appeared to impede his advance to sovereignty; he succeeded in supplanting Nunjeraj, the Minister, by whom he had been elevated, and in a short time took under his management the territory and revenues of Mysore; reserving only a moderate provision for the personal expenses of the Rajah, whose life and liberty were now dependent on his will.

In 1767 Hyder Ali was brought into hostilities with the English, by an attack they made on the Mysore territory, in conjunction with Nizam Ali. Hyder Ali dexterously managed to alienate the Nizam from his British allies, under the pretence of restoring the Mahommedan power in India, and to unite with his forces against them. The British routed the combined armies at Trinomaly. Hostilities were, however, continued for nearly two years; the principal forts in Coimbatoor, Salem, and part of Mysore, were taken and retaken; until Hyder suddenly made his appearance before Madras, demanding peace; a demand which was joyfully acceded to by the English Government, whose armaments and treasury had been exhausted in the unequal struggle.

In 1778 the war was renewed, and was, in one respect, remarkable above all others for the atrocious cruelties inflicted by Hyder Ali, on his English prisoners, in the Forts of Bangalore and Seringapatam. At one time, Hyder's army ravaged and pillaged the whole country to within five miles of Madras. In 1783 Hyder Ali died, and was succeeded by his son, Tippoo Sultan, with whom peace was made in 1784. The services of the celebrated Missionary, Swartz, as interpreter, were engaged by the Madras Government, in the negotiation of this peace with Tippoo Sultan.

Within a few years, the aggressive spirit of Tippoo Sultan led him to attack the territories of the Rajah of

Travancore, an ally of the British Government. This step was the cause of resumed hostilities on the part of the British; the Governor-General of India, Lord Cornwallis, assumed the personal command of the army destined for Mysore in 1791, and succeeded in conducting it, completely equipped and provisioned, to the table-land of Mysore, without firing a shot.

The first object was the reduction of Bangalore, which was successfully accomplished; but not without a tremendous struggle with the troops of Tippoo, some of whose best soldiers fell in defence of the Pettah and the Fort. Bangalore was taken in March, 1791.

In the following May, the army was put in motion towards Seringapatam, which Tippoo had made his capital; having destroyed the old citadel of Mysore, to obliterate, as much as possible, the memory of his own and his father's usurpation.

Tippoo's forces were brought to a general engagement within sight of Seringapatam, and suffered an entire defeat. They retreated into the fortress; and Lord Cornwallis, not having either provisions or sufficient support, was unable to follow up his victory by an attack on Seringapatam, and was under the necessity of conducting his army back towards Bangalore. They were employed for some months in the reduction of the most remarkable hill-forts in the Mysore country, many of which, until that time, had been considered impregnable.

Having been joined by the expected reinforcements, Lord Cornwallis again appeared within sight of Seringapatam, on the 5th of February, 1792. Within a few weeks, the skill and valour of the British troops had placed it beyond a doubt, that Tippoo Sultan's capital must surrender; when the wily tyrant proposed terms of peace, which Lord Cornwallis accepted; at the same time, taking charge of two of Tippoo's sons, as hostages, one of them ten, and the other eight, years of age; who, after two years' detention, were restored to their father. Many English prisoners were released from Seringapatam during this siege; but it is to be feared that many more were left to pine in cruel and hopeless captivity.

Tippoo Sultan's hatred of the English now led him to the adoption of a measure which issued in his discomfiture and death; and, in its results, tended more perhaps to the firm establishment of the British power in the south of India than any other event.

He dispatched an embassy to the Mauritius, then a French colony, proposing to the Government of that Island, and through them to the Government of France, that they should assist him, with men and ammunition, against the English, with the avowed object and purpose of their utter extermination, and to put an end for ever to their power and existence in India. This occurred in 1797.

The Earl of Mornington, afterwards Marquis Wellesley, had newly arrived in India as Governor-General. He saw the necessity of immediate proceedings against Tippoo, and promptly prepared for the anticipated struggle. Two armies were assembled, one in Madras, under General Harris, and another in Malabar, under General Stuart. These armies were united before Seringapatam, in April, 1798. Having made the needful approaches and preparations, the assault was made on the 30th of April, under the command of Major-General Baird, who had formerly, for several years, been a prisoner in Tippoo's capital. Seringapatam was carried, after great loss on the side of the English, and dreadful slaughter among the troops of Tippoo. He himself was numbered with the slain, and his family became prisoners of war.

The permanent command of Seringapatam was intrusted to Colonel Wellesley, brother of the Governor-

General, who had taken an active part in the siege. It was thus in India that the peculiar character and brilliant talents were nurtured and matured which have rendered the Duke of Wellington so conspicuous, both in the camp and in the council, as the hero of his country, and the deliverer of Europe.

The representative of the ancient Royal Family of Mysore, whose rights had been usurped by Hyder Ali, was now sought for. He was found, a child about five years of age, in an humble dwelling, near the ruins of the old palace of Mysore, from which the family had been removed, that it might be converted into a granary. He was saluted, and acknowledged as heir to the throne of Mysore, to the exclusion of the family of Tippoo Sultan. The same Prince still occupies the throne; and his patronage and approval have been given to the operations of the Wesleyan Mission, now established in Mysore; one of the principal Mission-schools being exclusively supported by himself.

Bangalore is situated in the heart of the kingdom of Mysore. It is about two hundred miles west of Madras, little more than seventy miles north-east of Seringapatam, and eighty from the town of Mysore, the present capital of the kingdom.

The Fort, and the Pettah (a name common to towns adjoining forts in India) of Bangalore, are chiefly occupied by natives, who use the Canada or Canarese language, in number perhaps thirty thousand; but there are amongst them many Mahommedans also, the descendants of the former invaders of the country, or of those who were made to embrace Islamism by the violent zeal of Tippoo.

The Cantonment, built for the accommodation of the British force maintained here, is about a mile from the Fort and Pettah; and is usually occupied by several native regiments, and two of English, one of horse and one of foot. The bungalows occupied by the officers and their families, and other British residents, stand apart from each other, surrounded by gardens, and present much the appearance of a neat English village.

Connected with the Cantonment, are the bazaars and huts, built and occupied chiefly by the native followers of the army, of all religions, trades, and professions: the greater part, having accompanied the troops from Madras, or some other part of the Carnatic, use the Tamul language; but the Teloogoo and the Hindostanee are also extensively spoken.

Bangalore is said to be nearly three thousand feet above the level of the sea: the climate is accounted healthy; the mornings and evenings are cool, but in the course of the day the sun is very powerful.

In deciding on this station as favourable for the establishment of a Mission, we were influenced by the consideration of the salubrity of the climate, the accessibleness of the natives of every class and description, the immediate vicinity of Seringapatam, Mysore, Oosoor, Nundidroog, and other populous towns and villages; as well as by its being a central mart for merchandise from various parts of India.

Mr. Close returned to Madras, after having visited Seringapatam. I remained in Bangalore, and was kindly entertained by the Rev. W. Malkin for several weeks, whilst waiting the arrival of Mr. Mowat, and until I could engage a house for our residence.

I deferred any arrangements for the commencement of Missionary labours in public, till my colleague could arrive, that we might in all things act in concert. The man I employed to assist me in Tamul reading and composition, hazarded some advice on the subject, very illustrative of his own character as a Heathen and Hindoo.

I had finished a sermon in Tamul, which had cost me considerable pains, both as to matter and composition; and to ascertain its intelligibleness and its effect, I read it to my teacher, who thus criticized it:—"The people will not hear it, because it tells of Christ: when I, who can explain things better, mention him, they say it is *all lie:*" he then proceeded to recommend that I should first acquire great influence among the people, and then attempt the promotion of Christianity.

Whilst residing with Mr. Malkin, I usually rose early; and, finding I could bear the heat of the sun for two hours after its rise, I gratified my curiosity, and enlarged my acquaintance with the immediate neighbourhood of Bangalore, by taking long walks in every quarter successively. Study of the Tamul language employed me during the day; and in the evenings I was generally accompanied by my kind host to some neighbouring gardens, kept by natives, for the growth of the aromatic and pungent herbs used for curry; of roots of various kinds; and of the *kerbuja*, or water-melon, usually the object of our inquiry, which, though seldom brought to the tables of Europeans in India, is a most pleasant and refreshing fruit.

In one of these evening excursions I was near setting my foot on a serpent; it was creeping on the other side of a hedge, which I had taken a leap to cross. I cleared the dangerous reptile, and gave warning to Mr. M. not to follow. The serpent concealed himself in the hedge; we disturbed him, and he twined up one of the shrubs: again he found a hole in the ground, from whence we dug him up with a gardener's spade, and despatched him. He was about three feet long, and was said to be of a venomous kind, whose bite frequently occasions death.

The garden I was most fond of visiting was one (the property of a wealthy and respectable old Hindoo) in which there was an abundance of fruit-trees of various kinds; but its chief attraction was the clearness of the water in its stone tank, and the profusion of roses which adorned it, in almost every season of the year: these latter were, I believe, made an article of profit, being sold for the manufacture of rose-water, of which the natives make plentiful use on festival occasions.

The numerous tribe of monkeys inhabiting the jungle round the Pettah of Bangalore, sometimes attracted my attention, and induced me to enter the jungle and observe their habits. Some were as large as a good-sized mastiff. They seemed very fond of plantains, and would crowd around me at the distance of a few paces, when they saw my hands filled with them; but none would approach near enough to receive them from my hands, except the females with young ones clinging about them. I was amused with the appearance of order and government maintained amongst them; the largest or oldest always claiming to be served before the younger. A smart junior, one day, stepped nimbly before one of his seniors, and snatching up a plantain I had just thrown, thrust it into his mouth, hoping to retire with it in safety; but in a moment found himself in the gripe of his offended and grinning superior, who threw him to the ground, and, thrusting his hand into his mouth, drew out the plantain, and safely deposited it in his own. These animals seemed to have a great dislike to dogs, perhaps because frequently robbed by them of the rice or other food placed for them by pious Hindoos.

After Mr. Mowat's arrival, I commenced reading my sermons to the people in the villages, who, in general, were not unwilling to hear. A Christian native of Tranquebar accompanied me, to explain my intentions more fully than my present acquaintance with the language enabled me to do. Several of them attended the service in our own house on Friday evenings, when we talked and prayed with them in the manner we thought best calculated to interest and benefit them.

Having received an invitation to Seringapatam, which place we had purposed to include in our Mission, I set out in my palankeen on Wednesday, the 25th of July, and passed that day at Kingairy, a large village with a fort in ruins, and an excellent bungalow for the accommodation of travellers. The bungalows erected by the munificence of the Rajah of Mysore, on every road likely to be travelled by English gentlemen, throughout the whole of his territory, render it much more pleasant and easy to be traversed than many other parts of India.

A general invitation to the inhabitants of Kingairy was successful in bringing a room full of natives, to whom I read a sermon in Tamul, which one of them undertook to explain in Teloogoo to those who did not understand the former language. I presented to them four different tracts in Teloogoo, with which I found they were more generally acquainted than with Tamul: they were all read aloud, and excited attention and interest.

I now passed through a rough, desert-like country, uncultivated in most parts, and apparently incapable of cultivation. Early in the morning of Thursday, parched with heat and thirst, we stopped for a few minutes in front of a heathen temple, to avail ourselves of the water of the tank in its neighbourhood: I purchased two cocoanuts for *forty cash*, not quite a penny, and was much refreshed by the water which they contained within the kernel.

About ten A.M. we arrived at the bungalow, near Chinnapatnam, which, as its name imports, is a small town, having a neat little Fort. I was immediately visited by the Cutwāl, a sort of head Police Officer, a venerable old Mahommedan, with a white beard, who spoke Tamul, and was very communicative as to the history and present state of the town. I asked him if he could read Tamul, or Teloogoo; he boldly replied he could read both; but when I tried him, confessed he did not know a letter, and thus destroyed any confidence I might have been inclined to place in his previous statements. A heavy storm gathered in the evening, and prevented me from visiting the streets of the town to converse with the people, of whom I understood a good number were acquainted with Tamul.

The next day we were detained a short time by the swollen state of the Madoor river, occasioned by the rains of the preceding night. Its depth and rapidity made it difficult to pass, and perhaps dangerous also; the bearers exhausted their stock of objections, and after a little delay, carried me safely to the other side.

We found the town of Madoor fairly depopulated by that dreadful disease, the cholera morbus. The rain detained me at Mundium till nine A.M. on Saturday, when we again set out; and, for some miles, we travelled through such a wilderness as I had not hitherto seen,—uninhabited, rocky, and barren, with hardly a stunted shrub or a blade of grass to relieve the eye.

A little after noon we stood at the head of the valley, in which are situated the Fort and island of Seringapatam. Through this valley, the Cauvery, a river deemed sacred by the Hindoos, has its course; and, by separating, and again uniting, forms the island, (about four miles in length, and one and a half in breadth,) on which stands the most celebrated fortress in India. Canals, commencing from the river at some distance up the country, conduct the water to the higher grounds of the valley; and, by an aqueduct over the river, into the island and Fort itself, which would otherwise be without means of irrigation; and thus the verdure of cultivation is extended far beyond the immediate banks of the Cauvery. The lovely green of the fields and gardens that adorn the valley formed a most delightful contrast to the appearance of the desert country I had just traversed; and the sight of the minarets and towers within the Fort of Seringapatam excited most interesting historical recollections, with which the feeling gladly mingled, that this former seat of tyrannical usurpation, and cruel Mahommedan bigotry, was now in the peaceful possession of my own countrymen; for, though in the midst of the dominions of the Rajah of Mysore, the Fort and island of Seringapatam have been retained by the British Government ever since the successful siege and storming by General Harris, in 1799.

About three P.M. we entered the gates of the Fort. I was soon recognised, and conducted to the bungalow prepared for my reception. I waited on the Commandant, Colonel S., who received me with friendly politeness: the Fort Adjutant, Lieutenant Lawler, was not at home when I called at his house, but afterwards came to see me, and showed me many attentions. I was conducted to the chapel erected about twelve months before by the Protestants residing in Seringapatam: they are chiefly descendants of Europeans, and are employed in the gun carriage manufactory within the Fort. In erecting the chapel they were liberally assisted by the Honourable A. Cole, (at that time Resident at the Court of Mysore, now Member of Parliament for Enniskillen,) and by the officers of the garrison: it will contain a congregation of one hundred persons. They had been accustomed to assemble in it for prayer and reading every Sunday; but no Minister had preached there before Mr. Close, who visited them in May, and of whose services they retained a grateful recollection.

The following day being Sunday, I conducted divine

service, in English, in the chapel, morning and evening, and preached to an attentive congregation.

On Monday I received and paid many visits. In the evening I read a Tamul sermon to a large congregation, with more ease and pleasure than I had anticipated.

Desirous of making my visit as profitable as possible to the people of Seringapatam, I busied myself in receiving and conversing with all who came to see me during the day, and every evening had a public engagement in English or Tamul, either in the chapel, or in my own house; not without incurring considerable fatigue, and some degree of indisposition.

On Friday morning I walked to view the fortifications of this celebrated place, which was erected in 1642, about the same time that the first English Fort was erected in Madras: they are not very ruinous, except at the unrepaired breach at which it was stormed, in 1799. I should think the Fort was nearly three miles round; its population was once immense, but at present does not perhaps much exceed twenty thousand; many of its Mahommedan inhabitants having removed to Arcot or Madras; and the wealthier Hindoos having been drawn away to Mysore, the present seat of the native court.

The palaces and seraglios of Hyder and his son are occupied as barracks, hospitals, or private residences, by the British officers and troops.

No part of the remains of the former splendour of Seringapatam interested me more than the palace in the *Laul Baugh*, or royal garden, at the east end of the island, about three miles' distant from the Fort. This palace, or banqueting-house, now in ruins, was, thirty years ago, the most superb in this part of India. I went through the whole of its galleries and apartments, now entirely unoccupied. It appeared to have been highly finished, and very costly. The walls were plastered with *chunám*, the shell-lime of India,—firm, and bearing a polish equal to plaster of Paris; on this white ground a regular pattern of flowers was exquisitely finished with paint, and gilt; giving it the appearance of rich porcelain, and superior to the best paper used for rooms in England: many parts of it are still in good condition. The four principal apartments open with their full width to the court or garden; and being galleried on three sides, appear to have been intended for displaying and witnessing dances or shows. On the bank of the river is a smaller building, or rather a roof supported by pillars finished in the same style; all the sides are doors, which may be opened to admit the air, or shut at pleasure.

Near the entrance of the Laul Baugh, stands the mausoleum, in which are interred the remains of Hyder and Tippoo. It is a beautiful building, in the Moorish style of architecture; and, having the attention paid to it which the climate requires, is in excellent preservation. The open verandah or terrace round the mausoleum is supported by pillars of black marble, polished; the pavement is of the same material, and strongly contrasts with the rest of the edifice, which is plastered with *chunám*, nearly white. The whole has a solemn and imposing appearance, well suited to the character of the place. As I ascended the steps, I was desired to take off my shoes, the mark of respect paid in the East to places reputed sacred. I told the persons in attendance, that it was not my custom to do so; and, from the regard usually given to custom, was allowed to proceed without submitting to so great an inconvenience. The interior of the building is beautifully finished with embossed work in *chunám*: on the floor are three mounds, each about two feet in height; the middle one is over the body of Hyder Ali; one on the side over that of Tippoo Sultan;

and that on the other side over the body of *Sultanka Ma*, the mother of Tippoo. These mounds were covered with precious cloth from Mecca, and constantly adorned with flowers. A lamp was kept burning; the place was filled with a strong aromatic smell, very pleasant; and was attended by a respectable man, who seemed to be a Minister of the Mahommedan religion.

From the tomb I went to the mosque close by; in which the object that most interested me was a beautiful youth, reading the Koran, under the direction of a venerable old man. The whole establishment of the tomb and mosque to the memory of Tippoo Sultan, is, I believe, supported by the liberality of the British Government; with that national generosity, which, however peculiar, is much exemplified in India, honouring all that is great, although hostile, and having a more tender regard for the prejudices and superstitions of even a subjugated people, than for the appearance of consistency with the dictates of its own purer system.

In the evening I returned to the Fort, and formed into a class of catechumens, or probationers, a number of persons who appeared sincerely desirous of the advantages of religious communion, and of conforming to our rules.

On Saturday, August 4th, I passed, within the Fort, the famous Abbè Dubois, in his palankeen. He was dressed in a Moorman's or Turkish habit, and wore his own long black beard. By conforming, in some measure, to the customs of the natives, and by his acquaintance with their languages, he had acquired great respect and influence among them; though he complained, in the society of Europeans, and in his writings, that, during a thirty years' residence in the country, he had never been able to find or to make a real Christian among the natives; that the Hindoos did not want Christianity, and that, if they did embrace it, the change was for the worse.

One of the instances which he cites as illustrative of the insincerity of the native Romanists is, that Tippoo Sultan required many thousands of them to become Mahommedans, when they all consented, not one of them having the principle or courage to become a martyr for his religion! Such instruction as the Abbè and his fellow-Jesuits have been accustomed to give is not calculated to make men "faithful unto death."

One of the officers of the garrison was very desirous of witnessing an interview between the Abbè and myself, and drove to the Abbè's residence to arrange with him as to place and time; but found him preparing for an excursion through the country, to visit distant portions of his flock. He could not defer his journey, but sent for my perusal the manuscript of his "Letters on Christianity in India," which have since been published in England, with the expression of his regret that a young man, such as he had heard me described, should have devoted himself to so hopeless a task as that of the conversion of the Hindoos, and his earnest recommendation to me to take the earliest opportunity of returning to England.

I read his Letters; and whilst I saw the futility and contradictory nature of his arguments, could not but pity the man who had such sufficient reason to complain that he had "spent his strength for nought;" and regretted that a person of such constitutional energy and adaptation to the climate and circumstances of India, had not commenced his labours among the natives with clearer views, and conducted them on better principles. Had he laboured to found faith upon knowledge, and to displace idolatrous superstition by the worship of God in spirit and in truth, I doubt not he would have seen results the opposite of those he complained of: had he aimed at communicating a knowledge of the Holy Scriptures, and faithfully insisted on the peculiar doctrines and privileges of Christianity, his influence might have been more contracted, and his worldly honour less; but he would have found a full compensation in the conversion of some souls to God, and in the peaceful satisfaction of his own mind.

It forms a singular conclusion to the history of the strange inconsistencies of the Abbè Dubois, that on his return to Europe he accepted an appointment to a Seminary, or College, in Paris, where it is his official duty to prepare and educate Missionaries for employment in India; a country which he professed to believe was incapable of Christianity, and under the judicial curse of Almighty God!

Another Lord's day, August 5th, was, I trust, profitably employed by me in Seringapatam. We assembled in the chapel for prayer at seven o'clock in the morning; in the forenoon I read prayers and preached, and administered the sacrament of the Lord's supper, and held service again in the evening.

Monday the 6th, I set out early to Mysore, the present capital of the kingdom, about nine miles distant from Seringapatam. I alighted and walked through the Pettah of Mysore; the streets were very dirty, and the place did not appear to me so large and respectable as the Pettah of Bangalore.

I breakfasted and dined with the Honourable A. Cole, before mentioned as British Resident, or Political Agent, at the Rajah's court. He received me with his accustomed and well-known kindness and affability, and honoured me with a conversation of considerable length, on the object of my visit and of our Mission in general; in the course of which, he offered his influence in our favour in Mysore, if we were desirous of establishing ourselves there. The unassuming dignity and condescension of this gentleman commanded my high respect; and I could not but be gratified that my country's Government, in a foreign court, should have so able a representative.

In the evening I preached in the Pettah of Mysore, to a small congregation of the English and country people, in the service of the Resident and the Rajah.

I here received an invitation to visit Oonsoor, a place about thirty miles distant, with an offer of conveyance by means of elephants and camels; but, having made other arrangements, I was obliged to decline it.

Returning to Seringapatam next morning, I dined with Colonel S., at whose table I met most of the English officers and gentlemen in the neighbourhood. In the evening I again met those who were formed into a class, and was gratified by their earnestness and desire to learn the things of God.

On Wednesday I delivered another sermon in Tamul, and took leave of the affectionate and grateful people, both Indo-British and native, who had been the chief objects of my visit. Were no other ends to be answered by Missions to India, than the maintenance of Christian knowledge and feeling among those who already profess our holy religion, it is an object worthy of the beneficent liberality of the public at home, and of the laborious exertions of the devoted Missionary.

The following morning, having been supplied by the kindness of Mr. Cole with an order for the Rajah's bearers, to carry me post to Bangalore, I set out in company with Captain Monk, of the Hon. Company's service, who was going to the same place. We found relays of bearers waiting for us at every stage, having thus six or seven changes in the whole distance to Bangalore, which we travelled in twenty hours, averaging nearly four miles an hour; all the expense incurred being a present of two rupees, about four shillings sterling, to each set of bearers, consisting of twelve or thirteen persons to each palankeen.

Captain Monk was afterwards one of my fellow-passengers on the voyage home in 1828; and while on board ship, reminded me of a circumstance that occurred on the journey above mentioned. Soon after we had left Seringapatam, the Captain observed a native stranger in company with us, who carried a sort of knife or dagger; and thought it proper to inquire who he was, and why he had joined our company. He replied, that he was servant to a gentleman in Bangalore; and, understanding we were travelling to that place, only desired liberty to run along with the palankeens: being allowed to do so, he kept company with us the whole journey, and was with us when we reached the fort of Bangalore at day-break the following morning, having run a distance of seventy-five miles in twenty hours, without indicating any symptoms of excessive fatigue.

On my return to Bangalore, I found my colleague and his wife removed to a house more suitable and convenient than that I had first engaged. The garden attached to it was extensive, producing culinary vegetables, such as spinach, cabbages, cauliflowers, nolecole, lettuces, and onions. Peaches of an inferior kind to those grown in England, but still delicious, and originally, I believe, from Persia, were in such abundauce, that we could neither use them all, nor even give them away. The lacott, a Chinese fruit, not unlike a plum, was produced also in great plenty; it is sweet when ripe, and both used for tarts, and eaten as dessert. We had also the rose apple, a fruit whose taste resembles the scent of a rose, so far as there is any similarity between the perceptions of the two senses; the pomegranate was not uncommon, but its tart and astringent flavour disappointed the notions I had formed of it; mulberries were fine and abundant; the custard-apple, whose pulp is soft and delicious; the lime, the orange, the pumplemose, (a large fruit resembling an orange, but three or four times the size,) and coffee, were all grown in this garden, the extent of which might be five thousand square yards. It must be remembered, however, that the climate of Bangalore is more favourable to horticulture than most other parts of the south of India. We had a few English apple trees whose fruit was excessively small and poor. The guava, an agreeable fruit, not unlike a pear in shape and size, but very dissimilar in flavour, was a favourite with us when ripe; but the trees were often robbed during the night by flying foxes, a species of bat so large, that their wings from tip to tip extend more than three feet. For the house and garden we paid a monthly rent of about £4. 4*s.* sterling.

As an additional means of communicating religious knowledge to the natives, we frequently assembled those who were occasionally employed in our house and garden to hear the reading of the Scriptures, and prayer, in their own language: the *bandi káran,* or the man who had charge of the bullocks used in drawing our palankeen carriage, excused himself from attending family prayer on the ground of its being against his caste.

I continued my evening walks for the purpose of road-side conversation with the natives, and village preaching; sometimes I found attentive hearers, sometimes I was unheeded, sometimes complimented.

One evening, walking out to Alsoor, a neatly-built village near Bangalore, I approached a school of well-dressed children, assembled in the front verandah of a respectable native house. The moment I addressed the Schoolmaster, he rose and presented a bit of carpet, on which he begged me to be seated. I complied, and, enjoying the shade, for the sun was still hot, I took off my hat, and tried to converse with him; but found that it was to some disadvantage; for, though he seemed to understand my Tamul, his answers, being in Teloogoo, were quite unintelligible to me.

Whilst thus trying to converse with each other, a very black, but good-looking, native, with the triple mark on his forehead as a worshipper of Vishnoo, and an ola-book in his hand, more like a man of learning than of wealth, joined us, and offered his assistance to interpret for us from Tamul to Teloogoo, and from Teloogoo to Tamul. Several other persons also came, and stood or sat to listen. Our conversation turned on the subject of religion, and led me to expose the absurdities of the Hindoo system, especially those arising from the doctrine of metempsychosis, or transmigration of souls, for which I found them great sticklers. They at length referred to the authority of their Puranas, or sacred historical books, next in repute to the Vedas: I acknowledged I had not read them, not having had opportunity, but had no objection to do so. The man who had acted as interpreter offered his assistance to me in reading them, which I accepted, and invited him to our house.

Next day he came, and agreed to attend me for a monthly sum of fourteen rupees, (£1. 8*s*. sterling,) but objected to commencing any thing of importance on Friday, it being an unlucky day. I allowed him to take his own way, and, when he was ready, began to read with him the Sree Maha Bhāgavatham, a Vaishnava Purána of great note, containing an extraordinary medley of mythological fables, morals, and metaphysics, and a particular history of the god Krishna, from his birth to his death. Govinda Moodely, my new friend, plainly "showed the work of the law written on his heart," while reading with me this heathen scripture: he pointed out the beauties of the composition; he boasted of the excellent morals here and there inculcated; but was often ashamed of the follies, absurdities, and wickedness attributed to those who are considered objects of worship. We were often quite opposed to each other in sentiment, and entered into arguments which gave me an opportunity of stating my views, and the authority on which they were founded. On these occasions he exhibited much keenness and temper, and was frequently so intent on his argument, that though engaged to attend me only two or three hours in a morning, he would wait while I dined, to continue the dispute, and not leave me till sunset.

As one proof of the truth of the Hindoo system, he adduced, and professed to believe, a vague story common among the natives, that there are *yogis*, or "monks," in the caves of the mountains, who have been living there without food, in a state of abstraction from the world, for several hundred years; and would not admit its fallacy, till I offered to travel any distance, and to pay all expenses, if he would conduct me to the abodes of any of them.

He endeavoured to account for the unmingled excellency of the Holy Scriptures, without allowing any especial or superior inspiration of the writers, by attributing their purity, consistency, and truth, to the judicious revision of Europeans, who, he professed to think, had taken pains to purge out every thing contradictory or absurd; and knew not how to escape the argument, that they were for the most part written whilst Europe was in a state of barbarism, and that they had not since undergone any alteration.

I read with him the whole of the Bhāgavatham, and several other native compositions in verse and prose; and as he was a studious and well-read man, I could not have had better assistance; his entire ignorance of

English made it necessary to carry on all our conversations in Tamul, which thus became valuable exercises as to a ready apprehension and utterance of the language, and gave me a fair opportunity of observing the native method of argumentation.

This person attended me four or five months as Tamul teacher, in the course of which he appeared quite as desirous to know the national customs and peculiarities of the British, as I was to learn those of the Hindoos: he was particularly interested by our systems of astronomy and geography, and seemed convinced of their truth, chiefly from the practical uses to which they were evidently applicable. I gratified him by an account of my own family; in his questions on this subject it was evident he wished to ascertain whether the office of Minister was hereditary amongst us, as amongst the Brahmans, or if we had any distinctions analogous to those of caste. He inquired into my education, and listened with extraordinary interest to an account of my voyage to India, and my subsequent movements and pursuits. As a man of learning, he was, of course, a poet; for all esteemed Tamul compositions, of science as well as of fiction, are in a poetic form; and even at the present day, a Tamulian can lay no claim to literary taste or eminence, if he does not possess poetic talent. My friend did not rank himself in the lowest class of poets; and often treated me with specimens of his composition, pronounced in the sort of chant with which the natives always recite their poetry. As a proof of his abilities, he threw the main circumstances of my story, within two or three days after he had heard it, into a poetic form, and recited and presented the verses to me with a countenance indicative of the pleasure he felt in his performance: a copy of the first stanza is given in English characters in the note. The reader may observe, that a stanza consists of four lines or verses, of six feet to each verse, and that (extraordinary as it may appear) the rhyme, as in all Tamul poetry, lies in the commencement, and not in the ending, of the line; the similarity of the endings of some of the lines is accidental, and not necessary to the poetry: it is impossible, by writing, to convey an idea of the cadence with which it is pronounced.*

Govinda paid a visit to Madras a short time before I left in 1828, when I reminded him of our former conversations; and regretting that he still wore the mark of Heathenism and idolatry on his forehead, pressed him to yield to his convictions of the truth. He said he still kept the Bible in his house, and sometimes read it; he acknowledged himself much indebted to me for his acquaintance with many things, and for a great improvement in his circumstances, but intimated he would never become a Christian, unless made so by the irresistible power of God!

Bangalore, though not possessed of any splendid establishment of temples and Brahmans, contains sufficient of both to interest and affect the curious and Christian observer. The largest temple is in Alsoor, the village already mentioned. Govinda Moodely procured my

* "Ilajavûl pâdhiriâr pêril
Asiria viruttam.

"Ta*ng*adaningileesu—latineeburugreeku—tagamei peravê unarndu
sabeiinil aneyvarum—manamagizhavê pira—sangamathuvê purindu
Va*ng*amathilêriyat—tireienakadalinil—varumalavil teevarindu
vandidumalavinil—idiathu vizhundusilar—mâlavê kappal vendu
Si*ng*alattêyamathil—sagariôdaruvipai—tiringumalei tannil vandu
sezhikindra pêrgoley—kandavamirundu pin—sevvey sêrurey pugandroi
I*ng*ilândenunteevil—lancashirenumpâlil—manchesterenumooril vâzhinia vôlandu vûl—manamagizhavê petta—vilajavûl enum magibanê."

admission into it; but I believe repented of his kindness, when he found what I thought of the abominable figures displayed within its bounds, and the too clear illustrations of the nature of idolatry thus furnished by himself.

The origin and progress of another temple in that neighbourhood, were curious. I had observed a mound, on a small piece of waste ground by the road side, sometimes decorated with flowers, and which I was told was the burial-place of a Heathen man or woman. Within a short time a sort of heading to the grave was built, with a hole for a small lamp, which was sometimes lighted; and flowering shrubs were planted about it. I saw women and carmen, passing with fire-wood, throwing each a small stick, or faggot, as an offering; and was told that loads of bricks and tiles passing that way, generally left a tribute of one brick or tile, the carman not fearing to rob his master for so pious a purpose. Within a few months, by these contributions, a small temple rose, having its idol, its servant, and its worshippers, whose festivals were generally more noisy than any other in the vicinity.

One day, before another small temple, I observed a man performing the ceremony of *shāstāngam*, or prostration of the eight members, repeatedly lying flat on his face on the ground. Several natives also were watching him: presently he appeared convulsed, and, as though possessed by the old serpent, writhed over the ground in an extraordinary manner, heedless of his turban, which loosened its folds and fell into the dust, and of the stones and prickly shrubs encountered by his partially naked body. He had not the appearance of drunkenness, but was strongly agitated; and, if under no uncommon influence, was a most clever hypocrite, powerfully reminding me of the pretended inspirations described by the Greek and Latin poets.

Occasionally I saw religious mendicants: some with their cheeks and tongues bored, iron or wooden spikes passing through them; some with lighted fires on their heads, so hot as to make it surprising how they endured them; and others with iron frames, a foot, or a foot and a half square, rivetted about their necks, rendering it impossible to rest the head in lying down. I saw one man with spikes thickly set in the soles of his sandals, his foot resting on their points, (which, however blunt, must have occasioned considerable pain,) walking apparently on a pilgrimage; and many others of both sexes and of all ages, who seemed to have abandoned every idea of home and comfort, to secure the fancied advantages and merits of this mode of abstraction from the world. All I witnessed impressed me with a deeper horror of that system, professedly religious, which not only allows, but sanctions and extols, such gross departures from every thing that is reasonable and worthy of man, and so dishonourable to the gracious purposes and mercy of God as revealed to man under every dispensation; but especially as manifested in the atonement and mediation of Christ for our redemption and salvation.

The burning of a widow alive, on the funeral pile of her husband, occurred in the neighbourhood, whilst I was in Bangalore; but I was not informed of the circumstance until it had taken place. A horrible instance of this practice was witnessed there, on the 9th of June, 1826, by Mr. England, our Missionary then on that Station. This is, however, a rare occurrence in this part of India, even under a native Government; and it is, I believe, quite unheard of within the Government of Madras; the custom having fallen into disuse, from the strong disapprobation expressed against it by the British authorities during the government of the Earl of Mornington.

In November, 1821, we applied to the proper quarter for the grant of a small piece of ground, in that part of Bangalore occupied by the followers of the army, for the purpose of a school, and place for preaching to the natives. The spot we selected had been formerly appropriated to the same object by a member of our society, temporarily residing in Bangalore, who had erected a building of mud walls and thatch, of which there were still some ruinous remains. Our application was successful; and a small building, little more than thirty feet in length, and thirteen feet in breadth, suitable to the purpose, was commenced and completed under the direction of Mr. Mowat.

In January, 1822, I again visited Seringapatam, and remained three weeks, occupying myself as on my former visit, and dividing my attentions between that place and Mysore. From both English and native congregations, I received every demonstration of affection and respect: rooms were prepared for my reception; and on the days I was not engaged to dine with the officers of the garrison, or other English residents, the poor people vied with each other in preparing for me a comfortable meal in my own apartments, by a plan they had laid down amongst themselves.

Some Romanists publicly avowed their renunciation of Popery, and were received into the Protestant Church; several adult natives also professed Christianity, and were baptized by me.

The person I had appointed at my former visit to lead the class having died, its meetings had been discontinued; and I found, what I have since observed to be the case in many other places, that, however useful and acceptable to the people my occasional visits might be, there was little hope of maintaining the regular discipline of a Christian society, without the residence and immediate superintendence of a Missionary. I gave them the best advice and directions I could, and promised to use my influence with my brethren in India, and with the Committee at home, to obtain for them a resident Missionary, or to allow me to come and remain among them myself.

On the 9th of February, I received a polite invitation from the Honourable the Resident at the Court of Mysore, to come over that evening to be present at a *durbar*.

A *durbar* is a levee or court held by the native Princes on especial occasions, when a display is made of their splendour and magnificence.

I hastened to the Residency at Mysore, and joined the party of ladies and gentlemen already assembled there. The uncle of the Rajah paid a complimentary visit to the Residency; and shortly afterwards His Highness the Rajah's carriages, accompanied by elephants, carrying immense tomtoms, or drums, and by numberless torch-bearers, were in readiness at the door to convey us to the palace.

The darkness of the night, relieved by the light of the flambeaux, the sounding of the music and tomtoms, and the firing of guns, increased the imposing effect of the procession. We found the native military drawn up in front of the palace; a great number of elephants were in attendance, and hosts of dancing-women, and of officers peculiar to Hindoo Courts.

We were conducted up a staircase to the gallery of a large apartment, opening with its full width to the area in front, and crowded with native attendants and visitors. In the centre of the gallery we found His Highness, Kistnah Rajah Oodiaver, seated on his *musnud*, or throne, a square couch of about two feet in height: he was a good-looking man of dark colour and complexion, and appeared to be about thirty years of age.

The British visitors, both ladies and gentlemen, were successively presented by the Resident, Mr. Cole, to His Highness, and shook hands with him, a ceremony which he performed in a hearty, good-humoured manner; and then, taking seats on chairs placed near the *musnud*, we gazed on the splendour around us and in the court below, while Mr. Cole and the Rajah conversed in a language I did not understand.

The Resident then proceeded to adorn the person of the Rajah with rich presents from the Honourable Company, of cloths, shawls, and jewellery; which were successively taken off, and carefully preserved by the attendants who stood behind the Rajah.

His Highness then directed his British visitors to be adorned with garlands of sweet-scented flowers, which was accordingly done to each of us by his servants.

At intervals a powerful voice was heard beneath the gallery, which I supposed to be that of a herald proclaiming the royal descent, and the titles and dignity, of his sovereign.

An infant child of the Rajah, covered with jewels of immense value, was presented to us.

At length we took leave of His Highness, again shaking him by the hand, and retired to an apartment of the palace, where a splendid table was set for us. At the dessert after dinner, there was a profusion of ices, and of English preserves and jellies.

During the whole of our repast, a female dancer, of superior elegance and grace, attired in the usual costume, but with the addition of a girdle about her waist, broad as a ribbon, and apparently of solid gold, performed the native dances.

After rising from table, we were taken through the palace: the more costly of its furniture and ornaments are of English manufacture.

In the most splendid apartment, we found seated a holy Hindoo *San-yasi*, or Monk, so nearly naked, that one of the gentlemen threw a handkerchief over his lap while the ladies passed him: from this apartment a door was opened to another, to give us a sight of the sacred cattle, bulls or cows, kept by the Rajah. They were large, white animals, and appeared in very good condition. The whole establishment presented an odd mixture of Hindoo peculiarities and European improvements.

I slept that night at the Residency, and the following day returned early to my work in Seringapatam.

CHAPTER XIV.

FEBRUARY AND MARCH, 1822.

JOURNEY FROM SERINGAPATAM TO MADRAS.

WHILST on my late visit to Seringapatam and Mysore, I had received a letter from Mr. Lynch, the Chairman of our District-Meeting then assembled in Jaffna, communicating the decision of the Meeting, that Mr. Squance should return to England, in consequence of the entire failure of his health; that Mr. Close, whose health had also suffered considerably, should proceed from Madras to occupy Negapatam, in the hope that change of place, and some degree of relaxation from labour, might prove beneficial to him; and that I was appointed to Madras, to labour in the Mission there.

I did not receive this intelligence without considerable regret. I had been assisting to lay a foundation for Missionary labours in the neighbourhood of Bangalore, and was desirous of witnessing the results; and was also exceedingly unwilling to be again separated from my excellent colleague, Mr. Mowat.

There was, however, no alternative. On the 22d of February, 1822, I left Seringapatam, and returned to Bangalore, having been favoured, by the kindness of Mr. Cole, with the Rajah's bearers both in going and returning. I then prepared for a further journey to Madras; and, taking an affectionate leave of my friends, set out on the 4th of March.

For four days I travelled through a country inhabited by persons using the Cannada or other languages with which I was not familiar; and, meeting with very few who spoke Tamul, had no intercourse with the people worthy of being recorded.

On the 9th of March, I arrived at Chittoor, a considerable native town, and the residence of several English families, connected with the Provincial and Zillah Courts established there, and other departments of the Honourable Company's service. It is situated in a fertile valley at the foot of the Ghauts, hemmed in on every side by bare rocky hills of a very bold character, rendering more remarkable the beautiful green of the fields and gardens. Mangoes, strawberries, and other fine fruits, are produced in great abundance at Chittoor, and the land appears capable of any production suitable to the climate. It was then esteemed healthy; though the heat is great, and I could fancy an insufficiency in the air, occasioned by its rarefaction. But it was, perhaps, more from the delightful retirement enjoyed by the English residents here, than from other circumstances, that it had been denominated, The Happy Valley.

I was welcomed with kind hospitality by Joseph D'Acre, Esq., a gentleman high in the service of Government, and much esteemed in the church of Christ. From his peculiar engagements, and his long residence in the country, he spoke Tamul with the ease of a native, with greater fluency even than he spoke English. Being himself a devout man, and possessing a zealous Missionary spirit, the faithful discharge of his arduous official duties as Judge did not prevent him from devoting such a portion of his time and talents to the promotion of Christianity among the natives, as, by the blessing of God, to make him instrumental in converting some hundreds of Heathens and Mahommedans to the faith of Christ.

Mr. D'Acre had been resident in Chittoor many years. When he first came, there was perhaps not one native

Christian in the place: he read the Scriptures, and conversed with his native servants on the subject of religion; he established schools in his garden, and employed Masters and Catechists; but was not satisfied concerning the propriety of addressing the natives publicly, until after some conversation with Mr. Lynch on the subject of lay-preaching, which encouraged him to adopt this method also, in which he proved very successful.

He was surrounded by the objects of his bounty: one was a Brahman widow, who had been saved from the funeral pile of her husband; another, a fine boy, whose mother, an entire stranger in Chittoor, had died on her arrival there, leaving him destitute. Many were his converts, or their children, whom he assisted in various ways to procure a livelihood.

He pressed me to stay; and I remained with him eight days, much delighted with what I witnessed. Every morning and evening about one hundred natives, including the children of the school, assembled to family prayer. On each of the two Sundays, I read prayers and preached in the Court-House to the English residents, and held divine service with the natives in a wing of Mr. D'Acre's house, devoted to that purpose. I administered the Lord's supper to about sixty native communicants; I baptized, during my stay, more than thirty persons, chiefly adults, and married eight couples. Such successful endeavours to introduce Christianity among the natives I had not hitherto seen in actual operation. No doubt Mr. D'Acre's wealth and rank had great influence among the people, as well as the truths he delivered; but it may justly be inquired whether the influence of wealth and rank can serve a more important purpose, than the deliverance of men from the yoke of Heathenism and falsehood, and their introduction to the enjoyment even of the outward privileges and blessings of Christianity; and whether it ought not, in a country like India, to be more frequently thus employed than it is.

It was with difficulty I could prevail on my kind host to allow me to proceed on my journey. I left Chittoor on the night of Monday, March 18th, and the following morning reached Arcot, where I was most kindly entertained during the day by the Rev. R. Smith, M.A., Chaplain of the Station. In the evening I again hastened on my journey, passed the following day in a very hot, uncomfortable choultry, and two days after, on the morning of the 22d, arrived in Madras.

At the Mission-house in Royapettah, I was affectionately received by Mr. Squance and family, who had already arrived to take their passage to England; and by Mr. Erskine, another of our Missionaries, who was here on his way from Ceylon (where he had been labouring from the first establishment of the Mission) to New South Wales, to engage in our Mission there. Mr. Lynch had not yet arrived from the District-Meeting in Jaffna.

I commenced my labours on my new Station the day of my arrival, by going to Black-Town, four miles distant, and delivering a Tamul sermon in the evening to the native congregation; thus entering on that department of the work most pleasing to me, and in which I felt it my duty to be chiefly engaged.

A detail of our labours for a few days will serve to give some idea of the extent of our exertions in Madras at that time.

Sunday, March 24th, at seven o'clock in the morning, I heard Mr. Squance read prayers and preach in English to a small congregation in the Royapettah chapel; at ten in the forenoon I preached to the natives in Tamul, and met the native class; and at seven in the evening preached in the same chapel to a small English congregation. On the same day there were also two English services in our chapel in Black-Town.

Tuesday, 26th, I went to St. Thomas's Mount, six miles distant, and took with me a Tamul sermon, expecting to find a congregation of natives; but found, in our small school-room there, an assembly of soldiers and others, to whom I preached in English, and afterwards addressed the Master and boys of the native school, in the Tamul language.

On Thursday evening, 28th, there was English preaching, and meeting of class in Black-Town.

Friday, 29th, I read a sermon in Tamul to our native congregation in Black-Town, whose appearance made me long for greater fluency in their language, and for divine assistance in my labours.

On Saturday evening an English class met at the Mission-house, Royapettah.

Sunday, 31st, I drove to Black-Town, and at seven o'clock in the morning read prayers, and preached in English: one reason for holding services so early in the morning is, that the great heat of the mid-day sun would render it uncomfortable for our English congregation to assemble later; and another, because we find it more convenient to our native congregations to come together in the heat of the day, and therefore reserve that time for their public worship. In the forenoon I met the native class in Royapettah; and in the evening again preached in English in the same chapel.

This day I received a kind letter from Joseph D'Acre, Esq., enclosing one hundred and fifty rupees, to be laid out in the way I might think best calculated to promote the great object he had at heart,—the conversion of the natives.

Monday, April 1st, I attended the monthly Missionary prayer-meeting, held by the Missionaries of the London

Society, and of our own, at their chapel and at ours, alternately. This evening it was held in Pursewaukum chapel, where I had the pleasure to hear the Rev. E. Crisp, of the London Society, then just arrived from England, deliver an address appropriate to the occasion.

In general, my engagements in Madras required me to deliver four or five, and sometimes seven, sermons each week, in English and Tamul, and to attend to many other meetings, public or private, of a religious character, besides the superintendence of schools. My labour was considerably augmented by the necessity of paying unceasing attention to reading and composition in Tamul, with a view to the attainment of such a proficiency as should enable me to converse in it with ease, and to preach without the use of written sermons, that I might thus be better fitted for more extensive exertions among the vast heathen population of Madras, and the surrounding country, which lay open to us as a field of labour, but into which the number of efficient Missionaries who had entered was very small.

Before I had been many days in Madras, I was invited to attend a meeting of the Sub-Committee of Translations of the Bible Society, for the revision of the Tamul version of the Holy Scriptures, and was elected a member of the Committee. The venerable Dr. Rottler presided; and at his house the meeting was held, consisting of Missionaries of all Societies, who understood the language, and of such lay gentlemen of the Committee of the Bible Society, whose leisure, and knowledge of Tamul, enabled them to give their services: we were assisted also by the cleverest Moonshees and Pundits of the College of Fort St. George, and by valuable correspondents in different parts of the country.

The Rev. T. Nicholson, of the London Missionary Society, was at that time Secretary to the Committee.

His health was delicate, and he died in the course of a few months, greatly lamented. I was then desired to take the office of Secretary; and, although a great additional responsibility, I thought it of too much importance to be refused or neglected, and, accepting the office, continued to act in it until I left Madras, in 1828.

Before the end of March, 1822, Mr. Squance and his family embarked for England in the ship "Barossa," followed by the prayers of his brethren, and of the people to whom he had ministered. A few days after his departure, Mr. Lynch arrived at Madras, having been so remarkably detained, both by sea and land, on his journey to and from the District-Meeting,—which in this year also (1822) had been held in the island of Ceylon,—that he had been three months absent from the Station.

CHAPTER XV.

APRIL—DECEMBER, 1822.

MISSION IN MADRAS.

FROM the first establishment of the Wesleyan Mission in Madras, in 1817, the Rev. James Lynch had laboured there with much acceptance and usefulness, among people of all classes. He had built by subscription the chapel already mentioned, in the Mission premises at Royapettah; but in Black-Town, the most populous part of Madras, and where the largest congregations assembled, the services had been held in various incommodious and unsuitable places; one of these, where Methodist meetings were first held in Madras, was a stable altered for the purpose.

A plot of ground, with some old buildings upon it, situated in Popham's-Street, or, as it is usually called, Popham's Broadway, being one of the widest and best streets in Black-Town, was at length purchased; and the principal building, a low room about sixty feet in length and ten feet in breadth, was appropriated to the purpose of public worship: many are the pleasing feelings which will ever be associated, by both Ministers and people, with the recollections of their assembling in that place.

It was, however, too low and confined to be comfortable to the congregation; and the Minister was usually drenched in perspiration almost as soon as he commenced his work; and the service was much disturbed by passengers and carts passing close by the doors and windows, open the whole length of the building; while both Minister and congregation were grievously annoyed by the thousands of musquitoes and other insects, that found this a suitable habitation, or were attracted by the lights used at evening service.

The society and congregation agreed with the Missionaries that a chapel was necessary, and engaged to subscribe towards its erection. A more appropriate plot of ground than that already occupied, could not be procured; and it was sufficiently large to allow of a new chapel being built, without interfering with the building then used as such, the only one in which the congregation could assemble.

It was resolved that the chapel about to be erected should be raised one story from the ground floor, to secure a free circulation of air, and to avoid the annoyance from insects, and from the noises of the crowded streets.

The character and object of our Mission were so well known, that Mr. Lynch found no difficulty in obtaining encouragement and liberal subscriptions from many of the servants of Government, and other highly respectable residents in Madras, as well as from those who had profited by the ministry of himself and colleagues. Contributions were ultimately raised to the amount of about seven thousand Madras rupees, or £700 sterling. The cost of the erection, and fitting up of the chapel, was more than ten thousand rupees; the original purchase of the land and premises had been upwards of three thousand five hundred rupees.

In digging for the foundation, it was found that the nature of the ground was such as not to permit the safe erection of such a building as that now contemplated, without more than common precaution. Wells were therefore sunk to the depth of about twelve feet, and partly filled with sand; from this artificial ground arches were turned, and on the arches the building was erected: the expense was considerably increased by the necessity of such a foundation.

The whole was substantially constructed of bricks and chunam, and entirely plastered with chunam within and without. The accompanying elevation gives a correct idea of the chapel and premises.

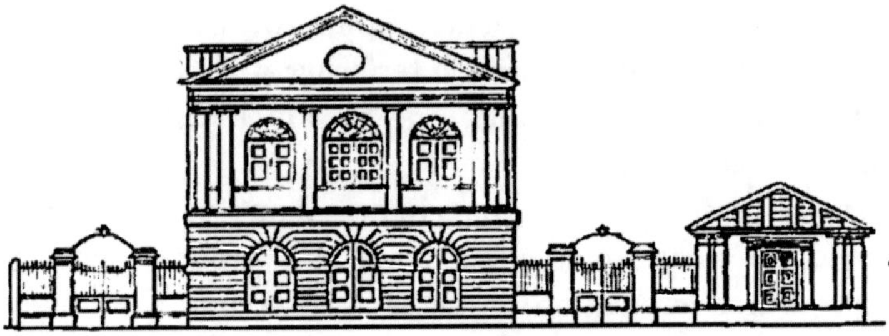

THE CHAPEL AT MADRAS, ERECTED 1822.

The upper story, which is the chapel, is fifty-seven feet long, independent of the covered verandah or porch in front, about seven feet, and thirty feet in breadth; and is capable of accommodating a congregation of three hundred persons: more than that number have assembled in it on especial occasions. The roof is of teak-wood, and covered with tiles; but within, has an arched ceiling of boards, the centre of which is nearly nineteen feet from the floor, which is also of teak-wood.

The lower apartments are dry and commodious: the front one is used as a vestry; that to the left is occupied as the Depository of the Madras Religious Tract Society; that on the right is used for Committees and class-meetings.

The small building to the right of the chapel is the place formerly used by the English congregation as a place of worship, and which has since undergone some improvements and alterations, and continues to be valuable for Portuguese and Tamul preaching, and for day and Sunday schools, both English and native.

The chapel was opened on the 25th of April, 1822. On this occasion a lively and extensive interest was excited among our friends. Before the hour appointed, the chapel was quite filled; and in the congregation we had the pleasure to recognise many Missionaries of other Societies, either resident in Madras or occasionally visiting it: about four hundred persons found room; but a great number had to return from the door without gaining admittance.

The service was commenced by the hymn beginning with, "Jesu, we look to thee," &c. The Rev. C. Loveless, of the London Society, then read the Liturgy and appropriate lessons; the Rev. C. Traveller, of the same Society, next offered up an extemporary prayer; and Mr. Lynch preached an appropriate and impressive sermon on Matt. xviii. 20: "Where two or three are gathered together in my name, there am I in the midst of them." After sermon the Rev. T. Nicholson prayed, and gave an address, stating the expense of the building, and the amount of contributions already made, and urging the necessity of further exertions: while he spoke we made the collection, which amounted to about £40 sterling. Mr. Erskine then offered up a prayer, and concluded the service.

Thus was another house dedicated to the service of the living God, in the midst of a heathen and idolatrous population: it is the largest Wesleyan chapel yet erected in Continental India. It was an interesting occasion to ourselves and our society, and was the means of increasing the favourable opinion already existing in Madras with regard to our Mission.

In a short time afterwards, we were invited to erect a chapel in another quarter of Madras, by two gentlemen who would have subscribed liberally; but our hands were already full; we had occupied more ground than we had strength to cultivate to our own satisfaction; and, however desirous of enlarging our sphere of labour, we were under the necessity of giving a refusal.

In the beginning of May, Mr. Erskine left us to proceed to Calcutta, from whence he embarked for New South Wales; having waited in vain at Madras for several months for a vessel direct to that part of the world. His labours had been very acceptable to our congregations, and were a great assistance to us: by his departure, the full work of the Station devolved upon Mr. Lynch and myself.

The Assistant Missionary, who had formerly been very serviceable in Madras, as interpreter and superintendent of schools, having returned to Ceylon, his native place, it rested with me to conduct the Tamul services entirely, and fill up all our engagements among the natives.

I was still under the necessity of writing my Tamul sermons: my plan was to compose four or six pages daily. A learned Brahman attended me early in the morning, and corrected what I had written; of which I had then to make a fair copy, and to prepare another portion for correction on the following morning. I thus found the composition and transcribing of one sermon, in Tamul, each week, as much as I could accomplish, in addition to my other numerous engagements.

But unequal as we had felt our numbers and strength to the work before us, they were now to suffer a diminution. The hopes which had been indulged of the recovery of Mr. Close, by his removal to Negapatam, were severely disappointed; he never regained the vigour he had lost by his zealous labours in the sultry climate of Madras. His favourite son died in Negapatam, soon after their arrival there; Mrs. Close sustained considerable injury by being thrown out of a gig; and, notwithstanding the advantages of relaxation, and the society and affectionate attentions of our excellent friends in Negapatam, Mr. Close's health continued to decline, till it was declared necessary for him to leave the country. He accordingly came up, with his family, to Madras, in July, to embark either for the Cape of Good Hope, or England. Here their afflictions were increased by the sickness and death of their only surviving child. Of their Madras friends who visited them during their stay with us at the Mission-house, none, I believe, departed without shedding tears of Christian sympathy over the afflictions and altered appearance of Mr. and Mrs. Close.

The comparative claims of Negapatam and Bangalore now became matter of serious deliberation; for we were reduced to the painful necessity of giving up one of those Stations, at least for a time. The society already formed in Negapatam, and the prospect of immediate and extensive usefulness, especially among the Dutch and Portuguese population, gave that Station a character of considerable importance. It had also been occupied by us previously to Bangalore, and was not the residence of Missionaries of any other religious body. By the influence of our excellent friend, J. Cotton, Esq., an allowance had been obtained from Government of about £100. per annum, for the performance of Chaplain's duty, by our Missionaries, in Negapatam, which, being a considerable contribution to our general fund, we thought ought not to be forfeited without due consideration.

It was with great reluctance that I gave my consent to the temporary abandonment of our Mission in Bangalore; but there appeared no alternative. Soon after the embarkation of Mr. and Mrs. Close for England, in the commencement of August, Mr. and Mrs. Mowat came down from Bangalore, and proceeded to Negapatam.

Meantime we had pleasing indications of success, and of the divine blessing on our labours, in various quarters of the extensive Circuit of Madras.

A favourable opening presented itself in St. Thomè, a large and populous neighbourhood on the sea side, about one mile south of the Mission-house. This place has a large heathen temple, whose annual feast is attended by many thousands of strangers, as well as by its own native inhabitants, who are very numerous, and have among them a considerable appearance of wealth and respectability. The descendants of the Portuguese, who, more than two hundred years ago, occupied St. Thomè as their chief Station in this part of India, are numerous also: many Indo-Britains reside there, sufficient to form a good English congregation; of these some had occasionally attended our English services in Royapettah; and, in the hot season, a great number of invalid or convalescent European visitors resort to St. Thomè to enjoy the advantages of its pleasant situation, and salubrious air.

The remains of the old Portuguese Fort are still to be seen on the beach; and, hard by, is the Romish cathedral, a building of considerable magnitude, with extensive premises adjoining connected with the establishment, consisting of the palace, or residence of the Portuguese Bishop, who receives his appointment from Goa, and accommodations for the Priests and students.

Adjoining the east end of the cathedral is a small chapel, similar in outward appearance to a heathen temple. The tradition concerning it is, that it was formerly a heathen temple, but was granted by the native Prince of Mielapoor (the Tamul name of St. Thomè) to St. Thomas the Apostle, who is said to have preached the Gospel in India, to have suffered martyrdom in this neighbourhood, and to have been interred in this chapel. When I entered the chapel on one occasion, the reputed grave of the Apostle was shown to me, being a deep and wide excavation, having its entrance within the chapel: the excavation has been occasioned by the holy earth having been from time immemorial taken away in small quantities to preserve voyagers from storm and shipwreck, and to answer other purposes of superstition.

A poor fisherman of St. Thomè, who, though the son of an Englishman, lived among the natives, and had a native wife, constantly brought his family to our Tamul services in Royapettah, and was a member of our native class. His wife was now a member also, but had formerly been a Romanist. A circumstance which occurred before she became a Protestant will serve to mark the character of her husband, and the view he took of Popery. She was desirous of attending the annual Romish festival in Pulicat, twenty-five miles north of Madras; her husband acceded, and resolved to accompany her. When they set out on their journey, which, as they were foot-travellers, would occupy them two days in going, and two in returning, he persisted in leaving his hat behind him, and walked bareheaded. When questioned as to his reasons, he said he knew well, that when they entered the church at the end of their journey, he should be required to take off his hat; and rather than uncover his head on entering a place of idolatrous worship, he preferred making the whole journey bareheaded.

This person, though not able to read himself, sent his children to our schools, and invited a few of his neighbours to hear the reading of the Scriptures and prayer at his own house: the number of this evening assembly increased, and he erected a *pandal* for their accommodation.

About the same time he pressed a respectable inhabitant of St. Thomè to attend our English preaching. This gentleman, though born in India, had enjoyed many advantages, having received a classical education at Harrow school. He began to attend our preaching early in April, and became for some time an altered character. He occasionally attended the English class, and expressed his surprise, that religious instruction should have enabled persons who had received so little education to speak on divine subjects with an ease and propriety to which he found himself inadequate.

He invited us to make use of one of his houses in St. Thomè as a chapel. We gladly embraced the offer, and commenced our regular services there, on the evening of Wednesday, August 28th, 1822.

At a few hours' notice an assembly of more than two hundred persons of various descriptions, but chiefly natives, was collected. Mr. Lynch commenced with prayer and a short address in English. I then preached to the native part of the congregation in Tamul, and concluded by prayer in the same language. We regularly continued a stated service of the same kind for several weeks, and saw some fruit of our labours in the increase of our Royapettah congregation, and in the number of Heathens, and others equally ignorant, who were brought under the sound of the word of God.

At length it was found advisable to have the English and native services separate from each other. It was proposed to us to purchase the premises we had occupied, which, though the situation was rather obscure, were the best we could expect till our means should be enlarged. The indigent, but zealous, man, before mentioned, solicited and obtained subscriptions from the poor as well as from the rich: the house was purchased, and altered for the purposes of public worship. Regular English service has been ever since held in it twice or thrice each week; and Tamul and Portuguese sermons have been occasionally preached in it to attentive congregations. Two schools, one English and the other Tamul, were established, and an English society was formed. The house, thus converted to a chapel, has been found incommodious for the English congregation; and from the increasing interest lately exhibited by our friends in that neighbourhood, I have no doubt that if they had a little encouragement from England, they would exert themselves to raise a building more suitable to the sacred purpose, and better adapted to the character of the place.

One evening about this time, passing along the road near our house, my notice was attracted by an immense assemblage of people, and preparations for the feast at which certain devotees swing on hooks thrust into the muscles of the back. On this occasion none came forward to swing, but a poor sheep was made to act as substitute. This absurd and painful ceremony is chiefly observed by the lower classes; and is generally practised in consequence of vows made in time of danger, or for the obtaining of some desired object.

In the month of September, Mr. Stead, from Jaffna, paid us a visit in Madras; and, by his seasonable assistance, in some measure lessened our toil, and enabled us to extend our sphere of exertion. My increased familiarity with Tamul now enabled me to begin delivering sermons without the aid of written notes. I commenced out-door preaching in the villages and roads, and distributed many tracts among the natives. The cholera morbus, which raged dreadfully at this time, seemed to have the effect of awakening the attention of the people to those subjects which relate to God and to eternity. But in the mass of human beings around us, our utmost endeavours seemed to be as insufficient to produce a general influence, as a pebble dropped into the ocean would be to produce an agitation of the whole. An oppressive conviction to this effect is, I believe, felt by every Missionary scattered throughout the vast population of India. But their faith regards the promises and the prophetic declarations of God; and their hope is turned to the land of their nativity for a supply of more labourers to enter into the harvest.

About the end of the year, at the request of the Madras Religious Tract Society, I engaged in re-translating into Tamul a considerable part of a large tract by the late Mr. Nicholson, "On the Truth of Christianity proved by the Resurrection of Christ:" the larger portion of the fair copy he had prepared for the press having been unfortunately lost. I made also a translation of the Rules of our Society; and of the Account of Mr. Wesley and the Rise of Methodism, contained in the tract of the Rev. V. Ward, entitled, "Facts," &c.; to which I added, the View of the Doctrines of Methodism contained in the same book, making those omissions and alterations required by the different circumstances of our people in Madras, for whose use and information the translation was designed.

In December, Mr. Lynch paid a visit to Chittoor, leaving Mr. Stead with me in Madras. We laboured with much comfort and harmony in our studies, as well as in our public engagements; and had reason to believe that the divine blessing accompanied our exertions. Mr. Stead found in Madras books, and various assistances for advancement in the knowledge of the language, which he had not been able to obtain in Ceylon; and showed how he regarded them, by the industrious application with which he improved the opportunities afforded to him.

On the last day of the month, Mr. Lynch returned from Chittoor. We closed the year 1822, and commenced the new year, in our chapel in Black-Town; where a large congregation assembled to be present at the interesting services connected with what is called a watch-night; a service peculiar to the Wesleyan Methodists, but exceedingly suitable to the occasion, and to the feelings of the sincere Christian at a season so favourable to solemn and devotional thought.

CHAPTER XVI.

1822 AND 1823.

TAMUL LITERATURE.

The Brahman I had employed as Tamul teacher, being a Moonshee of the College, was soon promoted to a higher class; and, receiving engagements which removed him from the neighbourhood, was prevented from any further attendance on me except as an occasional visitor. I subsequently engaged three or four other Moonshees, of whom some notice may be introduced in the proper place. During the whole of my residence in Madras, I always considered it necessary to have a learned native assistant, on whom, though not wholly employed by me, I could rely for help in any difficulties which might occur in Tamul reading or composition.

A friendly intercourse with some of the chief Moonshees of the College was highly valued by me. Among other advantages accruing from it, was the obtaining copies of rare and valuable books, which probably I should not otherwise have met with.

One of the first books in my course of Tamul reading in Madras, was part of the *Rāmāyanam,* one of the eighteen *Purānas,* or "Sacred Histories of the Hindoos." Its chief subjects are the exploits of *Rāma,* whose worship and festival I before mentioned, and whose history is adorned with fables too extravagant, I should have thought, even for an eastern imagination, and with mysticisms sufficiently abstruse to exercise and satisfy the acutest metaphysician, ancient or modern.

I fell in also with some of the works of Robertus de

Nobili, of whom some account has been already given, in the Seventh Chapter, under the head of "The Jesuit Mission in Madura." From the number of Sanscrit terms occurring in his writings, it would appear that he was well acquainted with that tongue, as well as with the Tamul language. He translated the Romish Liturgy as it is still used in the native churches, and entitled *Mantramālei,* or "Garland of Prayers." A work called *Atma Nirnyam,* or "The Determination of the Soul," by the same author, is a valuable book: I had a copy of it neatly transcribed, which formed a small quarto of nearly a thousand pages. In this work, which is almost free from the peculiarities of Popery, the author shows himself an acute disputant and metaphysician. In treating on the origin and nature of the soul of man, he successfully and ingeniously exposes the fallacy of the various opinions held by the different sects of Hindoos with regard to the soul; such as,—that the soul is God, that it is from eternity, that it is matter, that it dies with the body, that it transmigrates from one body to another, that there is no difference between the human soul and the souls of beasts, &c. On the last two points his arguments are particularly ingenious, and well calculated to strike and convince the mind of a Hindoo. The statement of Hindoo doctrines and authorities thus elicited, and the refutation of them advanced and enforced in the peculiar style of Hindoo argumentation, make the book valuable, and worthy of being possessed and perused by every Tamul Missionary.

But his most famous work is entitled *Nyāna ubadhēsam;* and consists of a course of lectures on theology, in a style peculiarly his own, and evidently displaying the hand of a master. It was, I believe, from the publication of this work, that Robertus de Nobili was styled by the natives, *Tatwa-bōdhaca-swāmi,* or the "Teacher of the

Divine Attributes." Two extracts from it, with a translation annexed, are given by Mr. Ellis in his translation and commentary on the Kural, pages 26, 28.

Mr. Ellis remarks: "Although the style of this work does not entitle it to rank among compositions in the superior dialect of the Tamul, the following extracts are so immediately connected with the present subject, and afford such lively specimens of the peculiar spirit of this Indo-European writer, and of the felicity and precision with which he has rendered into Tamul the phraseology of the schools, that they cannot fail to be acceptable both to the Tamul and English reader. The first passage forms the concluding paragraph of the third lecture, and contains the exposition of the third attribute, the immateriality of the Deity: the second is an abridgment, preserving the words of the author, of the fourth lecture on the fourth attribute, or the goodness of the Deity."

The extracts are as follows:—

"If we consider the Omnipotent to be self-existent and eternal, we cannot say that he has a body like our bodies; for when a being exists connected with a body composed of limbs finite in their nature, there must exist some one by whom those limbs were formed and united together. Therefore a self-existent being cannot be corporeal; and, consequently, the self-existent Lord of all cannot be admitted to be a corporeal being. Thus it is established that immateriality is the third attribute of the Deity. As this is so, to admit that the Omnipotent has a female on his head, (as Sivá,) or on his breast, (as Vishnú,) that in one place he contracts marriage, and in another he frequents the house of a prostitute, and that he amuses himself with these, and idle vagaries like these, there is no doubt, can arise only from defect of understanding, and must be productive of the greatest turpitude. As the Omnipotent is self-existent, eternal, and immaterial, it will be proper to describe what form he really has; and this I shall explain in the fourth lecture."

"On this subject there is one thing especially necessary to be known, that is, that, as it is said that all virtues are given to the effect by the cause, it must also be said that the cause produces the effect. The virtue afforded by the cause may exist in the effect in two several modes. One mode is, when the whole virtue inherent in the cause exists in the effect; as, for example, fire produces fire; a lion begets a lion; a man, a man. In investigating this species of cause and effect, it appears that the entire virtue inherent in the cause exists equally in the effect, being in degree neither more nor less. This species of cause and effect may be denominated the univocal cause and univocal effect. Besides this species of cause and effect, there is another; this is when the whole nature, and all the virtue pertaining to the nature, of the cause, does not exist in the effect; but, of the several qualities inherent in the cause, some one only is communicated to the effect; thus,—the statuary has made a statue; the potter, an earthen vessel; the sun is the cause of the lustre which exists in precious stones. On investigating this species of cause and effect, the understanding, strength, and the other qualities, mental and corporeal, inherent in the statuary, who is the cause, are not found to exist in the statue, which is the effect; the form only, a quality proceeding from the understanding of the statuary, and none of the other qualities pertaining to him, is communicated to the statue. It is the same, also, in the instances of the potter and the sun. This species of cause and effect may be denominated the equivocal cause, and the equivocal effect. Senseless people, not comprehending the mode of equivocal cause and effect, as thus explained, are accustomed to speak thus relative to the Almighty, and on the subject of creation." "And, in consequence of this notion, they assert that, without Parvati, Lechmy, and other females, no honour, nor glory could accrue either to Sivá or Vishnú, who are worshipped as the Almighty; and that otherwise, neither Sivá nor Vishnú could enjoy happiness. If we admit that the only God is of the male or female sex, because he created male and female, we ought to say that God is also a dog, fox, and the like, because he created dogs, foxes, and the like. To confute this blasphemous notion, it is sufficient to say, that the statuary and potter cannot be the statue or vessel of which they are the equivocal cause, and that the sun cannot be identified with the brightness united with a particle of earth. Thus, also, because the Almighty is the equivocal cause of the distinction of male and female, and of all other things, we ought not to say or think that he is either male or female. Therefore, let us admit that, as that sole goodness, which is the Almighty, contains in itself, in the highest degree, as has been already shown, all the virtue pertaining to the infinite number of existent beings; so, also, that same Almighty Being, who is the manifestation of goodness, is the equivocal cause of all things."

The translator then further proceeds to say:—

"It is worthy of remark that though power, goodness, wisdom, &c., are common to all the preceding series of attributes, justice is found in none. By the Catholic writers, desirous, it is probable, to allure their proselytes by the idea of an all-merciful, rather than to alarm them by the representation of an all-just, God, it is included, with a variety of other qualities, under the general attribute of goodness. On such a subject, omission and defect are not surprising; for in enumerating the attributes of the all-pervading Spirit, both European and Indian writers can select only what may appear to each the more prominent. His attributes, as various as his energies, are beyond the grasp of the human intellect. As he is by his nature, therefore, incomprehensible, every attempt to investigate his essence, or to determine his qualities, can, at the best, be only an approximation to the truth."

I perused also with much interest the works of a still more celebrated Indo-European author, C. J. Beschi, another Italian Jesuit, who came to India about the commencement of the eighteenth century. His name is familiar to Oriental scholars, from two excellent Grammars of the dialects of the Tamul language, written by him in Latin, and since translated into English; by use of which, the servants of Government, and Missionaries, have found the Tamul language of comparatively easy acquisition. But he is known to the Hindoos by the name of *Veera-mā-muni; Veera* being a translation of his Christian name, Constantine, and *Mā-Muni*, honorary additions, signifying "The great holy person." His chief works in Tamul are the *Saduragrādhi*, or, "A Dictionary of the Tamul Language, in four Parts;" *Tonnool Vilaccam*, a "Grammar of high Tamul;" *Védhiar Ozhuccam*, "Rule for Catechists, or Instructions for Teachers of Religion; *Védha Vilaccam*, "Illustration of Religion," being a clever attempt at an exposure and refutation of Protestantism, then spreading by the labours of the Missionaries of Tranquebar; and *Tēmbāvani*, "The Unfading Garland," an immense poem embracing the history of the Old and New Testaments, and innumerable Romish legends.

These works are all admirably performed, and, regarded only as literature, are invaluable; they deserve to be considered as models of composition; and, as such, to be attentively read, and to form part of the library of all who wish to excel in Tamul. I wish I could speak so favourably of the tenets enforced in them, and the effect they have produced, and must continue to produce, on the minds of the people: they are the favourite literature of the native Romanists.

Next to the Grammar and the Dictionary, the most unexceptionable of the writings of Beschi is the *Védhiar Ozhuccam*, or "Rule for Catechists:" it contains clear definitions, offers powerful motives, and presents affecting appeals, with regard to the work of this class of teachers. It is divided into twenty chapters. The first chapter treats of the nature of the office of Catechists; the second, of its importance; the third, of its universal obligation; the fourth, of the preparation to the office; the fifth, of the necessity of self-government in those who would save others; the sixth, of caring for others in order to self-preservation; the seventh chapter shows that the first means for the salvation of others is personal piety; the eighth, the second means is prayer; the ninth, the third means is desire; the tenth chapter presents motives to quicken a desire for the salvation of others; the eleventh treats on self-diffidence, and entire reliance on God in the execution of the office; the twelfth, on regarding the souls and not the outward condition of men; the thirteenth, on showing love to others; the fourteenth, on showing no desire for the wealth of others; the fifteenth, on regarding the proprieties of time and place; the sixteenth, on yielding to others in order to win them; the seventeenth, on not giving way to discouragement from want of success; the eighteenth, on unity among themselves; the nineteenth, on helps to the office of Catechist; the twentieth is an exhortation to attention to these instructions. The whole concludes with questions and assistances for self-examination, with regard to duty towards God, personal piety, family religion, duty towards Ministers, duty towards the church, duty towards the Heathen, duty towards dying persons, duty with regard to hinderances in the performance of the office; and a number of pithy proverbs to be fastened on the memory.*

The *Védha Vilaccam*, or "Illustration of Religion," by the same author, is of a very different character. In attempting to refute Protestantism, he pays no regard to truth or candour; and so colours even the facts which he adduces, as to make them produce a contrary impression to that which would be made if they were fairly told.

The first chapter treats on the rise of Protestantism, and foully calumniates the character and doctrines of Luther and his coadjutors; the second chapter recounts the divisions in the Protestant Church; the third defends the worship of saints; the fourth, the worship of the Virgin Mary; the fifth asserts the antiquity of such worship; the sixth defends the worship of images; the seventh asserts the antiquity of such worship; the eighth is on the decrees of the church; the ninth, on the infallibility of the church; the tenth asserts that the Romish Church is the only true church; the eleventh is on purgatory; the twelfth, on the sacraments generally; the thirteenth, on the sacraments particularly; the fourteenth, on transubstantiation; the fifteenth, on the sacrifice of the mass; the sixteenth, on the holy Scriptures; the seventeenth, on the miracles of the church; the eighteenth, confirmation of what had been advanced; the work concludes with a confession of faith on the principles defended in it.

* My copy of this work is beautifully written on *olas*, or palmyra-leaves.

The spirit, style, and doctrines of the work may be gathered from the following extracts; the first is a translation of the thirty-third paragraph of the book, being the sixth of the fourth chapter. After commenting on the answer of our Lord to the woman who exclaimed, "Blessed is the womb that bare thee," &c., (Luke xi. 27, 28,) he thus proceeds:—

"If what has here been advanced be considered, the well-informed will neither think nor affirm that the Lord Jesus disapproved of the praise ascribed by the woman to the divine mother, or forbad that she should be worshipped and praised, but rather that he approved and commended it; though to a person who has lost his senses it may appear the contrary. Let us, therefore, unite with that spiritually-enlightened woman, in praising the heavenly divine mother, that we may turn back the darts which those adversaries, the heretics, have hurled at the divine mother, and that we may pain the wounded minds of those who have already suffered a defeat. Let us say, Hail, womb that bare the God-man! Hail, womb that gave fruit not destructive of the flowers of virginity! Hail, breasts that poured nectar to the Instructer of every soul! Hail, thou who didst embody the Immaterial, to rejoice our eyes! Hail, thou who didst supply the blood that was shed for our salvation! Hail, Queen of the inhabitants of heaven! Hail, Strength to the weak! Hail, Beauty of the heavenly world! Hail, Life of the earthly world! Hail, Mistress of the fiery world! Hail, Splendour, displaying religion! Hail, Sea of grace, preserving the soul! Hail, Medicine, healing disease! Light, dispelling darkness! Joy, assuaging grief! Shore of heaven! Help of earth! Diamond of grace! Life! Nectar! Grace! Hail, Mother universally praised! Hail, Mother, worthy of universal praise! Hail, Mother, heavenly and divine!

Hail, Heroine, feared by heretics! Hail, O Bountiful, hated by heretics! Hail, Queen, who shalt destroy heretics! Hail!"

The next extract I shall make, is the conclusion of the work, headed thus:—

A CONFESSION OF FAITH, BEING THE SUM OF THE ILLUSTRATION OF RELIGION.

"SOME say that Annam," (the fabled swan of the Hindoos,) "separating milk from the water by which it has been adulterated, drinks pure unmingled milk. This must be difficult; but is it not much more difficult to separate the falsehood which has been mingled with true religion, by various sorts of heretics, and to receive the divine mysteries without adulteration? Knowing this, and that we may save the soul that has taken poison mingled with milk, we have laboured thus far, in this work, to refute all the adulterating falsehood of heretics, especially those of the present day; as though we presented to you and poured sweet nectar from a golden dish, we have exhibited to you, unmixed, the divine mysteries which are to be believed. All that we have here so diffusely written, the Council assembled in Trent, in the days of Luther, exhibited briefly in a confession of faith to be repeated by all. We, therefore, now render it for you into Tamul, as an abridgment of what we have advanced, and as a divine form of faith prescribed by that Council, to be received by all who are desirous of salvation. Let every one esteem this the form of his faith, and repeat it often during life; but especially in the hour of death, if it be possible, let him repeat it with entire devotion of mind. It is as follows:—'I, ——, believe with a firm faith all the divine mysteries contained in the articles of the belief of holy Roman

Church; that is, I heartily receive all the observances and commands observed in the holy Church, and that have been handed down by tradition from generation to generation from the days of the Apostles. Moreover, I receive as the holy Church receives, the seventy-two books as Scripture; and as it belongs only to the holy Church to interpret Scripture, I receive also the interpretation given by the holy Church. I receive the interpretation of the divine mysteries, given by the agreement of the Doctors of the holy Church; and I never at any time give any other interpretation. Moreover, I do firmly believe, that there are seven sacraments, ordained by our Lord Jesus Christ, necessary to the salvation of man, though all are not necessary to each person; and that they are these: baptism, confirmation, the Lord's supper, penance, extreme unction, holy orders, matrimony; that they communicate grace; and that these three, baptism, confirmation, and holy orders, cannot be repeated without sin. I accord that the whole manner observed by the holy Roman universal Church, in administering the seven sacraments, is good. Without any reservation, I receive all that was taught and established by the holy Council of Trent, on the subject of original sin, and the forgiveness of sins. Moreover, I affirm that in the sacrifice of the mass there is a true sacrifice offered to God for the quick and the dead; and that in the Lord's supper there are not signs, but truly the body, and blood, and soul, and divine nature, of our Lord Jesus Christ; that the nature of the bread perishes, and becomes his body, that the nature of the wine perishes, and becomes his blood, and that there is a transmutation according to the doctrine of the holy Catholic Church; and that though the properties of the bread only be received, or the properties of the wine only be received, the Lord Jesus is entirely received, and there is a perfect sacrament. I firmly believe in purgatory; and that the prayers and the alms of the holy Church are beneficial to the souls there detained. I also affirm, without doubting, that it is right to worship and to pray to the saints that are in heaven with the Lord Jesus, and that they intercede for us with God,—and to worship their holy relics; and that it is right to set up images of Jesus Christ, and of the ever holy Virgin, the divine mother, and of other saints in heaven, and to worship them in a suitable manner. I certainly affirm, that the Lord Jesus gave power to the holy Church to establish a fund of merit; and that great benefit doth accrue to all within the pale of the holy Church from the merits thus established. I am certain that the universal, Catholic, Roman, holy Church. is the mother of the holy Church spread throughout the world, and the head Church to instruct all others; and receive, that the holy Pope, reigning in the city of Rome, being the regular successor of the chief Apostle, St. Peter, is the head of the holy Church, and in the place of the Lord Jesus; and I swear that I will submit to him, and obey all his commands. Moreover, I heartily and without any doubt receive all that has been taught and established in General Councils, and in other decrees of the holy Church, and especially in the decrees of the Council assembled in Trent. And like as the holy Church has detested, rejected, and cursed every thing contrary to this, and the evil systems of all heretics, I also do detest, reject, and curse them. And because there is no salvation to any but to such as thus believe, as I receive in my mind, and firmly declare and confess by my mouth, this universal faith necessary to all, I do promise to God, and swear that, by the help of God, I will receive it in my mind, and declare it by my mouth even to death, without diminishing or altering, and will labour according to my power, that all who are under me may receive, affirm, and teach the same: so let God and his holy Gospels be my help.'

"The confession of faith, the sum of the Illustration of Religion, is ended."

The book then closes with the particulars of the place, date, and quantity of the composition, and the author's name. It is dated 1728.

I have both laughed and wept when perusing this book: the ridiculous falsehoods and mis-statements advanced in it cannot but provoke a smile; but the peculiar excellence of its style, and the want of other information on the part of those to whom it is addressed, give it a force and influence among the natives over which I could not but mourn.

The publication of a Church History in Tamul, an octavo volume of more than three hundred closely-printed pages, by the Missionaries of Tranquebar, afforded perhaps the most suitable answer this work could receive. I was told at Tranquebar, that a copy of that History was sent to Beschi, and he never ventured to impugn its statements.

An analysis of Beschi's great work, the *Tembāvani*, or "Unfading Garland," would be more than could be entered upon here. He professes this poem to be a translation from the work of a holy woman, called Mary of Agirth; but its perfectly Tamul style and matter prove this to be a mere pretence.

In his Grammar of high Tamul, speaking of this kind of poem, which has by some been denominated epic, he says: *Attamen quas Latini tradunt Poëmatum regulas non observant, &c.* "In these compositions, they do not follow the rules prescribed by Latin critics; they generally take up the narrative or fable *ab ovo*, 'at the beginning.' It is also an invariable rule, after the invocation, and the statement of the subject, to open the poem with a description of the hero's country, and the capital where he is supposed to have reigned or flourished; and these are represented in the most favourable colours; not such as they are believed to have been, but such as the poet chooses to describe them. In this description, the rains which descend upon the mountains, the streams which flow from them, and the consequent fertility of the country, never fail to have their place." *

Of this poetical licence he has availed himself to the full extent, in the composition of *Tembāvani.* It was intended to supply the place of a translation of the holy Scriptures; but every doctrine, fact, and superadded legend is so accommodated to the notions and circumstances of the Hindoos, that the whole might be supposed to have been the composition of a native, who had never set his foot beyond the boundaries of his own country; and whilst it recognises many important and sublime truths, it has a tendency, at the same time, to confirm and establish innumerable errors.

The hero of the poem is Joseph, the reputed father of our Lord. The particulars of his life, and those of the life of the blessed Virgin, are recounted with pretended accuracy; and innumerable miracles are feigned, to heighten the interest. The colouring given to the facts of the extraordinary birth and infancy of the divine Redeemer must shock any one who has tasted the simplicity of the Gospel-history; and is calculated to reduce it, in the estimation of the Hindoos, to the rank of one of their own mythological fables. The Old-Testament history, both canonical and apocryphal, with many fabled particularities, is related to the holy family, on the occasion of the flight into Egypt and the return, chiefly by

* Babington's Translation, p. 112.

angels supposed to attend on the infant Saviour. The New-Testament history, and the legends of the Romish Church, are given in the form of prophecy, to satisfy the inquiring mind of Joseph before his death.

As a specimen of the style, we select a few verses out of the second canto, relating to Jerusalem, to the description of which city the whole of the canto is devoted.

"This city, from its universal advantages, may be compared to religion; from the brightness of its ornaments, may be compared to day; from its extent, it may be compared to the world; from the keeping of its walls, it may be compared to a pure virgin; from its crowded state, it may be compared to the sea; to its enemies, it may be compared to the anger of saints; for goodness, it may be compared to heaven, and heaven may be compared to this city.

"Like as the great sea surrounds the golden world," (earth,) "so was the beauty of the wide moat, varying its bright waves, and surrounding the walls," (of Jerusalem,) which shone like a multitude of the solar rays, rose like a mountain to the water of the clouds, and pierced the sky.

"This extensive moat, at the foot of the heaven-reaching walls, seemed like a silver shackle to detain the beauteous city on the sea-girt earth; for fear it should esteem the earth an unsuitable situation, and ascend to heaven as a more appropriate place.

"This moat was deep as the deeply-rooted affection of the great; the green weeds in it played on its surface unstable as the affection of the mean; and the lotus, outshone by the beauty of the damsels, could not stay within the city, but here opened its tender leaves, and breathed its fragrance.

"There were swarms of contending crocodiles, showing teeth sharp as swords, and curved like the fair new moon, opening their fleshy mouths, and flashing fire from their eyes, as though the moat had formerly been deepened to hell, and the demons lying there had assumed, and wandered about in, a terrifying form.

"The beauty of the golden walls was as though the ever-fair earth, on a day of rejoicing, had put on a crown of pure and radiant gold: they were no more to be surprised than the temper of holy men, who are filled with goodness beyond desire, and who keep their minds.

"As the golden mountain is surrounded by clouds, the city, surrounded by a wall enclosing all wealth within it, had a gate which, when opened, was as though the earth had opened a casket, in which all its treasures had been collected with a desire to display them for universal advantage."

The remaining part of the description is equally imaginative; designed to please the fancy of a Hindoo, rather than to convey a knowledge of facts.

The following extract will exhibit the method in which doctrine is inculcated in the *Tembāvani:* the first two verses are represented as the words of the Saviour, addressed to Joseph; the third contains Joseph's reply.

"Embarking on the ship of true renunciation of the world, and setting up therein the tall mast of strong determination, spreading the two broad sails of devotion and godly fear, whilst the breeze of the excellent gifts of God blows upon them, the pilot of unceasing meditation steering them through the sea of this sinful world, they shall reach the desired haven of eternal bliss.

"But whilst the ship of renunciation thus sails along, some, by corruption of the penance they had commenced, will sink into the sea of sin and perish, as though by the up-setting of the vessel; some among them, (one or two only,) seizing with earnestness the raft of repentance, and floating in a sea of tears, directing their course straight forward, shall obtain the joys of heaven. Thus, although it is difficult rightly to perform penance, it is far more difficult for those who leave off that which they had commenced, to reach the shores of heaven.

"Joseph the possessor of the branch which blossomed with honey-dropping flowers, attended to all the divine Son uttered; and, by the mouth of his ear drinking in the nectar poured from the vessel of truth, thus replied: 'We may consider the wicked like to an unbaked earthen vessel, which, when broken, it is easy to join again, and to bake in the furnace of penance; but as it is impossible to join again a vessel broken after it is once baked, so it is most difficult for those who have left off to be penitent to be restored.'"

Amazing ingenuity, indefatigable industry, and the zeal of a mind worthy of a better cause, may be traced in every page of this work: it is so extensive as to form two large and closely-written quarto volumes. As a literary composition, and as an amusing book, it is invaluable; but when regarded as the masterpiece of the most celebrated Romish writer that has appeared among the Hindoos, and as the best information, as to Scripture history and doctrine, supplied to them by the talented men sent from Rome for their evangelization, it conveys a revolting but correct idea of the regard to expediency, rather than to truth, and to the inclinations of their converts, rather than to their best interests, shown by that body, whose exertions and successes were for a time the astonishment of Europe.

CHAPTER XVII.

JANUARY TO JUNE, 1823.

MADRAS AND WALLAJAHBAD.

Before the middle of January, 1823, Messrs. Lynch and Stead set out on their journey to attend the annual District-Meeting, about to be held in Jaffna.

They travelled on horseback down the coast as far as Negapatam. From thence they visited Trichinopoly, for the purpose of opening a small chapel, erected in the cantonment of that place by the exertions of the religious soldiers of His Majesty's Royal Regiment, about forty in number, who were kindly assisted and encouraged by the excellent Chaplain, the late Rev. Mr. Banks, and many of the officers of the station.

On their return from Trichinopoly to Negapatam, their embarkation for Jaffna was delayed several days by the dangerous illness of Mr. Lynch, whose exertions and exposure in preaching and travelling had brought on a severe attack of fever. On his recovery he proceeded to Jaffna. The result of the arrangements of the Meeting was, that Mr. Stead was appointed to Batticaloa, on the Island of Ceylon, and Mr. Lynch and myself to Madras, without the additional help we had hoped to obtain.

Meantime, the whole labour of the Station devolved upon me for more than two months. I have since sometimes wondered how I bore the fatigue of three services every Sunday, and of engagements every evening in the week. I was under the necessity of devoting all my time to the work of the Mission, but never experienced more pleasure in its performance.

On Sunday, the 16th of February, at seven o'clock in the morning, I conducted English service in the Black-Town chapel; returned to Royapettah, and at ten commenced the Tamul service, in the course of which I read prayers, baptized two adult natives and two children, married a native couple, preached in Tamul, and administered the Lord's supper to the native members of the society. At seven in the evening I preached again in English, and celebrated the sacramental service with the English society.

The two adults whom I baptized on that day had been brought for that purpose from Ellichpoor, nearly eight hundred miles from Madras, by a family of our Christian natives, who had been there in the service of an English gentleman, and now attended him on a visit to Madras. This is one of many instances in which our people, scattered through the country by their temporal occupations, have given us proofs, on their return, that they had not forgotten, during their absence, the spiritual interests of themselves and others.

Before Mr. Lynch's return to Madras, I received occasional assistance in the English services from the Missionaries of the London Society; the Rev. William Sawyer, of the Church Mission, also offered me the help of one of his native Assistants. The union of spirit and affection generally exhibited in Madras by the Missionaries of the different Societies, whilst it is quite compatible with a conscientious preference for their own religious communions, affords a pleasing proof of their Christian temper, as well as zeal; and has often been to each other a rich source of gratification and comfort.

In the month of April, we sustained a serious loss, by the death of Mr. Aylward, a young man employed in one of the Government offices, who for several years had given us his assistance as a Local Preacher and Class-

Leader. He had been particularly useful to the military part of our congregations, both in the Fort and at St. Thomas's Mount, and in diligently maintaining a religious correspondence with those members of our society who had been removed to distant parts of the country.

Being now, by the degree of proficiency I had attained, relieved from the necessity of constant attention to the study of Tamul, in the months of April and May, I employed a Teacher of the Portuguese language; and, by a little application, gained a colloquial knowledge of that tongue, in the corrupt form in which it is used in India; and translated and composed in it a number of sermons, in hope of finding some opportunities of usefulness among that part of the Portuguese population whose knowledge of English was not sufficient to enable them to profit by our English services.

Though it was not till subsequent to this period that we commenced public preaching in Portuguese in the neighbourhood of Madras, I found my new acquisition of immediate advantage, in my daily intercourse with the people. The language, as it is commonly spoken, can afford no literary pleasure; it is calculated rather to excite a degree of disgust; but as a means of conveying spiritual instruction to many hundreds who are otherwise inaccessible to a Missionary, it is well worth the trifling labour necessary to acquire it.

On the 19th of May, I assembled our Mission-schools in the chapel of Royapettah, for the purpose of a public examination. The circumstance of their being at several miles' distance from each other, had hitherto deterred us from bringing them together; but, thinking it would promote the general interest, and, by creating some degree of emulation, rouse both masters and children to greater activity, I devoted this day to that purpose, and presented clothes and books as an encouragement and reward to the most deserving of the children. Amongst them were a few native girls, whose docility and improvement were remarkable, and made us regret that we had at that time neither means nor suitable Teachers, to attempt even one separate school for native female education.

These difficulties no longer exist to the same extent: the education of Hindoo females has become a subject of great interest with the Christian public; and the increasing number of those who have been thus educated is lessening the difficulty of obtaining persons competent to teach, and diminishing the prejudice which still exists in India against females being instructed at all.

The month of May is reckoned, in India, the hottest in the year; the wind from the west, called at Madras "the land wind," blows hot and dry, and sometimes prevails a considerable time without intermission day or night; whilst the thermometer ranges from 90° to upwards of 100° in the shade. The season is usually rendered more tolerable by the alternating of the sea-breeze, which springs up towards evening, struggles against the land-wind, and, though sometimes overcome, generally prevails to a few miles inland, and, affording some mitigation of the heat, seems to refresh every thing that has life. Birds and cattle, as well as man, are sensible of its effects: its approach is often announced by the cawing of the crows, till then drooping their wings in the shade, and gasping for breath with their beaks wide open.

The land-wind produces little effect on Europeans whose constitution is good: invalids are much exhausted by it; and are commonly removed to houses near the beach, for the full benefit of the sea-breeze. The most usual plan for mitigating the heat, is to fix over the open doors and windows, on the windward side of the house, mats of grass, or of the root of the cusa-grass, which latter yields, when wet, an aromatic smell: natives are employed to throw water on these mats, and the hot wind passing through them occasions evaporation, and causes a delicious coolness in the air. I never adopted this method; and am doubtful whether it is suitable for persons whose avocations make it necessary frequently to leave the house thus cooled, and pass through an atmosphere of very different temperature.

The heat of this season had not been remarkably great; but it occasioned an indisposition which confined me to the house for some days. The prickly heat and biles from which I suffered were painful and disagreeable; but I recovered sooner than some of my friends who were laid up from the same cause.

In June I took a short journey, the chief object of which was, to visit the society formed in His Majesty's 69th Regiment, then recently removed from Cannanore, on the Malabar coast, to Wallajahbad.

Wallajahbad is a military cantonment, about forty miles west of Madras; and is considered only a night's journey from that place for a palankeen with a full set of bearers.

I employed only six bearers on this journey, as I intended to make two or three stages of it, and to take the opportunity of conversing with the natives, and distributing religious tracts.

On the 5th of the month, on my way to Wallajahbad, I proceeded to St. Thomas's Mount, and in the evening preached in the school-room. After supping with my hospitable friends there, I entered my palankeen, and travelled as far as Serapanumchairy, a small village about eighteen miles from the Mount.

As soon as I arrived, early in the morning, I had a small congregation, in a number of persons who came to tell me of a man who had been attacked and died there of the cholera morbus on the preceding day. The subject of death led me to speak of the origin of death, and the remedies and hopes afforded by Christianity. I read to them a Tamul tract on the Last Judgment: they heard me attentively; and remained under the tree where I rested till I desired them to leave me, that I might take breakfast undisturbed. In the course of the day I was visited by many others: reading, conversation, and the distribution of tracts employed me till evening; and I was encouraged to hope that many of the people would remember the things they had heard.

At five o'clock in the morning of Saturday, the 7th, I arrived at Wallajahbad; and whilst looking for some person to direct me, was met by Surgeon Gibson, who kindly invited me to his house, insisted on my company to breakfast, whilst he sent for the Leader of our society, and engaged me to breakfast with him every morning during my stay.

I waited on Major Leslie, the commanding officer of the 69th, who desired me to conduct divine service for the regiment on the following day: he had already directed an unoccupied part of the officers' quarters to be prepared for my accommodation. I preferred this arrangement, as it left me perfect master of my time, and more at liberty to pursue the objects of my Mission, than if I had been entertained by any private individual.

In the afternoon, according to previous engagement, I preached in Tamul, to a congregation of natives, chiefly the wives of English soldiers, professing Christianity, though few of them had heard the Gospel in their own language. They were very attentive, and some of them appeared much impressed. One of them said, that she feared she should have laughed to hear an European preach in Tamul; but, on the contrary, she was cut to the heart by what she heard. They were thankful when I promised to preach again to them at the same hour the next day.

In the evening more than sixty persons were present at an English prayer-meeting: many of the soldiers took part in the service, and prayed with great fervency and propriety.

The sea-breeze not reaching Wallajahbad, the night proved dreadfully hot, and I arose feverish and unrefreshed. It was Sunday; before sunrise, the regiment was on parade, and formed into a square; seats for the women and children were provided within the square; the great drum was placed as a reading-desk to support the Prayer-Book and Bible; the band played church-music; and thus, in the open air, I read prayers and preached to a large congregation of my military countrymen, including the officers of the regiment.

In the forenoon I met the class, in which I found about forty members; and addressed an exhortation to a number of others, who had requested permission to attend.

At three P.M. the natives assembled more numerously than the day before. Several who appeared affected by the truth, gave us reason to believe, by their subsequent conduct, that the word had not been preached to them in vain.

Returning to my quarters, I was so overcome by the heat and fatigue, that I knew not what to do. I spread the palankeen-mattress on the ground, and, throwing myself upon it, requested to be left alone; but, after trying to rest for two hours, I did not feel much refreshed.

In the evening I preached to the soldiers in a long, narrow room they had engaged for their religious meetings: it was exceedingly crowded; and more than could hear stood outside, round the door and windows. The communicants, who remained at the celebration of the

Lord's supper, after the conclusion of the evening service, quite filled the room: many others thought it hard they were not allowed to remain as spectators. It was a solemn and profitable season; and especially so to many who, before that day, had never seen a Missionary of the society to which they had for some time belonged. I was myself much cheered and animated by the services of the evening.

Monday morning, at seven o'clock, I again met the pious soldiers to take leave of them. In the course of the day I visited the Hospital, and found one of our society under severe affliction, but enjoying the consolations of the Gospel. Many of the invalids were attentive, while I read prayers and gave an exhortation. I visited an old native Heathen, who had requested the praying soldiers to make use of his bungalow to meet in: he had seen them engaged in reading, or other devotional exercises, under the shade of trees in the neighbourhood; and, though he could not speak English, made them understand that they were welcome to his bungalow as a place for prayer. When I inquired into his motives, he said he thought them pious men; that when they were engaged in worship, he used to attend to pay his respects to their God, and then return again to his labour. When I asked where he thought their God was, he said he supposed in the book, meaning the Bible, which he had seen them read attentively. He appeared pleased that I took some pains to inform him on the nature of Christianity; and thankfully received a few tracts.

This day I refused to baptize a child whose parents were living in concubinage; a crime too common in India, and which, I am persuaded, would be considerably checked, if all Ministers would refuse baptism to the offspring till the unlawful connexion should be dissolved, or the parents made man and wife by marriage. By constantly refusing to baptize such children except on these conditions, I believe our Missionaries have, in some instances, remedied much evil, and promoted the comfort and improved the morals of many of our countrymen.

I entered the palankeen at sun-set; my six bearers, induced by the promise of an extra rupee, carried me to St. Thomas's Mount by the following morning, a journey of thirty-two miles. I rested there during the heat of the day, and reached home in the evening a good deal fatigued, but thankful for the favourable openings presented to me in my excursion of the past five days.

Towards the end of June, we celebrated the fourth Anniversary of the Wesleyan Missionary Society in Madras. The Missionaries of the London Society, as on former similar occasions, kindly afforded us their valuable assistance. The collections amounted to about £30 sterling, being more than those of any former year; a good feeling was exhibited by the people, and in every department of our work we saw reason to hope for prosperity and increase.

CHAPTER XVIII.

JULY TO SEPTEMBER, 1823.

TEN WEEKS' TOUR IN THE TAMUL COUNTRY.

I NOW prepared for a Missionary excursion of some months through the interior of the country, for the purpose of visiting a number of small congregations, consisting of English, Portuguese, and natives, who had rarely the opportunity of coming to Mission-stations; and could seldom enjoy the privileges of the Christian church, except by the occasional visits of travelling Missionaries. The hope also of valuable opportunities of conversational intercourse with the heathen natives on the subject of religion, and of recommending Christianity to those who had never before heard of it, or were ignorant of its nature; of scattering more widely the seeds of knowledge and true religion, by the distribution of tracts and portions of the holy Scriptures in the languages of the people; of enlarging my personal acquaintance with the country in general, and obtaining information on the comparative importance of different places to which our attention as Missionaries had been directed; induced me the more readily to undertake this journey. It was considered also that my state of health rendered it necessary to relax for a time from the confinement and labours of the Madras station.

Mr. Mowat, who was still at Negapatam, fully accorded with our views; and kindly consented to part for some time with his Assistant, Mr. Kats, that he might come to Madras, to attend to the native societies and congregations, under Mr. Lynch's directions, during my absence;

only urging that, in the course of my journey, I must visit Negapatam.

I was detained a few days after Mr. Kats's arrival, to be present at the re-opening of our place of worship at St. Thomè, which had been somewhat enlarged and beautified, and furnished with a pulpit and seats. One of the sermons on the day of re-opening was in Portuguese; and attracted an audience so considerable, as forcibly to show the importance of establishing regular services in that language.

On Monday, the 7th of July, 1823, I passed the day in conference with the Missionaries of our own and other Societies, who afforded us the pleasure of their company at the Mission-house in Royapettah. We went thence in the evening to the monthly Missionary prayer-meeting, held in Black-Town. We returned; and at midnight I entered my palankeen, and set out on my journey, reflecting on the innumerable advantages, both as to myself and my work, I had enjoyed since I arrived at Madras; and the solemn responsibilities devolving on me, from the character to be sustained and the work to be performed, whether dwelling among my brethren, or travelling as a Christian stranger through a heathen land.

On the following day, I found no protection from the heat in the choultry at Tripatoor, though it served to screen me from the direct rays of the sun: a severe pain in my head was the consequence; but I was not hindered from conversing with some natives who came to see me, and gladly received a few Tamul tracts. We resumed our journey in the evening, and proceeded to the neighbourhood of Mauveliveram.

Mauveliveram, or *Maha Bali pooram*, "the city of the great Bali," (one of the former monarchs of India, styled also *Bali Chakkra Varti*, or "Bali, Lord of the universe,") was once, it is said, a great and very populous city; but is now no more than a small village, inhabited chiefly by Brahmans, who are here surrounded by monuments of the antiquity and influence of their system of superstition.

On Wednesday, as soon as day dawned, I walked from my resting-place to look at these ancient remains, which have so often been described; and was soon surrounded by a number of Brahmans, one of whom undertook to be my guide.

A little to the north-east of the village is a temple built of hewn stone, partially in ruins, its base being continually washed by the sea, which, the Brahmans told me, by a sudden irruption had overwhelmed great part of this ancient capital. The form of this temple is pleasing to the eye: its numerous stories or steps lessen to the top, which is surmounted by a fine black stone. Its style differs much from that of the modern temples; and many of the sculptured figures on it have much of the European feature, and are represented with bushy heads of hair.

To the south are scattered rocks, sculptured in the form of idol-cars and temples, of no great height or extent, but displaying the marks of considerable labour and skill, and illustrating the wild mythology of the Hindoos.

One of the bas-relief sculptures, on the side of a rock, entirely exposed, but in good preservation, is remarkable for the completeness of its idea and execution: it is several yards high; its length may be two or three times its height. The subject is the penance of Arjuna, one of the ancient warriors, performed to obtain the *choolam*, or trident, the all-powerful weapon of the god Siva. He is represented as standing with his hands joined over his head, his hair and beard grown long and shaggy, and his body wasted to the bone, by the long-continued extremity of his penance. Heaven, earth, and hell are moved by his extraordinary perseverance. Siva stands beside him with the weapon in his hand, gods and goddesses are descending from heaven, various kinds of sublunary animals, as well as man, are assembling, and demons are rising from the abyss, to witness the results. The symmetry and proportions of these figures are remarkably just; and the characters of many of them seemed to me to be well preserved.

There are inscriptions on some of the rocks, in a character not understood by any present inhabitant of the place; but which, I was told, had been pronounced to be of the ancient Cannada language, by some learned natives who had formerly visited Mauveliveram.

The appearance these sculptured rocks present at sea has gained for them the name of the Seven Pagodas.

As Mauveliveram is only thirty-five miles from Madras, it is not unfrequently visited by parties of pleasure. Some of its former visitants had been mindful of the interests of Christianity, for the Brahmans were quite aware of the general subject of the tracts I presented to them. A present of a rupee gratified the Brahman who had acted as Cicerone; but I could not silence the clamours of the rest, who also wanted presents, until I reminded them how ill it became men professedly devoted to spiritual things to be so anxious to obtain a little money.

My palankeen had followed me while I walked among the rocks: when I had seen all, I entered it, and proceeded to Sadras, where, as on a former journey, I was kindly entertained by F. P. Regel, Esq. At four P.M. I preached in English, to a small, but attentive, congregation; and, in the evening, conducted divine service in Portuguese, at the close of which one of the men begged hard for the sermon I had read; but my stock in hand was too scanty to allow me to spare it to him.

I slept soundly in a tent pitched for my accommodation in front of Mr. Regel's house, and resumed my journey early in the morning of Thursday. In the evening I rested in the cabin of a mixed family of Roman Catholics in Alemparva, who did not object to my praying with them, and reading and talking on religious subjects.

On the morning of Friday I rested under a tree, near a noisy and bustling bazaar. As the most likely method of attracting attention, I called one of the natives, and inquired if he could read: he proved to have a very strong voice; and, when he commenced reading, attracted a crowd of people around him. He read the whole of a Tamul tract on "The Way to Heaven," another on "The Last Judgment," and considerable part of a third on "The Ten Commandments." He then said he was tired; and I rewarded him by presenting him with the tracts he had read. He went away, but soon returned, saying he had forgot something: it was to ask me to recommend him to Government for some office. This gave me a good opportunity of telling him, and the people around, the object of my mission; that whilst every man cared for worldly things, very few cared for the more important concerns of their souls; and that my only business among them was to awaken them to think on these subjects, and to point out how they might secure their eternal interests.

On Saturday, as I passed through Pondicherry, I distributed several tracts, which were eagerly received. Crossing a river in a boat filled with passengers, I called for silence, and read and talked to them till we reached the opposite bank. When we got ashore, one of them followed me to beg a tract, urging that his child could read, though he himself could not: he then begged a few more for some Christian families, that, he said, lived in his village. I gave him what he requested, and sent him away quite satisfied.

I passed the middle of the day under the shade of a tree, and was much employed in conversation with the natives who visited me. Among them was a Fakeer, or Mahommedan religious mendicant, who seemed ashamed of his ignorance, and a San-yasi, or Hindoo monk, a strong hale fellow, who was not able to give any reasonable account of himself, or of his principles. I advised him to quit his idle and vagabond mode of life. Here also I distributed many tracts, which were eagerly received. In the evening I proceeded to Cuddalore.

On Sunday, 13th, I attended the Mission church at Cuddalore in the forenoon; and, in the evening, preached in a bungalow to a congregation consisting chiefly of English pensioners, with their wives and children. Several military officers were present.

I set out at sunrise on Monday, 14th; and when the day became advanced, rested at the same choultry where I had passed a Sunday when I travelled this way before. After a little refreshment, I walked to the native choultry opposite, and began to converse with the people. A Pandaram, a Hindoo religious mendicant, took part in the conversation; and, in their usual way of treating such subjects, began to ascribe every thing to God, both good and evil. When I stated my views, he seemed convinced of their correctness, and acknowledged it before many who listened to our conversation. He thankfully received some tracts, and hastened after his companions, who had commenced their journey some time before. I distributed a few more tracts to those who could read, and endeavoured to impress on the minds of all, the great importance of eternal things, and the folly of allowing temporal considerations to interfere with their spiritual interests; and was heard with attention.

One man followed me to my palankeen. I asked, "Where are you going?" He replied, "To Ramisseram." "For what purpose?" "To see the god there." "What sort of a god is he, brass, wood, or stone?" "He is self-existent." "But of what substance is he?" "Stone." "Has he eyes?" "Yes." "Can he see?" "No." "Has he hands?" "Yes," &c. "And do you say, that this is God?" "It is the image of God." "Impossible! As God is a Spirit, and omnipresent, it is impossible for any image to represent him. You may make the likeness of a man, a dog, a beast, or a serpent; but you can never make the likeness of God." To this he assented; and I then proceeded to say, "All adoration rendered to idols is an insult to God. By pursuing your present intention, you will provoke his anger, rather than gain his favour. How foolish it is for you to expose yourself to hunger, and thirst, and weariness, by so long a journey; and, after all, displease the Almighty! Take my advice,—sit down awhile, and consider that God is present here; and that he is equally so in Madras, whence you are come. Pray him to give you wisdom; and do not take another step of your journey, for such a purpose, to Ramisseram." I then left him to reflect on what he had heard, and to read a tract which I put into his hand on "The Incarnation of Christ."

Tuesday, July 15th. In pursuing my journey southward, I experienced some delay by the swollen state of the three branches of the Coleroon river, which entirely filled their wide beds, and rushed rapidly towards the sea. On the banks were hundreds of natives waiting for an opportunity to cross, to visit, or return from, the Hindoo feast then holding at Chillumbrum, a large pagoda, whose high towers I had noticed as I passed on the road. There is a most fertile tract of land about a mile in breadth between the branches of the river: on each branch I found only one large and clumsy boat, towards which, when it reached the shore, the rush of people was so great as to occasion some danger of its being upset: a military guard restrained the people in some measure; but, after all, the boats were so filled, that I was apprehensive of accidents. Some of the people told me they had been waiting there three days. I was thankful to get safely to the south side of the river, and could not but wish, that, when I travelled this way again, it might be neither the Chillumbrum feast, nor the flood of the Coleroon.

I passed the day on Wednesday, in Tranquebar, in company with Mr. Schrievogel, a Missionary who had long laboured in that place, but appeared to have met with little else but discouragements in his work. In such circumstances, it is a cheering consideration, that the labourer is responsible for his faithfulness only, and not for the results of his endeavours. It is God alone who giveth the increase.

The following morning I arrived in Negapatam, happy again to see my fellow-voyagers, Mr. and Mrs. Mowat, and to be occupied a short time on the Station where I had formerly resided, and where I should have an opportunity of witnessing the results of the labours of my highly-respected brethren.

In the course of my journey thus far from Madras, I had met with many native Romanists who gladly heard me, and conversed with me. One poor fellow was extravagant in his expressions of joy at what I said, exclaiming to all around, "It is one religion, one faith, one Saviour, one baptism," &c. It is not to be doubted, that many of them, notwithstanding the superstitious fear they entertain towards their Priests, who uniformly denounce our native schools and religious books, gladly avail themselves of all safe opportunities of obtaining an enlarged acquaintance with Christianity from the Scriptures and tracts in their own language, and conversation with passing Missionaries.

Whilst particularly engaged among the heathen natives, I deeply felt the necessity of that ardent zeal and unwearied patience which should characterize the true Missionary. It is not enough that he pass through the country, and declare his character and the object he has in view: to induce the people to hear the Gospel with attention, he must converse with them, and encourage them to free conversation by answering their inquiries; many of which, as it may be easily conceived, are widely remote from the chief subject to which he is desirous of directing their attention. When a Missionary thus displays a patience and a condescension not usually witnessed in Europeans, the people are apt to take troublesome liberties, and to contrive how to promote their own present advantage. When spoken to with great earnestness on the most awful and important subjects, they would sometimes reply, "Will you take me into your service?" "Will you recommend me for a situation to the Collector, or to Government?" Or, "I am very poor, and will thankfully accept any thing you will please to bestow." And they did not generally appear well pleased when I told them, that these things I had nothing to do with; that my religion condemned an inordinate care about temporal matters; and that, till they obtained more just notions about another world, they never would be content with their circumstances in this. In some cases, I thought the first enunciation of divine truth made an impression on the minds of the hearers; and though the deceitfulness of the people is almost proverbial, I indulged the hope, that, in some instances, "the good seed" was received "into good ground."

I have often, on these occasions, inquired within myself, How are the Hindoos to be converted? Miracles would not be successful; for they would refer them to the art by which their jugglers every day perform their wondrous feats. The extraordinary relations of sacred history fail to excite their astonishment; for their own books record most marvellous events, with which the truth of things will bear no comparison. Their prevailing prejudices with regard to caste, the antiquity of the Brahmanical system, and the necessity of continuing in the profession of their forefathers, appear contrived to prepare them to reject the Gospel from the first of their hearing it preached; or, if it makes some impression, to cause it to be immediately effaced. There is nothing but their accessibleness favourable to the introduction of the Gospel amongst them; for though they respect the character of European Christians residing with them, their own interests and practices generally remain unchanged. It must then be one of the purest and greatest triumphs the world ever witnessed, when the Hindoos shall bend to the yoke of Christ. And the conclusion to which I have arrived is, that whilst an improved system of education, and the diffusion of general knowledge, may have their share in preparing the way for some change in their religious system, the truth will only be ultimately successful in the hands of men of irreproachable conduct, residing among the people, and so setting forth the doctrines of Christianity by public preaching and conversations, that its light may strongly contend and contrast with the widely-prevailing darkness of Heathenism.

Let the command of the Divine Author of the Gospel be perseveringly obeyed, by unceasing endeavours to promulgate a knowledge of it amongst the adult Hindoos; and we may justly hope that those endeavours will be succeeded by the gracious influences of that blessed

Spirit, without whose energy we are assured that no man, of whatever nation, can be effectually turned from the error of his ways.

In Negapatam I remained eighteen days; and, during my stay, relieved Mr. Mowat, whose health was delicate, from the chief part of his public labours, English, Portuguese, and Tamul.

Several persons who had formed part of our congregations when I formerly resided there had died in the interval, leaving behind them a pleasing testimony that they had not heard the Gospel in vain. Many who were then members of society continued faithful; and, by their conversation and conduct, gave proof of their having valued, and profited by, the advantages of the faithful ministry established among them: the minds of some others also, not immediately connected with us, seemed to be undergoing a favourable change.

I was much pleased with the regularity and progress of several native schools Mr. Mowat had succeeded in establishing, into which the use of the holy Scriptures and Catechisms, as school-books, had been fairly introduced. In visiting the schools, we had several opportunities of addressing the people who crowded round to witness the examination.

But not the least interesting of my engagements, on this visit, was the addressing in Tamul a large crowd of natives, assembled and seated under the trees of Mr. Mowat's garden. They consisted generally of the poor of the neighbourhood; though there might be some strangers and professed beggars among them. They assembled every Saturday, to receive each a small measure of rice from the bounty of Mr. Mowat, and of other respectable inhabitants of Negapatam, who made him their almoner; and as none who came were turned away, their number generally amounted to about two or three hundred. The hour being fixed, they came usually at the same time; and their attention to the addresses delivered to them was secured, by deferring the distribution of the rice till the conclusion. I preached three times to this congregation; and though not sanguine as to the success of such a conjunction of means for their benefit, nor hearing of any decided results, I could not witness the serious attention and apparent good feeling of many, without hoping that, among these poor to whom the Gospel was preached, there might be some who should believe to the saving of their souls.

On the evening of Monday, the 4th of August, I quitted Negapatam. I now travelled nearly due west, on a road raised many feet above the land-level, to make it practicable for travellers, when the country for many miles round is under water: the cultivation of rice requires the irrigation of the land, which in this part is rendered exceedingly valuable and productive by the waters of the river Cauvery.

Mr. Mowat drove me in his *bandy*, or gig, about four miles out of Negapatam; I then entered my palankeen, and he returned home. The following day was passed in a retired village; where, being free from interruption, I took the opportunity of preparing communications for England, relative to the state of our Mission, and the necessity of further help.

At Pundi, on Wednesday, the 6th, I was visited, soon after my arrival, by a respectable native, who, from his conversation, appeared to have thought seriously on the subject of religion. I gave him a few tracts, and desired him to invite the chief people of the village, to visit and converse with me in any place most agreeable to themselves. The invitation was delivered and accepted; two chairs were brought to the choultry, and placed opposite each other, one for the Merasi, or land-owner, and the other for myself.

The Merasi, a fine, stout, respectable-looking man, soon appeared, accompanied by a number of Brahmans, and other attendants, who stood about him whilst he took one of the chairs: a crowd of the common people followed, and almost filled the choultry in which we sat.

I seriously felt the importance of the task before me, whilst I rejoiced at such an opportunity of declaring the truth of God. In order that all might hear what was said, and to leave no room for doubt or misrepresentation, I spoke throughout in a loud and distinct manner.

I commenced the conversation by asserting the value of the soul, and the importance of its salvation; and stated that it was my business to raise a concern for its welfare in all to whom I had access; that by sin we were exposed to death and hell, but that the one true God who had made us, not willing that any should perish, had found a ransom, and had given us a true *Vedam*, or holy Scripture, teaching us how to obtain and keep the blessings purchased for us by Jesus Christ; that the truths of the Bible claimed regard as the objects of faith, and its precepts were to be received as the rule of practice; that, in obedience to its commands, I endeavoured to make it known to all, and that I now felt pleasure in declaring its truths in their hearing.

He heard me patiently to the conclusion, and then replied: "You call your religion the true religion: does that imply that our religion is false?" I asked whether it was probable that one God would give to the same race of beings, all in similar circumstances, different laws and religions. He did not admit the truth of the assertion, that there was only one God; he thought there might be more than one; but supposing there was only one, he thought he might with propriety give different religions to different nations of the world. When I again objected to this, on the same ground as before, he inquired, "Who, then, must judge which is the one true religion, and which are false?" I argued, that the authors of some systems, both by their writings and actions, had shown themselves to be, in many respects, ignorant and wicked men; that a religion whose authors were acknowledged to have been guilty of many enormities could not proceed from a holy God; and that a system sanctioning and enforcing contradictions could not be the work of a God of wisdom and truth; that it was our business to exercise the understanding he had given us to discern and to choose the right way.

In replying to these and similar arguments, he sometimes spoke with apparent vehemence and passion; but was, I believe, merely making the experiment as to the effect such a manner would have on me. For, if an Englishman, in conversing with a Hindoo, allows his resentment or indignation to be roused, there is an end to all argument, and the Hindoo triumphs as having won the day; but they profess to be great admirers of stern imperturbability of mind. When the Merasi found that I was immovable, he became quite mild, and allowed me to warn him of the condemnation arising from a wilful neglect or rejection of divine light; and to recommend to his serious consideration the subjects of our conversation, and some tracts I had put into his hand. He rose to go away, saying, "It is true that there is only one God, and he is Siven, Vishnoo, Bramha, or Christ, or whatever you please to call him."

None of his attendants would receive any tracts, from a fear, I supposed, of displeasing him. Though the result of my efforts was often, to all appearance, no more satisfastory than in this case, I felt pleasure in *attempting* to accomplish the objects of my Mission; and indulged a hope, that what I advanced on these occasions was not without effect on the minds of many of the silent and attentive hearers.

On the evening of the same day I proceeded to Tanjore, and was again hospitably entertained in the Mission-house.

The following day, Thursday, the 7th, I preached in the church within the Fort to the native congregation. I felt it an honour to enter the pulpit of the venerable Swartz, and to address a congregation containing some whom he had been the means of converting to the truth. The people were respectably dressed, and behaved with decorum. I observed that they were chiefly of the Soodra caste; and was informed by Mr. Kolhoff, that three-fourths of the native Christians in Tanjore are of the same class.

Many of them visited me in the evening, and thankfully received from me some of the publications of the Madras Religious Tract Society. Our walk round the Mission-garden was rendered more interesting, by the company of several of the Christian natives. The conversation was in Tamul; in the course of which, some doubt having been expressed as to the use of a certain word, Mr. Kolhoff observed, that such were the peculiarities of the Tamul language, that, though he had been now using it fifty years, he still considered himself merely a learner.

Early on the morning of the 8th, I quitted Tanjore, and arrived, about nine o'clock, at Puthupet, a village of the Christianized Kollers, to which I had been directed by Mr. Kolhoff.

The Kollers, literally, "thieves," are a numerous people, who formerly paid a tax for the privilege of thieving; and in the exercise of their profession sometimes became formidable to the Rajah himself. When the country fell into the hands of the British Government, that tax was no longer exacted: Mr. Swartz preached the Gospel to the Kollers; and many of them, by the influence of good government and instruction, "steal no more," but cultivate their land, and subsist on its produce. There are amongst them several small Christian congregations. Many of those who continue Heathens still pursue their old profession: upwards of twenty of them were, about this time, taken at once in the street of Trichinopoly; and I was assured there, on the most respectable authority, that every house occupied by an European family was under the necessity of employing one or more watchmen of this class of people, that they might recognise their fellow-thieves, and give warning of their approach; but that it was very rare for any house thus guarded to be attacked by them.

George Borrow, the enterprising author of "The Bible in Spain," maintains that the Gipsies are of Eastern origin, and that the primary stock is to be found among the Hindoos. Some coincidences are remarkable, and perhaps worthy of being recorded. He calls the Gipsies, *Caloro;* these people are called *Koller.* The Gipsies call blood *errate;* these, *iratta.* The Gipsies say, *chachipe,* for truth; these, *chattiapech.* *Jockey* is a Gipsy word, derived from the name of a whip; which this people would call *jowk.* I think, if George Borrow had met with the Kollers, he would have pronounced them Gipsies.

No better evidence of the advatageous results of Missionary exertions in India need be adduced, than the conversion and improvement of a large portion of this people, who considered it their birth-right to defy the just laws both of God and man.

Whilst I rested in the vestry of the church of the village of Puthupet, a very small squirrel dropped from the roof to the floor; but, uninjured by the fall, was so active as to make it matter of some difficulty to catch him. I succeeded, however, and secured him on the table. The piercing cries of the old one, when, from the roof, she saw her young one taken prisoner, induced me to set him at liberty. The mother then hastened down the outside of the building, and, entering by the door or window, seized the young one in her mouth, and carried him back in safety to his place in the roof. These squirrels are grey, and not so pretty as those of England. They abound every where in India; and, if a little encouraged, come boldly into the house, and nibble at the food on the table. A pair of them, finding themselves unmolested, formed a nest in one of my book-shelves in Royapooram, and there reared their young, till I was obliged to dislodge them, for trying their teeth on the bindings of my books. The Portuguese call them *rato das palmiras*, or "the palmira-rat."

At ten o'clock a congregation of the Christian Kollers assembled in the church, to whom I preached: though rude and simple, they received the word with much attention. The Catechist residing here assured me that many of them are sincerely pious.

I afterwards visited some of them in their huts; and in conversation found the name of Swartz very dear to them. Some amongst them had been baptized by Swartz himself.

The morning of the following day, Saturday, the 10th of August, I arrived at Trichinopoly. Mr. and Mrs. Rosen again very kindly received me, and entertained me during my stay at the house adjoining the Mission-church within the Fort.

In the evening I went out to see the chapel, erected in the cantonment, about two or three miles distant, by the soldiers of the Royal Regiment connected with our society. It is a small but neat and substantial building, with a tiled roof. I found in it a number of the soldiers engaged in prayer; and gladly took the opportunity of uniting with them, and of giving them a short address.

On Sunday I preached twice in this chapel to very attentive congregations of the English soldiers and their families; and in the afternoon assembled as many natives as I could to attend a Tamul service. They were chiefly Heathens connected with the regiment, and formed an uncouth congregation; but so anxious were they to prevent any disturbance, that the crying of a child created almost general confusion, every one was so desirous to silence it. It was apparent that they understood me well; and I learned afterwards, that some of them were affected by what they heard.

On Monday, before sun-rise, Mr. Rosen and I set out to see the famous temple of Seringham, about four miles distant. This temple stands on an island which, like the island of Seringapatam also, more than two hundred miles up the same river, is formed by the separation and re-union of the Cauvery, a holy river in the estimation of the Hindoos. The island itself is accounted sacred; and abounds with traces of superstition, with numerous temples to the honour of different idols, and choultries for the accommodation of pilgrims.

The outer wall of the great temple of Seringham is said to be nearly four miles round. We alighted at the principal entrance or gateway, which is constructed of stone, in a style very striking and magnificent. Some of the stones used at the front, and placed across the roof, are twenty, and some more than thirty, feet in length, and five feet thick. We ascended to the top of the staircase, constructed inside the wall, much like that of a church-tower, but wider. The tower over the gateway is evidently unfinished; and we were told that the design was to have raised it to four or five times its present height, which may be fifty or sixty feet. When I looked at the extraordinary magnitude of the stones, and the boldness of the design, I was not surprised that one of the Hindoos who accompanied us should say, that it was the work of the gods.

There is no doubt that the large stones used in this building were raised to their places by means of the inclined plane, a method still in use by native architects. One of the natives said, that the mound used to raise these stones was constructed of cotton.

We descended from the porch, and entered the sacred enclosure, which we found occupied by streets of bazaars and dwelling-houses, crossing each other, and leading to the different quarters where the towers are erected, and religious ceremonies are performed. We passed under several of the towers, in going to the Thousand Pillar Choultry, an immense room, the roof of which is supported by a thousand pillars of stone, and, I suppose, designed to accommodate the devotees and pilgrims who assemble at annual festivals. The chief curiosity of this choultry is the workmanship of some outside pillars, which have projecting from them, in full relief, a variety of figures, such as a man on horseback, almost as large as life, contending with an elephant, a tiger, or some other ferocious animal. These figures are of one stone with the pillar. Indescribable care and skill must have been required in the sculpture, as well as in the removing and raising of the immense masses of stone of each of which they form a part.

We were conducted to the flat roof of the Thousand Pillar Choultry, that we might thence see the gilded dome, erected over the shrine of the principal idol, which we were not allowed to approach. In passing and repassing through this temple, our eyes were continually offended by the most indecent and monstrous figures in plaster, or paintings on the walls of the same character; which might have been intended for personifications of sin, but are, in the estimation of the Hindoos, the legitimate ornaments of their places of worship. Such is the character of Hindoo idolatry! We were also favoured with a sight of the crown and other regalia belonging to the idol, which are only used on festival occasions: they were of pure gold, and richly set with uncut precious stones. They were said to be worth several hundred pounds sterling. The monkeys inhabiting this vast building are of a large size, and very bold. We were told that, but a few days previous, one of them had run towards a gentleman standing on the top of the principal gateway, as though with the intention of casting him down; and that it was probable he would have done so, but for the number of the attending natives, who scared him away.

On leaving the temple, we were beset by a crowd of Brahmans, who, as usual, were not ashamed to beg hard for a little money. On these occasions, I always rewarded my conductor; but abstained from further liberality, lest it should be misconstrued into an offering to the idols of the place, under which character it was, in fact, generally solicited.

When we came to the bank of the river, we found the large boat in which we had crossed it at a great distance, and therefore entered a smaller boat of very peculiar construction: it was quite round, made of wicker work, and covered outside with leather or skin. From its circular form, it turned round in the water, till I should sometimes have been puzzled to tell which bank of the river we were approaching; but, being very light, it was exceedingly manageable, and carried us safely to the opposite side.

Mr. Rosen took me to see another large temple, within the Fort of Trichinopoly, which is now quite deserted, having been polluted by the military during the war. I found several Europeans soldiers and their families residing under its vast roof: they had built slight partition-walls, to render their quarters more snug and private.

On Wednesday I again met my favourite congregation, the natives. They were improved both in numbers and behaviour: some of them seemed to think seriously on the subjects brought before them. At the conclusion of the service, one of the women came to the vestry-door; and, by her attitude, showed that she wished to be noticed, though she feared to intrude. I asked her what she wanted; she said she had been in darkness till now; but as she had received light, was desirous of acting by it, and to make a profession of Christianity by baptism. Another then came, and begged me to baptize her little girl, the daughter of an European soldier, who had returned home some years ago. I asked if she herself had been baptized; she replied, "No." "Why, then, do you wish your child to be baptized? Is it not enough if she is as you are?" The tears began to trickle down her cheeks. Another native woman was brought by her husband, who was an Irishman. He had married her, though a Heathen; but, having lately become serious, aud joined the society, was anxious that she also should be instructed and baptized: she appeared to be equally desirous of it.

Although I had no reason to doubt the sincerity of any of these individuals, I did not feel at liberty to baptize them without further knowledge, or before they had been more adequately instructed. I therefore gave them some suitable advice, and recommended them to Mr. Rosen. He sent his Catechist to instruct them in the principles of Christianity; and ultimately administered baptism to them and to one or two more, who had not come forward so prominently on that day; and I have since several times heard concerning them, that they continue to adorn their profession. This was the more remarkable, as the previous character of two or three of them had been notoriously bad.

Soon after six o'clock the same evening, I preached to the English congregation; and afterwards met the classes, a service which occupied me till ten o'clock; the officers of the regiment having kindly granted permission to the men to remain out of their quarters till that hour, if necessary. In this meeting I was greatly encouraged by finding reason to believe, that my visit and ministrations among them had not been in vain. As during my stay, so also at parting from them, I received every demonstration of affection and regard.

I had intended to proceed from Trichinopoly, through Salem, to Mysore and Seringapatam, and to return to Madras by way of Bangalore; but, receiving letters from Mr. Lynch at Madras, desiring me on many accounts to hasten my return thither, I was induced to relinquish my intention, and to choose a nearer route.

On Thursday, the 14th of August, I quitted Trichinopoly, and travelled through a beautiful country. Nearly the whole, with the exception of the roads and hedges, was under water, from the swelling of the river Cauvery; which occasions an annual irrigation as valuable and necessary to that part of India, as the overflowing of the Nile is to Egypt. The bright green of the newly-sprung *paddy*, or rice, just rising above the surface of the water, was refreshing to look upon; the air was in some measure cooled by the universal irrigation; and clumps of trees, of a dark green foliage, sheltering the cottages of the cultivators, studded the country at intervals, as far as the eye could reach. In such scenery, and at such a season, the providential goodness of God is mightily displayed; but the people who enjoy its blessings do not in general know the Author of them, but attribute the whole to the river, or to the idols, the objects of their worship.

I rested in the middle of the day at Kowiladi; and in the evening, resuming my journey, travelled towards Comboconum, nearly fifty miles on the road from Trichinopoly to Madras; and was there received with brotherly affection by the Rev. Mr. Barenbruck, of the Church Missionary Society.

I had there, also, the pleasure to meet J. Cotton, Esq., of Negapatam, on an official tour through his district, who, with his usual kindness, offered me his tent whilst I remained at Comboconum; as Mr. Barenbruck had not sufficient room even for his own family, in the small bungalow he was then occupying as a temporary residence.

On Sunday, Mr. Barenbruck's house was well filled with the native congregation; a considerable part of it was composed of the young men of the Christian native seminary under his care, whose appearance and order did much credit both to themselves and their instructor.

The following day the young men were catechised on the sermons they had heard; and were able to give a good account both of that delivered by myself in the morning, and of that by Mr. Barenbruck in the evening.

In my walks with this clergyman, through the streets and neighbourhood of this large town, I could not but observe, that his character appeared well known to its inhabitants. We met with many Heathens, who were quite willing to hear and to converse on the subject of religion. I had not hitherto seen so entirely respectable a native population, or one among whom there seemed less bigotry, notwithstanding the large proportion of Brahmans.

There are in Comboconum several temples, and an old palace, well worth notice; but the object which most strikingly illustrates the superstitions of the people, is a tank or pool, into which they believe that the Ganges miraculously flows once in ten years; though that river is nearly one thousand miles distant.

Many natives visited Mr. Barenbruck during my stay; and I never saw him omit the opportunity of conversing with them about their spiritual interests: it was evident that his object was well understood, and his character generally respected.

On the evening of Tuesday, the 19th, Mr. and Mrs. Barenbruck accompanied me a short distance in their *bandy*, or gig, and then returned, whilst I continued my journey. I and my bearers were soon under the necessity of seeking shelter, for a few hours, from a heavy fall of rain, accompanied by lightning and thunder. We travelled about twenty-four miles in the course of the night; and about seven o'clock on Wednesday morning, arrived at the large town of Myaveram.

I immediately walked down to the bank of the river, which was crowded by natives washing themselves and their clothes in the Cauvery, or performing their morning ceremonies under the porches and on the steps leading down to the water: some of them seemed to regard me with proud contempt, and others with some degree of curiosity.

I was naturally led to speak to them on the subject of purification; I admitted that the waters of the Cauvery would cleanse their bodies, but questioned their efficacy as it regarded the soul, which they profess to believe is also purified by daily washing in this river; and endeavoured to turn their attention to the "fountain which is opened in the house of David for sin and uncleanness," as the only means of cleansing from sin, and communicating that "holiness without which no man can see the Lord."

Whilst I enlarged on this subject, one man interrupted me by saying, that the eternal happiness or misery of the soul was entirely determined by the destiny written on the forehead by the finger of God. I begged him to beware of attributing an arbitrary partiality to the holy and just God; and endeavoured to illustrate the undistinguishing regard of God to the whole human race, by the love of a father to his children, who, without excepting any, wishes equally the happiness of all. To this he objected, that God was like many fathers, who were fond of one or two of their children, and cared not what became of the rest: on this he laid much stress, and seemed to think he had the better argument. I asked him if he was himself a father. He said he was not. "But," said I, looking on the crowd around me, "there are many fathers here; I appeal to them whether what you say does not sound like folly; I am sure there is not one who does not wish the welfare of all his children." This doctrine of God's universal love appeared to be heard with pleasure by all except the disputant, who was obliged to content himself by quoting several Sanscrit verses to prove what he had advanced. I then told them, I had some books on the subject of the religion I recommended to their acceptance, which I would give to any who desired; but though many had heard with much curiosity and attention, none seemed desirous of tracts.

I returned to my palankeen to breakfast, and was soon followed by a man who wished me to give him, or recommend him to, some lucrative situation. I advised him to seek the favour and blessing of God, as being of the first importance; and assured him, that if he secured them, he should not want for any good thing. He replied, "I cannot see God, nor do I know him; you I know, and to you I look." This was intended for flattery; but it contained an awful truth, and discovered a deplorable state of mind.

After breakfast, I went to a *mandabam*, in the main street, leading down to the river: it was a platform of stone raised about five feet from the ground, having no walls, but a number of stone pillars supporting the roof, on which was erected a small tower adorned with images.

Intending to remain here for the day, I began to converse with an individual who stood near. Several persons passing and re-passing stopped to hear our conversation, till, at length, a large congregation was assembled. I then took the opportunity to address them all on the concerns of their souls and eternity; and concluded by recommending to their acceptance and attentive perusal some tracts which I held in my hand; but they seemed afraid, and would not touch the books till an old devotee coming up, ridiculed their fear, and took one of the tracts into his hand; but, through age, could with difficulty see to read it.

Sitting down on the ground, in the native fashion, I entered into conversation with this man, whilst the rest of the people listened attentively. He appeared to have no sense of piety, nor even a fear of God; but to be an infidel as to all religions. From his language I concluded him to be a man of some learning, and of good common sense, who, from the absurdities of the Hindoo system, and his inability to account for the evil and misery existing in the world, on the supposition that it is governed by an almighty, just, and merciful God, had adopted atheistical notions, or, what is nearly allied to atheism, the opinion, that if there is a God of justice, there is another of opposite principles.

I related to him the history of the fall of man, and of the redemption of the world by the Lord Jesus Christ. I desired him to look at the works of creation and of providence, and acknowledge the existence and supremacy of one God who is over all. He replied that it was all in vain; that the truth could not be known; neither would he receive any tracts from me, because he thought they no more contained the truth than did the numerous books he already possessed on the Hindoo system.

The circumstance, however, of his taking a tract into his hand seemed to embolden the surrounding crowd; and I was soon under the necessity of applying to my stock in the bungalow to satisfy their demands. I was thus busily employed till noon, conversing, reading aloud, and distributing tracts; and became so much the object of attention, that I could with difficulty get time to eat. After dinner, I was similarly engaged till I set out on my journey: the clamour and press for tracts then became so great, that my bearers were quite angry, and, pushing rudely through the crowd, rushed with the palankeen into the river, and carried me to the other side. Several persons forded the river after us to obtain a tract, like their more successful neighbours, and ran alongside my palankeen, till, at length, I gave away every tract I had access to without unpacking my luggage. Of the numbers who this day conversed with me, or listened, and received tracts, a great proportion were Brahmans, or men of other high castes.

The following day I arrived at Sheeally, and took shelter from the sun in a bungalow kept by a native, who introduced himself to me as a Christian, and seemed to pride himself in the name, but refused an invitation to join me, in the evening, in reading the Scriptures and prayer in Tamul, saying, that he was a

Roman Catholic. Though called by the name of Christ, he did not appear either to have, or to desire, even the "form of godliness."

At night I continued my journey, and, travelling about forty miles, reached Cuddalore, where I was kindly welcomed by Mrs. Sim and family.

Being requested to preach on Sunday at Cuddalore, both in English and in Tamul, I determined to remain for that purpose.

On Saturday morning, I visited the school for the children of the European pensioners residing there, supported by their own voluntary subscriptions: it contained few children, but appeared to be conducted in an orderly manner. At the house of one of the pensioners with whom I breakfasted, I found a considerable number of maimed, and halt, and blind native men and women, waiting for their weekly dole of rice and money. I called on them to look to their heavenly Benefactor for the "bread which endureth to everlasting life." Some of them seemed stupidly indifferent to the importance of what was spoken, others gave the most serious attention. On such occasions, I endeavour to give a clear view of the plan of salvation, to call sinners to repentance, and direct penitents to faith in the Lord Jesus Christ. It is seldom that I have had heathen women among my out-door hearers, except when the congregation has been of this description, as it would be deemed indecorous for females, married or unmarried, to stand in the streets or roads listening to a stranger. There is, therefore, little opportunity of trying whether they would be more readily convinced of the truth than the men; and though I have known some instances to the contrary, I have generally observed, that they make little difficulty of professing Christianity, if their husbands embrace it.

In the evening the lady of the house assembled her

servants, who were chiefly Christians; and herself, another lady, and two English officers, made part of the company, whilst I read, expounded, and prayed in Tamul.

Captain K., one of the officers, expressed himself as agreeably surprised at the easy flow of words and sound so obvious in the Tamul translation of the New Testament, which he had never before heard read. He told me he should be very glad if I would see his head servant, a most honest, trust-worthy man, and, as he thought, a real Christian, whose zeal in conversing with his countrymen on religious subjects was very remarkable, and, he thought, had been successful: he was sure he would be glad to see a Missionary, and that he would send for him.

When the man came to me, I was happy to recognise in him a member of our native society in Royapettah, who, though, by his engagements with his master, he had been many months absent from the public means of grace, had not lost his piety or zeal. One fact relating to him when he lived in Madras will serve to illustrate his character, and at the same time exhibit some peculiarities of the natives.

My colleague, Mr. Lynch, had heard that this man had been beating his wife; and sent for them both, that he might ascertain the fact, and afford them suitable admonition. He inquired from the man, "Is it true that you have been beating your wife?" "Yes, Sir." "What was your reason for doing so?" "Why, Sir, you know that my business requires me to be at my master's house by six o'clock in the morning; and as the distance is four miles, I must set out from my own house at five o'clock. If, then, I must read and pray with my family before I go, it is necessary for me to rise at four o'clock; which I do, and awake my wife also, that she may join me in my devotions. But whilst I read and pray, she falls asleep again: and for this I have beaten her." Mr. Lynch inquired from the woman if all this were true; she replied, "Yes, Sir." "And do you think your husband did right to beat you for sleeping during prayer?" "Yes, Sir." Mr. Lynch commended the man's practice of family worship; but, of course, advised him not to treat his wife so severely.

On Sunday morning I preached in the church of Cuddalore, first to the Tamul congregation, which was very small and irregular, and then to an English congregation, composed of almost all the residents of the place. One of the gentlemen said, he had not heard the Gospel for many years before that day. At night I again assembled the natives of Mrs. Sim's household, for Tamul reading and prayer. I have often wished that wherever a Missionary visited or lodged, arrangements, as in this instance, might be made for the native servants also to hear the message he would gladly deliver to them.

Before quitting Cuddalore, I will relate a circumstance in its history which connects it with the name of one of the most remarkable potentates in Europe.

In June, 1783, a vigorous attack was made by the French, under M. Bussey, on the English army, which, under General Stewart, had taken up a position to the south of Cuddalore. Not a single advantage was gained over the English, and the French sustained a heavy loss. An incident connected with this attack, and which, in addition to the interest derived from its romantic character, merits notice from the historical reputation of one of the parties, is thus related by Colonel Wilks:—

"Among the wounded prisoners was a young French Serjeant, who so particularly attracted the notice of Colonel Wangenheim, Commandant of the Hanoverian troops in the English service, by his interesting appearance and manners, that he ordered the young man to be conveyed to his own tents; where he was treated with attention and kindness until his recovery and release. Many years afterwards, when the French army, under Bernadotte, entered Hanover, General Wangenheim, among others, attended the levee of the conqueror. 'You have served a great deal,' said Bernadotte, on his being presented; 'and, as I understand, in India.' 'I have served there.' 'At Cuddalore?' 'I was there.' 'Have you any recollection of a wounded Serjeant whom you took under your protection, in the course of that service?' The circumstance was not immediately present to the General's mind; but on recollection he resumed: 'I do, indeed, remember the circumstance; and a very fine young man he was. I have entirely lost sight of him ever since: but it would give me pleasure to hear of his welfare.' 'That young Serjeant,' said Bernadotte, 'was the person who has now the honour to address you; who is happy in this public opportunity of acknowledging the obligation, and will omit no means within his power of testifying his gratitude to General Wangenheim.'" The Serjeant had become one of the most distinguished Generals of France. It is almost unnecessary to remind the reader, that he subsequently attained the exercise of sovereign power in Sweden.

The moon shone brightly at two o'clock in the morning, when I set out on my journey, and the air had been made deliciously cool by a thunder-storm during the night. At six o'clock I reached Pondicherry; and, hearing that high mass was to be celebrated in the French church at seven, curiosity induced me to go, as I had never before witnessed it. It was the festival of St. Louis: the servants of the French Government were required to attend; the church was therefore well filled. The service was conducted by a noble-looking French

Priest, who wore a long beard. When the host was elevated, I looked round the assembly, and seeing that every individual except myself was in a posture of worship, either kneeling or standing, I concluded that I was the only Protestant present. The whole service was imposing in its character. But of what avail are good singing, the ringing of bells, changing of posture, and splendid garments, where there is nothing to inform the understanding, or to engage the heart? It concluded by both Priest and people three times exclaiming, *Vive le Roi!*

On returning to the house where I was entertained, I found some natives waiting to speak with me; to whom I presented tracts, and desired them to meet me in the afternoon.

I dined with a large and mixed party of different nations. English, French, Portuguese, Tamul, and, I think, Hindostanee also, were spoken at the table; but the number of languages did not much assist us in communicating with each other. However, it did not appear that those parts of the conversation not understood were any great loss: the intermixture of French and Hindoo blood does not seem to have formed a graver character, than that usually attributed to our continental neighbours.

In my own room I met a small company of natives, who attentively heard the word of God, and thankfully united in drawing near to a throne of grace. Captain K.'s servant was one of them. When another, who resided in Pondicherry, complained of the want of opportunities for Christian instruction and edification, no Protestant Missionary or Teacher residing in that place, he replied with his usual energy, "What can you expect here?" *Ithu Babylon, allava?* "This is Babylon, is it not?"

Having heard from Madras that my return was not immediately necessary, I thought I could not be more usefully employed than in traversing other parts of this extensive and populous country, to converse with the people at all opportunities, and scatter among them the Gospel and tracts in Tamul which still remained of the large supply I had carried with me when I set out. Altering my course, therefore, I proceeded in a north-western direction towards Wallajahbad.

We left Pondicherry at three o'clock in the morning of Tuesday, the 26th of August; and, missing our way, travelled eight hours and a half before we reached the small town of Permacoil, about twenty miles from Pondicherry; where, though much tired, I had an opportunity of pursuing the object of my journey by conversation, and distribution of tracts.

In the afternoon we proceeded a few miles further to Matrantam Sheoor, a small village, where we had hoped to find shelter for the night, my bearers being too much tired to go on to Atcharawauk, the regular stage. We found, however, no choultry, but a mud-built shed, with a thatched roof, so low, that it would not even admit the palankeen. Whilst at a loss where to find shelter from the rain, which now threatened to fall in torrents, a kind old Heathen offered to admit my palankeen into his house, though he could not allow me to sleep there, and to accommodate me with a board in the choultry, on which I might spread my mattress, and rest till morning.

I walked into his house, and found several women employed in spinning a coarse description of cotton, and another winding the yarn off the cop into hank. He told me that they received raw cotton from their employer, a native manufacturer, and returned it in hank, their delivering the whole being ascertained by the weight. Out of one *vis* (about three pounds) of cotton, they spin sixteen hanks, and receive for their labour eight *fanams*, about fourteen-pence, English money. One woman spins only one to one and a half hank per day; and consequently earns one penny, or a fraction more, as her daily wages. I did not ascertain the length of their hanks; but as the yarn appeared to me to be about the fineness of No. 6 English yarn, and they spun sixteen hanks from three pounds of cotton, I should suppose their hanks to be about the same length as our own,—eight hundred and forty yards. Of course, there is, in the south of India, much finer spinning than that now described; but I never found so favourable an opportunity of inspection as in the instance now referred to. The instruments they used for cleansing, loosening, and spinning the cotton, are remarkable for their ingenuity and simplicity. A wish to gratify my friends at home with a sight of what differs so entirely from their complicated and scientific machinery for the same operations, induced me afterwards to procure and bring home specimens of them, which are now deposited with my friends at Manchester, where they have been seen and admired by some of the most eminent spinners of the day. Drawings of these machines have been executed by a much-respected artist and fellow-townsman; from which accurate sketches have been taken, and, with a description, are presented to the reader on a subsequent page.

I tried to explain to my native host and this family of female spinners the superior method by which the same kind of work was done in my own country. The women expressed great astonishment at hearing of so many spindles turned by the same power, but the man seemed to understand; he, however, in his turn, was much surprised at learning, that the cotton to be spun was not held in the hand, but supplied also by machinery.

He returned with me to the place I was to occupy for

the night, and remained in conversation with me for several hours. An inquiry from me whether he could read, elicited a reply in the negative, and an explanation of the cause which very considerably interested me. He said that his parents had sent him to school, and would have given him an education; but the troops of Hyder Ali scouring the country, had driven the whole family, consisting of forty or fifty persons, from their home. They fled to Sheeally, where they all died of disease or famine, except himself and three other young people; and consequently he had had to struggle with many disadvantages in early life. To show me, however, his regard for learning, he called his eldest son, who had just come in from following the plough; the *Barada Purana*, written on olas, was sent for, and I listened to his reading for about half an hour. In return, I took out my Tamul New Testament and tracts, and for some time read and explained to them. He had already begged me to allow him to prepare supper for me. About nine o'clock it appeared. There was a large quantity of boiled rice, in a brasen dish; two kinds of curries, on separate leaves; in another leaf, stitched into the form of a cup, was *ghee*, or clarified butter; and in a brasen pot was *mulugu tanni*, a hot vegetable soup, made chiefly from pepper and capsicums. A number of leaves (I think, of the banyan-tree) stitched together, formed a plate such as the natives of all classes eat from, never using the same more than once.

I thrust my hand into the rice in native fashion, and put some handfuls on my plate of leaves. My host stood near, with the *mulugu tanni* in his hand, which he poured out at intervals, and the *ghee* also, to moisten the rice to my taste; and recommended me to try first one curry and then the other, with a politeness most pleasing, as being quite natural and unaffected. He was amused by my want of expertness in eating with my fingers; but appeared highly gratified that I ate with confidence, and made a hearty meal. After some further conversation, he retired, and I slept soundly in the open shed, without the least fear or alarm.

The subjoined wood-engravings are executed from correct drawings of the complete set of Hindoo cotton-spinning machinery, which I procured at Madras, and brought over to England, as mentioned in page 248.

No. I. is a cotton-cleanser, or gin, consisting of two rollers of teak-wood, through which the cotton is

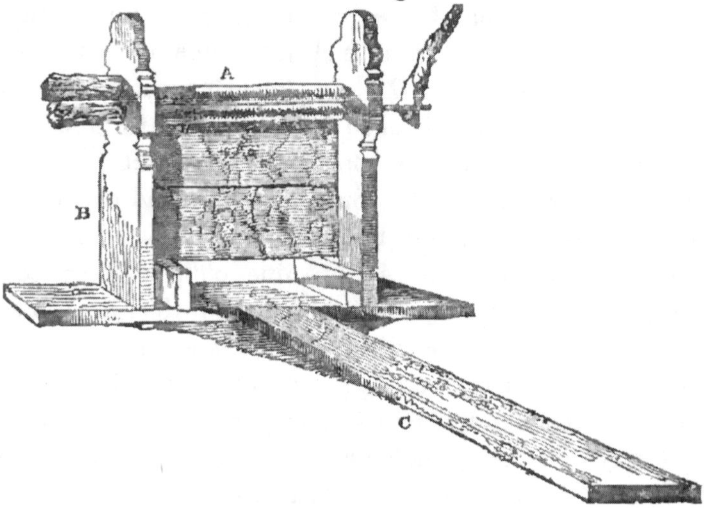

NO. I. COTTON-CLEANSER.

passed, in order to cleanse it from the seeds, and make it fit for use.

No. II. is a cotton-bow; and has a great resemblance to the hatter's-bow, used for bowing wool in our own country. The cotton being spread underneath this machine, the string, which derives elasticity from a complicated arrangement of strings on the frame of the bow, is struck with a heavy mallet of wood, causing it to vibrate strongly amongst the cotton, which is thus reduced to a loose, fleecy state: and this simple operation serves the purpose of that of carding in England.

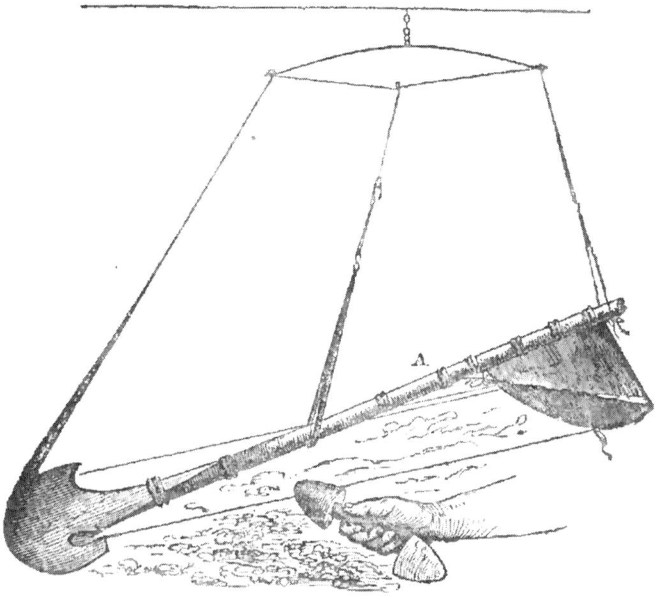

NO. II. COTTON-BOW.

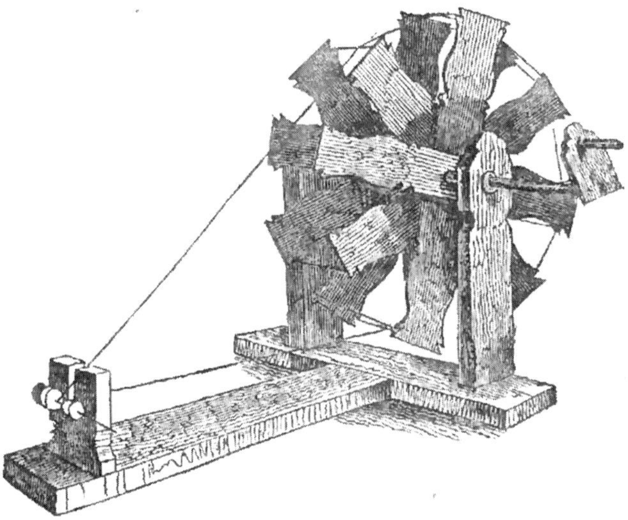

NO. III. SPINNING-WHEEL.

No. III. is the spinning-wheel. The wheel itself is composed of two sides, formed of cross pieces, connected at the extremities by strings, to serve in lieu of a circular frame; so that it is, in fact, an octagonal wheel. This machine is of teak-wood, extremely heavy, and strong in proportion to its size. The spindle, which is very small, is fed by the hand with the cotton prepared by the bow, No. II.*

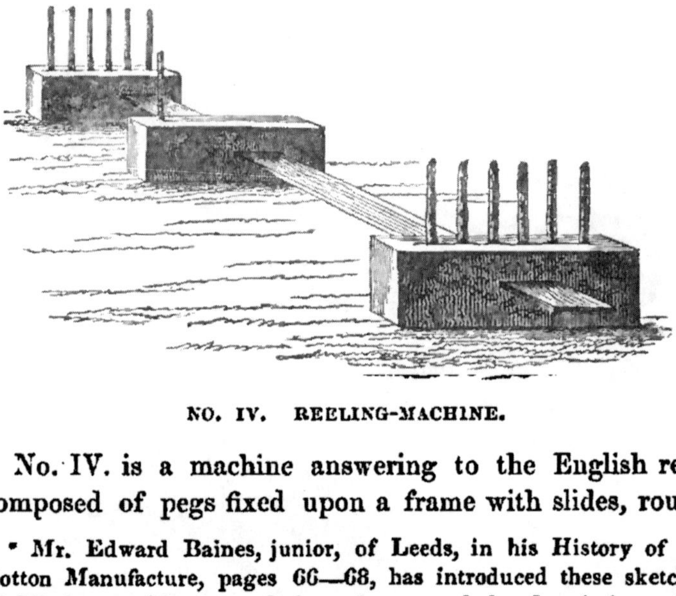

NO. IV. REELING-MACHINE.

No. IV. is a machine answering to the English reel, composed of pegs fixed upon a frame with slides, round

* Mr. Edward Baines, junior, of Leeds, in his History of the Cotton Manufacture, pages 66—68, has introduced these sketches of Hindoo machinery, and the substance of the description, without any acknowledgment that he found them in the first edition of my "Personal Narrative." For the correct sketches thus appropriated, I was indebted to my early friend and school-fellow, Michael P. Calvert, Esq., the talented artist, of Manchester. The description was written by my brother, Mr. Holland Hoole, of Manchester, with whom I deposited the machinery, and some beautiful specimens of Hindoo manufacture, at the mills of Messrs. Philips and Lee, in Salford. Mr. Baines acknowledges his obligations to many persons for assistance in the compilation of his book; but omits to mention from what quarter he obtained the information and sketches, here described, which strike every reader as most curious and original.

which pegs the cotton yarn is formed into hanks. I am unable to explain the precise mode of using this machine; but am informed, by very good authority, that in Russia linen yarn is reeled upon a similar principle, but the pegs are fixed in the wall.

The cost of the whole of this complete set of machinery for spinning cotton, was about thirty-five shillings sterling.*

It may well excite our surprise, that, with such rude machines, and from cotton of a peculiarly short staple, the Hindoos should be able to produce the fine yarns required for the manufacture of the Arnee muslins. But such is the fact; and it affords proof of their extraordinary skilfulness, and patient application, in those pursuits to which they have been trained from their childhood, and which they have inherited from their forefathers.

The scheme of introducing British cotton-spinning machinery into India will, I think, be attended with many difficulties. The habits of the Hindoos must undergo a mighty change, before they will submit to the

* A literal copy of the invoice of these articles, in the imperfect English of the native broker whom I employed to purchase them, may amuse the reader:—

Rev. E. Owl, Dr.

One Cotton Cleanzer	Rs.	5	4	0
One Wheel Gig		3	8	0
One Worldy Gig		1	12	0
One Cotton Bow		7	0	0
Two Iron things and four Lather things ...		0	12	0
Cooly hire for Do. office to your Geordon-house		0	2	6
Three Gony-bags, ℘ Packing		0	8	8
	Rs.	18	15	2

Madras, Contents Receved,

8th Feb. 1828. P. Condapah.

confinement and regular labour of a cotton-mill. And, on the Coromandel coast at least, it may well be doubted whether the machinery itself can be kept in working condition, on account of the extreme moisture of the atmosphere, which rusts and corrodes every thing made of iron to such a degree, that it is likely the cotton will adhere to the rollers, &c., and the work be spoiled. It is probable, however, that many improvements may be effected in different branches of the native manufactures, in the course of years, by the gradual and judicious application of machinery. This may also greatly assist Missionary objects, if the converted Hindoos should be able to find employment in the establishments of Europeans, so as to avert the ruin which now generally would result in their temporal affairs, on their embracing Christianity, and the prospect of which at present deters multitudes of them from obeying the convictions of their judgment and conscience.

27th.—A journey of five hours brought us to Atcharawauk about nine o'clock. The burning sun did not permit me to venture out, so I conversed with only a few individuals, and distributed some tracts.

Early in the afternoon we proceeded to Carangooly, a large and neat village. It was *tiru-nál*, or "holy-day;" the inhabitants were carrying an idol in procession, and the streets were thronged with holiday-people. Having determined to remain for the night in the choultry, I began to converse with one of the first persons I met; but he could not or would not stay to hear much. Another was more patient and attentive, and I was soon surrounded by a great number of people. I endeavoured to declare to them the love of God in giving his Son for the redemption of mankind, and to make them feel it their duty to consider and return that love. Their attention seemed fixed, and I continued to improve the opportunity by reading and commenting on a tract. It then grew dark, and I wished to dismiss them from the front of the choultry, where they had crowded together. I distributed all the tracts I had in my palankeen, and had to assure them I had no more at hand, before they would go away. Still many of them waited, whilst I took tea, and unpacked a box to obtain more tracts. The news, too, seemed to have spread; for the people flocked together, and kept me fully employed in answering their questions, directing their attention to the truths of Christianity, and distributing tracts, which were very eagerly received, till past ten o'clock; and even after I had laid down to sleep, several persons came, begging to be excused for disturbing me; but they had only now heard of me at some distance, and had come wishing to receive tracts, and to hear what I had to say.

28th.—We travelled about sixteen miles further, to Sallawauk, another large village, having on the road passed several places of the same character. I took up my abode for the day in the vestibule of a heathen temple, which contained some tolerable sculptures, but seemed partially deserted. I had soon a number of visitors, sent, I suppose, by my bearers, who had now some notion of my object in travelling, and took a pleasure in seeing me employed. They sat down at a short distance during my breakfast, and diligently read, and talked over, the Tamul and Teloogoo tracts I handed to them, returning them as they perused them, and requesting others larger, and more comprehensive, on the same subjects.

One of these people desired to be allowed to prepare dinner for me: he did so, and showed himself an excellent cook, and would receive no money for his trouble; he only begged copies of the tracts he had read; I added a few others, and he appeared quite delighted, saying, he had never before heard the doctrines of Christianity. Many others were anxious to learn all they could, and begged for such books as would best teach them the right way.

The willingness of the people of that place, and of some others, through which I had passed the preceding days, to hear the Gospel, and to receive the books I had for distribution, surpassed my expectations; and was some compensation for the disappointment I had felt in being recalled from Trichinopoly, instead of proceeding thence through Salem to Seringapatam and Bangalore, and other parts where a visit was expected.

The following day I arrived at Wallajahbad, and took up my quarters as on a former visit; the pious soldiers were rejoiced to see me, and the officers of the regiment showed me considerable kindness and attention.

My engagements, for a few days, were frequent and laborious, but exactly such as accorded with the character and pursuits of a Missionary.

On Friday, the 29th, I conducted two services, one in Tamul, the other in English. On Saturday morning I was engaged some time in solemnizing marriages and baptisms; one of the persons baptized was an English invalid, advanced in life, the son of Baptist parents, who had not presented him for that ordinance in his infancy. In the after-part of the day, I had another Tamul service, and in the evening again assembled with the soldiers for prayer.

On Sunday, before sunrise, the regiment was marched to the Fives Court, which, being enclosed with walls, made it easier to speak and hear than on the open parade-ground, as well as affording some shelter from the rays of the sun, which are hot from the moment of its rise. The place was rather a strange substitute for a chapel; but both officers and men stood with great attention whilst I read prayers, and delivered a sermon.

In the forenoon I was engaged two hours in meeting the class of about thirty members. At four in the afternoon, I again addressed the native congregation, and was glad to observe indications of some impression having been made on their minds; and at night preached in the mess-room, kindly lent by the officers, for the purpose, to a congregation of three times the number that could have been accommodated in the room we had hitherto occupied. Several officers attended this service, and one, who seemed not to have forgotten the good lessons taught him at his then distant home, partook with us, after the public service, of the sacred memorials of the death and passion of our Lord.

On the succeeding Monday and Tuesday, the 1st and 2nd of September, I was similarly employed as on the preceding days. There were several baptisms: I preached a few times more to the English and Tamul congregations; and had some opportunities of serious conversation with several of the officers and their families. When I mentioned my intention of soon returning home to Madras, one lady exclaimed, "Have you indeed a home? I have heard of you in all parts of the country, and thought you were always employed in travelling about." I was surprised that she had thought me so entirely a wanderer; for she and her husband had requested me to baptize their infant child.

I quitted Wallajahbad about midnight, and when I awoke, at day-break, the following morning, found myself in the neighbourhood of the great temple of Conjeveram: a Brahman soon appeared, and offered his services to show me the whole establishment. I was first conducted to a *Mandabam*, a sort of porch opposite the entrance to the temple, but at some distance from it: this was a new erection not quite finished, and entirely of stone; said to have cost fifteen thousand pagodas, or upwards of £5000 sterling. It consisted simply of pillars supporting a square roof, surmounted with characteristic devices. Each pillar is of one stone, about twenty feet in height, and two feet square, sculptured on every side with Hindoo gods and goddesses: the bare indecency of many of these sculptures proves, that notwithstanding English influence and the general diffusion of a small degree of Christian light, the Hindoos are unchanged in their moral and religious character, and will remain so even under their increasing advantages, till they entirely cast off their own abominable system, and embrace the pure precepts and doctrines of the Gospel. The temple is large, and of similar construction to other Hindoo temples of like magnitude. It has an outer and inner wall of great height, on which, at irregular distances, are erected pyramidal towers, several stories high. The extensive prospect to be seen from the top of the highest tower, is a sufficient reward for the fatigue of the ascent. Within the walls are shrines for the different objects of worship, and shelter for thousands of people: there is also a large tank, with stone steps on every side, down to the bottom. Much of admirable workmanship and skill is displayed in the architecture and sculpture of its various parts: a particular examination of the whole establishment would be the work of many days.

On returning from the temple, I was accompanied by a considerable number of Brahmans to the place where I intended to pass the day. I drew out some tracts, and entered on my usual topic, the necessity of the atoning sacrifice of Christ to reconcile man to God, and to give a title to heaven: some were attentive, but most of them did not seem to like the subject; and, on the whole, did not form a promising congregation. After breakfast, I recommenced reading and speaking, and continued till a native reader belonging to the Church Mission in Madras, visiting the schools in this neighbourhood, came up and afforded me very seasonable relief; he also read and spoke a considerable time. I distributed many tracts; and, as at several other places, found it necessary to deny the importunity of some who were not content with one or two, but desired a specimen of each sort in my possession.

In a dispute with one Brahman, I was asked, "Is God a Spirit? How then did he create matter? Is the soul God, or something distinct from God? Is the soul immortal? Then it is eternal; for what has no end can have had no beginning; but if the soul is created, it must have had a beginning, and is therefore perishable." Many of them delight to speculate and converse on such subjects, rather than to have their sinful and dangerous condition pointed out to them, and the will of God concerning them stated and enforced.

Intending to visit Vellore, I proceeded from Conjeveram to Cauverypauk, about seventeen miles, where I passed the middle of the day; but, though I went out into the streets, found little even of curiosity among the people of that town to hear what an European stranger had to say on the subject of religion. In the evening, a journey of about ten miles brought me to the large town and cantonment of Arcot, where I was kindly received by the Chaplain, as on my former visit.

On the evening of the 5th, I had a small, but attentive, Tamul congregation, consisting chiefly of persons professing Christianity. I am not aware that any Missionary was ever stationed at Arcot, though the place and its neighbourhood are very populous; and less has been attempted there among the natives than in any quarter offering equal advantages.

The following day I proceeded to Vellore, where I was hospitably entertained during my stay by Commissary Penn. Within the Fort of Vellore is a large Hindoo temple, containing specimens of native device and sculpture, as admirable as those of any I ever visited: it is now entirely out of use as a temple, and occupied as an arsenal by the British.

Vellore has long been visited by the Missionaries of the Society for promoting Christian Knowledge, residing at Madras. I found the Rev. Mr. Falke, of that Mission, diligently labouring in a large and well-conducted school: he seemed to have met with some discouragements during his visit, which he had protracted to several weeks. He had been told on the one hand, that he had nothing to do with the English inhabitants, and on the other, had been warned against public preaching and conversation among the natives; but his diligent zeal had found means and opportunities of attempting to benefit the inhabitants of all classes. On Sunday, the 7th, I heard him read prayers and preach in English, and remained, with considerable part of the congregation, at the celebration of the Lord's supper. In the after-part of the day I had attentive congregations, both English and Tamul.

On Monday I returned to Arcot; and, in the evening, preached in a private house to the same congregation as before. On the evening of Tuesday I again reached Conjeveram, and had many applications for tracts from natives who had seen or heard of those I had distributed the previous week. About eight o'clock at night, I received a polite invitation from A. Maclean, Esq., assistant Collector and Magistrate, and the only European residing in Conjeveram; on whom I had not waited, because I had no acquaintance with him, or letter of introduction. He was surrounded by his assistants and officers, and was diligently discharging his duty as Magistrate; his acquirements in the languages enabling him to do it with ease, and without the assistance of interpreters. I remained with him the following day, and visited the temple of Little Conjeveram, a place of great celebrity among the natives, but containing nothing superior to those temples which I had already seen.

Whilst resting at Amrambaidoo, on the following day, on my way to Madras, I was recognised by a native Brahman, who said he had heard of me from a great distance as distributing tracts, and conversing about religion. I think I was applied to by all in the village who were able to read.

In the evening of Thursday, September 11th, I reached the Mission-house in Royapettah, having travelled about six hundred miles, and been absent nearly ten weeks, during which I had been chiefly engaged in conversing with strangers. In few parts of the world could I have travelled so long with so little annoyance; and though a professed Teacher of a strange religion which I was anxious to propagate, my movements seemed to excite no jealousy among the people. May the bread thus widely cast upon the waters be found after many days!

CHAPTER XIX.

SEPTEMBER, 1823, TO MARCH, 1824.

THREE MONTHS' TOUR TO THE SOUTH AND WEST.

Returned to Madras, I again entered into the regular work of the Station, and found cause for encouragement and perseverance. In the native department especially, an increase was apparent, both in the number of hearers, and in the interest felt by the congregations. At the Tamul service, in Black-Town, on Friday evenings, the doors and windows were usually occupied by Heathens or others who desired to hear the Scriptures read and explained, but did not dare to enter our place of worship, either on account of their own scruples, or because they feared persecution or inconvenience if they identified themselves with us. Some of these were regular in their attendance; and though I never saw them, except on those occasions, I hope the partial knowledge of Christian doctrines and principles which they must thus have acquired, will not have been entirely in vain.

In our labours among the natives, our principal deficiency, at that time, was the aid of an active native Assistant; who might follow up, by conversations and familiar intercourse with the people, the public and stated exertions of the Missionary. Those members of our native society, whose acquirements qualified them to act as Schoolmasters, were already engaged in that capacity; and we could only hope and pray, that the help we required in this important work might in some way or other be raised up for us.

On the 14th of September we were gladdened by the safe arrival of Mr. England, a brother Missionary, sent to our assistance by the Committee in London.

The relief from considerable part of the English work, afforded to me by Mr. England's arrival, gave me an opportunity of commencing the study of the Teloogoo language.

In my late journeys I had found, that a knowledge of that language would have enlarged my sphere of usefulness while travelling. A great part of the population of Madras also use this language; but none of the Missionaries, at that time residing there, had paid any attention to it. Another reason which urged me to the acquisition of Teloogoo, was its similarity, in many respects, to the Cannada language, vernacular in the Mysore country, whither I was directed to proceed by the letters Mr. England brought with him from the Committee; and although it would then have been impracticable for me entirely to quit our native societies and congregations in Madras, for want of a Tamul supply, I did not conceive it improbable that circumstances would, in a short time, favour my proceeding thither, to re-commence our exertions in the neighbourhoods of Bangalore and Seringapatam.

My Teloogoo teacher was a poor Brahman, of the neighbouring village of St. Thomè, whose chief peculiarity seemed to be a thorough and sincere belief of all the absurdities of the Hindoo system. I think he was the only native of tolerable education I ever met with, so blind and entire in his attachment to idolatry and all its concomitant observances. He was generally unwell from bathing every morning in the public tank; because, in his opinion, it was more meritorious to bathe in cold water, and in the open air, than to use warm water within the house, though the latter was permitted in case of indisposition. He was one day taken very ill whilst attending me; but though apprehensive of the cholera morbus, which at that time was raging dreadfully on every hand, his scruples would not permit him to take the specific I offered him; though he knew it had been successful, in other instances, in checking the disorder.

The laxity of the notions of some Hindoos, and the miserable subterfuges with which they quiet their minds on religious subjects, may be illustrated by the following circumstance:—

An old acquaintance of mine, a Brahman Moonshee of the College, came to see me, with one or two others: they found me in the burial-ground, contiguous to the chapel in Royapettah, superintending the opening of a grave. Desirous of improving the opportunity, I adverted to the solemn subject, naturally occurring to our minds from the appearances of the place in which we stood, and pressed on them the importance of ascertaining whether our systems of faith and practice were calculated to promote and secure our happiness in the eternal world. My friend did not seem much at ease whilst I talked on this subject; but replied, that one religion was as good as another; that every man would be right if he could only think so; and illustrated his meaning by kicking a clod just thrown up, and saying, "Let a man believe this earth to be gold, and keep it as such, it will make him as happy as though it were gold in reality." I replied, "Yes; but if he take his clod to the bank, or to the mint, and present it as so much precious metal, he will soon be undeceived as to its value; and exactly thus shall we be brought to trial in the day of judgment, when our eternal destinies shall be fixed. The inquiry then will not be, how we esteemed our different systems, but what both they and we are in the just estimation of the Almighty: and how awful will it be, to continue under delusion till it shall be too late to remedy the evil!"

By frequent conversations of this description, the views and objects of Christian Missionaries become extensively known among the natives; and though the result may not appear in any decided success, the raising of doubt, and excitement of inquiry, are almost necessary consequences, and may be calculated to have their effect on the general mind and feeling of the people.

In November, Mr. Lynch opened a small room in Chintadrypett, (a populous neighbourhood between our house and Black-Town,) erected for the purpose of a school and occasional preaching. I preached several times to attentive companies of natives in this place; but was not able to give it regular attention, in addition to the engagements of equal or greater importance already formed in other quarters.

It being still considered desirable that I should visit our society in Bangalore, and the affectionate people in Mysore and Seringapatam, before Mr. Lynch, who intended returning to Europe, should take his departure, and make it less practicable for me to leave Madras, I prepared for another journey; in the course of which I purposed to visit the hills near Salem, which had recently become the subject of general conversation, as possessing a cool and salubrious atmosphere, and being peopled by a race of different character from that of the surrounding lowland districts.

It was now the middle of what is usually the wet season in Madras; but the rains had this year entirely failed, and the whole country was parched with drought. Rice, the aliment of the natives, had become very dear, and great distress was felt as the consequence in almost every class of the community. But though in other respects unseasonable, the weather was favourable for travelling.

As on all similar occasions, I was liberally supplied with tracts and books in various languages, for gratuitous distribution among the natives, by the active and valuable Bible and Tract Societies existing in Madras. I carried with me on this journey more than one man's load of these publications, being in all several thousand copies.

Early in the morning of Wednesday, the 3d of December, I again left Madras; deeply impressed with a sense of the mercies hitherto vouchsafed to me, and with humble trust for a continuance of them in the journey before me. I felt the necessity of divine influence and blessing to my individual happiness, and to insure successful results to the labours in which I was engaged.

In the forenoon I reached Poonamallee, about thirteen miles from Madras, where there is a Fort and cantonment, and a large native village; there is also a small village of pensioners from the British army, who have retired here with their families to end their days in peace. Some of these had expressed a wish that we should come and preach to them. They assembled soon after my arrival in the humble cottage of one of their number, when I took the opportunity of speaking to them individually on their spiritual concerns, and of leading their addresses to the throne of grace. Many of them shed tears whilst they recounted their long-continued course of ignorance and sin, and spoke of the greatness of that mercy which had called them at the eleventh hour. I rejoiced at the grace of God manifested in the change that had taken place in them; and, drawing out a class-paper, took down their names as members of society on trial, with a confidence, which the event has proved well founded, that this would be the beginning of a good work in that place.

From this time they had a claim on our attention as Missionaries, which has invariably been paid to them. Several who were present on that occasion have since exchanged worlds, in the enjoyment of the assurance and consolations inspired by a belief of the truth; and their places have been more than filled up by others who have joined themselves to those who remained. We have now in Poonamallee a very neat bungalow, which is used as a chapel and school-room; and at one end has a separate room, which accommodates an English pensioner and his family, who acts as Schoolmaster, and takes care of the premises.

At that time, however, we had not a foot of ground in Poonamallee; but obtained for our services in the evening the use of the native church, a thatched building of mud, erected for the accommodation of the Christian natives, by the Rev. James Hough, a pious and zealous Chaplain, formerly resident in Poonamallee, who is now the perpetual Curate of Ham, the diligent author of the "History of Christianity in India." The place was crowded by a mixed company of Europeans and natives. The latter waited patiently till I had dismissed the English part of the congregation, and I then exhorted and prayed with them in their own language. The good influence resting on the whole assembly was indicated by their seriousness and attention from first to last.

Towards midnight I left Poonamallee, and proceeded about eighteen miles further, to Tripassoor, where I arrived in the morning of the 4th. This is also a station for the residence of European pensioners, who occupy several lines of buildings within the Fort, now in ruins. Fishing seems to be the favourite occupation of the pensioners residing here, the immense tanks and lakes of the surrounding country affording plenty of fish. The exposure incurred in this pursuit has given to many of the men an extraordinarily ruddy complexion, not confined to the face only, and seeming to justify the appellation of "red men," which the natives in some places give to Europeans. I was met by three of them some miles before I reached Tripassoor, so anxious were they to show how much they valued the visit of a Christian Minister. The round bungalow, erected on a bastion of the Fort, for the accommodation of travellers, being occupied by some who arrived before me, I took shelter for the day in a choultry at a short distance, in the coolest part of which the thermometer rose to 90°. In the evening I preached in the school-room, which was well filled. After baptizing a child, and dismissing the English congregation, I addressed in Tamul the few natives who had assembled; and afterwards went to the house of one of the pensioners, to converse individually with such as wished to become decidedly religious.

I then entered my palankeen, and travelled towards Wallajahbad, which is nearly forty miles distant from Tripassoor. The sun was hot the next day before we reached Chellampatri Cotoor, a Teloogoo Romanist village. In the first place which I entered, to seek shelter from the heat, I was welcomed by some hundreds of fleas, which covered my legs in an instant, and would soon have covered me entirely, had I not hastened away. I was kindly conducted by the inhabitants to a verandah in the church-yard, where I soon became an object of curiosity and attention, and passed a pleasant and, I trust, an useful day.

The Schoolmaster, a Romanist Brahman, and many other sensible and inquiring men, conversed very freely on religious subjects; and gave me an opportunity of speaking plainly and closely, of recommending to them the pure Gospel, and pointing out the folly and danger of trusting in any thing for pardon and salvation, besides the blood of Christ our Saviour. The Brahman thankfully received a copy of the Gospels and Acts in Teloogoo; to others I presented tracts.

On the morning of Saturday, the 6th, I arrived at Wallajahbad, where the forenoon was occupied in waiting on the families with whom I had been acquainted at previous visits; in the afternoon I looked at a piece of ground which we thought eligible for the site of a chapel and school-room; in the evening I preached with much liberty to a crowded congregation.

On Sunday, from half-past six till eight, I was employed in meeting part of the class; at ten, I attended divine service, conducted by the Chaplain, the Rev. Mr. Boys; at one P.M. I met the remainder of the class; most of the members of it were happy in the enjoyment of the privileges connected with clear views of divine mercy, and a personal reception of its blessings; I then addressed a congregation of natives, most of them camp-followers, Protestants, Romanists, and Heathens, altogether about fifty, who attentively heard the Gospel in their own language. I was then just in time to hear the Chaplain's afternoon sermon, which, like that of the forenoon, also contained sound doctrine, and was impressively delivered. After dining with the Chaplain and his excellent lady, I hastened, at seven in the evening, to the meeting-room, which I found crowded inside, and surrounded without at every opening where any thing could be heard, and preached till the sound of drum and trumpet warned the military part of my congregation to attend the roll-call.

After service, as I was speaking to the Leader about erecting a room to serve as a chapel and native school, it was mentioned by a person present, that the Collector would probably give some assistance, by permitting trees to be felled for the roof and other parts of the building; and he added that if no other place could be procured, he would give part of his own garden to erect it upon.

Accordingly, on Monday morning, I went over to Conjeveram, and mentioned to Mr. Maclean the object of my visit. He exceeded my request by recommending a larger and more substantial building than that I had contemplated, and kindly engaged to supply all the material, if we would find labourers. Encouraged by this success, I returned to Wallajahbad, and waited on the Commandant, who immediately offered to give any spot of ground that might be most eligible. The following day I measured the part I had selected, and received a written grant of it to the Mission. I headed a paper for subscriptions, to which about £45 was ultimately subscribed, chiefly by the military officers and men stationed in Wallajahbad. The chapel was soon completed; and, though possessing no furniture besides an excellent pulpit, the gift of a lady in Madras, and a few rude benches, it is useful as a place of worship to the pious Europeans or natives, occasionally forming part of the fluctuating military population of Wallajahbad; and is often occupied by interesting and attentive congregations at the quarterly visits paid to that place by our Missionaries in Madras.

In visiting the hospital, I found an encouraging instance of the benefit resulting from our exertions. A soldier, who lay to all appearance near death, but waiting patiently for his change, in the blessed prospect of eternal life, said that at my first visit to Wallajahbad he was awakened to a sense of his sin and danger, and that at the second visit he found peace to his troubled conscience in receiving the sacrament. Whilst I was engaged with this man, the Surgeon came in, and uncovered the face of a man apparently dying, to whom he called my attention. He was a Romanist, who had before objected to see me; but was now willing. His prejudices seemed to give way to a sense of his spiritual wants whilst I spoke to him; and he made no objections to being prayed with.

On Tuesday afternoon I again met the native congregation, and recommended them to assemble regularly till my return; leaving them a few manuscript Tamul sermons, to assist them in conducting their religious services. During the whole of this visit I received many kind attentions from the inhabitants of Wallajahbad of all classes; and though quite worn out by the active labours required from me, I could not but rejoice in the full opportunities for useful exertion with which I had been favoured.

In the evening of Tuesday, the 9th, I quitted Wallajahbad. We rested in the open road for several hours in the middle of the night; and at ten the next morning we arrived at a small village called Puthucheri, where we took shelter from the sun, in a fine shady grove of tamarind-trees. Here I passed the day in necessary rest, conversing with any natives who came to see me. The chief subject of their conversation was the dearness and scarcity of rice, in consequence of the dryness of the season; a topic of mournful interest to them. For though, in regular seasons, the poorer natives can by their daily labour procure a comfortable sufficiency of food, many of them were now suffering extreme privations; and famine, which for some months after carried off many thousands of them, had now begun to stare them in the face. A tract which was received by one visitant was afterwards found deposited on one of the boxes near; some unexpressed fear had deterred the man from carrying it with him.

On our journey on Thursday morning, we passed through a country beautifully varied by hill and dale.

The jungle of the uncultivated parts was of a rich and bold character, having a considerable proportion of lofty trees interspersed in it; but the whole was equally parched for want of rain; and the crops had perished, except here and there, on a low spot of ground watered from a neighbouring tank or well. I rested for the day at Wandewash, a Fort in ruins, about thirty miles from Wallajahbad. This was formerly a place of great importance, but is now entirely deserted. The bungalow for travellers is built on the walls of the Fort, and commands clear air and an extensive view, and is quite retired. I passed the day in reading and revising some Tamul composition. I set out early in the evening, and distributed several tracts as I passed through the town.

At ten o'clock on the morning of the 12th, I rested in the tamarind grove to the east of the northern hill of the fortress of Ginjee, or, as the natives called it, Tchenjee. During the heat of the day, I had the opportunity of conversing with a few natives. At four P.M. I went into the fort; the walls are several miles in extent, enclosing three high hills, and three or four low ones, all strongly fortified in the Hindoo manner, but entirely deserted. A man, with a sharp pruning-knife in his hand, went before me to clear a path through the jungle, with which this once-busy spot is now almost entirely overgrown: we were not without apprehension of disturbing some serpents in our path. I ascended a kind of tower of eight or ten stories, which I thought of Moorish architecture; and at the highest story was surprised to find a contrivance for a continual supply of water, by earthen pipes, communicating under ground with a reservoir at the top of one of the hills, at a distance of many hundred feet.

After visiting a large building, which my guides called the granary, and another, which they said was the boxing-court, I proposed ascending one of the hills, to see the buildings at the top. My attendants wished me to attempt the southern one; but finding, on inquiry, that a chasm in the rock, over which there was at present no bridge, would interrupt us before we reached the summit, I decided on the northern one, because it appeared most interesting and easiest of ascent. Several persons who had accompanied me thus far, refused to ascend the hill; nor was I astonished at this, when I had made the trial myself: I was obliged to rest three times before I reached the top; and my head bearer, whom I had never known exhausted by the longest march, complained of weariness and aching legs.

The ascent is by steps, partly cut out in granite rock, of which the hill consists, and partly built of the same material. At the top I found temples and choultries, and palaces and granary, all of elegant and durable structure: the stones and rubbish about part of the foundation of one of the temples, had been recently disturbed, probably by some person in search of hidden treasure. There was water in a reservoir which was said to be inexhaustible.

Whilst taking rest, and enjoying the extensive prospect afforded from so elevated a spot, I inquired into the history of the Fort, and had a number of traditions recounted to me, differing much, as might be expected, from the written accounts we have of it. My guide said that it was commenced and completed by one King, in whose family it continued three generations only; that the last of the three, Derasingha Rajah, was besieged by the Nabob of Arcot for some arrears of tribute, when the Fort stood the siege as long as would be required for a tamarind-tree to be raised from the seed, come to perfection, and bear fruit,—a period of not less than twelve years. At that time the Fort was throngly inhabited, and contained twelve thousand houses; but from what I observed, I should suppose there is not a twelfth of that number at present, in all the neighbourhood about Ginjee. The Fort itself is entirely unoccupied, except by innumerable monkeys, of a very bold character, and which bound unmolested from rock to rock.

The side of the hill was so steep, and many of the granite steps so slippery, that before descending, it was necessary to take off my boots, as a precautionary measure; for one slip might have been fatal. It took us half an hour to descend. On my way back I saw a good deal of sculpture, highly finished in the Hindoo style; an immense smoothly-wrought slab of granite, probably intended, like that in the Fort of Chunar, as a seat for the tutelary deity of the place; and a cylindrical roller of the same stone. Many sculptured pillars and blocks were lying near the gate, as though dragged there for the purpose of removal, and seemed to me of the same description as those I have seen in Pondicherry, and which I was told were brought from Ginjee when that place was in the hands of the French.

Though I passed three hours within the walls of Ginjee, I saw but a small part of it; so many days would not more than suffice to examine all that is worthy of attention. It is, however, not very safe to linger about such places; fevers of the worst description are often taken, by breathing the air of undisturbed jungles and uninhabited buildings. I was much tired, and thought myself unwell after my return: I soon retired into my palankeen under the shade of the trees, with my mind filled with solemn reflections, excited by the review of those silent and stupendous monuments of the vanity and instability of human power and greatness. It is scarcely possible that the Christian, contemplating such a scene, should not call to mind the words of Christ, "Heaven and earth shall pass away, but my words shall not pass away;" and, "He that doeth the will of God shall abide for ever."

A large and well-executed oil-painting of the ruins of Ginjee hangs in the staircase of the East India House, in Leadenhall-street.

A run of about four hours, the following morning, brought me, about nine o'clock, to the village of Anantapooram. It had a clean appearance, and the surrounding fields and gardens seemed well cultivated. On my arrival, my attention was attracted by the sound of children repeating their lessons. I soon found my way to the school, and had some conversation with the master and others who came in. The curiosity of the people seemed roused, and they kept me employed the whole day, in reading and speaking to them: many listened attentively to my detail of the main facts and doctrines of the Gospel.

In the course of the forenoon, an old man, with a head and beard of shaggy grey hair, brought me a present of flowers and pomegranates; the latter were of the best I ever tasted. I followed him to his hut, in a garden, whose produce, he said, was the whole subsistence of himself and family, except what he received as alms. I asked why he did not shave; he said, he had a vow upon him, made in sickness, five years ago, to present the sum of five pagodos, (about £1. 15*s*.,) if he recovered, to the temple at Tripetti, which he had not been able to perform, and until he had performed it, it was not lawful for him to shave or dress his hair.* I endeavoured to persuade him, that all the good he had ever received must have proceeded from the one true God, the only proper object of worship, who could not be pleased by any observances which gave his honour to graven images.

I distributed several tracts in this place; with the Prayogithen, or astrologer of the village, I left a copy of the Gospels and Acts, in Teloogoo, and with another person, St. Matthew's Gospel, in Tamul.

* Is not this illustrative of what is referred to in Acts xxi. 23?

In the evening we travelled on to Tricaloor, and found a good bungalow, in which to pass the night, and to enjoy the following day, which, being Sunday, I had determined should be a day of rest from travelling both to my bearers and myself.

In the morning of Sunday, the 14th, I rose refreshed, and very thankful for all the mercies I had hitherto experienced on this journey. I walked out to look at the temple, which is very large: on the whole, Tricaloor seemed a place of more importance than I had imagined. Several peons visited me: the head peon was very polite and complimentary: he said, they expected the Padre's (Missionary's) coming would give them some rain, of which the country was so much in need; there was, indeed, more appearance of rain than there had been for a considerable time.

At ten o'clock, I collected my bearers and others as a congregation in the bungalow, and, though all heathens except one, they were very attentive, as were also some standers by, whilst I read and talked to them about an hour. I could hardly help smiling at the humble, simple look of the only native Christian in the company, when he found he made himself the object of attention and curiosity by repeating after me, aloud, the Confession and the Lord's Prayer. The poor fellow could neither write nor read, and from fear, I believe, of making mistakes, made several.

A young native, of some literary acquirements, who at Wallajahbad had prevailed on me to allow him to accompany me as reader and amanuensis on this journey, after considerable reading and conversation, this day expressed his wish to become a Christian. I advised him to read and pray, that he might obtain the necessary information and decision of character, reminding him of the consequences of taking the profession of Christianity. I was not quite satisfied as to his motives and sincerity. He travelled with me several weeks, and after I returned to Madras, corresponded with me from Bangalore, where he had procured a situation. I saw him last in Madras, where he had some engagement in the college, but still remained an idolater: he is one of many instances in which I declined administering the initiatory rite of baptism to persons who wished to unite themselves with us, lest their instability or insincerity should bring a disgrace on the cause.

About noon, I was visited by Rohonautachariar, a young Brahman of some respectability: he came on horseback, and had a long-poled parasol of red silk, two or three times as large as an umbrella, held over his head by an attendant, who walked by the side of his horse. He professed to be better acquainted with Sanscrit than with any other language; but received a tract in Teloogoo, and the Gospel of St. Matthew, in Cannada. There was a degree of honesty and candour in his countenance and bearing, that quite attached me to him. After we had conversed some time, he asked my opinion of idolatry, and listened very attentively without attempting to controvert what I advanced. He said he had never before been acquainted with the nature of Christianity; and, as he went away, invited me to his house, saying, he would send me word when he was at home, as he was now going about some business which might detain him.

In about two hours he returned with two of his Brahman friends, one of them past middle age, of an honest, open countenance; the other was bold, quick, and very disputatious. We had a long conversation on the nature of God, of the soul, of true happiness, of heaven, of sin, and of the torments of the damned. The young and the old Brahman seemed pleased with my arguments; and if they said any thing, it was by way of inquiry; but the disputatious one kept up the argument as long as he could with propriety. I found it of great advantage not to allow him to wander from the point in dispute, which the natives are very apt to do, and to remind him of what he had himself admitted. At last he acknowledged, that I was perfectly right; and said, that the same doctrines were to be found in some of their Shastras, but that they contained opposite doctrines too, which must also be received. I endeavoured to point out the folly of embracing contradictions. I spoke of the doctrine of atonement, and contrasted the powerless and inefficient observances and ceremonies of the Hindoos, with the provisions of the Gospel of Jesus Christ. They were very attentive, and appeared struck with my earnest and serious manner.

I then walked with them to their own village, about two miles distant, and endeavoured, by the way, to apply what they had heard and admitted to be reasonable and good, and to show them the beauty and consistency of truth. Their houses were very respectable brick buildings, with flat roofs; they had spacious verandahs in front, where they received me, and where a considerable crowd of men soon assembled: the women, and girls, most of whom had probably never before seen an European, peeped out of the doors, or leaned and listened from the house-tops. I proposed that we should read and converse about a Teloogoo tract on "Regeneration:" it was read, and entirely approved. Having been with them about an hour, I prepared to leave them, but not before I had reproved the gross flattery and impiety of one of them, who, quite in consistence with their pantheistic notions, told me that I was the Supreme Being. They would not let me depart without receiving a brasen dish full of the betel leaf, and areka nut, which are chewed by the natives, and which I handed to the bearers who had followed me, and a quantity of native sweetmeats, which were far from disagreeable. They gave me a general invitation to come and see them whenever I should again pass that way. Several of them accompanied me out of their village, and I did not leave them before I had exhorted them to forsake their lying vanities, and turn to that one true God whom they had now in words acknowledged.

What a blow would it be to Heathenism, if the population of a Brahman village like this should be converted to the faith of Christ! But how hardly can this be? Their pride of caste forbids it. Those who embraced Christianity would be discarded by their friends and families; and, as their present income is derived from houses and lands given to them in consideration of their performing certain duties in connexion with idolatry, if they forsook the one, they must lose the other, and most probably be reduced to poverty and want. However, I could not but hope, that the information and books I had given them would lead to inquiries and discussions that would not be without their use.

On Monday morning we travelled on to Pillirombatti, through a country for the most part uncultivated, and covered with wild and luxuriant jungle. The greater part of that which was cleared for cultivation, and which this month should have been covered with a crop ready for the sickle, was neither ploughed nor sown, in consequence of the long-continued drought, and did not even yield a sufficiency of grass for the cattle, which were driven about in large herds to great distances in quest of pasture. The people of a village where we stopped a few minutes to procure a guide, were loud in their complaints on this subject. I told them it seemed to me, that God was entering into judgment with the inhabitants of this country for their impiety and idolatry, and that the present distress was a call on them to repent.

I had not been long in Pillirombatti before a considerable number of people came round me. I addressed myself to one man particularly, who appeared the most attentive, whilst the rest listened to our conversation. I was thus employed two or three hours in reading and speaking; and, judging from their countenances, could not help thinking, that a lasting impression had been made on the minds of some of them. As I passed along the road in the evening, two men looked earnestly, and followed after me. I called them, and gave each of them a tract, and a few words of advice, which they received with great respect.

At seven P.M. my palankeen was put down in the open street of a village called Palacheri, where I was soon visited by a number of people, who seemed to have no object but to satisfy their curiosity by gazing on me. I spoke to them, but it seemed in vain; either they did not comprehend what I said, or were stupidly indifferent to it. At length I was visited by a Brahman, who entered freely into conversation on religion. Several others made their appearance, and seated themselves in the verandah of the house opposite to which my palankeen was standing, and the street now became thronged with attentive listeners.

Having brought them to acknowledge the necessity of an atonement of infinite value in order to the reconciliation of sinful man to God, and perceiving I had gained their serious attention, I preached the Gospel to them with as much feeling as I ever had in addressing any audience: their inquiries showed how much they were interested and impressed by what they heard. I endeavoured to display to them the deformity and sin of idolatry; and they heard with the countenances of men who assented to the truth. They begged I would give them books, that they might keep these things in remembrance. "But," they said, "what can we do if you do not come again for twelve months, or even for six months?" I told them, that if they were truly desirous to know more of these things, I would visit them again, and pass a few days among them; they said, "Come, and we will prepare a place for you, in which the people may assemble together to hear." Although I had now been engaged with them three hours, I hardly knew how to send them away; but refreshment and sleep were necessary to fit me for my journey the following morning. I therefore dismissed them with a prayer, that God would show to them, and incline them to walk in, the right way.

Notwithstanding my wish again to visit this people, and redeem my promise to them, our deficiency of strength in Madras and its neighbourhood never permitted me to do so; nor, as far as I have heard, has any Missionary since visited them. Nor, indeed, except the number of stations and labourers be considerably increased, is it probable that many of those to whom I preached the Gospel on this journey, will ever hear it again; for, including the Missionaries of all Societies labouring among the Tamul people, there is, on an average, only one Missionary to about a million of souls. Wherever we turn, we find towns and villages in which the Gospel was never preached, and thousands of sinful, but immortal, beings who never heard so much as the name of the only Saviour of sinful man.

For the succeeding three days I travelled slowly by way of Calcourchy, Chinna Salem, Tallivashell, Autoor, and Pootrampollium, employing myself in the manner already described, conversing with all who would converse with me, and leaving tracts in the hands of such as could read them, and were desirous of having a succinct statement of the important doctrines and facts brought to their notice. Complaints of poverty and distress in consequence of the drought were made to me in almost every place; the whole of what is considered the wet season, from October 15th to December 15th, having passed away without a single shower of rain.

On December 19th, I arrived at Salem, having been seventeen days from Madras, during which I had not travelled, on an average, more than fifteen miles per day.

Mr. Cockburn received me in a friendly manner, and had the kindness to offer me the use of a bungalow on the Sheravaraya hills, for any length of time I might choose to remain there. In the evening he took me out to see a few tumuli, (of the hundreds there are in that neighbourhood,) which he had directed to be opened. They were each found to contain a large earthen jar, or rather globular vessel, generally filled with dust; but, in one instance which I saw, bones were found also, establishing the fact, that these tumuli were graves, perhaps for the ashes remaining after the body had been consumed by fire, the usual mode among the Hindoos of disposing of their dead. If the bodies were buried entire, it must (from the size and form of the receptacle) have been in a sitting posture, with the knees bent close to the person. None of the sects of the Hindoos inter in this manner at the present day. The natives who attended us knew, from common report, that these tumuli were graves, but had no information as to what nation or class of people they were who had practised this method of interment.

On the morning of the 20th, I proceeded to the foot of the Sheravaraya hills, about two hours' run from Salem; and at eight A.M. began to ascend on foot, by a steep and rugged path, which required care and exertion at every step. Much of the road was zigzag, and sometimes circuitous; the whole, however imperfect, had been made by great labour; some skill also had been used to make the ascent as easy as possible. The sun was burning hot, and would have rendered the toil too great for me, had it not been for the almost continual shade afforded by the trees and bamboos which flourish on the sides of the hills. The notes of the jungle fowl, (which, in appearance, are so like our domestic poultry, that when I saw them, I thought some traveller had lost his live stock,) the antics of the monkeys, and the widening prospect which I sometimes turned about to enjoy, combined, in some measure, to beguile the way, but could not persuade me it was either short or easy.

I met several of the mountaineers, whose appearance and manners verified the description given of them. They were robust, good-looking men; each of them, in addition to their cotton dresses, carrying a long, thick, woollen cloth or camblet, a covering which their climate renders necessary. They seemed of a taciturn disposition, and answered my questions in as few words as possible, without showing any desire of holding further communication. They spoke Tamul in a manner rather different from the people of the low country, but quite intelligibly; and it was evident that they understood what I addressed to them.

After a walk of about three hours, we stood at the top of the pass. From the moment I reached this point, which was said to be an elevation of about five thousand feet, the weariness I had felt in the ascent was entirely dispelled by the bracing effect of the clear atmosphere, between twenty and thirty degrees colder than that of the valley; and I was delighted with the varied and extensive prospect commanded by such an elevation.

When I reached the bungalow, it wanted about half an hour to noon. My thermometer packed in my box, still stood at 83°; but, exposed to the open air, fell immediately to 68°.

Most of the houses or huts erected on these hills, for the accommodation of those who occasionally visited them, were constructed of the rough stones which lie scattered on every hand, but which, from want of roads and skilful workmen, cannot be gathered and piled on each other, to form a building, however rude, without considerable trouble and expense. That erected by Mr. Cockburn, for himself and family, was of squared trunks of trees, fixed perpendicularly side by side into the ground, to form the walls, and roofed by tiles, brought up the hills with immense labour. The bungalow I occupied for a few days, was about thirty feet in length and sixteen in breadth, constructed chiefly of bamboos: mats of split bamboo formed the walls; the upright stakes of bamboo to which they were fastened, supported the roof, which also was framed of bamboo rafters, and cross pieces, and thatched with long grass.

During the night, I was awoke several times by the cold; all the clothes and covering I had being insufficient against the wind, which pierced through every crevice. When I arose, the thermometer which was hanging near me stood at 54°, a low temperature for 12 degrees north of the Equator; and I found it necessary to move about quickly to maintain any degree of warmth. My walks in the course of the day introduced me to many beautiful spots; the whole country is very romantic; in the valleys the soil is rich and deep, producing wheat and other species of grain; and in the gardens, planted by Mr. Cockburn and others, English vegetables, of every description, were cultivated with success; most of the hills are rugged and rocky, but covered to the top with trees, among which the cedar is said not to be uncommon.

The mistrustful policy of the natives has led them to

forsake their villages in the immediate neighbourhood of the situation chosen by Europeans: there are no traces to be found of one large village, described by a gentleman who pitched his tent near it in traversing these hills some time ago. The hill country is, I understand, twenty or thirty miles in length, and five or more in breadth. My native informants said, that these hills were governed by three different chiefs, each of whom had his village, and separate district; that there are no Brahmans among them; that none of them are able to read, and that their chiefs decide all their disputes; so that there had not yet been an instance of their bringing any cause into the English courts.

One of the mountaineers I conversed with this day was more than ordinarily communicative; he admitted their general ignorance, and seemed pleased when I spoke of schools for the instruction of their children. A Christian, servant to one of the gentlemen, overheard our conversation, and, when I left him, took up the subject; the man replied, "The gentleman speaks very kindly; but does he not wish to instruct us, that he may ship us off to his own country?"

On my way home in the evening, curiosity brought a number of them about me, and kept them attentive, while I called them to forsake their idolatry, and accept the offers of divine mercy, by faith in the only Saviour, the Lord Jesus Christ.

On the 22d, I was kept within doors great part of the day, by the state of the atmosphere: a dense cloud rested on the hills, which would have speedily wet me to the skin, had I ventured out; and would not have allowed me to find my way to any certain point, by the devious foot-paths of the jungles and mountain sides.

Meantime, I found it necessary to send one of my bearers every day to Salem, a run of four hours, to bring what I required for daily consumption: nothing but milk and honey being to be purchased on the hills; bread, rice, fowls, mutton, and even the ingredients for curry, had all to be brought from that distance. No wine or spirits could be procured even in Salem; and, as I found my store too low to last me to Seringapatam, I was under the necessity of dispatching another of my men to Trichinopoly, which, though almost ninety miles distant, was the nearest place at which a supply of these articles could be had.

At sunrise, on the morning of the following day, I set out with one of my bearers to visit Tulasiwillie, (the Sweet-Marjoram Village,) the nearest principal village of the mountaineers. We walked a considerable distance without meeting any one: the first person we met, told us we were in the wrong path, and, after some intreaty, and the promise of a reward, reluctantly undertook to conduct us. He took us up the mountains and down the valleys, by a rugged and narrow path, impassable to any but persons on foot, and admitting only one abreast, through a romantic country, the lower grounds of which were here and there beautifully cultivated, the fields manured, and the furrows deeper than those I had generally observed in the ploughed fields of other parts of the country; the hills and higher grounds were uncleared, and covered with trees and thick underwood. When we approached the village, my guide was very unwilling to proceed; we came upon it all at once, its situation being so sheltered as to conceal it from the view on whatever side it may be approached.

I sent my unwilling guide to present my respects to the Gavunden, or chief, and to say I wished some conversation with him; meantime I observed that the village was very still; not a sound proceeded from it. It consisted of about thirty houses, all constructed in the same manner; they were of a circular form, made chiefly of split bamboo, interwoven with upright stakes fixed into the ground: these wicker walls are plastered with mud in the inside, so as to exclude the wind; and, with the roof, which is a thatch of strong grass continued almost to the ground, form a habitation that keeps out the weather, and has considerable appearance of neatness and comfort; the whole was much superior to many of the villages of the plains.

My guide returned with the intelligence, that all the men of the village were absent on a hunting excursion, and no one knew when they would return. Elks, stags, bears, and other wild animals abounding on these hills, were, I suppose, the objects of their pursuit. I was told that ten or fifteen miles further at Palacâdu, was another large village; but my guide refusing to accompany me, and as I doubted the possibility of finding my way through such an extent of wilderness, I returned to the bungalow about mid-day.

Soon after two o'clock, I set out to see the temple of Sheravaraya. A walk of about an hour and a half brought us to the foot of the hill, whose summit is the highest point of land in the whole range.

A good part of the way up, we had to push through the bushes, as there was no path; the whole was so steep and rugged, that my guide, one of the mountaineers, turned about and complained that he was tired, whilst the bearer who accompanied me was left behind, at a considerable distance. At length we gained the summit, and found an extensive piece of table-land, on which there were very recent marks of bears, probably the long-snouted ant bear, from the holes they had dug in the earth. There were also, on the summit of the hill, two cars of simple construction, to be borne on the shoulders of men at their idolatrous festivals.

I returned a little way down the hill, by a paved road

of large rough stones, to the entrance of the temple. The temple is nothing more than a dark cave in the side of the mountain; the entrance to it six or eight feet wide, and four feet in height; surrounded by a thicket, and a few huts or sheds, entirely without inhabitant. I was told I could not enter the cave without giving great offence, and was therefore not able to ascertain its extent; but, looking into it, I could see a few small stone figures of bulls; and, besides some other idols in the usual style of Hindoo workmanship, at the extremity of the visible recess, an image of Vikkinespuren, the god of accidents and hinderances. As there are no Brahmans among this people, they themselves perform their own religious ceremonies, which are probably very few. The place had about it an air of solemnity and mystery, calculated to impress the minds of a simple and superstitious people.

The first village we passed on our return was perfectly deserted; our guide said that the people were gone to their work: the next village had some inhabitants; one man, at the request of my bearer, ran up into a tree to gather a few wild oranges for me, which he did with astonishing agility, stepping from one branch to another with as little difficulty as if he were walking on the ground. The women and children kept at a distance, except one woman who brought a quantity of milk for me, in a measure formed by part of a joint of the bamboo: not wishing to defile the vessel in her estimation, by drinking from it, I put my hands together to form a channel to my mouth, in the manner customary with the natives, whilst one of the men poured out for me to drink. I had soon drunk enough; but both hands and mouth being occupied, I had no means of expressing myself, and was obliged to continue drinking till I had finished the whole.

My guide now hastened us onwards, as the day was fast declining; he took us by a better road than that we had before walked over, and brought us home just at dark, when I was thoroughly tired by my day's journeyings. Though the direct rays of the sun had been hot, the continuation of a cool breeze throughout the day had enabled me to take the longest ramble on foot I had enjoyed since leaving England.

On my return, I found a letter from Madras waiting for me at the bungalow. It had been forwarded from Salem; to which place, as to every station occupied by Europeans, there is an established post. The mail-bags are carried by men, who run singly from stage to stage about ten or fourteen miles each, having no other weapon for defence than a staff, with a few links of iron chain at the upper end, whose sound, they say, frightens serpents out of their path: at night they frequently carry a lighted faggot of eight or ten feet in length, whose blaze enables them to choose their way. Nothing was more common, in whatever direction I traversed the country, than day and night to be passed or met by these posts at full trot, who, in the south of India, are usually called Tappâls; in the north they are called Dawks. These mails, at an average, are carried about a hundred miles in twenty-four hours; and the letters are charged about four anas, or sixpence, for every hundred miles.

Parcels of small weight are forwarded to the principal stations by the same sort of conveyance, but not quite so quickly: the post for the conveyance of parcels is called the Banghy; the expense is regulated by the weight and distance.

On the following day, I had an opportunity of speaking to several persons on divine things; and in the evening I read the Scriptures, and prayed with the natives about me.

On the 25th, being Christmas-day, I held service twice in the bungalow, with my own attendants, and such strangers as we could prevail upon to attend: they were very attentive to what they heard. I was much pleased by a visit from two Heathens, in the service of a gentleman then visiting the hills. One of them had been for some time inclined to Christianity, but had wavered between Popery and Protestantism; the other had been awakened to a sense of the sin and folly of idolatry, by a tract I had presented to his fellow-servant, when he had before come to me for conversation and advice. Both desired baptism; but as my acquaintance with them had been short, and as I understood they were going to Madras, I gave them a letter of introduction to our Missionary there, hoping that, on trial, they would be found suitable candidates for that sacred rite.

In my evening walk I met a poor native, whom I discovered by his conversation to be a Romanist: he had been baptized about twelve months. He proved deplorably ignorant; but, appearing sincere and teachable, I sat down and gave him some instruction as to the nature and intention of the Gospel of the Lord Jesus Christ, to whose church he wished to belong. He heard very thankfully what I said; and seemed to want words to express his obligation to me, when I had knelt down and prayed with him and his companion, who, being a Heathen, had now probably for the first time bowed his knees to worship the true and living God. Returning home, I passed a company warming themselves at a tile-kiln. I asked them if any man could endure the fire even for one day; and, by the terrors of the Lord, endeavoured to induce them to quit their idolatry, and turn to the only true God.

I walked out again to Tulasiwillic, in the afternoon of the 27th. The Chief was not at home; but a party of the people were working in the threshing-floor, with whom I had a long conversation. I proposed establishing a school for the instruction of their children; but they said it was not necessary, for neither they nor their forefathers had ever learned to read. They were attentive to what I said to them about God; and especially with regard to the present drought and scarcity, as being under the direction of his providence, and a token of his righteous displeasure towards a guilty people, who refused to acknowledge and to serve him. I spoke also of sin and its deserts, of heaven and of the only way to it; but they seemed to have sat down contented in the dark valley of the shadow of death. Yet I rejoiced in the hope, that one day, even here, Christ shall be known, and his name loved and revered.

My bearer was now returned from Trichinopoly with stores for the journey. In the night, hearing loud singing in the shed where my people slept and ate, and kept a large fire to warm themselves, I walked out to see who was indulging in such vociferation; and found it was the bearer, who, though but just returned from so long and hasty a journey, was treating his companions by reciting a poem which took him two or three hours. He had bared himself to the waist; and, seated before the fire on the ground, moved his body backwards and forwards, as if to keep time, intent on nothing but the subject of his song. In answer to my inquiries afterwards, he said he could not read, but had learned that long poem by having had it recited to him. Its subject was one of the Hindoo mythological romances.

On the 28th I again visited the Roman Catholic and the Heathen I had seen a few days before; and invited them and some others to assemble for divine worship in the evening. In consequence, I had a good congregation, who heard me read and speak with considerable attention. I thus took leave of the natives of these hills, leaving behind me a few tracts and a Gospel in Tamul;

hoping that my residence there of eight days had not been without its use, and that some correct knowledge of Christ, however faint, had been introduced among them. May it prove to them the savour of life unto life!

About seven o'clock on the following morning we began to descend from the hills of Sheravaraya. When I set out, my face was blue with cold; but a walk of two hours brought me to the valley, where the thermometer stood at 84° in the shade. On the top of the pass I met the Collector, Mr. Cockburn, coming from Salem; whence he had been driven by indisposition to seek the cooler atmosphere of the hills. He had ascended on horseback, without having had to alight very frequently, being mounted on a Pindaree pony, an animal accustomed to climbing.

My people being too much tired by descending the hill, to allow them to set out immediately on our proposed journey to Mysore and Seringapatam, I passed the remainder of that and the whole of the following day with the gentlemen of Salem. A man with whom I had met and conversed in coming down the hill waited on me for further conversation, and to receive the Gospel and tracts I had promised him. The words of eternal life are thus scattered abroad among the Heathen, with the hope that they may not be entirely without special and lasting effect.

On the 31st of December I quitted Salem, and rested for some hours in the middle of the day in a village, where the people continued to loiter about me, but would not give their constant and serious attention to what I had to say. Amongst them was a begging Pandaram, or religious mendicant, fantastically dressed and ornamented, carrying, as is the custom with some of them, a round plate of metal, which, struck by a stick, served as an accompaniment to his singing, and gave notice of his approach to those who were charitably disposed. He asked me some questions, which fully elicited his ignorance; and was so serious in listening to what I said, as to give me hope that some impression had been made on him. When I paused, however, he commenced striking his substitute for a bell, and singing aloud. I desired him to desist; he begged me to give him alms of cloth or money; and appeared astonished when I told him it would not be charity, but sin, to give him either the one or the other. An explanation of my meaning led me to expose his character as an useless member of society, and a professed beggar, in such a manner as to increase his embarrassment, and make many of the people laugh aloud, an evidence that they were not very bigoted. He asked what he must do, if he gave up this way of life; his question was easily answered by asking in return, "What do others do?" He persisted in his request till I dismissed him with a peremptory refusal; recommending him to prefer the welfare of his soul to the idle ease of his vagabond mode of life.

Some Brahmans came, who said they had heard of me at a distance, as conversing with the people and distributing books. I gratified them by letting them hear for themselves, and giving them a few tracts.

Though the last day in the year, and at a season which is accounted comparatively cool, the thermometer stood at 90° in the shade. The drought seemed general throughout the country. I passed several extensive groves of fine palmira-trees; and was now and then delighted with a green paddy-field, or a garden watered from wells; giving the eye some relief from the barren glare and dreariness of the country at large.

On the morning of the 1st of January, 1824, I arrived at Sankerrydroog; a place whose rocky hill and almost inaccessible fortress made it of importance during the time of war, but, in the present peaceful state of the country, entirely useless and forsaken.

The bungalow for the accommodation of travellers being in a retired situation, I passed the day in the study of Teloogoo.

In the evening I walked to the Pettah, a mean-looking village. Seeing a small Roman Catholic church, I went towards it; and was observed by a man, who ran round and opened the door for me to enter. It presented nothing more than the paltry ornaments usually found in small native churches. I asked the man if there were any Christians in this place; "Yes," he replied; "I am a Christian, and the Minister of this church." I told him, I must doubt his veracity both as to the one and the other. He seemed astonished; but I explained my meaning by asking him what was indicated by the mark he wore on his forehead,—a mark confessedly heathen in its origin, and designating the wearer as belonging to one or other of the idolatrous sects of the Hindoos. These marks are considered part of the full dress of a Hindoo; and, though belonging to heathen idolatry, are worn by many who, though Christians in name, are more anxious to maintain their caste and respectability, than their consistency as professed followers of Christ. I have seen so many Roman Catholics wearing these marks, that I am doubtful whether their Priests have ever required them to lay them aside.

This Catechist, or Teacher, finding I would not consider him a Christian so long as he wore that mark, acknowledged that he was wrong; and, taking a corner of his cloth, wiped it from his forehead, saying he would never wear it again. We entered into conversation; and I found him amazingly ignorant of even the first principles of Christianity. The qualifications necessary to a

Teacher of religion seemed never to have occurred to his mind; the only reason he could give for filling that office was, that his father had filled it during his life, and that it had fallen to him by way of inheritance.

He followed me to the bungalow, and continued with me till late at night. I presented him with a Gospel in Tamul, solemnly charging him to read it as the word of God; and a tract exposing the image-worship of the church of Rome.

Much reliance is not to be placed on the assent or approval of a native, expressed in conversation: their notions of politeness often deterring them from fully expressing their real sentiments: however, I could not but hope that whatever effect my conversation with this man might have produced, the perusal of the word of God would be blessed to the enlightening of his understanding, and the amendment of his heart.

I felt that the indulgence of hopes like this was necessary to reconcile me to my present circumstances. Whilst I wandered a solitary stranger in a heathen wilderness, weighed down with a sense of my unworthiness; whilst I bore and scattered around the precious seed of God's holy word; I remembered my native land, and its rich privileges; and could not but long after the opportunities enjoyed by my brethren, even in Madras, of assembling with the pious people of their charge, and recounting together the mercies of the past year, with united prayers and determinations for increased faithfulness and zeal in the year now commenced. I was encouraged by remembering that, though absent from them, I should not be forgotten in their addresses to the throne of grace; and that in thousands of assemblies in my native country, the cause in which I was engaged would, on these days, be pleaded with faithful and persevering prayer.

On the morning of the 2d of January, I travelled for

some hours along a road which, like the country around, appeared entirely of a kind of alabaster rock, barren, rugged, and sharp. I observed two of my men, laden with books and other luggage, quite barefooted, after having been three hours on the march on this rough and pointed road, sportfully running a race with their burdens on their heads; strongly illustrating how custom inures the human frame to what at first sight would be considered next to impossible.

We rested for the day in an excellent bungalow in Bhawani, a village delightfully situated on the junction of the river Bhawani with the Cauvery. It contains some considerable temples, and the inhabitants appeared wealthy and respectable. The soil of the neighbourhood is good; and, notwithstanding the dry season, the vegetation was very beautiful.

Soon after my arrival, I was visited by some of the chief officers of the temple, attended by music, and about twenty dancing-women. I received their compliments, and wished to dismiss them; but they were unwilling to go, without having performed for me. I assured them I could not enjoy their performance, and did not approve of their mode of life; that my business was to recommend men to turn from their idolatry, of which this was a part, and worship the only one God in spirit and in truth.

They went away, I suppose to some service in the temple, and returned in about an hour, crowding into the room where I was writing: they behaved respectfully, but were very inquisitive about my watch, and compass, and thermometer, which were lying on the table. I answered some of their inquiries, talked to them on religious subjects; and finding that some of the women also could read, having been taught for the purpose of learning the songs used in the service of the temple, I gave them a few tracts, and sent them away.

In the afternoon, I was visited by one of the principal officers of the temple. He acquiesced in what I advanced on the subject of religion, and observed that it was said, that one day all the world would be of the same faith. I told him that this was a subject of inspired prophecy, and that we were expecting its accomplishment. He mentioned the tracts I had given to the dancing-women, and afforded me an opportunity of explaining the subject of them, and the intention of their distribution: I concluded by presenting to him a Gospel in Tamul. I now set out to continue my journey, and finding some persons waiting outside, distributed a few tracts amongst them.

A journey of about six miles in the evening brought us to Tarepollium, a poor village, with nothing to invite the traveller's stay, except a shed in which his people may rest for the night. Seeing some holes in the ground, I inquired the occasion of them, and was told that the people had been hunting rats, which they make an article of food. I asked one of the villagers what religion they were of; he answered that they had no religion, and that none of them were able to read: he excused himself from calling his neighbours to hear what I had to say, though he had himself listened attentively to what I said on the will of God as to the eternal salvation of man, and the love he had displayed in the gift of his Son Jesus Christ.

In this remote district of Coimbatoor, the influence of the Brahmanical system seems less general than it is to the north and east; and among the thousands of its inhabitants, there are great numbers who, in receiving Christianity, would have less falsehood to unlearn, and fewer prejudices to overcome, than those of their more educated and polished countrymen. But no Mission has yet been established among them.

On the morning of the 3d, I travelled about five hours

through a well-cultivated and fruitful country. We rested at Gopaulchittypollium, a large and respectable village. A number of Brahmans and others came round me; and for two hours I endeavoured to deliver my soul, by faithfully instructing and warning them. One of them said, he would take the tract I gave him to his superiors, to consult with them on the subject.

It was near midnight when we reached Sattimungulum, where I had determined to rest the whole of the following day. My bearers, aware of my practice of resting on the Lord's day, made an extra effort to reach this populous neighbourhood, where they knew there was a good bungalow, and they should find comfortable accommodations for themselves.

I rose before sunrise on Sunday, the 4th, and had a delicious and refreshing bathe in the river, which I enjoyed, unconscious of any danger. In the course of the day, however, I was warned not to bathe in the river, because it is infested with alligators: if there were any, I escaped their notice.

Never did I feel a greater horror of Heathenism than was produced in my mind on this morning, by an examination of the idol-car belonging to the temple of Sattimungulum: as such cars generally are, it was covered with carved figures, representing different characters and actions, not only highly indecent, but so monstrously abominable, that they could not, I conceive, be imagined even by any who are unacquainted with the mysteries of iniquity, unfolded by the mythology and rites of the Hindoo superstition.

On my return to the bungalow, I sent a messenger into the streets, to distribute a few tracts, and recommend them to the perusal of the people, and to invite them to come and converse with me on the subjects they referred to.

I soon had a return to this invitation, in a visit from some Brahmans and others, to whom I opened my commission. The obligations of man to God, the divine perfections, particularly that of holiness, the great evil of sin, the inefficiency of any good works or of ceremonies to remove its guilt, the necessity of an atonement of infinite value, the mercy of God displayed in providing such an atonement in Jesus Christ, the difference between Christianity and Heathenism in their nature and effects, and the present and eternal advantages resulting from a sincere acceptance of the Gospel, were the topics of my discourse. They heard attentively; and the answers I made to some objections advanced by them, would serve to impress these important subjects more deeply on their minds. I felt thankful that I was not ashamed of the Gospel of Christ, from a conviction that, when fairly stated, it would commend itself to every man's conscience in the sight of God.

The neighbourhood of Sattimungulum is infested with tigers: the natives pointed out to me a small cave on the opposite bank of the river, that had been the haunt of a very fierce one, which had been shot not long before by an English gentleman. It was reported that one had carried off a man that day at noon, at a distance of only six miles from Sattimungulum, and on the road I had to travel the next day; another person had been seized and carried off, it was supposed by the same tiger, but a few days previous.

On Monday, the 5th, I did not succeed in getting my bearers to set out till after sunrise; such was their dread of tigers and wild elephants, which abound a little further on the road I had to travel, that, till I reached Mysore, they would not travel except in open day.

We rested during the hottest part of the day, under the shade of luxuriant trees and jungle, on the banks of the Bhawani. The thermometer stood at 89° in the shade.

On the morning of the 6th, we were four hours in ascending the romantic mountain-pass of Gujlehutty, the road being steep and difficult, though much labour and skill had been used to clear and level the path, to make it as easy as possible. I was told that a gentleman ascending this pass with a fowling-piece, and followed by a native servant, was met near the top by an enormous tiger, which he was fortunate enough to shoot dead, in the act of crouching to spring upon him; but when he turned to his servant, he found that by excess of terror the poor fellow's reason was irrecoverably fled; and that he still continues in the neighbourhood in the same state, subsisting on a pension settled on him by his master.

At the top of the pass, I was surprised to see an English burial-ground, containing tombs, and a considerable number of graves; and was informed that it was the place of interment of the English officers and pioneers, who had died whilst employed in the unhealthy task of clearing away the jungle, and constructing the road up the pass.

My day's rest in the bungalow at the top of Gujlehutty, was the more delightful from the lower temperature of the atmosphere, when compared with that of the plains below: the thermometer fell to 73° in the shade.

For more than an hour the following morning, we travelled over beautiful table land, a good part of it cultivated, and the rest appearing well worthy of the labour of cultivation: I thought it one of the most delightful spots I had seen in the interior of India. We then stood on the edge of the hill, from whence to the north we had an extensive view of the country of Mysore, on which we were now entering. We travelled till noon, when we reached the village of Ardanhully, the frontier village of the territories of the Rajah of Mysore. The most suitable place I could find wherein to take shelter from the sun, was a small mandabam, or open platform, covered by a roof supported by four stone pillars. Here I had several visitants, and endeavoured to improve the opportunity by conversing with them on the usual topics. Thermometer 76°.

The following day I rested under the shade of trees, on the border of a large tank, in the village of Coinoor: the water of the tank was nearly exhausted; what remained was dreadfully filthy, but was yet drunk by the cattle and the poor thirsty sheep and goats, and carried away in pots apparently for culinary purposes, by the women of the village.

At night I slept at Nanjungode, and on the morning of the 9th, arriving at Mysore, found at the Residency the usual kindness of reception, and the rest and refreshment I required, after the exposure and privations of the journey of the preceding nine days.

On Sunday, the 11th, I preached twice in English, in the house of one of the servants of the Rajah, to an attentive congregation of Indo-Britons and others.

The next day I was desired to visit a sick man, and found, under the influence of a wasting fever, a Franciscan Friar, a Portuguese native of Goa. He told me that in the course of his journeys through the country, he had visited Chittoor: there he had been presented with a New Testament in Portuguese, by one of the servants of Mr. D'Acre, who at the same time pointed out to him the errors of Popery. The things he had heard and read so impressed his mind, that when he returned to Tellicherry, he publicly renounced Romanism, and attended the Protestant church. He was now on his way to Madras, in the hope of being received into the service of one of the Missions established there; but, having fallen sick by the way, and all his money being expended, he had sent for me, hoping I would render him some encouragement and assistance.

The frankness of his manner, and the corroborating testimony of several persons who had known him in his ecclesiastical character when he formerly passed through Mysore, left no room for doubt as to the truth of his story; and I cheerfully engaged to assist him on his journey to Madras, leaving him at liberty on his arrival there to follow his own plans.

In the house of a medical man in the service of the Rajah, a child was shown to me perfectly fair, with light hair and eye-brows, and a tinge of pink in the eyes: he was the son of native parents of dark complexion, who had other children, and, esteeming it a misfortune to have a child of this description in their family, had given it to the Doctor to bring it up as he pleased. The facts were so well attested, that I could not doubt their correctness. It is a rare circumstance; but, I was told, not a solitary one: the colour of the hair and eye-brows clearly distinguish such children from the offspring of Europeans by Hindoo females.

On Tuesday I went over to Seringapatam, and, on that evening and the following, had very attentive Tamul congregations; several of the heathen inhabitants having assembled with those professing Christianity from curiosity to hear an Englishman preach in their language.

Returning to Mysore on the morning of the 15th, I was overtaken on the road by a procession of several elephants attending one of the Rajah's kinsmen who had been down to the Cauvery to wash. These enormous animals moved more rapidly than the pace of my palankeen bearers; and although they are known to be perfectly at the command of their drivers, I was not sufficiently familiar with them to dismiss all sense of alarm, as they were urged past the palankeen, and quite close to it; for my bearers thought it enough just to make way for them, without going out of their road.

At Mysore I had an opportunity of addressing a considerable party, assembled at the baptism of a child.

The next day I again went to Seringapatam, where I baptized a child of native Protestant parents, and in the evening preached in Tamul.

I was told that some of the Heathens who formed part of my attentive congregation on this occasion, when they had their usual visit the next morning from the *prayogithen*, or astrologer, whose profession it is to announce to each family the lucky or unlucky nature of the day, told him they did not wish to hear his nonsense; he could tell them nothing about their souls, but that the white Padre had given them good advice: to some of the Christians of the congregation they expressed a wish that they could embrace Christianity. In this, as in almost every other, neighbourhood in India, the encouragement and countenance that would be afforded by the constant residence of a Missionary are all that is required to induce many natives to embrace the profession of our holy religion.

At this my last visit to Seringapatam, I found many houses thrown down, and many thoroughfares obstructed by operations which were in progress for the discovery of treasure, under the direction of the Rajah of Mysore. It was supposed, that large sums had been secreted under the former Rajah's, or Tippoo Sultan's, reign. It was curious to see the old temples and houses which the excavators discovered twelve or twenty feet below the level of the present surface. Much property was damaged or ruined, and many streets rendered almost impassable; but no treasure was found. Since my return to England, I have been informed, that not one European now resides in Seringapatam, and that it is almost forsaken by the natives themselves. Thus has it been with respect to very many far-famed capitals in the East.

On the evening of the following day, (Saturday,) having returned to Mysore, I preached in Tamul to a crowd of native Heathens, who had assembled to witness the baptism of a native man, and his wife and child: the man had long been reading tracts and other books in Tamul, that had been supplied to him by his Christian master, from an anxious desire for his conversion. It was a solemn occasion; and I thought a lasting impression in favour of Christianity was effected on the minds of the Heathen who were present.

On Sunday, the 18th, I preached twice in English, and had about twelve communicants at the celebration of the Lord's supper. Both here, and in Seringapatam, I had again the most pressing entreaties to remain, or to use such influence as to get for them a resident Missionary. But as we had not yet been able to re-occupy Bangalore, I could not encourage very sanguine hopes of the accomplishment of their wishes.

Being favoured by the kindness of Mr. Cole with an order for the Rajah's bearers, on the 19th I set out for Bangalore. As I travelled post, I had little opportunity of speaking to the people; but being detained a short time at Madoor, I had a conversation with the Cutwal in the hearing of a crowd of natives, on the nature and excellency of the Christian religion, at the close of which he received a copy of the translation of the Gospel of St. John in the Cannada or Canarese language.

The following day I arrived in Bangalore, where I was hospitably welcomed and entertained, as at my first arrival there, by the Chaplain, Mr. Malkin.

In Bangalore I remained seven days, and in the course

of them preached seven times to very attentive English and Tamul congregations. Our small building, formerly described, was too small to accommodate all who attended.

The English society was under the care of a sensible and faithful Leader, who afterwards fell, with many of his religious comrades, in the expedition against the Burmese. The class had not been long formed; but the advancement and steadiness of its members indicated the peculiar suitability and usefulness of that mean of grace among military men, when far removed from the public ordinances of religion.

Among the natives who attended the Tamul services was a young man whom I had baptized in Madras, and who was now employed by some pious gentlemen in Bangalore, to sell or otherwise distribute religious tracts and books to the natives. He afterwards came again to Madras, and, under the direction of the Missionaries of the London Society, continued zealous and faithful in his endeavours to promote among his countrymen the knowledge of the Gospel. It is worthy of remark, that he was the son of an English officer by a native woman, and, like too many under similar circumstances, was left entirely to the care of his mother, who brought him up a Heathen; but being found and instructed by some of our people, he thankfully embraced the profession of that which his convictions assured him was the truth. Though aware of his parentage, he continues to dress in the native costume, as being more economical, and better suiting with his engagements and circumstances.

When I quitted Bangalore on the morning of the 27th, I felt very unwell and feverish, and did not take my usual morning's walk. Not apprehending any serious consequences, I continued my journey, as also the following day, when I lost all appetite, and was unable to take any thing but toast-water. Several of my bearers also fell sick; but, meeting with a supply of others, and hoping to succeed in procuring post-bearers a little further on the road, I continued to press towards Chittoor, the nearest place where medical aid could be obtained.

I was carried into Chittoor on February 1st; and, in the house of Mr. D'Acre, received all the attention that could be paid to me. The fever was one incident to the hills and jungles of India; and, being frequently fatal, my friends were apprehensive it would have proved so in my case. I took no food for a fortnight, and was wasted almost to a skeleton. Mr. D'Acre's assiduities and medical skill contributed greatly to the preservation of my life at this critical juncture. At length, by the divine blessing on the means employed, the disorder took a favourable turn; and although I was left so weak as to be unable to rise or walk without assistance and support, some hopes began to be entertained of my recovery.

Meantime I was cheered by the kind attentions of my friends, who gave me as much of their society as possible. The Rev. W. Reeve, of the London Missionary Society, on his way from Madras to Bellary, passed several days in Chittoor, and animated me by his brotherly conversation, his sympathies, and prayers.

The kindness and concern on my account displayed by the Christian natives of Chittoor, surpassed any expectations I had from them. This is a fact which justice to them forbids me to omit mentioning, and the recollection of which binds them to my heart in the ties of gratitude and affection.

Having gained strength sufficient to bear the motion of the palankeen, on March 1st I proceeded on my journey to Madras; and, on the morning of the 3d, was met at Sree Permatoor by my brother Missionary, Mr.

England, who had kindly come thus far on the road to meet me. We passed the day together in the bungalow there, and in the evening proceeded to the Mission-house in Royapettah.

In the course of that month I had a slight relapse of the fever, whilst on a visit at the house of my friend, Mr. Crisp, in Kilpauk; but, by care, and the beneficial influence of the sea-breeze, continued gradually to recover, and was soon enabled to resume some share of the labours connected with the Mission.

Subsequently to my last visit to the Mysore Country, as recorded in this chapter, the Wesleyan Missionary Society resumed their Mission in Bangalore, where there are now two Stations, one for the Tamul department, and another for the Canarese. A printing-press is in full operation, and the Mission is in a most encouraging and prosperous state. The city of Mysore, likewise, is occupied as a Mission Station; as are also Goobee and Coonghul.

Salem has been taken on the list of the Stations of the London Missionary Society.

CHAPTER XX.

REMARKS ON FACILITIES FOR MISSIONS.

THE attentive reader of the preceding pages must have been struck with a few very important facts which it has been their chief design to illustrate,—facts connected with the best interests and welfare of one of the largest and most remarkable portions of the human race,—a numerous and partially civilized people, who in the course of divine providence have been brought under the influence of the British Government, and whose state and prosperity are nearly related to those of our own country, and will probably affect them closely to the end of time.

It will appear, that there is no direct political hinderance to the spread of Christianity among the Hindoos. The Missionary is allowed unrestrained intercourse with the people: within their temples, in their towns, their villages, by the road-side, he can converse with and address them; and though he possess no advantage beyond that of the European character, which generally insures him attention and respect, and can bring no influence to bear upon them other than that of plain truth and argument; yet, this being all a good cause can require, and having already been partially successful, there is no room to doubt, that, in the end, it will prove effectual to the accomplishment of the object.

The natives themselves are under no restraint with regard to availing themselves of the opportunities afforded to them, by Missionary establishments, of obtaining Christian or general knowledge for themselves or their children. They have nothing to fear from being known to converse with us, or from sending their children to our schools.

As the whole country is open to Missionary exertions, it would be endless to point out where additional Missions might be advantageously established, even within the circle described in the preceding narrative. Stations occupied by Europeans have comforts and facilities not to be found on stations entirely native. The society of fellow-countrymen, medical attendance, and the ready procuring of the necessaries of life, make a residence on European stations in many respects desirable; but of these, there are many still entirely unoccupied. Wallajahbad, Arcot, Vellore, Seringapatam, and the French settlement of Pondicherry, (if the French Government would permit an English Missionary to reside and labour there,) are all places of importance, with populous neighbourhoods, offering the advantages above mentioned. In such large native towns as Conjeveram, Chillumbrum, or Tricaloor, or on the Sheravaraya Hills, Missionaries might reside with the certainty of commanding the attention of a considerable proportion of their numerous inhabitants.

But notwithstanding the accessibleness of the people, and the facilities enjoyed by the Missionaries already residing among them, it is a fact which should be plainly stated and clearly understood, that the mass of the people of India remain in the same state of ignorance and superstition as ever. Some, but comparatively few, have been converted to Christianity; and a degree of general knowledge both of religious and scientific truth has been partially diffused; which, though enough to raise doubt as to the correctness of their own systems in the minds of thousands of the Hindoos, has not been sufficient, either in degree or operation, to convince and determine them to alter their profession, to forsake their own system, and embrace the Gospel.

The reasons of their continuance in their ancient professions are not difficult to be assigned. Independently of the natural enmity of the human heart to doctrines so humbling to the pride of man as those of the Gospel, the Hindoos have many particular causes of attachment to their own system. Their education is decidedly religious; consequently, their earliest associations are connected with their superstitions and idolatrous worship. The wealth of their religious establishments, their vast temples, their ponderous cars, the immense concourse of people assembling at their splendid annual festivals, and the general example, cannot be without an imposing effect on the minds of the lower and uneducated classes; whilst the intimate connexion of their most favourite literature, and every department of their philosophy and science, with their system of religion, tend to impress it on the minds of the educated, and to identify it with their interests and literary honour. The system of caste, too, is dear to the higher classes, as securing certain degrees of superiority and respectability, entirely independent of personal character, or of the possession of wealth or learning. It has been strongly argued, that Hindoos taking the profession of Christianity should relinquish the peculiar observances necessary for the maintaining of their caste, and give up all the advantages connected with it, as being part of an idolatrous system. But whether this be enforced upon them or not, it is equally certain to the mind of a Hindoo, that, when he becomes a Christian, he shall be disowned by his friends, separated from his family, deprived probably of his portion of the paternal inheritance, and excluded from the circle in which he has been accustomed to move. There are but few individuals who have courage to make these sacrifices, even when convinced of the truth; and a great proportion will wait till knowledge and conviction become so general, that whole families, and villages, and tribes shall agree at once to renounce idolatry, and seek for admission into the Christian church. Many with whom I have conversed, and who have assented to the truth of Christianity, have declared that they only waited for such an event.

There is little room for doubt that this will be ultimately accomplished; but the means at present in operation are very inadequate to the hastening of such desirable and extensive results. Of the Missionaries sent to India, a certain proportion may be calculated to fail from the baneful influence of the climate, it being ascertained that the average length of Missionary life in India is not more than seven years; others fail to acquire the languages, which are necessary for familiar intercourse with the people. And when such acquisitions have been made, and the confidence of the natives secured, the removal or death of the Missionary will often disappoint the fairest hopes of harvest; and his successor will find himself under the necessity of acting as though at the very commencement of the work. The Missionaries already engaged find considerable difficulty in widening their sphere of action amongst the Heathen, from the attention and care demanded by the small societies and congregations already formed; whilst their labours among these also are not so fully efficient or widely successful, as they would be rendered by more enlarged means for the erection of chapels, the possession of burial-grounds, and the more extensive establishment of both male aud female schools.

It is a natural inquiry of the people, "What shall we do with our dead?" The want of a burial-ground on two of our Stations in India has deterred many, both Roman Catholics and Heathens, from uniting with us, as they would thus exclude themselves from the privileges of their own communions, without, in this respect, securing tantamount advantages in ours.

In addition to these causes, it must be remembered, that the number of Missionaries in India is extremely small; for, taking those of every Society into account, the proportion is not that of one to each million of inhabitants; their most zealous and well-directed exertions must, therefore, be unequal to even the partial instruction and information of the great mass of the natives.

It will be understood that our exertions have not been confined to natives only; but that our own countrymen and the descendants of Europeans have shared the attentions, and been benefited by the labours, of those who have been sent forth as the messengers of the churches. The improvement and evangelization of those parts of the community of India will have their corresponding effect on the surrounding heathen population. Many of the natives have already learned to distinguish those of our countrymen who are truly Christian in their character and deportment; and they must increasingly feel the force of the truths attempted to be propagated among them, when their due influence is exemplified before their daily observation.

Patriotism, therefore, and Christian benevolence, demand the continued support of the Missions already established in India, and will dictate also the propriety and necessity of their multiplication and increase. With this object in view, these remarks are offered, which, it is trusted, are authorized by the simple details of the preceding pages; and their correctness, it is hoped, will be further established by the remaining part of my Narrative.

CHAPTER XXI.

1824.

TOURS AND DUTIES OF 1824.

The year 1824 was remarkable for circumstances which will cause it ever to be remembered by all who at that time resided in Madras and the south of India. The continuance of the drought, which, even in January, immediately after what ought to have been the wet monsoon, had been already so destructive to vegetation, that I had seen many of the houses of the natives unroofed, for the purpose of giving the old thatch as fodder to the cattle, in the hope of keeping them alive till rain should again renew the face of the earth; the consequent scarcity and famine by which, notwithstanding the liberality of the Government, and the extraordinary exertions of private charity, both European and Hindoo, many thousands terminated a miserable existence; the prevalence of the cholera morbus, whose ravages were not confined to the starving population, but extended to all classes, and carried off some of the highest officers of the local Government, occasioning mourning in every circle, if not in every house; the expedition against Burmah which took from us many dear and highly-valued military friends, who were never to return:—all combined to form an era not easily to be forgotten.

The reader who has not witnessed a drought in a tropical climate can hardly imagine its effects: men and cattle were to be seen lying dead; and the latter, being frequently allowed to remain unburied, tainted the air with noxious effluvia; the fish at the bottom of the tanks and rivers having no means of escape, became a seasonable prey to the kites and crows, and ultimately these latter not unfrequently dropped dead from the wing, exhausted by heat, and want of sustenance.

In many instances the prejudices of the Hindoos gave way to the stress of their necessities; persons whose difference of caste would under other circumstances have been an entire bar to intercourse, might be seen crowding together to partake of the food prepared for them by the hand of charity. There were, however, many exceptions, sufficiently illustrative of the iron reign of superstition over the Hindoos. One day, whilst we were at dinner in the Mission-house, in Madras, a woman, much worn by hunger and fatigue, came into the garden, and, standing opposite our door, gently lowered from her back a tall lad, reduced to a mere skeleton, unable to stand or move without help, imploring pity and assistance. I immediately directed the rice and curry on the table to be taken to them; but the woman both rejected it herself, and refused it to her famishing child, because it was against the rules of her caste to eat any food cooked or touched by Europeans!

An excursion through Tripassoor, Wallajahbad, and Poonamallee, in the month of April, in company with my colleague, Mr. England, afforded us many opportunities for preaching in English and Tamul, for conversation with the natives, and for distributing a number of portions of the holy Scriptures, and tracts. It was our decided conviction, that itinerancy, reduced to a system, and regularly attended to, would greatly forward the objects of our Mission among all classes: we accordingly gave some intimations of our intention to revisit some of the places after a certain time, which subsequent events, however, did not allow us to fulfil.

In May, Mr. England and myself travelled together

down the coast to Negapatam, to attend a District-Meeting to be held there. Our journey both going and returning was chiefly remarkable for the intense heat we had to endure, whether we rested under the shade of trees, or in the choultries, and bungalows. Sickness was prevailing to a great extent: we had in consequence many applications for medicine, which was sometimes administered by Mr. England, and received by the people with a confidence in its efficacy, which, though almost ludicrous, no doubt contributed to the advantage of the patients.

In Pondicherry we waited on the Romish Bishop, who received us with great dignity and kindness. As he was not much more master of English than I of French, we soon adopted Tamul, in which he conversed fluently, as the medium of communication. As it was merely a complimentary visit, I had no intention of entering into any discussion; but when he adverted in terms of disapprobation to the labours of the Bible Society, and their agents, in the hearing of a number of natives who had surrounded the entrance to witness the interview between their Bishop and a heretic Missionary, I entered into the dispute, and challenged him to point out any of those essential errors he professed to complain of in the Tamul translation of the holy Scriptures, and invited him to co-operate with us in the revision of the new translation then in hand.

About twenty miles south of Pondicherry we visited the famous pagoda of Chillumbrum. This structure, which is held in high estimation by the Hindoos, is said to extend 1332 feet by 936, and is entered by a lofty gateway, under a pyramid 122 feet high, built of enormous stones forty feet long and more than five feet square, and all covered with plates of copper, adorned with a variety of figures neatly executed.

After inspecting the interior of this extraordinary monument of Hindoo superstition, on our return to the outer gate, I preached to a large assemblage of Brahmans and others, and delivered a testimony against their absurd idolatries and superstitions, which they did not misunderstand. Some of the Brahmans became rather abusive; but for this we cared very little. The good seed was deposited in the memories of many, and perhaps in their hearts also. The event we leave with God. The accompanying sketch gives a correct representation of one part of the interior of the temple of Chillumbrum.

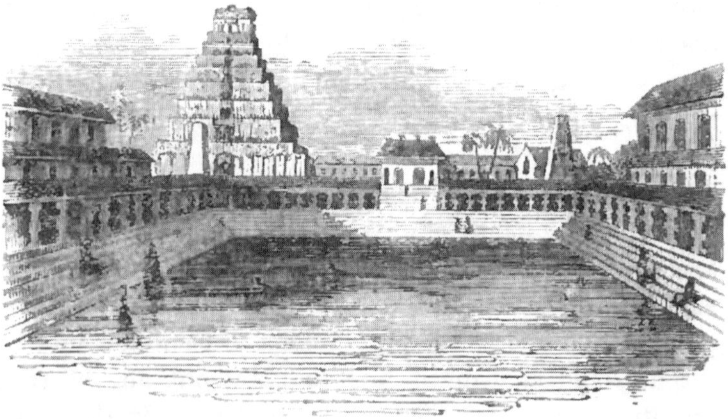

BRAHMAN BATH, WITHIN THE TEMPLE OF CHILLUMBRUM.

At Negapatam we were met by four of our Missionaries from the north of Ceylon, who, with ourselves, were partakers of the attentions and hospitalities of Mr. Mowat, and the other British inhabitants during the meeting. Mr. Lynch announced to us his intention of returning home,—a failure of health, and other circumstances, having rendered advisable a visit to his native land. He accordingly embarked from Madras in the following July, with the blessings and prayers of hundreds, who had been benefited by his ministry, and had a high regard for his character.

Soon after the arrival of Mr. Carver, who, in August, came over from Jaffna, in Ceylon, to supply the vacancy occasioned by Mr. Lynch's departure from Madras, I accompanied him through the Circuit we usually travelled, in which Conjeveram (mentioned page 257) is one of the most important and interesting places.

The Collector's bungalow at this place, where we were entertained, is built on the bank of an extensive pool, then quite exhausted of water by the drought, but retaining sufficient moisture in the mud to emit a noxious air, and promote the production of insects. At night the heat within doors was so great, and the insects so annoying, that both Mr. Carver and myself removed into the open verandah, and stretched ourselves on the floor to sleep. I awoke with a burning fever, which confined me for two or three days, and then passed off without doing me further injury.

This indisposition hindered me from witnessing an absurd ceremony performed at that time in Conjeveram, in the temple of Vishnu. At the bottom of a deep tank within the courts of the temple, was an idol of wood, which, according to tradition, had lain there undisturbed for forty years, and was now only rendered approachable by the dryness of the season. At a time appointed, the mud was opened, and the multitude gratified by a sight of the object of their worship: gallons of milk and *conjee*, or rice-water, were poured on the image, which was then adorned with sweet-scented flowers, and covered with a fine muslin cloth, bordered with gold. Thus ornamented, he was visited and adored by thousands of persons, many of whom had travelled a considerable distance for the privilege. Afterwards he was again consigned to his favourite residence, the mud at the bottom of the tank.

Much of the superstition of the Hindoos, like that of the ancient idolaters, is connected with their hopes and fears in reference to the seasons, the supply of rain, and the success of their agriculture. One evening, on this visit to Conjeveram, whilst standing at the entrance of a temple, and surrounded by a crowd of Brahmans, I told them, that the time was approaching when they and all mankind would agree in worshipping the only true God. After some whispering among themselves, one of them said, "You worship only one God in your country: does it rain there?" implying a doubt, that the seasons could be regular in a country where one God was worshipped. One of them asked, "Why does it not rain here?" By way of answer, I pointed to a boy who stood near, and asked, "How many fathers has that boy?" They replied, "Only one." "But suppose he should call several men father, and honour them as his father should be honoured; and, absurder still, should say to that tree, and to that stone, 'Thou art my father,' and neglect and disobey his real parent; would he not justly be angry with him, and chastise him?" "Certainly." "This is exactly your case. You neglect God, your heavenly Father; and, choosing gods after your own imagination, pay honour and worship to senseless idols: is it a wonder, then, that God chastises you by sending you no rain for two years?" One of them observed, "We also acknowledge one Supreme God;" but all were silenced, and seemed ashamed, when I inquired, where they had a temple to his honour, and what worship they offered to him. In their professed knowledge of God, and their practice of idolatry so inconsistent with that knowledge, the Hindoos come peculiarly under the description of the Gentiles, given by the inspired Apostle: "When they knew God, they glorified him not as God, neither were thankful; but became vain in their imaginations, and their foolish heart was darkened. Professing themselves to be wise, they became fools, and changed the glory of the uncorruptible God into an image made like to corruptible man, and to birds, and four-footed beasts, and creeping things." (Rom. i. 21—23.)

The severe indisposition of Mr. England, which continued some months, and prevented his taking a regular part of the engagements of the Station, necessarily confined our exertions, for a considerable time, within their ordinary circle.

In the month of October, our little band of labourers was diminished by the death of Mrs. Mowat, in Negapatam. Independently of the attachment arising from our having been companions on the voyage from our native country, and fellow-sufferers by the destruction of our vessel, the amiableness of her disposition, and her regard for the work of the Mission, caused her loss to be much deplored by myself, and, in fact, by all who had known her. Our deep sorrow was only mitigated by the cheering assurance afforded by her character in life, and the dispositions manifested even in the delirium which preceded her dissolution, that the event which we mourned was to her one of infinite advantage.

Mr. Mowat was now alone on his Station; and it was thought advisable that I should visit Negapatam, to relieve him for some time from his engagements, and afford him the cheering influence of society.

Nothing of particular interest occurred on this journey to Negapatam, (which I commenced on November 3d,) till the third night, when I reached the banks of the inlet of the sea near Alemparva, and, finding neither boats nor boatmen, was obliged to commit myself to a very rude raft with three of my bearers; the palankeen and the rest of my party were, by the same means, got over with some difficulty.

The few hours I passed in Pondicherry were employed in inquiring for books; and I fear the result affords too correct an illustration of the state of literature among the inhabitants of that settlement. I was directed to a little, dirty shop, where perfumery and other small articles were vended: amongst them were a few soiled volumes of French novels, which seemed to serve the double purpose of a circulating library, and a stock for sale. The object of my search being noised abroad, I was met in the street by two men, who offered for sale Thomas à Kempis, in French, and the Dialogues of Fenelon, in Portuguese; which were the most valuable books I saw in Pondicherry, except the library of a medical man lately embarked for Europe, from which I selected a good copy of the Vulgate, and a curious English Bible, in black letter.

At Cuddalore I passed a Sunday of rest and enjoyment in the society of some friends then resident there; one of them recently returned from Burmah, where the severities of the campaign had been destructive to his health, and induced a disease which shortly hastened him to a premature grave. The circumstances of the following day formed a contrast to the pleasures of the preceding, not uncommonly experienced by the English traveller in India. Instead of the comforts of a house, and the society of agreeable friends, I had to take up my quarters in a ruinous shed, from which I had previously dispossessed two ragged horses.

The last two days of my journey I suffered the inconveniences of a deluge of rain, which swelled the rivers, and laid miles of the country under water: in many places we found deep and rapid torrents, where a few days before scarcely a drop of water could be obtained,

Those that were fordable were passed without boats by the native passengers, the women as well as the men wading fearlessly breast or shoulder high, retaining only one fold of their cloth about their persons, the rest being carefully borne on the head, to afford dry clothing when the opposite bank was gained; the part of the cloth that had been wet would then be wrung and carried in the hands, spread out to the sun and breeze to dry. The costume of the natives is thus admirably suited to the climate and circumstances of the country; the boots, stockings, &c., which the English traveller retains in India, are in general of more inconvenience than use.

Some of the torrents were not fordable, and, not being supplied with boats, had to be crossed by rafts of a very peculiar description. These rafts consisted of a number of common earthenware pots, such as are used by the natives for carrying water and boiling rice; many of them had the appearance of having been recently employed in cooking: they are of a globular form, with short necks and rather narrow mouths, of the capacity of three or four gallons each. A slight frame of split bamboo, fastened about the necks of twenty or thirty of these pots, disposed into a square, served to keep them together, and to form a sort of deck. This frail float was generally managed by two men, one on each side the river, who, by ropes attached to the raft, guided and drew it across, with the passengers who were adventurous enough to risk themselves and their property upon it. In the middle of some of the torrents, where the water was exceedingly rapid, it was with no small interest we watched the water eddying about the mouths of the pots on which we were standing: it would not have required a much greater agitation of the water to have filled them, and, at best, to have made it necessary for us to swim for our lives. Through care, however, and the protection of Providence, we met with no accident.

On this journey, I employed the leisure it afforded me in translating some of our hymns into Tamul. Those hitherto used in our congregations were the work of Danish or German Missionaries, and of course adapted to metres and tunes imperfectly known to us. In my translation from Mr. Wesley's Collection, I retained the English metre of each hymn; and we soon had the gratification of hearing our Tamul congregations, at public worship, utter the same sentiments and unite in the same melodies with our English congregations throughout the world. These translations, beside having the approbation of the brethren of our own Mission, were adopted by J. D'Acre, Esq., of Chittoor, who purchased a considerable portion of the edition printed at Madras in the following year, and introduced the use of these hymns into his congregation. The published copy contains seventy-three hymns, to which I have since added about thirty, which were incorporated in subsequent editions.

The following specimen will afford the reader some idea of the degree in which Tamul may be accommodated to English metre and rhyme :—

ENGLISH VERSION.

"Now I have found the ground wherein
Sure my soul's anchor may remain,—
The wounds of Jesus, for my sin
Before the world's foundation slain;
Whose mercy shall unshaken stay,
When heaven and earth are fled away."

TAMUL VERSION.

Ippoth'en âtmâ nileyâi
Tarikkum nilattey kandên,
Yêsu en pâvangalukkâi
Kâyapattâr end' arivên,
Vânam bûmium ozhindum
Averin irakkam nirkum.

I may here be permitted to express my satisfaction and thankfulness, that, by the translation of our Hymns and Catechisms, which have gone through several editions in the Tamul language, as well as by the publication of many other Wesleyan works in the same tongue, so much has been done to place permanently before the reading Hindoos clear statements of divine and saving truth, and to furnish them with suitable forms for public, social, and private worship.

On the 11th of November I arrived at Negapatam, where I found my bereaved colleague requiring all the consolation and assistance I could afford. In taking from him the burden of the public and private services, I had opportunities of observing the effects of his exertions amongst various classes of the inhabitants, and rejoiced to find that he had not laboured in vain.

A new chapel, erected by subscription on land presented for the purpose by an inhabitant, was a testimony to the usefulness and acceptable nature of Mr. Mowat's ministry. I had the pleasure of opening this chapel on the 21st of November. My sermon was in Portuguese, as the chief part of the congregation were persons using that language; several of the English residents also were present, to show their approbation and afford their assistance. On the Tuesday evening following I preached in Tamul in the same place. The chapel was principally intended for evening services in Portuguese and Tamul, as the church in which the English congregation assembled was too large for frequent services, and was not convenient to be illuminated for evening worship.

I thus continued in Negapatam till the close of the year 1824.

CHAPTER XXII.

1825

TOURS AND DUTIES OF 1825.

In the beginning of January, 1825, Mr. Mowat's family and myself were visited by a fever which had been prevalent for several months throughout the whole of India. The attack usually commenced with severe pains in the joints and limbs; it continued only a few days, rarely proved fatal, but in many instances left effects very difficult to shake off.

Being tolerably recovered by the 8th, I commenced my journey to return to Madras, and passed the following day, being Sunday, at Tranquebar with one of the Church Missionaries then stationed there. At his request, I preached in one of the churches erected by the venerable Missionaries of former days; but, though pleased with the appearance and attention of the congregation, I could not conclude favourably on the state of religion among the people, when, out of upwards of a thousand who profess Christianity, not more than one hundred attended public worship. A faithful ministry of the word of God, and a vigilant pastoral superintendence, are equally as necessary to the prosperous continuance as to the commencement of a Mission.

The rains of the monsoon had now ceased, and had left a delicious coolness in the earth and air, affording some respite from the burning heat which is the general character of this unenviable climate, and of which we had experienced such an undue proportion for the past two years. The thermometer now ranged from 76° to 80° in the shade; the land was covered with the promise of harvest, trees of all descriptions had put on their new and best foliage, and the brisk and merry movements of the beasts of the field, and of "every bird of every sort," indicated that they also enjoyed the temperature of the season. January and February are the pleasantest months in the year in the south of India, during which the European hopes to gather new strength, to enable him to bear the succeeding heats.

My journey to Madras was shorter as well as pleasanter by the mildness of the season: we were only seven days in travelling one hundred and eighty miles; which, however tedious it may appear to the mere English traveller, is good running for one set of palankeen-bearers.

I found Mr. England in Madras still indisposed, and consequently a good deal of work awaiting me. Encouragement, however, was not wanting; several Roman Catholics began to attend our Tamul preaching, who subsequently united themselves to us, and became steady and useful members of our society.

The attention and opposition of the Romish church were more particularly roused about this time, by our commencing a Portuguese service in St. Thomè, in which Mr. Martins, the Franciscan Friar, (mentioned page 301,) who had now lived with us twelve months, and had afforded evidence of his sincerity and conversion, took a part. He had held some communications, whilst residing with us, with Frè Clemente, the head of his order in Madras, a very respectable and somewhat clever man. I have now one of his letters addressed to Martins, in which, after labouring to convince him of the errors into which he had fallen by embracing the Protestant faith, Clemente concludes with the following questions:—

1°. *Quæro. An tua ecclesia sit antiqua vel nova?*

2°. *Vera Christi ecclesia aut fallibilis aut infallibilis?*

3°. *Vel homines possunt salvari in ecclesia Romana vel non possunt?*

4°. *Ecclesia Lutherana, si fuit in mundo ante Lutherum, vel erat visibilis vel invisibilis?*

5°. *Vestra ecclesia si fuit in mundo ante Lutherum, vel fuit sancta, vel non sancta?*

6°. *Scriptura sacra non est nata cum Luthero, sed eam accepit ab ecclesia Romana quando ab ea defecit in anno* 1517. *Quæro igitur hoc modo ecclesia Romana a qua Lutherus accepit scripturas sacras, vel fuit tunc temporis vera vel falsa ecclesia?*

It is not my object here to enter into the controversy, but to show that there is some activity among the Romanists of India, and that they did not part with Mr. Martins, or, as they called him, Frè Jose de Santa Anna, without an effort; and that Missionaries to that part of the world should be prepared not only to labour amongst the Heathen, but to enter into the lists, and combat with some advantage against the advocates of the Romish faith.

Our schools, having now a regular proportion of our attention, began to revive: the means of Christian instruction afforded in them received a valuable addition by the introduction of the "Wesleyan-Methodist Catechisms," of which copies had reached us from England. A translation of the First Catechism was soon in the hands of our native children; the excellency and suitableness of this epitome of Christian truth were evinced by the readiness with which the whole was understood and committed to memory by them. I found a translation of the Second Catechism a work of more time; it was, however, subsequently finished, and extensively used in our schools; and it was also read with great interest by our adult natives. I had not completed a translation of the Third Catechism when I quitted India.

The St. Thomè school, chiefly composed of children of Catholics, was for some time in an irregular state, from the threats of the Priests against those who attended our preaching, or sent their children to the schools: after a little opposition, it recovered itself, and improved considerably.

In the month of February, Mr. Crisp, of the London Society, who had been dangerously ill, came with his family from another part of Madras to reside with us at our Mission-House, for the benefit of a change of air. The advantage he derived was greater than could have been anticipated, and strongly evinced the salubrity of our situation, which, though low, is free from the stench of the burning-grounds, where the bodies of the dead natives are consumed by fire, (the general method of disposing of the dead amongst the Hindoos,) and from the other annoyances common to crowded neighbourhoods in India, and from which few situations in the vicinity of Madras are exempt.

Whilst Mr. Crisp occupied my rooms in Royapettah, I made the experiment of living in Black-Town, with the design of giving more attention to our societies and congregations there: the object I had in view was for a time accomplished, but at a considerable expense of rest and comfort. I occupied one of the rooms under the chapel in Black-Town, which during the day was agreeably cool at this season; but in the evening and throughout the night, the hosts of musquitoes that filled the air, and indefatigably laboured to satisfy their thirst for blood, defied all attempts at repose. I endeavoured to screen myself by curtains, but I found it impossible to keep them all outside; as a farther security, notwithstanding the heat of the climate, I enveloped myself in a boat-cloak, which was yet an insufficient defence against their attacks. These troublesome insects will insert their sharp probosces through the slightest crack in a boot, and of course triumphantly avail themselves of any larger aperture. After a few nights of defensive warfare, I was fairly beaten out of my town-quarters, and never attempted to take them again.

As the only Tamul Preacher on the station, I was so much occupied by the regular engagements of the Mission, that I had little opportunity of following my inclination for general itinerancy through the country, to scatter more widely the seeds of Christian truth. In February I travelled no farther than Poonamallee and St. Thomas's Mount. In March I again visited the same places, accompanied by Mr. Martins, who preached and conversed in Portuguese, whilst I attended chiefly to English and Tamul. On this visit Mr. Martins waited on the Romish Priest residing at Poonamallee, but found him too strongly entrenched in bigotry and self-importance to allow of any intercourse with a heretic.

From Poonamallee we extended our excursion to Tripassoor; the hot sun and deep sand made it a journey of more than half a day, though only a distance of eighteen miles. Here I preached in English and Tamul, and baptized a native woman, who had been married to an Englishman, without any inquiry, on the part of the Minister, whether she was a Heathen or a Christian. On conversing with her, I found reason to believe that she was a suitable candidate for the sacred rite; and as the party assembled on the occasion was a mixture of Europeans and natives, I repeated some portions of the service in both languages.

Meantime I had caused to be published to the Portuguese, that Mr. Martins would preach to them; but being Romanists, they let us know that they would not assemble except in their own chapel, and that if he would perform mass or preach to them there, they would attend.

On our return by way of St. Thomas's Mount, we had an opportunity of conversing with many Romanists. The worship of the blessed Virgin and of saints is certainly considered by the common people as more important than the worship of God through Jesus Christ.

The great day of the annual heathen festival at St. Thomè, held in April, occurring this year on a Sunday, gave us an opportunity of making our message and intentions known to a great number of strangers. We had made it a practice, every Sunday morning, about an hour before the commencement of public service, to place a man at the gate, with a handful of tracts, whose business it was to invite passengers to attend the chapel, and to give away the tracts to any who might be desirous of them. On the day of the feast, many were induced to enter and inquire; we calculated that upwards of a thousand persons received tracts and portions of the holy Scriptures in their own language. Some who resided in the neighbourhood came again afterwards for more tracts or further information; and many who came from a distance no doubt carried with them to their quiet habitations, something better calculated to inform their minds and mend their hearts, than the gaudy pageant they had come to witness.

In my evening walks in our own neighbourhood for conversation with the natives, I sometimes met with persons who thought themselves quite competent to argue on the subject of religion, and were ready to stand forward as champions of Hindooism. The following is a tolerable specimen of their mode of argumentation and defence.

I had walked out with a handful of tracts, and had distributed several, with a few words of conversation or advice to the persons who received them. Passing by a door where two natives were sitting in the shade, I asked if they ever read: "Yes," replied one, "when we have a little time to spare, we read." "That is a good custom," I said; "by attending to your daily occupations, you procure a livelihood and support your families; by reading, you cultivate and improve your minds." "Yes," answered he, "but learning assists us also in our business." I replied: "Of course it does, and therefore is valuable; but as the soul is immortal and more valuable than the body, that learning which has reference to the soul and its eternal welfare is of the greatest importance; 'What shall it profit a man, if he gain the whole world and lose his own soul?' I therefore recommend these books to you; for they treat entirely on these subjects." "O," said the speaker, "I know the sum and substance of those books; it is that a man cannot be saved except he become a Christian; but we know better than that. It is said in your Scriptures, 'that it is easier for a camel to go through the eye of a needle than for a rich man to enter into the kingdom of God;' and yet you Europeans who profess to believe this, have taken one kingdom after another, and are amassing wealth till you have possession of almost the whole world. You have likewise many excellent precepts, but do not obey them; we have the same; so in the end, what difference is there between your religion and ours?" I told him there was one especial point of difference to which I was desirous of directing his attention; it was, that the Gospel pointed out a clear way whereby a sinner might find acceptance with God, and obtain ability to obey those precepts which so few attend to; and thus find eternal happiness in the enjoyment of God;—that this was the plan of salvation by the Lord Jesus Christ. He would not allow that this constituted any essential difference, and maintained that it rather established the superiority of their system; for Christianity taught only one incarnation, but Hindooism had many. I then endeavoured to show, from the characters and actions ascribed to those incarnations in their sacred books, that, even supposing the history of them to be true, they had no reference to the salvation of the soul from eternal perdition to the enjoyment of perfect holiness and happiness in the presence of God for ever; that the works of the infinite God, like himself, are perfect; that what he had once done did not require to be repeated; and that thus "Christ had *once* suffered for sins."

After much controversy, which attracted a crowd of people around us, he exclaimed, "The great God who made all the nations of the world, has made also all the religions of those nations; and as they are all his work, it is unnecessary to go from one religion to another: I have a well in my own house, why then should I go to another house to draw water?" I replied, "Suppose God should make a great well in the middle of the town, and declare that there was something so divine in the waters, that those who drank of them should never be sick, but constantly healthy and vigorous, would not the people be quite right to leave their private wells, and draw out of that to which God has invited them?" He saw I was about to draw the comparison, and interrupted me by starting another subject; so I arose, and offering some tracts to the bystanders, walked towards home, for the night had overtaken me.

With such arguments as these they satisfy themselves and silence those Europeans who, without having the conversion of the people at heart, or making the subject a matter of thought, sometimes venture to recommend Christianity to the natives, or, by drawing a comparison between the two systems, endeavour to show the superiority of their own. It is not an uncommon thing to meet with gentlemen well acquainted with the native languages, and otherwise well informed, who plainly avow that they dare not converse with the natives on the subject of religion, from an inability to meet the arguments which they use.

In the month of May, Mr. Carver and myself took a journey of ten days through the interior: besides our intercourse with the people by the road sides and in the choultries, we had attentive congregations of all descriptions of persons at Chingleput, Wallajahbad, and Tripassoor.

At Wallajahbad, we found our schoolmaster suffering from the cholera morbus, from which it is probable he would not have recovered, had not our arrival afforded him the requisite medicines.

From thence we proceeded to Conjeveram, to witness the procession of the Hindoo festival, held there annually. We reached the town an hour before day-break on the morning of the 30th of May; but, early as it was, and notwithstanding the torrents of rain that had been falling that night and the preceding day, we found the roads and streets crowded by strangers, who had assembled from all the country round to attend the feast, or, as they expressed it, "*to see God.*" Many of them wearied by their journeys and privations, were lying promiscuously on the damp ground in the open air, with no other covering than their thin cotton cloths: when we saw this, we did not wonder that many who attend these festivals, from even no greater distance than Madras, never live to return to their families.

At six in the morning we proceeded to the temple to witness the commencement of the procession. At a signal given by loud explosions of gunpowder and native music, the lofty gates of the entrance were thrown open, and the idol was presented to view; it was worshipped by a simultaneous lifting up of hands, a cry of *Sâmi! Sâmi!* or, "Lord! Lord!" from the assembled multitudes, and was carried in procession along the street.

The idol represented the human figure, under the full size, profusely decorated with ornaments, and seated on a platform borne on the shoulders of men. Several Brahmans were on the platform with the idol, greatly increasing the burden of the carriers; several were employed in fanning the object of their worship, as though to keep him cool during this unusual exertion, or to prevent him from being annoyed by flies: one of them held in his hand a sort of crown, apparently of brass, and almost in the form of a bell, which, as the procession moved along, he was incessantly employed in applying to the bare heads of those who presented themselves for the purpose.

A number of sepoys and peons were employed under the direction of the Collector, or English Magistrate, to moderate the rush of the people, as on former occasions many persons had been killed; on this, a woman was much hurt by one of the elephants (attending the procession) inadvertently putting his foot upon her. It was extraordinary that we heard of no other accident having occurred in the movement of so vast an assemblage: it was calculated that the people occupying the main street, leading to the entrance of the temple, and commanding a view of it, amounted to eighty or a hundred thousand.

The people were dressed in their best clothes and gayest ornaments; they appeared to attend the procession without any act of devotion, more than the occasional lifting up of their hands and crying as above; and manifested much the same feeling as may be observed in England in the dissipations of a fair or a wake.

A grand display of fire-works, in which the Hindoos

excel, had been prepared for the evening; but the torrents of rain which fell hindered this intended addition to the attractions of the festival.

On the 2nd of June we visited Trivalloor, about three miles from Tripassoor, where there is a considerable temple, and a number of Brahman families.

I sat down in front of the temple, and, being surrounded by Brahmans, asked a number of questions concerning their god, and drew acknowledgments from them which assisted me in exposing the absurdities of their system and worship. They endeavoured to defend idolatry by urging that God has a body or form; that if not, an image may express some of the divine attributes, and that at least idols are necessary to assist ignorant people in their worship. The coincidence which exists between the arguments of these Brahmanical advocates of idolatry and of those who advocate the idolatry of the Romish church is worthy of notice. The Brahmans disagreed among themselves, however, as to what part of their system was defensible, and by what arguments it should be supported. At length they asked why we erected places of worship if we abhorred idolatry; for if we worshipped God without body or form, invisible and omnipresent, he might be worshipped in all places alike. This question gave me an opportunity of explaining the nature of Christian worship, and of stating some of the principal doctrines and facts of our holy religion. Many showed great attention, and at the close a few received copies of the Gospel in Tamul: others refused them.

On our way home in the night, we alighted from our horses, in the vicinity of a temple and a large tank, to refresh ourselves. Whilst there, we had another illustration of the prejudices of the people. A poor man, who appeared to be very lame, told us the history of his misfortunes. I held the light, and Mr. Carver put out his hand to examine the man's leg that was hurt; but the poor fellow started back with horror, exclaiming that he was a Brahman, and must not be touched by us!

In July I was again left alone on the Madras station, by the departure of the brethren Carver and England, to attend the District-Meeting to be held in Jaffna; but, on the 16th of that month, was relieved and cheered by the arrival, from England, of Mr. and Mrs. Williamson, who came to assist, as fellow-labourers, in the great vineyard.

Mrs. Williamson was of a peculiarly amiable disposition, and rendered herself a favourite wherever she was known: she was, however, too tender a flower to be so far transplanted from her native soil. Though not subjected, like most of us, to the exposure and fatigue of removals and travelling in India, she finished her course on the 19th of July in the following year, having been only twelve months in Madras.

Mr. Williamson did not last much longer: though apparently of a robust constitution, he soon felt the influence of the climate. At the demise of Mrs. W. he was labouring under an indisposition, from which he never recovered, an attack of inflammation in the liver, which rendered severe treatment necessary. I witnessed the operation of opening the abscess in the liver, by a deep incision with a surgical knife, A sea voyage was recommended, and he embarked for the Cape of Good Hope; but, before he arrived at that place, he sank under the influence of disease, and was consigned to a watery tomb.

Thus early were this young couple snatched from life, and from a field of labour, in which there was reason to believe they were fitted for considerable usefulness. Such circumstances remind us of the sovereignty and independence on all human agency, of Him, who, whilst he commands us to labour in his vineyard, would have us salutarily to feel that we are not necessary to the accomplishment of any of his great and gracious designs.

The brethren, on their way to the District-Meeting, suffered considerably from sickness and detention by contrary winds. They did not reach Madras again till the beginning of September. We rejoiced that arrangements had been made to divide our District, so that it would be no more necessary either for us, or the Missionaries on the Island of Ceylon, to cross the seas for the purpose of attending a District-Meeting.

The month of August proved a sickly month in Madras: several members of our congregations died; and in the composure and triumph with which they met death, gave proof that they had not listened in vain to the declaration of the truth.

The services connected with our Missionary Anniversary were this year rendered additionally interesting, by being made the occasion of introducing to our native congregation a knowledge of the general state and numbers of our society throughout the world. This was accomplished by means of a report, drawn up in the Tamul language, and read by myself to a numerous and attentive audience. Much interest and evident surprise were excited among the natives by the statement of the extent and numbers of our society, and by the descriptions of the condition of the Heathen, in other parts of the world. The report, when printed, was much sought after by the heathen as well as Christian natives. A similar meeting has been held, and a report in Tamul published, every year subsequently; which have tended to excite inquiry among the natives, and to diffuse general knowledge; nor have they failed to produce corresponding liberality according to the means of the people. By the statement of the Madras Report, for 1828, the natives had contributed in that year nearly £10 to the funds of the Society. It is not a little remarkable that several of the contributors are Heathens, making no profession of Christianity.

A visit to Wallajahbad in September was not distinguished by any circumstances essentially differing from those previously described. My journey in November was more interesting.

On the 21st of November, I went to Poonamallee, and found the congregation, to whom previous notice had been given, assembled in the court-yard of one of the pensioners. On late visits to Poonamallee, not having any house or building that would accommodate the congregation, we had held the services in the open air.

On this occasion, it was a clear and beautiful evening; the air was so calm as to allow of lamps being hung in the trees, which formed extensive and convenient chandeliers; the chairs and benches, brought together from various quarters, were soon well filled by persons of all hues, from the pale worn-out European to the black Hindoo. I took my station in the verandah, raised two or three steps from the ground, and felt it a pleasure to preach to a people amongst whom religion was making daily progress. I was afterwards called to visit the dying chamber of one of our congregation. It was cheered by peaceful resignation and a good hope through grace: the last end of several persons in this place alone, has been to us an encouraging proof that we have not laboured in vain, and of itself would have been a sufficient reward for our dangers and toils. To every quarter, however, of the occupied field, we can look with pleasing recollections of some who escaped thence to a better world; we see others also preparing to follow them; and in the language of the holy Apostle may say, "Now thanks be to God, who always causeth us to triumph in Christ, and maketh manifest the savour of his knowledge by us in every place."

I proceeded to Wallajahbad and Chingleput; at both which places the English congregations were attentive, and the native congregations more numerous than usual.

On my way from Wallajahbad to Tripassoor, I passed through Keelcheri, a village which I had never visited before, chiefly inhabited by Romanist Teloogoo natives: it contains a neat chapel also, and was the residence of a Romish Priest. The latter personage, a Frenchman, whose name is Austrey, welcomed me kindly, and gave me a good deal of his company. Being the only European residing in the neighbourhood, he seemed to have conformed himself in a good measure to the native mode of living. His dress was only a shirt of coarse calico, and a pair of loose drawers of the same; a rude staff assisted him in walking; a slight ailment in one of his legs rendering its support necessary; otherwise he was a strong hale man, though seventy-eight years of age. His residence was a square of the verandah of the chapel, only large enough to contain his chair, table, and couch; his library consisted of a Latin Vulgate and a few volumes of Cicero. He conversed in Latin with fluency and ease, and was very communicative.

He told me he had left France in 1788, and, referring to the Revolution, he said he thought it attributable to the assistance and countenance afforded by Louis to the American colonies in their struggles to throw off the British yoke. During his residence in India, he had made many proselytes; he had now under his care three thousand souls, scattered through about twenty villages, among which his colleague was itinerating. I asked if he was acquainted with the Abbè Dubois; O yes, he replied, he knew him exceedingly well, they had been colleagues many years: he had neither seen nor heard of the publication of the Abbè's "Letters on Christianity in India;" and when I told him of the character the Abbè gave to the Hindoo Romanists, he said it was not correct of them all. When I inquired if he belonged to the order of Jesuits, which I had reason to believe he did, he replied, *Societas Jesu extincta est.* I referred to the smallness of his habitation, and the absence of many comforts; but he said, *Satis est, satis est.* In him I found a realization of what I had often fancied might be the character and state of many of those talented men, who, when they were driven from Europe, with a zeal worthy of a better cause, penetrated into the interior of countries than very partially known, and raised from amongst the heathen population a community and an influence in some measure compensating for what they had lost in Europe.

The proficiency in religious knowledge he required in his people, did not extend beyond the Creed and Catechism; with regard to every thing else, they were taught to say, that they believed as the holy Roman Catholic Church believes. It was no wonder, then, that when I conversed with some of his people, among whom was a catechist, and others employed as assistant teachers, I found them ignorant of the essential doctrines of Christianity. They listened, however, with candour and attention to my statements concerning justification by faith in Christ, and the influences of the blessed Spirit of God, on both which subjects they seemed to have been in profound ignorance. Such, there is reason to apprehend, is the state of the great majority of the Romanists of India. With little knowledge, much of superstition and ceremony, and an absence of all that is vital and sanctifying, it cannot be expected that their moral or religious character should stand higher than that of their heathen neighbours; nor is it a matter of surprise, that the difficulties in the way of Protestant Missionaries should have been considerably increased by the unworthy associations thus connected with the name of Christianity amongst the Hindoos.

My host got very warm on the subject of the Reformation and Protestantism; he wondered at the presumption of men in rejecting doctrines which had been received by the church for ages, and confirmed by such a host of saints and learned men, and became angry when I told him that the heathen priests had just the same arguments in their favour. However, we parted friends, and with mutual expressions of good-will.

Setting out before sunset, I could not but admire the situation chosen by the Priest for his church and place of residence: it is a high spot, in the midst of a fertile country, commanding a pure free air, and an extensive view. Were equal judgment exercised by Europeans in general, in the choice of their residences, it is probable they would more frequently enjoy robust health, similar to that of my aged friend.

The 30th, I passed at Tripassoor, and was led to contrast the present state of the place, with its religious condition when I first visited it. It was then unnoticed, and hardly known, even by name, to the Missionaries of Madras. A feeling of compassion for the religious destitution of such a number of our fellow-countrymen as are pensioned here, and the probability of being serviceable to their native wives and their rising families, appeared now to have roused the zeal and attention of the Missionaries of different Societies. Those of the Church had frequently visited them, and assisted in their school; those of the London Society had given them some attention, and formed a religious society of some of the more serious and steady amongst them. At every visit I thought I discovered improvement, but at none more than at this, when the gratitude of some of the people seemed to have no bounds.

On the 18th of December, I opened another place for Tamul preaching, in the centre of Black-Town, in Madras. It was only a bungalow, or temporary erection of bamboos and palmyra leaves: but being in a populous neighbourhood, and near a crowded market, it was calculated to afford opportunities of addressing multitudes, to whom we otherwise should have had no access. The result proved that we had not miscalculated in this respect: the shed itself, for it was little better, would accommodate one hundred and fifty persons; we calculated there were as many in it at its first opening; and the open front and side were generally crowded by Heathens, or others, whose prejudices and fears would not permit them to enter a place dedicated to Christian worship.

This place continued to be useful as a school and preaching-house, till the middle of 1828, when, from its frail construction, having been a second time blown down by a hurricane, as we had not the means of constructing it more durably, we removed the services to the old chapel, on the Mission premises. It is still, however, a desirable object with us, to see a place for Christian worship, of a more permanent character, in that part of Madras, for the special use of the natives; conversations in the streets and bazaars are of use in drawing attention and awakening inquiry; but stated and regular instruction must be given under circumstances more favourable to thought and devotion.

CHAPTER XXIII.

1826.

TOURS AND DUTIES OF 1826.

In January, 1826, we held our District-Meeting, in Madras, for the first time, and took the opportunity of all the brethren being assembled, to wait on the Governor, Sir Thomas Munro. Our visit appeared to interest and gratify him; he inquired into our operations and prospects, and dismissed us with assurances of the full protection of Government, and his own good wishes for the success of our labours.

My engagements were now chiefly among the natives, and I had the pleasure of seeing considerable improvement both in the schools and congregations: still, however, it was seed-time rather than harvest; a time of scattering abroad the means of knowledge and happiness, more than of gathering many souls into the church. The congregations, especially in the bungalow mentioned in the last chapter, were considerably increased; many hundreds of Heathens, of all classes, there heard the word of God read and explained, and some of our own people were roused into increased activity by observing the interest and inquiry thus excited amongst them.

In February I again left Madras, for an excursion among the natives in the interior. On the 22d I passed the day under a tree on the banks of a large tank, where I was visited by several persons, who listened to my conversations. Among other applicants for tracts, was a

Mahommedan religious mendicant, or Fakeer, who appeared in some measure convinced of the truth. He said, he would translate the tract I gave him into Persian; and inquired where I lived, with a view to visiting me at some future time.

The person who had charge of one of the temples in the neighbourhood presented himself before me; his body disgustingly daubed over with holy ashes: in his hands he held a metal dish, filled with the same substance, into which he desired me to throw an alms for the temple. I told him, that I did not believe the idol of the temple to be God; and that, as its worship was hateful to Him, I should be doing wrong if I complied with his request. He appeared satisfied with my reasons; but rejoined, that gentlemen generally gave something. It is not an uncommon thing for Europeans, by a thoughtless liberality, to lead the Heathen to suppose that they approve of their absurd customs and impious worship.

When I had commenced my journey in the afternoon, I was overtaken by a young man, who requested a larger book than the tracts he had received. I gratified him by a copy of St. Mark's Gospel, and was rejoiced at the opportunity of leaving in that heathen neighbourhood so suitable a portion of the word of God.

I passed two days at Chingleput, where I preached in Tamul, and had the attendance of several Europeans who understood the language. In Wallajahbad, I passed three days in the usual manner, and was encouraged by the numbers and attention of the congregation.

On the 28th I proceeded to Conjeveram, where, from my frequent visits, I was pretty well known. A circumstance occurred here illustrative of the inquiry and gradual change taking place in the minds of some of the natives. It should be remembered, that there was still not one Christian in the whole population, though consisting of some tens of thousands.

Two of the men who came to me brought with them a copy of the Tamul translation of Mrs. Sherwood's "Indian Pilgrim." They said, it was borrowed; and that, within the past two months, they had read the whole of it by lamp-light, being obliged during the day to attend to their occupation of weaving: their object now was, to get an explanation of some parts of the book that to them appeared obscure. They said, it was eight years since they first heard of Christianity; that within that time they had read many tracts, distributed here by Missionaries, and had perused the whole of the New Testament, which had been lent them from one of the schools. They once visited Madras, for the purpose of seeing a Missionary; but, not knowing under what name to inquire for him, except as Master of all the charity-schools, they traversed that extensive town and neighbourhood, and returned home, a distance of about forty miles, worn out with fatigue and disappointment at not having accomplished their object. When I told them, that it was their duty to be baptized, and make an open profession of what they believed to be the truth, one of them readily answered, that the Apostle had said, that "Christ had not sent him to baptize, but to preach the Gospel;" thus showing, that he had read the New Testament with attention, though he misapplied the passage. They said, they were not ready to make the sacrifices a profession of Christianity would require; and asked, if it were not possible for them to be saved without baptism. I gave them my views on the subject, and prayed with them before I sent them away.

On the road, in the evening, I was met by a man who requested a tract, reminding me that I had given him one about twelve months ago.

On the 2d of March, I arrived in Chittoor, and was welcomed in a hearty and Christian manner by Mr. D'Acre, who had sent his people out several miles to meet me.

Here I remained thirteen days, enjoying all the pleasure that could be afforded by Christian society and a prosperous religious establishment.

Every morning and evening, at family worship, more than one hundred persons were present; the congregations on Sundays consisted of several hundreds, and twice, when I preached in the open air, there were upwards of a thousand natives present; many of them prisoners in the jail, who were allowed to assemble in their irons to hear the word of God; and I certainly never saw a more attentive assembly.

The number of native females in the school was upwards of one hundred; many of them read with ease and fluency; when I examined the school, more than twenty married women attended, and gave proof that, though they had entered on the cares and concerns of life, they retained their skill and diligence in reading the word of God. It was with no common feelings I congratulated them on the privileges they enjoyed above their fellow-countrywomen, and pointed out their duty in consequence.

I baptized upwards of twenty natives on this visit, and married several couples.

When I left Chittoor, I was accompanied by Mr. D'Acre as far as Vellore, where I found a wide field for exertion, both among the natives and Europeans.

Before the end of the month I returned to Madras, gladdened and encouraged by what I had seen of the progress of the truth, and by the opportunities afforded to me of proclaiming the Gospel to thousands of Hindoos and Mahommedans. I was persuaded that a change was silently but perceptibly taking place in the views and feelings of a portion of the vast population of India; that many hundreds are convinced of the folly and sin of idolatry, though their hearts are not sufficiently affected by the truth to induce them, for its sake, to forego those social and civil privileges from which they would be immediately excluded if they avowed themselves Christians. A removal of such impediments would soon add thousands to the visible church; but it is, perhaps, more desirable that our numbers should be comparatively few, and consist of those who are ready to "count all things but loss for the excellency of the knowledge of Christ."

During my absence from Madras, Bishop Heber visited the Presidency, and won all hearts by that devoted and cheerful piety for which he was distinguished: when our brethren waited on him, he expressed great interest in our Missions, and spoke in high terms of what he had seen of them in Ceylon. I was in hopes of meeting him on his proposed return to Madras, which, however, was prevented by his untimely death at Trichinopoly, an event which was deplored by all classes in India as a general calamity.

My routine of engagements, in Madras and its neighbourhood, were now uninterrupted, till we were all thrown into deep affliction by the demise of Mrs. Williamson, on the 19th of July. Mr. W. became also dangerously ill, as before mentioned, and, for a short time, my own health was in danger of suffering by our increased anxieties and constant labours.

Mr. Williamson's indisposition, and the entire absence of native assistance, made it necessary for me to devote myself to regular work. With the exception of one visit to Wallajahbad, I did not leave the precincts of Madras, till the close of the year. On the 23d of December, Mr. W. embarked for the Cape of Good Hope, but died at sea, as already stated.

CHAPTER XXIV.

1827 AND 1828.

TOURS AND DUTIES OF 1827 AND 1828.

In the commencement of 1827, I removed from the Mission-house in Royapettah, to Royapooram, a village about five miles distant from the former, but only one mile north of the town of Madras, to which I was desirous of paying closer attention.

This arrangement lessened my exposure to the sun and rain, and afforded to Mr. Carver and myself opportunities of establishing some additional services, both English and native. The schools in Black-Town became more efficient, and, in the course of twelve months, more members were added to the society than for some years previously.

In March, Mr. Bourne arrived from England, and proceeded down the coast to Negapatam, to assist Mr. Mowat.

In the course of a journey I commenced on the 13th of June, I visited many places where I had before preached the Gospel. A few particulars shall suffice.

At Poonamallee I found one, who was suffering much from sickness and pain, and not far from death, exhibiting the same holy dispositions as those observable in believers, under similar circumstances, in our own highly-favoured land. He shed tears of joy, and his face beamed with holy triumph, whilst he related his feelings and prospects; and, referring to the dealings of God towards him, he said, "Whilst he afflicts with one hand, he supports with the other."

It was about midnight when I reached Tripassoor; but I was even then visited by one of my old friends, and, in the morning, had breakfast hospitably provided for me, as my own boy had failed to come up.

I preached here three times: in visiting the school, I heard about twenty of the children repeat by heart the twenty-fifth chapter of Matthew.

On the night of the 15th, when sleeping at a choultry, between Tripassoor and Wallajahbad, I was awoke by the cry of *Pambu, pambu!* "A serpent, a serpent!" My bearers were all on the alert, the serpent had passed between them and me, without touching any one. Having ascertained that it was not the hooded serpent, or *cobra de capella*, which their superstitious reverence will not allow them to destroy, though it is one of the most deadly reptiles in existence, they killed it, and then found that it was the *kazhuthei virian*, literally, "ass viper," a serpent whose bite is fatal.

We far less frequently hear of injury sustained by the bite of serpents, than might be anticipated from their numbers, and the practice of the natives of sleeping on the ground. During my residence in Madras, five serpents of a venomous kind were killed on the Mission premises, but no person was injured by them. A short time before I left Madras, a man, who brought me a note from Mr. Carver to Royapooram, was, on his return, bitten by a serpent, near the gate of the town: though it was midnight, he obtained assistance from the chapel-keeper, and a native doctor succeeded in checking the influence of the venom; which in two or three days seeming to have recovered its power, he was affected as at the first, and, becoming dangerously ill, requested to be baptized, that he might die a Christian, as he had for some time been a candidate for admission into the Christian church. The same doctor was again called to him, and, by means of his specifics, was successful in restoring him to perfect health.

Singular as it may appear, the natives suffer more from the attacks of rats than of serpents. The former, which exist in great numbers and variety, take advantage of the men being soundly asleep, and eat the skin from the soles of their feet, so near the quick, as often to make it difficult for them to walk for some days afterwards. I was awoke and astonished one night, by something tugging at my ear; it was a rat: the moment I stirred, my visitant made good his retreat: had my sleep been more sound, I should probably have suffered severely.

At Wallajahbad, I was employed as usual, in the chapel and in the school, for four days.

On the 20th, I set out for Vellore. In passing through Arcot, I was recognised by a native, who said he had formerly seen me at Conjeveram, and now again wished for tracts. I exceeded his request, by giving him a Gospel also.

At Vellore, I was kindly entertained for three days, by Captain Wahab; and had an opportunity of preaching to attentive congregations, English and native. From thence I proceeded to Chittoor, where I could not long remain; but again, for a short time only, enjoyed the society of my friends, both English and native. A journey, as rapid as circumstances would allow, brought me back to Madras, on the morning of the 30th of June.

This was the last time I had the pleasure of seeing Mr. D'Acre. In the beginning of 1828, he fell a victim to a severe fever, which, from the description I heard of it, was similar to that of which I was cured at his house, four years before, in a great measure, by his attentions and skill. In him the Government lost a valuable servant, and the cause of Christianity in India a liberal and laborious friend.

In the course of the year 1827, our Tamul schoolmaster in Black-Town, a native Portuguese, who had become a Protestant about two years before, evinced more than ordinary zeal in publicly reading the Scriptures and other Christian books, and in refuting both heathenish and Romish idolatry, and calling the natives to repentance and faith in the Lord Jesus Christ. When I arrived at the chapel on Sunday mornings, to conduct Tamul service, I usually found the front of it crowded with natives, listening to his reading and exhortations.

Spontaneous exertion on the part of the natives is what we particularly wish to see; as likely to proceed from right motives, and being an encouraging indication of the workings of divine influence. We have not been without several valuable instances of this kind, both among our immediate congregations and those members who had been removed to a distance from us: and may not some important results be anticipated from the labours of a few faithful men, though their number and character may, to a casual observer, appear unworthy of notice? The walls of the city have been compassed, and though the force be apparently inadequate, let them continue to be compassed in the name of the Lord, and they will one day fall down suddenly, so that every man may go up into the breach that is before him.

Another means which has been employed by the brethren at our different stations, and which should, perhaps, have been before adverted to, is the establishment of daily morning service, at an early hour, either in the chapel or the Missionary's house, at which we had not unfrequently an encouraging attendance of strangers, as well as of our own people and the children of the schools. By these frequent services, by school examinations, and continual intercourse with the natives, the Missionary becomes familiarized with the people and the language;

and there are perhaps weeks and months in which he reads and speaks more in the languages of India than he does in his own.

The hurricane which occurred in December, 1827, was the most violent that had been experienced in Madras for some years. On the 5th I had left home early, married a native couple at the chapel, and had gone thence to Perumboor, the residence of the Rev. W. Sawyer, of the Church Missionary Society, to be present at the opening of a beautiful little church he had erected in his garden, for Tamul worship. In the afternoon a singular murky blue line of clouds near the horizon, to the north-east, attracted my attention, and, together with the extreme coldness of the day, led me to expect rough weather. I postponed an engagement I had that evening, and hastened home; but did not reach it before the rain had commenced, the wind being from the north-west, which continued till towards midnight, when it blew a tremendous hurricane from the north-east. I lay down, but not to sleep; the increasing violence of the wind filled me with anxiety for the shipping in the roads, and for the many thousands of inhabitants of fragile dwellings on shore. I once rose to satisfy myself whether the tremendous roaring was that of the wind only, or whether the sea had not passed its bounds, and was ready to swallow us up. The storm increased in violence; and, giving up thoughts of rest, I stood where I was not much exposed to the tempest, to watch its progress. Large trees in the garden were torn up by the roots, and others were laid prostrate on the ground. In a grove of cocoa-nut trees opposite, several were torn up, and others snapped in the middle; they waved to the wind like so many stalks of wheat. All the natives in the garden left their more imperfect shelter and came into the hall, where they lay on a heap; the dog appeared to sympathize with their fear, and crept whining into a corner. The storm continued unabated till after sunrise; but in the midst of it I saw naked natives, who might have been imagined to be demons of the storm, hurrying away with fruit, timber, or any other wreck they could lay their hands on.

Wishing to have a view of the sea, I tried to ascend to the top of the house, by the flight of steps outside, leading to the terraced roof; but was obliged to return for fear of being carried away. I ventured up when the storm was somewhat abated, and had my fears for the shipping increased by the violence of the surf, and the distance from the shore at which it began to break.

I now ventured out to see the damage which had been done; the road, in many places, was obstructed by the uprooted trees; our chapel in Black-Town was partially unroofed, and consequently drenched inside; the bungalow for school and preaching lay prostrate on the ground. In another part of the town, the beautiful high front of a new Romish church had been blown down upon the roof, which was forced in, and the expensive furniture of the interior destroyed. A Romanist, who witnessed the destruction of my temporary chapel, exclaimed, "There goes the Protestant religion:" when his own chapel gave way, he assumed a more serious tone. On the beach, large stones, heavier than a man could lift, were thrown up to a considerable distance; heavy boats had been blown from their moorings, and rolled over and over, throwing down walls and palisades in their progress for several hundred yards. Five vessels lay complete wrecks within three miles of each other on the coast; but the crews had in general got on shore. I saw one poor native woman who had been killed by the falling of a strong wall; but, on the whole, fewer lives were lost than might have been apprehended.

The hurricane extended with equal violence to forty or fifty miles in-land, but not to so great a distance either north or south.

At the close of 1827, I prepared to pay a visit to my native land, but was induced to defer that pleasure for another year, by the wishes of the brethren, expressed in the District Meeting of January, 1828.

A journey in February to Wallajahbad, in which I visited several places frequently mentioned, accompanied by the schoolmaster, whose character has already been adverted to, did not present any incident of unusual interest. In the course of it I distributed about fifty Gospels and nearly a thousand tracts. My engagements, both at home and abroad, continued to be such as before described.

In March I became the subject of some indisposition, which unfitted me for my work; Mr. Bourne came up from Negapatam, on the 1st of May, to supply my place. I now made trial of change of air, and followed medical advice until July, without experiencing any amelioration, when my friends agreed with my medical advisers that a sea voyage and a residence of some time in my native land had become absolutely necessary for my restoration.

Accordingly I embarked in the "General Palmer," on the 20th of July, 1828, and was accompanied to the vessel by Mr. Carver, who had displayed the greatest kindness to me during my indisposition, and several Brahman natives, whom curiosity led to visit and examine the ship.

I had then been, within a few weeks, eight years in India, more than six of which had been happily passed in Madras. I could not quit the scene of honourable labour, and some degree of usefulness, without regret; I never revert to Madras without feelings of pleasure; and flatter myself that the additional information concerning it, offered in the following chapter, will not be unacceptable to the reader who has accompanied me thus far.

CHAPTER XXV.

CONCLUDING REMARKS ON MADRAS.

Before entering upon an account of my voyage home, I lay before my readers some remarks on subjects not fully treated upon in the preceding chapters.

Madras is a place of greater political than commercial importance. Though it is the chief port in the south of India, the circumstance of its possessing no harbour or shelter for shipping, causes it to be shunned at some seasons, and renders it at all times less desirable to trade at than the other Presidencies; the coasting trade is difficult and limited. All goods being embarked and disembarked by Masoola boats managed by natives, English seamen are rarely seen ashore; and it would scarcely be possible to pick up an English boat's crew from amongst the whole population. It is said to have been nothing better than a fishing village, before it was fixed upon by the British as the seat of Government; and it is obvious that a great part of the site of Black-Town was formerly a part of the salt ditch, or back-water, which may be observed, a little way within the beach, for many miles both to the north and south; and of which Cochrane's canal is a part, deepened so as to make it navigable for boats as far north as Pulicat.

A view of the ecclesiastical establishments of Madras would afford some assistance in estimating its importance. The Romish Clergy are numerous, and are to be seen, as is never the case in England, walking abroad in the habit of their orders; the Franciscan with his gown and the cord about his waist, the Capuchin with his hooded cloak, &c. There are also some of the Clergy of the

Armenian Church, who, I was informed, have this peculiarity, that they must be married men to be eligible to these distant appointments; and that for ten years, the period of their engagement, they leave their families in their native land. Madras has now, for several years, been the seat of an English Bishop: previously an Archdeacon and several Chaplains supplied the churches of the established Church of England. Two Presbyterian Ministers, of the Kirk of Scotland, officiate at St. Andrew's. The Incorporated Society for the Propagation of the Gospel had two Missionaries in Madras; its affairs are conducted by a Committee of resident gentlemen. The Church Missionary Society had also two Missionaries, and a similar Committee. The London Missionary Society had two Missionaries, and the Wesleyan Missionary Society the same number.* The Male and Female Asylums, for the support and education of the orphans of British soldiers, contain many hundreds of children; and, together with the free-schools of Fort St. George and Black-Town, and those connected with the different Missions, provide for the Christian education of a considerable portion of the offspring of those persons, British and native, whose indifference or poverty would have consigned them to ignorance and Heathenism. The reading population is supplied with Bibles and tracts by the active local auxiliaries of the British and Foreign Bible and Tract Societies.

The British community of Madras consists chiefly of the members and servants of the Government, in active service, and a few lawyers and merchants.

The English congregations of the different Mission chapels are composed chiefly of descendants of Europeans,

* For the Statistics of the Madras Presidency, and a View of the Missions of each Society according to the most recent returns, see the Tables appended to the Introduction.

or Indo-Britons, a rapidly-increasing and important race, forming a link of connexion and communication between the British and the Hindoos.

The chief employment of persons of this class is, that of clerks in the different offices of Government. Being, in many instances, the children of persons holding high situations, and not having before them the example and circumstances of the lower and middling classes of English society, they are inclined to despise mechanical pursuits, as low and unsuitable to them; whilst, in point of fact also, their adoption of the English mode of living has made it impossible for them to compete with the natives in cheapness of labour, or to obtain a comfortable subsistence in such employments.

The moral and spiritual condition of the thousands of this portion of Indian society has been obviously improving for some years past. One of themselves, a very respectable and intelligent man, told me, that twenty years previous he did not suppose there were three families of this description in Madras, in which the sacred duties of reading the Scriptures and prayer were attended to; but now we could reckon many, who, in this respect and in the general consistency of their deportment, would bear a comparison with their Christian brethren in any part of the world. Many of them are liberal and active in religious and charitable institutions; valuable auxiliaries and assistants to Missions have been raised up from among them; and we doubt not they will, ultimately, bear a considerable part in Christianizing the aborigines of India.

The descendants of the Portuguese are not of such a promising character; these, with few exceptions, are kept in ignorance by their attachment to the religion of Rome; and their indolence secures their poverty. Their credulity and superstition were exemplified by the crowds who, in 1827, visited, with offerings and presents, the grave of a notoriously wretched woman in Royapooram, where miracles were said to have been wrought; the falsehood of which was so manifest, that the Romish Bishop of St. Thomè issued an order, that the practice should be discontinued.

The condition of the Hindoos, their prejudices and superstitions, have been, in some large degree, described in the preceding narrative. There is one annual observance of theirs briefly alluded to, p. 101, the full description of which ought not to be omitted, as I frequently witnessed it: the natives term it, *chedl audl*, "swinging," or, literally, "playing on a pole." This play, or sport of Heathenism, bears the usual characteristics of absurdity and cruelty.

In Royapettah, where I witnessed the observance for several years successively, a pole, thirty or forty feet high, was planted in the ground perpendicularly, having an iron pivot on the top, on which rested the middle of an horizontal yard or cross pole, which might also be about forty feet in length: this latter was managed by a rope attached to one end, reaching down to the ground, by means of which it could be made to turn upon the centre as fast as the people could run: near the other end of the cross pole, attached to a short rope, were two bright iron hooks; and at the extreme end was a short rope, about the length of that to which the hooks were attached.

By slackening the rope, for the management of the cross pole, the other end, to which the hooks were attached, was lowered to a platform, higher than the heads of the assembled multitude, from whence, when it was raised, was borne into the mid-air a man, with no other dress than a waist-cloth, and supported only by the muscles and flesh of the middle of the back, into which were thrust the iron hooks! When the cross pole, thus laden, had regained its horizontal position, it was turned quickly on the pivot, by the persons holding the rope at the other end, moving round with it at a good pace.

It was impossible to look at the deluded votary of superstition thus painfully suspended, without a sickening horror; not merely from an idea of the agonies endured by him, but also from a fear lest the flesh should tear by his weight, and that, falling from a height which would insure his destruction, he should, by death, complete the sacrifice thus offered to the infernal gods.

The rising of the flesh taken up by the hooks seemed to threaten such a catastrophe; and the short rope at the extremity of the pole being within reach of the person suspended, was, perhaps, intended to afford, in such a case, some chance of safety. Some of the persons thus suspended appeared fearful of falling, and held constantly by the rope; or, by this means, they perhaps hoped to relieve themselves of some degree of the pain which must be endured. Others, more bold and hardy, made no use of the rope; and, as though happy as well as fearless, thrust their hands into their cloth, and, taking out a profusion of flowers, provided for the occasion, showered them abroad amongst the people, who struggled to catch and preserve them, as though they had been blessings from heaven: one fellow, by way of additional bravado, fired a pistol, which he had stuck in his waist for the purpose.

I never pressed through the assembled crowds near enough to see the hooks put into the flesh; but was told that the only means used to deaden the pain was a smart blow, given with the open hand, on that side of the back into which the hook was to be inserted. From the indifference with which they mingled with the crowd after the ceremony, and the smallness of the streams of blood I have seen trickling from the wounds, I should suppose that a less quantity of blood than would be imagined is lost by the devotees. I think I have seen five or six persons swing in one day.

Swinging is neither practised nor sanctioned by the Brahmans; at least they have always disavowed it to me; and I never observed any besides the lower classes of the Hindoos conducting or participating in the ceremony. It is said to be observed in consequence of vows made in time of sickness or danger, or for the obtaining of children or some other desired object. It is not improbable that facts have afforded good ground for the observation common in India, that the persons who swing are generally notorious rogues, who thus manifest their gratitude at having escaped the punishment due to their crimes. Immorality is not inconsistent with the religion of the Hindoo system, as might be expected from the character of the objects of their worship. I have had repeated to me a prayer in doggerel verse, said to be used by some servants, in which assistance and protection in all sorts of peculation and thievery are expressly implored!

Another curious practice of the Hindoos is that of feeding the bird vulgarly called the Brahmany kite: this bird is considered the representative of Garuda, the bird and vehicle of Vishnu, as the eagle to Jupiter. Garuda is described as possessing something of the intellect and form of a man, as well as the pinions and habits of a bird; a well-executed brass cast of Garuda, as bearing Vishnu and two of his wives, is in the possession of my brother in Manchester. The time of feeding these kites is on Sunday morning, when many respectable natives may be seen on the public roads with small baskets, containing bits of flesh. They call out, "Hari! Hari!" one of the titles of Vishnu, till the kites, accustomed to the call, hover within a few yards of the ground, and stoop on the wing to catch the bits of flesh thrown up to them by their worshippers.

With the Mahommedans of Madras I had only occasional intercourse; they seldom appeared in our congregations, and their haughty assumption of superiority to all other men, especially in religious matters, renders them, humanly speaking, more unlikely to be converted to Christianity than the Hindoos. I have, however, known several instances of conversion among them, and have had hopes that the constitutional energy and superior mind of some of them would be successfully directed to the promotion of the faith they had embraced.

One Mahommedan, of great age and venerable appearance, had frequently visited me, and, notwithstanding his pretensions of superiority, allowed me to talk to him on religious subjects. The object of his visits was at last opened, by a very serious inquiry of how much I would allow him, monthly, if he induced a hundred Mahommedan families to embrace the profession of Christianity!

This reminds me of an account given to me by a respectable Roman Catholic native, whom I knew many years, of the manner in which his family were converted from Heathenism.

Several generations ago, before the English power in Madras extended so far as Poonamallee, there died in that village a Hindoo of the Velala caste, or class of farmers, leaving his property to be divided between his two sons, each of whom was already the head of a family.

The two sons disagreed about the division of the property; and the younger, thinking himself aggrieved, carried the cause before a magistrate, who determined that the case should be decided in the manner sanctioned by the custom of the country.

Accordingly, he and suitable witnesses proceeded to the estate which was the subject of litigation, and the two brothers were required to attend and point out their respective claims. A dish of burning coals was then provided, and the elder brother, who claimed more of the property than the younger admitted him to be entitled to, was required to take the vessel of fire upon his bare head and carry it over the land, on the supposition, that as soon as he had passed over as much of it as he had a right to, the dish would, judicially, become too hot to be endured, and that wherever it should be thrown down, there providence indicated should be the border of his possessions. The elder brother took the fire on his head, and ran with it from one end of the estate to the other: it was, of course, decided that the whole belonged to him, and that the younger brother had no just claim to any part of it!

Whilst the poor fellow was smarting under his loss and chagrin, a Romish Priest came into the neighbourhood: the man waited on him, and related the whole affair, entreating him to use his influence for the recovery of his property. The Priest engaged to do so, if he would become a Christian; and, on this assurance, the man brought all his family and dependents, to the amount of about fifty persons, to be baptized. After they had been received into the bosom of holy Church, when the Priest visited their house, the head of the family pointed out a figure of Pillciar or Ganesa, the elephant-headed deity of the Hindoos, which had long been the object of their domestic devotions, and with which the women and children were unwilling to part. "O," said the Priest, "that is no great matter; it may continue, only let them make the sign of the cross before it." After a time the crucifix was substituted in its place.

The condition on which, for several generations, the heathen and Christian branches of this family intermarried, affords a further illustration of their views of Christianity. It was, that a heathen female marrying into the Christian family should be baptized, and that a

Christian female marrying into the heathen branch should become a Heathen. It is but lately that the Roman Catholic part of the family has determined that no more of their relations should return to Heathenism: in consequence, the intermarriages have ceased, as the Heathens will not continue them under any other consideration.

It is scarcely necessary to add, that the Priest did not fulfil the expectations he had caused the poor man to entertain; and that the whole estate to this day remains in the heathen branch of the family.

The whole population of Madras, whose varieties of character and circumstances are thus attempted to be illustrated, presents a most open, extensive, and important field for Missions, and a field promising, ultimately, the greatest triumphs to Christianity. Every section of the Missionary force has already had its degree of success, and our own has had much reason to be encouraged.

The erection or purchase of seven chapels, two of them of good size, the others smaller, chiefly by contributions among the people,—the establishment of as many congregations, which, though not numerous, are affectionately attached to us, and zealously devoted to the cause,—the prosperity and increase of the eleven schools, superintended by our Missionaries, none of which were in existence twelve years ago,—are sufficient testimonies of the divine blessing having been on our Mission, and will justify the attachment of the labourers to the field, and the hopes which they indulge of an ultimately abundant harvest. These prospects, as well as the increasing facilities for Missionary operations afforded by the labours of the Bible and Tract Societies, should stimulate the zeal of the church to increased exertion, and lead us to "pray the Lord of the harvest that he would send forth more labourers into his harvest." "For the harvest indeed is great, but the labourers are few."

CHAPTER XXVI.

1828.

VOYAGE TO ENGLAND.

The passengers were all embarked by the evening of the 20th of July; but we did not get under weigh till three o'clock on the 21st. A strong breeze from the land occasioned a favourable commencement to our voyage, and Madras, with its spires and noble range of buildings on the beach, soon receded from our view. I could not leave India without feeling that I left behind much that was dear to me; and even the cheering thoughts of a visit to England, and the anticipations of restoration to health, were chastened and partially subdued, by a remembrance of the work, the friends and the colleagues, from whom I was to be separated, at least for a time.

The following day a stiff breeze considerably ruffled the sea, and occasioned much motion to the vessel: as I sat on deck, a heavy spray dashed over the weather side of the ship, and drenched me from head to foot; a fellow-passenger, more unfortunate still, trying to escape from it, fell heavily on the deck, to his considerable hurt and annoyance.

On Sunday, the 27th, at day-light, we saw the island of Ceylon. The mountain called the Friar's-hood, and the whole line of coast, as I had seen it from the ship Tanjore on my voyage out, were in view. I still look at Ceylon with pleasure, because I know that much has been done to free it from slavery and superstition, and that every day the champions of the cross are there successfully combating the powers of darkness.

The day proved excessively hot: the wind failed, we

lay still on the water, and all was calm, as though purposely to allow us to assemble for divine worship.

Great pains were taken to make a comfortable church, by the arrangement of seats, and by spreading out awnings to screen us from the sun. The passengers and crew, the women and children, were all in their cleanest and gayest apparel; my congregation consisted of about one hundred persons, the whole of whom paid great attention, whilst I read the morning service, and preached from, "Seek ye first the kingdom of God."

The confinement of ship-board, and the sort of fare to which we were necessarily restricted, had no tendency to hasten my recovery; and I continued to suffer much from indisposition.

Before many weeks had elapsed, the tedium of a sea voyage began to be complained of by the passengers; and some of my books were borrowed and perused by persons, who, under other circumstances, would have thought it severe drudgery to read religious works. Two or three years' old newspapers which I possessed, became highly valuable, and were borrowed in succession, and carefully returned, after having been entirely read over, from the advertisements on the first page, to the bottom of the last column on the fourth. Many of us were of opinion, that it would have been a profitable speculation for the Captain, or any of the officers, to have had on board a stock of books as a circulating library, to be available only to those who thought proper to subscribe.

We had a good deal of boisterous weather in August and the beginning of September. We were then in the neighbourhood of the Cape of Good Hope, well called by the Portuguese *Capo des Tempestades;* the thermometer ranged about 60°, and it was felt to be exceedingly cold by us who, for many months previously, had been living in a temperature thirty or forty degrees higher.

On Sunday, the 7th of September, it was a lovely morning; the wind was favourable, and invited us to crowd sail; about half-past ten all assembled to prayers. At noon we experienced a lull; the sun shone bright and warm, the surface of the waters was unruffled, and not a cloud appeared in any quarter: we were becalmed for several hours. In the midst of it the Captain astonished us all by taking in studding-sails and gallant-sails, and reefing top-sails, as though in expectation of rough weather. He had been consulting his glass, a barometer of peculiar and very delicate construction, and was right in his conjectures as to what might be expected: before midnight the severest gale we had experienced began to blow, and continued, with little abatement, for seven days: as it came from the north-west, it was direct against us, and it was with some difficulty we could maintain our ground.

The perils of eating and drinking, during a gale of wind, cannot be easily imagined by those who have never experienced them. We were one day taking lunch at twelve o'clock, when the vessel rolled so greatly, that the cheese could not be kept on the table: the Captain desired one of the passengers to put it on the swinging-tray, over the table, on which the decanters and glasses were placed: in doing as he was desired, he stayed the swinging of the tray with his hand, when, in a moment, by a roll of the vessel, decanters, tumblers, wine-glasses, cheese, and all, were poured from it to the floor, and involved in one general smash.

During part of the time this gale continued, the sky was cloudless, and the sun shone brightly; its rays passing through the showering spray, which was broken and scattered by the wind from the top of every wave, formed a sort of rainbow, presenting us with the beautiful phenomenon of a hundred miniature rainbows at one view.

On the 14th we saw the southern coast of Africa. On the 16th, one of the seamen on the weather top-sail yard, trying to ship the studding-sail boom, fell down into the main-top, and was severely hurt.

A favourable wind sprung up on the 17th. The passengers spent most of the day on deck, enjoying the sight of the land as we sailed along, from point to point, continually varying the bold and mountainous scenery, and sometimes coming very near the shore, much delighted at the fair prospect of at last accomplishing that difficulty of the voyage, doubling the Cape. We could discern nothing on the shore, except here and there a shrub on the sandy beach and bleak-looking hills.

At noon, on the 18th of September, we were fairly in the Atlantic Ocean, out of sight of land, and fifty miles to the west of the Cape of Good Hope, with a moderate wind and quiet seas.

Our voyage now became invariably delightful for many days, the weather allowing us undisturbed sleep at night, and permitting us, during the day, to occupy ourselves as we chose.

On the 28th and 29th more than usual care was observed in navigating the vessel. The longitude was ascertained with exactness; the log was thrown out every hour, to give the rate at which we passed through the water; and, during the night, the bell was sounded every hour, and answered by the man on the look-out at the bows of the vessel, by the cry of, "All's well."

On Tuesday, September 30th, before day-light, as I swung in my sea cot, I heard the cheering news of, "Land in sight! land a-head!" It was the island of St. Helena.

Our making this island had been naturally a matter of anxiety to us: our water was nearly expended, our live stock scant and poor, our Indian potatoes and yams had been long exhausted, and we had no substitute, except rice and maccaroni. Our hope of refit and refreshment depended on our sailing direct on the south-east part of St. Helena, a small island, whose extreme length is only about nine miles; (a mere speck in the vast ocean we were navigating;) and our touching there, under Providence, rested on the correctness of the chronometers, and the skill of the officers in taking solar and lunar observations. Instances were mentioned of vessels having passed it but a few miles to the west or north; and, when they discovered their error, having been unable to return at all, or having had to beat about for two or three weeks before they could retrieve their mistake; for the wind, all the year round, blows strongly, and, with little variation, from about the south-east, and renders a return to the island almost impracticable: it was delightful, therefore, to find that the land, when discovered, was direct a-head of us, to the north-west.

I did not leave my cabin before I had made every arrangement preparatory to going ashore. When I went on deck, we were a mile or two from land, which presented an appearance singular and awful. The accounts I had read, and the views I had seen, had certainly failed to convey an adequate conception of the scene then before me;—a dark rock, of amazing height, rising precipitously out of the sea, roughly jagged and peaked at the sides and top, without any vegetation, except here and there a patch of moss rendering the general barrenness more remarkable. As its appearance was uninviting, so its rugged steepness seemed to render it impracticable to land.

This is the side by which the island is always approached. While I gazed on it, I could not help imagining the feelings of the great warrior, whose name had made Europe tremble, when he came in sight of the gloomy rock where he was to be imprisoned for the remainder of his days.

Signal-posts on the top of a nearer, and of another a more distant, mount, bespoke the former vigilance of its possessors: we saw nothing about them to indicate that they are used at present. For about half an hour we glided round the north-east corner of the island, passing point after point of the same grand and gloomy character. At length we came in sight of a small fort, situated on a rock, rising abruptly from the level of the ocean, as nearly as I could judge, to the height of five hundred feet; whilst the back part of the rock assumed a conical form, and rose to three or four times that height. At this fort every ship must speak, before she is allowed to approach the anchorage. The rock on which it stands would seem to be of the same abrupt character below as above water; for we passed it fearlessly, under full sail, within, perhaps, fifty yards distance, and read, on the fortified point above us, the words, "Send a boat."

This it did not prove necessary to do, as several men appeared on the walls, one of whom hailed us with a speaking-trumpet, and inquired our name, &c. The Captain answered, and we were allowed to proceed. I could then uninterruptedly enjoy the scene, and thought it one of the finest I had ever gazed on: the lofty main-mast of the vessel, hung with sails, seemed nothing in height, when compared with the precipice under which we were passing, and from the top of which an orange might have been thrown by the hand upon our deck; or, by opening the guns, which we saw in war-like order, it would have been easy to annihilate us in an instant.

From thence we traced the road, winding and descending towards the valley, in the bosom of which lies James-Town, the only one in the island, and which formed the bay in which we must anchor. The town soon burst on our view; presenting, as the most prominent objects, the church and the Governor's house, surrounded by many other buildings of less magnitude, and of a neat and pleasing appearance.

With the exception of a few trees, of dingy green, the valley appeared as barren as the mountain-rocks on each side of it; but the eye was relieved in the back-ground by a plantation of firs round Alarm-House, crowning and adorning a point equal in height to any within view.

We had no sooner cast anchor than we were visited by the Doctor of Health, whose duty it is to ascertain whether there is any disease on board, before any person from the ship is permitted to land, or any from the shore to visit the vessel. After the usual inquiries, the hoisting of a white flag announced that communication with the land was permitted, and boats came alongside immediately, for the accommodation of passengers. The morning was remarkably fine; cloudy, without rain. We passed through the fortified gate of the town at twenty minutes before ten, whilst the musical band of the European regiment on the island was performing on the parade in front of the hotel, which we entered to order dinner and inquire for conveyances.

After an hour's delay, I and three others procured a low, open, four-wheeled carriage, drawn by two horses, in which we moved quickly through the town, towards the hill on the left. The ascent was rendered easy by a zigzag road on the side of the mountain, guarded, on the lower side, by a stone wall. As we ascended, the grandeur of the scenery and the apparent dangers of the road increased, till we came to one part which had not the defence of a wall; when the fears of a lady, who was one of the party, obliged us to walk the horses. To remove our apprehensions, the driver coolly assured us, that the horses knew the way as well as he knew it himself.

As we proceeded, we several times looked back, or rather down, at the diminished houses of James-Town, and at our own and other vessels in the harbour, which appeared but as specks on the water; till at length both they and the line of horizon became indistinct, and were lost in the distance and haze.

A neat little box, at the side of a hill before us, had attracted our notice, when suddenly the driver stopped the horses, and, directing our attention down the side of the mountain to the left, said, gruffly, "There is his grave," meaning Buonaparte's. We gazed down the steep; and, in a warm nook of the valley, beautifully green, and strongly contrasting with the general barrenness, beheld the spot which had received the remains of the most extraordinary man of his day, overshadowed by a weeping willow, and encircled by two enclosures, the outer one for the preservation of the tree and the grass-plot round the grave. This was a deeply-interesting moment: I gazed in silence and with solemn reflection on the wondrous ways of Him, who "removeth kings and setteth up kings," who "abaseth the proud," and "giveth the kingdom to whomsoever he will." The entire absence of monument and inscription seemed irresistibly to imply, that the extraordinary nature of his character rendered them unnecessary; and that the everlasting rocks and heights which form the island, would ever be chiefly famous as being his tomb, as they had before been as his prison.

We were told we should visit the grave on our return; and accordingly proceeded to the house in front of us, which had before attracted our attention, and which we learned had been the residence of General Bertrand, till a better house was prepared for him, in the immediate neighbourhood of Longwood. We alighted, and welcomed the refreshment offered to us by the woman of the house; for the low temperature of the mountain air had given unusual keenness to our appetites.

To Longwood-House, the former residence of Buonaparte, we now hastened. Its situation is on high table-land, commanding an extensive prospect, and insuring pure air, and a bracing temperature. The approach to it is through a long avenue of trees, of peculiar appearance, having long narrow leaves of a dark green hue, and branches hung with moss, as though but recently left by the waters of a deluge.

We alighted in a court-yard, where we already found a party of visitors; with a few of whom I entered a stable, and admired the strength and beauty of some English horses, kept for the purposes of the farm, to which the grounds about Longwood are now converted. I was about to retire, when the Doctor of the island, who was with us, observed, "This was Buonaparte's bedroom." "Yes," said one of the grooms; "and in this corner, where the horse stands, he was laid in state."

We were next taken to the house, for the most part constructed of timber in England, and sent out to be raised in St. Helena, for Buonaparte's immediate accommodation. It was then used as a barn; fodder for cattle and implements of husbandry occupied the apartments in which Napoleon had read, walked, and conversed.

The house subsequently erected for him, and which was scarcely completed when he died, was magnificent, and finished in good style; but its walls and passages were forsaken and silent, and its garden neglected. An officer occupied two rooms of it occasionally; and a French family, employed in the new experiment of the production of silk on the island, lived in some of the outbuildings. From the floor of the kitchen had been taken the three stones which covered Buonaparte's grave, and marked the spot of his interment. They have not been replaced by others; and their absence gave an air of dilapidation to the place, with which the feelings of the stranger accord, when he hears with wonder the strange cause of their removal. "It was a prison, after all," exclaimed one of our party, whilst we were admiring the building and its situation. There was nothing about the house, or the reflections to which it gave rise, to induce us to remain much longer; so we plucked a few flowers in the garden, and took our leave of Longwood.

Returning about a mile and a half, we came again to the nook in the valley where Buonaparte was interred, and walked by a circuitous, descending, and rather dangerous path, to take a nearer view of the grave.

It was a beautiful little spot, to which he used to retire to read, or to converse with Madame Bertrand; and it was because he had said, "If I die on the island I could wish to be buried here," that he was interred in this place rather than elsewhere.

The place was kept by an English sergeant; the walk was neat and clean, and the surrounding hedges filled with flowering shrubs. A beautiful spring gushes out hard by, from which Buonaparte was supplied with water: we all drank of it, and pronounced it excellent. Whilst others were making observations and inquiries, I walked round the grave, and, picking up a stone for a memorial, joined the party, now moving off towards the carriage, which waited for us at some distance.

The interest I had felt in visiting the monument of Hyder Ali, at Colar, and the forsaken palaces and mausoleum of his son, Tippoo Sultaun, in Seringapatam, appeared as nothing, in comparison to the deep interest excited by visiting the grave of him who had been the theme of every man's conversation from my earliest childhood, and in whose proceedings the fate of nations seemed to be involved. If kings should go on pilgrimage, let them visit this valley in the island of St. Helena.

In descending the hills, on our return, we used only one horse, and had a wheel locked. It was terrific to view the roads we had to pass; but we got down in safety. On approaching James-Town, we again noticed, at the head of the valley, a mountain-stream, which supplies water to the inhabitants and shipping. It leaps from its bed in the mountain, down a steep of considerable height, in a clear, connected stream: before it has fallen half the distance it appears scattered like rain; and seems to the eye to be lost, or evaporated, ere it reaches the bottom; where, however, it collects in a basin, called the Devil's Punch-bowl, and, again assuming its form as a torrent, hastens through the valley, which it fertilizes, and, passing through the town, empties itself into the sea.

At four o'clock we reached the hotel, and sat down to dinner, which was indeed a feast; the potatoes, cauliflowers, turnips, and other vegetables, to us who, in our passage from Madras, had been ten weeks on the salt ocean, out of the reach of such articles of food, had a more delicious flavour than any artificial dishes, and excited our thankfulness while we enjoyed them.

A call for brandy and water, so common a beverage in India, was answered, to our astonishment, by an assurance that they had no spirits, and were not allowed to sell any; that, by a local regulation, a limited quantity, for private consumption only, was allowed to be imported: we had heard of the sobriety of the Europeans on this island; it was now accounted for: but though the fact might be instructive, and the abstinence salutary, the sore complaints which were vented bespoke any thing but admiration of the bye-law, or an intention to profit by it subsequently.

Having tasted the blessings of the land for about twelve hours, we entered the Governor's barge, and returned to our vessel for the night.

On the following morning I re-visited the shore, and remained till past noon; the Government gardens and the stone-quarry were the most interesting objects I met in my rambles; the former were necessarily small and poor, from want of earth, the latter was more in character with the nature of the island, which seems to be one great rock.

I did not see any thing in the state of the people, whether black or coloured, that appeared to indicate the existence of slavery; and it was with surprise I observed against the wall, the following advertisement:—

"To be let by Public Auction,
On Monday, 29th September, 1828,
At ——
For one year,
Two male Slaves, one of them an excellent Fisherman.
Conditions to be mentioned at the time of sale."

On inquiry, I was informed that slavery was fast diminishing in St. Helena, chiefly by the influence of a regulation of Government, that all children born subsequently to the year 1818 should be free. The waiters at the hotel were pointed out as instances of the comfort and respectability of many of the slaves. None of them are allowed to be sold; but they may be let or hired, at the option of their owners, and, if desirous of their freedom, may usually purchase it by a few years' industrious attention to business. We saw coloured men, of very respectable appearance, who had thus liberated themselves.

The Africans, and the people of mixed race, with whom I conversed, seemed very ignorant on religious subjects;

many of them confessed their inability to read, though there are several schools on the island, under the auspices of Government. The whole population, about five thousand, is nominally Christian; there are two churches supplied by two chaplains of the East India Company, who are the only Ministers on the island.

Europeans appear to enjoy excellent health in St. Helena; their comparatively robust figures contrasted strikingly with the wan countenances and feeble frames of those of us who had been long resident in India. None of our party, however, were inclined to remain; and there appeared to be no regret when, at four in the afternoon of the 1st of October, we weighed anchor and set sail for our much-desired home.

The report of a piracy, recently perpetrated in these seas, which had been communicated to us at St. Helena, created a little additional excitement on board our ship; the invalid soldiers were mustered in military order, and the arms and ammunition examined and arranged, so as to be available at the shortest notice.

On the 9th of October we crossed the Equator, in 20° W. Long.

In the course of the night of the 10th, an old seaman died. He was committed to the deep in the usual manner, stitched up in his hammock, with a quantity of old iron, or other heavy material, to cause the body to sink.

On the 16th I seemed to have lost all the advantage which the voyage and our touching at St. Helena had afforded me, and became increasingly unwell: my indisposition continued to the end of the voyage; but I was carefully attended by the Surgeon and two other medical men, fellow-passengers. Confinement to my cabin was more tolerable to me than it would have been to many others; in the evenings I had usually the society of several of the passengers, who displayed much sympathy and kind attention. One of the greatest inconveniences I had to suffer, was the application of a large blister, when we had a great deal of motion from the violence of the wind and seas.

After the usual vicissitudes of fair and foul winds, of painful anxieties and cheering hopes, we discovered the Scilly lights, on the morning of the 17th of November, and, when day broke, had our eyes gladdened by a view of our native shores.

On the 22d of November, 1828, I landed at Gravesend, from whence I had embarked in May, 1820; and soon hastened to my friends, whose attentions, with the air and comforts of my native home, effected, in some measure, that restoration of health and vigour, which was the object of my return.

ON

THE RELIGION AND RELIGIOUS STATE

OF

THE HINDOOS.

It would be going beyond the plan and object of the present work to attempt entirely to unravel the pretended mysteries of the Hindoo Mythology, or to exhibit the system in all its parts; if, indeed, that may be called a system which abounds in the grossest absurdities and most evident contradictions. But were it desirable even to accomplish such an object, the want of sufficient leisure for the undertaking would render it at present impracticable.*

The intelligent and curious reader, however, will not be displeased to find a few extracts and translations from Tamul works, illustrative of the notions of the Hindoos on some most important subjects; and which may not be without their use and interest, as displaying the degree of traditional light which has been preserved amongst them for ages, perhaps from the patriarchal times; and the intricate paths and windings of error on divine subjects, into which the human mind has deviated, when not favoured, as in the ancient church, with continual revelations; or, as under the dispensation of the Gospel, with a full manifestation of the "whole counsel of God."

* All the information which can be desired on Hindoo Mythology may be found in Ward's "View of the History, Literature, and Religion of the Hindoos;" and in Dr. Duff's work on "India and Indian Missions."

These passages and observations have been reserved to this place, and been thrown together, rather than scattered through the narrative, as circumstances might have developed or suggested them, that they might be commented on with greater advantage, and referred to by the reader with readiness and ease.

NOTIONS OF THE HINDOOS CONCERNING GOD.

There are some among the Hindoos who, from the blinding and debasing influence of unrestrained licentiousness, and others who, from the scepticism naturally resulting from the absurdities and superstitions of idolatry, and the unfounded claims of false religions, or the proud assumption of superiority to vulgar prejudice, venture to deny the being of God, and refuse to acknowledge any moral difference between what is called good and evil, virtue and vice. The Hindoos generally, however, acknowledge the existence of one Supreme and Eternal Being, from whom all things have proceeded, and for whose pleasure they exist.

The two principal sects of the Hindoos, the Vaishnavas and Saivas, each strenuously contend for the supremacy of the chief object of their worship, and the consequent inferiority of the other.

DOCTRINE OF THE SAIVAS.

The Saivas, or worshippers of Siven, declare that the Supreme, the invisible Parabaram, appeared or became embodied in the form of Siven and Satti, the former male, the latter female, and made all things as well as all persons, including both Vishnu and Bruhma; and contend that these, and all other beings, shall finally be absorbed into the divine essence from whence they have proceeded.

The following translated extracts, the former from *Sivanyanasittiar,* and the latter from *Arunajala-puranam,* both of them works of the Saiva sect, will illustrate their sentiments.

SIVANYANASITTIAR.

"We will place upon our heads" (an expression denoting profound reverence) "the flowery gracious feet of the Mother, who dwells with the Father, the Lord, who, although without favour, or desire, or disposition, or enjoyment, having the power of love and pleasure; he, the resplendent immaterial, becoming material and assuming a form, becoming also female, becoming the earth and its riches, formed and blessed innumerable souls; dwelling amongst his faultless servants, having granted to them great delight, and freed them from mortal birth.

"We will continue and grow in perfect and boundless love, placing on our heads the blooming lotus of the feet of Param, who is without beginning, middle, or ending, the god possessed of boundless splendour, grace, and wisdom; and whom the inhabitants of earth praise, as pressing to his side the mother of the terrestrial world, and as the jewel of the crown of the blessed, who danced at Chillumbrum,* gloriously resplendent, adorned with the half-moon, and wearing long shaggy hair, red like coral."

* A large and much-famed temple on the Coromandel coast, one hundred and forty miles south of Madras, esteemed very sacred, and visited by multitudes of strangers at the annual festival. (See p. 221.) It was not regarded with great respect during the war, and is more open to European visitors than most principal temples I have visited; I have more than once proclaimed the truths of the Gospel within its walls. It is said that formerly three thousand families of Brahmans were connected with the temple at Chillumbrum, but that, at present, there are not more than three hundred.

ARUNAJALA-PURANAM.

"In the day of the dissolution of all things, Ari, (Vishnu,) Ruttren, (Siven,) Magesen, the gigantic Sathasiven, with the principles of life, sound, and power, shall be absorbed by Para Siven; Para Siven will remain in the possession of all surpassing attributes."

The worshippers of Siven say that he has five faces: in the character of the first, *Sattiyos'atham,* he creates; in the character of the second, *Tatpuradam,* he preserves; in the third, *Agoram,* he will destroy; in the fourth, *Esanam,* he governs; and by the fifth, *Vamam,* he illuminates.

They attribute to him the vilest human passions, and read with delight the filthy romances in which he is represented as the chief actor.

There are, however, some devotional compositions of his worshippers, in which, addressing Siven as the Supreme, they have attained to the truly sublime; and, in the most appropriate language, have displayed a correctness of sentiment and ardency of devotion, which we cannot but admire. It is only by the recurrence of the names of Siven and of Tiruperundurei, the place of the abode of the idol addressed, that we are reminded of the idol-worship in which the language is used. The following extracts are from a work, entitled *Tiruvasagam,* or Holy Reading: I adopt the translation given in Ellis's unfinished work on the Kural.

TIRUVASAGAM.

"O Lord! O my Father! even mine, who am the slave of those that love thee! Thou art the light of truth, which pervadeth both my body and my soul, which melteth my heart and dispelleth the darkness of falsehood!

Thou art a placid sea of honey, agitated by no wave, O Siven of Tiruperundurei!

"Thou who art pure intelligence, not requiring the aid of either speech or thought, O teach me the way in which I should speak of thee!

Thou art not fully comprehended even by the contemplative sages, the gods, or any order of beings;

Thou art the spirit which pervadeth all spirits; thou art the sure remedy against repeated births; *

Thou art the pure light, which shineth in the midst of expanded darkness, O Siven of Tiruperundurei!

"Thou art unqualified happiness,—what more can they require who are united to thee?

Thou art the full weight without diminution, thou art unadulterated nectar, thou art a hill of unextinguishable, eternal light;

Thou comest in the words and in the sense of the scriptures, and art for ever fixed in my mind;

Like undammed water thou flowest into my thoughts; O Siven of Tiruperundurei!

"O Lord, thou hast taken thine abode within me, what more can I ask?

O Sun, arisen in my mind, that by continual solicitation I may propitiate thee!

Thou art he whose lotus-feet are placed on the heads of the gods, O Siven of Tiruperundurei!

"The expanded ether, water, earth, fire, and air, these thou art not,

But, without form, art hidden among them; I rejoice that I have seen thee now with the eye of the mind."

In the last two stanzas, the author clearly distinguishes between the material universe and God, whom

* On the subject of repeated births, or metempsychosis, *vide infra.*

he regarded as the all-pervading Spirit, the soul of the world; a distinction not maintained by all Hindoo writers; nor, indeed, uniformly by those who seem sometimes to assert it clearly enough, the same writer at one time distinguishing between the universe and God, and at another time asserting that the universe is God.

DOCTRINES OF THE VAISHNAVAS.

The Vaishnavas, or worshippers of Vishnu, contend for the supremacy of Vishnu, and his superiority to Siven: they attribute the production of Bruhma, the creator, and Siven, held by them to be the destroyer, to Vishnu as the first great cause, and declare that all things have proceeded from him, and to him they will return.

They ascribe to Vishnu three dispositions, *Irasatham, Tamatham, Satuvigam;* by the first of these, as Bruhma, he creates; by the second, as Vishnu, he preserves; by the third, as Siven, he destroys.

In the *Irusameiavilaccam,* a Hindoo controversial work in the Tamul language, which, if translated into English, would, perhaps, throw more light on the general system of the Hindoos, and the different doctrines held by the contending sects, than any work that has yet appeared on those subjects, are the following verses, expressing the notions of the Vaishnavas:—

IRUSAMEIAVILACCAM.

"As the spider spins its thread from its bowels, and takes it in again, so the Vedas declare that all worlds have proceeded from glorious Vishnu, and that to him they will return.

"At the period when the earth, air, water, fire, the heavens, and the great systems, and the inhabitants of heaven faded and died,* Vishnu alone remained in exist-

* They assert that there have been many creations before the present, and that there shall be many more after this world is at an end.

ence; from the lotus of the navel of that glorious Vishnu sprang Bruhma (the creator); and in many places of the Ruku Veda it is said that Bruhma begat Siven."

My Tamul teacher, Govinda Moodely, belonged to the Vaishnava sect. He argued for the supremacy of Vishnu; and would sometimes assure me that all the worship offered to any being, was, in effect, received by Vishnu, as supreme, and that the worship of Christians was accepted by him.

The Vaishnava system is said to be more modern than the Saiva, and to have had its rise in a village about thirty miles from Madras, called Stree Permatoor, or the Town of glorious Vishnu. The literature of this sect is neither so extensive nor respectable as that of the Saivas. Of the eighteen Puranas, or scriptures for the vulgar, ten are Saiva Puranas, four only are Vaishnava Puranas, two are Bruhma Puranas, and the remaining two relate, one to the sun, and the other to fire.

It is scarcely necessary to observe, that the study of the Vedas, the books accounted most sacred, and which are said to be four in number, is restricted to the Brahmans; and that persons of lower caste cannot read them, or even listen to the reading of them, without being guilty of *maha pavam*, "a great crime." A suspicion, that the motive for concealing these books from the people is an evil one, prevails to some extent; and the most learned Tamul Heathen I ever met with, conversing with me on the subject, a short time previous to my quitting Madras, said, that he understood some of our learned countrymen in Bengal had obtained copies of the Vedas; and he trusted that, with their usual anxiety to promote general knowledge, they would publish them; because, in that case, the displeasure and threats of the Brahmans would would not deter him, though not a Brahman, and others of lower caste, from perusing them, and obtaining a knowledge of their contents.

The following extracts from *Tiruvaimozhi*, "Words of the Holy Mouth," the principal work in the Tamul language on which the tenets of the Vaishnavas are founded, will show how their principles differ from those of the Saivas, as illustrated by the preceding quotations. The translation is adopted, with little alteration, from Ellis's Kural.

TIRUVAIMOZHI.

"Thou art in the heavens, thou art above the mountains, thou dwellest in the ocean,

Thou revolvest in the earth; but though amongst all these, thou art every where present, thou art every where hid;

Thou art amongst other worlds, among systems beyond the reach of thought,

And thou sportest also in my soul: wilt thou ever thus remain concealed, without manifesting thy form?

"Thou art the water, thou art the earth, thou art the fire, thou art the air, thou art the extended ether,

Thou art the two regulating lights, thou art Siven, thou art Ayen (Bruhma);

Thou, who holdest a sharp disk and white couch, to me the sinner

Wilt thou not one day come, giving joy to earth and heaven?

"To rejoice earth and heaven thou assumedst a dwarfish form, and displayedst thy power;

O Father of the energy which supports the earth and heaven,

I perceive thee by meditation, and dance with delight;

Thou wilt assuredly one day approach me in this world!

"Who but he possesseth in the highest degree the highest virtue?

Who but he vouchsafeth clearness of understanding, to dispel the fantasies of the world?

Who but he is the lord of deities, free from all affliction?

Bow, O my soul, at his resplendent feet, by which the miseries of the world are removed.

"He removeth the impurity of the mind, and causeth the flower of purity again to blow;

His knowledge is eternal and immeasurable, but his knowledge is not derived from the organs of sense;

He is intelligence, he is perfect goodness; by the past, the present, or the future,

He is not affected; he who is my life hath no superiors.

"He who is himself all things and all persons; who, as every sect

Believe, is not connected with the five senses; who is the consecrated image of the mind,

The life of the soul; even he may be attained by attaining the power of perfect devotion, abstracted from all sublunary things."

CONCERNING BRUHMA.

Bruhma is one of the Hindoo Triad; to him are attributed the creation of the world and the production of the Vedas. He must not be confounded with Brahm or Parabaram, whom all allow to be supreme, though no worship is paid to him, except under the form of Siven or Vishnu, and from whom, it is generally acknowledged, that even the Triad themselves, as well as all other beings, have had their origin; the Vaishnavas and Saivas have both appeared desirous to identify their respective tutelary deities with Brahm, as the great first cause.

It may have been already observed, that the sects differ in their account of the production of Bruhma; the Saivas saying that he was formed by Siven; whilst the Vaishnavas relate, that as Vishnu lay sleeping on the sea of milk, a lotus grew from his navel, up the stalk of which Bruhma proceeded from the body of Vishnu, and, resting on the petals of the flower, performed his devotions to the being from whom he sprang: he then entered on the work of creation.

He appears, however, to have been ungrateful to his parent; for in the *Arunajala-purana*, it is related that Bruhma, entering Vygundam, the heaven of Vishnu, addressed him to this effect: "How is it, that I, who created all things, am not said to be the greatest, whilst it is affirmed that thou art the greatest in the world, and that I was born from thy navel? As it is impossible to execute a painting without a wall to paint on,* so, if I had not created, where would have been thy work of preservation? Cease, therefore, to boast thyself as being the preserver; if thou dost not, I will create another, who shall preserve in thy stead; and thou hadst now better plunge and hide thyself in the sea of milk, before the demons come and sink thee." Then commenced a desperate battle between them; they lifted and threw each other, and wrestled up and down till the universe trembled, the mountains became dust, the tanks for water were destroyed; the sun, moon, and stars were darkened; the old serpent, who bears the earth, no longer able to sustain the weight, stretched forth his head; and all the gods covered their eyes, thinking that it was the termination of the *Calpa*, or age, the time of absorption. Then all the gods, with Indra at their

* The paintings of the Hindoos are usually executed on the walls of their temples and houses, and not moveable as ours are, on paper or canvass.

head, complained to Siven. Siven immediately took the form of a great mountain (or pillar) of fire, entirely passing through all worlds. When Bruhma and Vishnu saw this phenomenon, they said, "Why should we fight thus? let us explore the depth and height of this mountain; and he that first succeeds shall be the greatest." Bruhma, changed into a bird, tried to reach the top; while Vishnu, transformed into a boar, tore up the earth with his snout and tusks to an amazing depth, to find the base of the fiery mountain: he was the first to give up the attempt, and concluding that it must be an appearance of Siven, he worshipped him. Meantime Bruhma fled upwards, his wings battered and wasted by the exertion, till he met a flower, falling from the garland that adorned the head of Siven, to which flower he told his distress, and prayed him to corroborate his testimony, when he should assert to Vishnu that he had seen the top. They descended together, and when Bruhma asserted he had seen the top, the flower said he told the truth. In a moment, the mountain of fire opened, and out darted Siven, who cursed Bruhma and the flower, but expressed himself pleased with Vishnu. Bruhma was convicted of lying, and on this account, it is said, his worship was abolished, and is discontinued to the present day.

An annual festival is held by the Hindoos, in commemoration of this appearance of Siven; lights are put up on the towers of their temples; and at Trinomaly, the mountain in the Carnatic, into which the fiery appearance is said to have changed, an enormous torch or lamp is lighted, that can be seen for many miles.

OBSERVATIONS ON THE HINDOO TRIAD.

It would weary the most indefatigable inquirer, were we to go into an enumeration of the various forms, relations, and modes, in which these deities are worshipped. It shall suffice to say, that from them are fabled to proceed the *muppattimukkodi devergl*, the three hundred and thirty millions of gods, in whose existence the Hindoos profess to believe, and from amongst which array of "gods many" they find little difficulty in selecting one for every occasion, and for every possible purpose.* It will be more interesting to inquire whether the notion be correct, that in this system we have a corruption of the scriptural doctrine of the Trinity.

There are some points in the two systems which may be paralleled and compared, and assist us in coming to a conclusion on this subject. The Hindoos attribute to the different persons of their *Trimurti*, or Triad, separate and distinct offices. Sectarian zeal induces them sometimes to assert what may appear contradictory to this ; but their general doctrine is, that Bruhma creates, Vishnu preserves, and Siven destroys. The intelligent and learned will judge what correspondence there is in this doctrine with that of the holy Scriptures, in which the work of creation and providence are equally attributed to the three persons of the ever-blessed Trinity ; Apollyon, or the destroyer, being a term applied only to the enemy of God and man ; whilst, instead of entire destruction being threatened to the whole universe, we are assured that eternal duration and conscious happiness are to be the portion of all holy and intelligent beings.

We have seen also that a temporary duration only is allotted by the Hindoos to their Triad : they had an origin ; they are to come to an end ; these, as well as other imaginary deities, and men, and the whole universe, being, according to their system, to be absorbed

* A native man, having observed one of my English friends in Madras say grace when about to sit down to dinner, said, "Ha, very good custom, *pray the god in the belly to digest the meat !*"

and lost in the divine essence, from whence, it is said, they did proceed. The Trinity of the Bible is eternal: "In the beginning God (*Elohim*, plural) created the heavens and the earth." The Spirit, in the language of Scripture, is the "eternal Spirit;" and to the Son the Father hath said, "Thy throne, O God, is for ever and ever." The holy and ever-blessed Trinity, "from everlasting to everlasting," is God unchangeable.

The Triad of the Hindoos, according to their own doctrine, exists separate from the divine essence, Brahm, the one-eternal God. In conversation with me, they have frequently insisted on this distinction, making the Triad inferior to Brahm, and dependent on him; superior only to all other beings in the universe, but inferior to the Great Supreme, into whom they, as well as all other creatures, are to be absorbed, to exist no more, unless he should choose again to afford to them, and the rest of the universe, a separate existence.

There appears, then, nothing in the character of the persons of the Hindoo Triad on which to ground the supposition, that this doctrine is a corruption of the scriptural doctrine of the Trinity. The offices attributed to Bruhma, Vishnu, and Siven, the limited duration assigned them, and the assertion of the distinct and independent existence of Brahm, the Great Supreme, all show this system to have been entirely of the imagination of man's heart, a structure of fables, having no part of its foundation in the great mystery of godliness, revealed to the patriarchs, and handed down to us in the Scriptures of truth.

If it may be still thought that the agreement of the number with that of the persons of the Godhead is a sufficient indication of the Hindoo doctrine having had its origin in truth; I answer, that this number is purely accidental; no sacred or mysterious signification is attached to it by them, as far as my knowledge extends; and we as frequently, perhaps more frequently, hear them speak of the *Panchakartar*, the five lords, (*vide supra*, p. 380,) than of the *Trimurti*, the three gods.

General remarks, on the probable origin and intention of the Hindoo system, are deferred to the close of this essay.

CONTEMPT FOR IDOLATRY EXISTING AMONGST THE HINDOOS.

General as the influence of Hindooism amongst its votaries may seem to be, it is not universal in its sway. In few cases does it appear to have any hold on the conscience; by the educated part of the community it is regarded as a system of priestcraft, by which they feel themselves enslaved; and by the Brahmans it is looked at and supported only as the means of securing ease, profit, and honour. I have conversed with many Brahmans on the subject of their professed belief and practice, but do not remember to have met with more than one, possessing such learning and information as are within the reach of them all, who maintained his belief in the Puranas, or defended, on other principles than those of expediency, their idolatrous worship and superstitious rites.

There have been writers in the Tamul language, and it may be in the other languages of India also, who, probably without any knowledge of Christianity, have boldly attacked and exposed the national superstition; the most eminent and popular of such writers in the Tamul language, is the author of Siva-vakkiam, a work of some antiquity, and very generally known.

Ellis, who, when writing on these subjects, appears almost to have fancied himself a Hindoo, says, concerning this work, "It may be doubted whether it is entirely orthodox: the author of it eschews alike the figurative mythology of the Puranas, and the mystical philosophy of the Upanishats and Agamas; he denies the efficacy of all religious ceremonies, whether prescribed by the Smritis, or invented in more recent times; derides the notion, that the Almighty could have made an inherent difference in his creatures, as in the Hindoo system of caste; and, finally, with the doctrine of metempsychosis, rejects most of the dogmas believed by the various sects of the Hindoos."

As a specimen of the style and tenets of this author, Ellis quotes the following five stanzas.

SIVA-VAKKIAM.

"Formerly, how many flowers have I gathered and scattered,
How many prayers have I repeated in a vain worship!
While yet in the prime of my life, how much water have I poured out!
And, moreover, how often have I encompassed the holy places of Siven!
This I have left off; for the wise, who knows the true God, the Lord of heavenly beings,
Believe not the idol of the temple, apparent to the eyes, to be God, nor lift up to it their hands.

"While taking up the water and throwing it again into the water (in performing the sandya and other rites) what is the object on which you think?
On whatsoever you think you have thrown all the water vainly;
Think on the root, think on the seed, and on the benefit arising from that seed;
When you are thus able to think, you may approach the feet of God.

"It is not Ari, (Vishnu,) it is not Aren, (Siven,) it is not Ayen, (Bruhma,)

Far beyond the black, (the colour of Vishnu,) the white, (the colour of Siven), or the red, (the colour of the Bruhma,) soars the everlasting cause,

It is not great, it is not small, neither is it male, nor female;

Beyond every state of corporeal being it is farther, farther, farther still.

"What, O wretch, is caste? Is not water an accumulation of fluid particles?

Are not the five elements one, and the five senses one?

Are not the several ornaments for the neck, the breast, and the feet, equally gold?

What then is the peculiar quality supposed to result from difference in caste?

"As milk, once drawn, cannot again enter the udder, nor butter, churned, be re-combined with milk,

As sound cannot be produced from a broken conch, nor the life be restored to the dead body,

As a decayed leaf, and a fallen flower, cannot be re-united to the parent tree,

So a man, once dead, is subject to no future birth."

I was never able to obtain a complete copy of Sivavakkiam, but have frequently heard verses of it repeated by the natives, and have met with quotations from it in Tamul works. The following I have translated from a Tamul manuscript, in which they occur as quotations: they will further illustrate the distaste and contempt for idolatry, and its accompanying superstitions, which have grown up in the midst of Hindooism, amongst some of the natives themselves; and prove that amongst the Heathen, there is a degree of knowledge and truth contending with ignorance and error.

SIVA-VAKKIAM.

"Though you read without interruption the four Vedas, and all the Shastras, you shall not thereby obtain a knowledge of God.

Abstain from concupiscence, and contemplate your own minds;

Then shall God dwell in you, in an imperishable form.

"Though you read the four Vedas without any inaccuracy,

Though you daub yourself all over with holy ashes, God will not appear;

Melt your mind, and mould it into God; proclaim his truth;

Then shall you reach and behold the immeasurable splendour!

"What, O wretch, is the holy mount? What, O wretch, is the Irukku (Rig) Veda (said to treat on ceremonial rites and cleansings)?

What, O wretch, is the lofty idol? What, O wretch, is the natural image?

What, O wretch, is the thread wound round the baked earthen pot (in idolatrous worship)?

Know that they are all as perishable as exquisitely wrought silk?

"What, O wretch, is the Veda? What, O wretch, is the interpretation?

What, O wretch, is the instruction? What, O wretch, is the Vedanta?

What, O wretch, is the divine foot? What, O wretch, are the distinctions?

Study, study to know thyself, and so instruct others!

"Hear, O ye (Brahmans) in whose mouth is the Veda.

Who kindle a fire, and pour into it clarified butter, who take pleasure in bathing daily in the water:

Reflect and discern the fire and the water (the evil and the good) that is within you:

Then shall ye approach the unmeasurable splendour.

"The adorning of the person, the furbishing of bells, the putting up of lights, the burning of perfumes,

All these are performed on the same principle, as that on which a butcher kills a sheep, cuts it up, and cries out for buyers;

What sort of worship is the offering of flowers,

In a building constructed of a multitude of choice trees?

"You bathe and dress the body,

You meditate and repeat prayers every day,

Is it in the Munda mantra, or Mula mantra?

In which mantra (or prayer) is it that God is present?

"Ye fools, who bathe in the water morning and evening,

And remain in the water a long time, like so many frogs,

Rise early in the morning, and acknowledge the Three-eyed (Siven) to be the first cause, and you shall get to heaven.

"Why do you sprinkle water, why do you stand (in the posture of worship, till your arms are tired?

Ye foolish men, who neglect to draw the water of your minds,

If you will take the water from the iron and separate the dross (Hindoo alchymy);

The light who is contemplated, and you and I shall become one.

"You were born in water, and you perform ceremonies in the water;

Of whom do you meditate when you take up water and sprinkle it in the river?

Attain to him who is the root, the seed, and the produce, and you will reach the feet of God.

"You are like buffaloes, (fond of the water,) but do not cleanse away the faults of the mind,

Like frogs you bathe in the pools,

Your Four-faced one (Bruhma) failed to obtain the vision of God, though he flew upwards like a bird,

But, whether or no, turn your mind inwardly, and you will behold it.

"To what purpose are flowers and water, and the pleasing temples?

The heart is the altar, the soul is the image, he is every where;

To him who is the five senses, the frankincense and the fire,

And who plays as a dancer, (an allusion to the history of Siven,) there is neither morning nor evening.

"You are distracted by the science of men, who, though born from the womb, pretend to know all things,

Consider for yourselves what is the nature of God, and the way to him; what consciousness or death remains to those who are absorbed into the Deity?

"The books read by disciples, ornamental and pleasing learning,

Idols and gods, and the four Vedas,

And all the senseless raving of books carefully preserved,

Were wholly regarded as vile, when I had seen God."

The expression of sentiments like the preceding, many of which are so opposite to the prevailing superstition, is not merely tolerated, but, in some degree, popular among the Hindoos. A regard to temporal interest, or the hope of averting affliction and calamity, may suggest the outward acts, and rouse and strengthen the inward principles, of an idolatrous superstition in the minds of many; but the better judgment of others leans towards the sentiments so boldly expressed by this author. Whilst such opinions are broached among themselves without affecting the general peace, it would be absurd to suppose that the judicious and well-directed efforts of Christian Missionaries are hazardous to the safety of the country, or calculated to disturb its tranquillity.

ON REPEATED BIRTHS, OR THE TRANSMIGRATION OF SOULS.

ONE of the absurdities of the Hindoo system, ridiculed by the author from whose writings the preceding extracts are made, is the doctrine of metempsychosis, or of repeated births of the soul.

The liability to repeated births is professed to be the great evil to which all creatures are subject, so long as they continue in separate existence from the divine essence; an absorption into Deity, and the loss of individual consciousness, being the only means whereby any creature can escape "the sea of mortal birth."

An European imagination can scarcely fancy the extravagance of the tenets held orthodox on this subject: the following statement of the number of births to which a creature is subject, is extracted from the Togei section of the Sadur Agaradi, and occurs under the head *Pirappu*—Birth.

"Births are divided into seven classes; those of gods —of men—of beasts—of birds—of reptiles—of fishes—

of things without locomotive powers, such as vegetables and minerals.

"In these births are enumerated different kinds, or degrees, to the amount of *eight millions four hundred thousand;* (through every one of which a creature may have to pass before he obtains absorption;) in those of the gods, one million four hundred thousand; in those of men, nine hundred thousand; in those of birds, one million; in those of reptiles, one million one hundred thousand; in those of fishes, one million; in those of things without power of locomotion, two millions. Some authorities, however, differ from the above, by attributing two hundred thousand varieties of births, additional, to the gods, and an equal number less to things without power of motion, making, in the aggregate, the same number of varieties,—eight millions four hundred thousand."

In the Nigandu, a literary work of great merit, the defects inseparably attaching to the beings subject to these births are thus enumerated.

NIGANDU.

"Imperfection of knowledge, obscuration of intellect, weakness arising from pain or pleasure, delusion of passion, designation by name, division into tribes or families, decay from age, and the impediments matter opposes to exertion; he who is free from these is Lord of all."

It is singular enough that they should hold the sentiment, that none but human beings can obtain freedom from these defects, or final deliverance from this almost endless repetition of births; that the gods themselves, in order to gain absorption into the Deity, must submit to human birth. Thus, whilst the system amuses an extravagant imagination, and lulls the natural apprehensions of man, in respect to an immediate futurity of eternal rewards and eternal punishments, as suggested by conscience, reported by tradition, and clearly revealed in the Scriptures of truth, it soothes the aspiring pride of his nature,—representing him as only one step removed from the Divine Essence, divided from it by a narrow boundary, which the initiated and persevering may successfully pass, by virtue of their own exertions.

NOTIONS OF THE HINDOOS CONCERNING THE DIVINE ATTRIBUTES.

If some of the preceding extracts discover a justness of thought and propriety of language relative to Deity beyond what we might have expected to find amongst such gross idolaters as the Hindoos, there are some other passages of their writings, which would serve to show that the nature of God has been made a subject of speculative inquiry, the results of which have been given with an air of accurate definition, and as laying claim to the character of entire and positive truth.

A modern Tamul author, partially enlightened by a knowledge of the Bible, speaking of the degree of information on divine subjects displayed by the Hindoos, observes:—

"It is evident that the ancient Hindoos held the existence of one supreme God, and attributed to him the eight qualities of infinite wisdom, infinite intelligence, infinite power, infinite happiness, having no name, no kindred, no decay, no liability to evil, thus implying his omnipresence, his omniscience, and his almighty power; yet it is equally evident, that when the sects took rise, they embraced the notion that the Supreme does not at all superintend the affairs of this world, but has under him certain inferior deities: these they worship; but to him whom they acknowledge to be the one Supreme, they render neither worship nor service, and only make mention of him to adorn their poetry, or to form a subject of argumentative discussion. It is true there are some called *Nyanis,* or wise men, and others called *Vedantis,* embracing the abstruse system of the Vedanta, who profess to rise above these sectarian dogmas; but as they mingle with the polytheists, observe the customs of their country, and do not form themselves into a separate body, nor bear witness to their own doctrines, their wisdom is small and of no avail."

In the Nigandu, a respectable literary work already quoted, the divine attributes are introduced and mentioned in an order and form exactly corresponding to the verse in which the defects of beings subject to birth are enumerated, as quoted above.

NIGANDU.

"He who is possessed of infinite wisdom, intelligence, power, and happiness,
Who is without name and without kindred or tribe,
Who is without age, and not liable to impediment,
He who possesses these qualities is Lord of the world."

The Kural of Tiruvalluver is a poetic work on morals, of great merit as a literary performance, and highly esteemed amongst the Tamul natives, for the beauty of its language and the truth of its sentiments: it consists of one thousand three hundred and thirty stanzas. The author, Tiruvalluver, commences his book with an acknowledgment of God, in a style which, in the production of an Heathen, we cannot but greatly admire; and throughout the whole he evinces a singular degree of freedom from many of the strong prejudices of the Hindoos, although he frequently illustrates his positions by allusions to the mythology and doctrines of the superstition of his country.

Mr. Ellis, in his unfinished work on the Kural, an invaluable manual to every Tamul scholar, has given a poetic version in English of some parts of this work: the following is a prose translation of the first chapter, which is entitled *Kadavul Vazhtu*, the Praise of God, and commences the section treating on Virtue. In this translation I have followed the gloss of Parimelazhager, who has written a Tamul prose version and a comment on every stanza. A manuscript copy of the whole of this heathen commentator's learned and ingenious work is in my possession.

KURAL.

"As A is the first of all letters, so the Eternal God is chief in all worlds.

What do men profit by learning, if they worship not at the feet of Him who is pure intelligence?

They who cleave to the glorious feet of Him who moves over the flower, (the heart of his worshippers,) shall live for ever happy in the highest heaven.

Never shall there be any evil to them who cleave to the feet of Him who has neither desire nor aversion.

The two deeds (good and evil) connected with ignorance, shall not cleave to them who render that praise which acknowledges the truth of the being of God.

They who continue in the path of the infallible law of Him who has not the five organs of sense, shall enjoy eternal bliss.

A deliverance from that anxiety to which the mind is subject is not possible to any, except those who cleave to the feet of Him who has no similitude.

To swim the sea of vice is not possible to any, except those who cleave to the feet of Him who is a sea of virtue.

The head which does not bow at the feet of Him who possesses the eight attributes, has itself no quality, but is like an organ of sense deprived of its distinguishing property.

They who do not cleave to the feet of God shall not be able to swim the sea of mortal birth."

Some degree of original truth, connected with subjects of the greatest interest to man, may be traced in many of their most highly esteemed compositions, the knowledge of which could not be attained by mere human ingenuity or conjecture, but must be attributed to the preservation, by tradition or otherwise, of some portion of God's revelation of himself. The Hindoos were, at a very early period, formed into a separate people, and were far remote from the highly-favoured nation to whom was vouchsafed a continual and miraculous revelation from God; yet they appear to have received, by tradition, some, at least, of that knowledge on divine subjects, which was, doubtless, preserved by the children of Noah, and handed down, entire, for some generations after the general deluge; and which, it may be safely conjectured, was universal amongst mankind, before the introduction of idolatry. These rays of divine light, however, are now so refracted by the whole atmosphere of error, the only medium through which they shine on the Hindoo, and so obscured by superstitious fancies, as to afford to the mass of the people no satisfaction of reason or judgment; and, consequently, they fail to have a due influence on their consciences and conduct.

The Christian easily seizes on those passages in their writings which express sentiments according with the system of revealed truth, happily so familiar to us; whilst the deluded and ignorant Hindoo attributes to those passages which we would select as excellent, either in doctrine or morals, no authority superior to that of others, which are absolutely false, and to the last degree absurd. Having no certain standard to which they may refer, no test whereby to prove all things, and hold fast only that which is good, the truths regarding Deity, of which they possess any knowledge, are to them almost without power and without value. The fact of no worship being offered by them to the supreme God is sufficient proof of the truth of this assertion.

CONTEMPLATIVE SAGES, OR ASCETICS.

THE characters most highly esteemed amongst the Hindoos for their religious attainments, are not those who scrupulously perform the numerous ceremonies enjoined by their superstition, nor even those devotees who inflict on themselves severe bodily torture, as elsewhere described; but the contemplative sages, who are said to retire from the world, and employ themselves in the exercise of meditation. What proportion of such characters there may be amongst them at present, or whether there be any at all, is difficult to be ascertained; descriptions of them abound in their books, the principles they are said to maintain are generally lauded and admired, and the full adoption of those principles in theory, and a practical conformity to them, are considered as securing the highest perfection of human nature on earth, and the certain absorption of the soul into the divine essence, whenever it may separate from the body.

These ascetics are described as cultivating and maintaining a more than stoical indifference to pleasure and pain, whether mental or bodily, an entire disregard to the rights of property, and an utter contempt for every thing connected with the present world: this part of their character is intimated in a pithy proverb, not unfrequently in the mouths of the Hindoos :—

"Nyanattukku ulugam pe,
Ulugattukku nyanam pe."

"The world is the devil to wisdom, and wisdom is the devil to the world."

Whilst it may appear strange that such stoical recluses, acknowledged to be entirely useless members of social and civil society, and securing no religious advantages to any but themselves, should be so highly esteemed; the respect entertained for them must be regarded as displaying the disposition subsisting in the human mind, even under the most unfavourable circumstances, to render homage to any system professing to deliver its adherents from the trammels of earthly desire, and the consequent dominion of passion; and to give a serenity, however cold, to the soul, which is to extend beyond the period of its connexion with the body, and its continuance in the present world.

The process by which a man may arrive at this state of perfection is distinctly and concisely described by Parimelazhager, in his commentary on the first stanza of the third chapter of the Kural. His language is thus translated by Mr. Ellis :—

PARIMEL-AZHAGER.

"A strict adherence to the proper rule is true devotion. By thus adhering to the rules appropriate to their respective tribes or states, virtue increaseth; by the increase of virtue sin is abated; by the abatement of sin ignorance is destroyed; by the destruction of ignorance the difference between time and eternity is known; and reflection on the evils of mortal birth, and disgust at the pleasures enjoyed, in transient succession, in this world, and in the heaven of inferior deities, arise; by reflecting on these the desire of eternal beatitude (or, rather, absorption) is produced; from this proceeds the abandonment of the fruitless works, which are the cause of mortal birth, and the practice of meditation; and from meditation true knowledge; the distinction of that which is external, as MINE, and of that which is internal, as I, then ceases, and these two affections are thus renounced with abhorrence. It is thus to be explained."

The disposition of mind thus described, and generally applauded as the highest perfection of human nature, appears to be exactly that of the suicide, who is disgusted and weary of the world; and, therefore, to use the common phrase, puts an end to his existence.

The following translations, by the same scholar, from the Tamul version of the Bhagavat Gita, describe the character and practice required in these ascetics; and the latter from Ozhivil-oduccam, intimates the sentiments with which they are said to regard even the religion of their country.

BHAGAVAT GITA.

"Than he who has performed every species of austerity; than he who has acquired every branch of learning; than he who has assiduously performed every religious rite, the contemplative sage is more excellent: adhere thou, therefore, to the practice of contemplation.

"Having, by the study of the various branches of the sacred writings, acquired a complete knowledge of them, and having overcome the deception of the objects of sense, he whose firmness no object can disturb, beholds, with the same indifference, gold and a broken potsherd, and viewing, unmoved, the vast dance of the illusions of this world, rests serene in the midst of it.

"He acts regardless of the fruit of his actions; he is alike affected towards his most intimate friend and his most bitter enemy; he is the same to all mankind, to him with whom he is connected, and to him with whom he is not connected; to him who walketh in the path of the sacred scriptures, and to him who acteth contrary to their precepts: such an one may be truly called a contemplative sage.

"Hear, now, the pre-eminent nature of contemplation, which leads to eternal happiness; having utterly rejected all desires, however difficult to resist, and considering nothing as his own; either in the cave of a mountain or in some other place, proper for contemplation, where he is not subject to any kind of disturbance,

"Here, having spread smoothly the sacred grass, (cusa,) having spread over it the skin of an antelope, and covered it with a clean cloth; being seated thereon; and, for the purpose of purifying his thoughts, having restrained his mind from wandering, and having wholly restricted the senses to the act by which he is occupied;

"Keeping his head, his neck, and body without motion, in one posture, fixing his eyes steadily on the point of his nose, divesting himself of all desire tumultuous as the waves of the ocean, and of all bodily fear, confining his wandering mind within itself, let him think solely on me, (Chrishna, as a form of deity,) This is (*yogam*, or) contemplation."

OZHIVIL-ODUCCAM.

"They shake their heads when they behold the powerful delusion which causes the distinctions of Vishnu, Bruhma, and Indra, of life and death, and they smile as they contemplate the frenzied dance of the illusions of the world,—those who have learned to know themselves."

The third chapter of the Kural, a work already quoted, is entitled *Nittar Perumei*, or "the Greatness of Ascetics," and will further illustrate the estimation in which this class of devotees are held.

KURAL.

"The perfection of lovely verse consists in displaying the excellency of those ascetics who walk by rule.

"Estimating the greatness of ascetics, is like counting the number of those who are born and die.

"The greatness of those who, knowing the nature of both worlds, put on virtue in this, is higher than the world.

"He who, by the hook of resolution, governs the elephant of the five senses, is a seed fit for the soil of heaven.

"Indra, lord of the inhabitants of the wide heaven, is witness to the power of him who restrains his five senses.

"The great perform things difficult to be done, the mean cannot perform difficult things.

"The world is possessed by the man who understands the properties and relations of taste, sight, feeling, sound, and smell.

"The sayings of scripture set forth the greatness of the men of weighty words.

"The wrath of those who have attained the summit of the hill of virtue, cannot be borne even for a moment.

"They are called (*andanar*, or) beautiful, because they extend their benevolence to all living creatures."

The following translations from different works illustrate the same subject, and particularize some of the advantages supposed to arise from the attainment of this character.

DEVICAL—OTTIRAM.

"He who hath truly attained the state of a contemplative sage, having diverted the organ of sense from pleasure to truth, and being released from transitory fears and delights, will obtain a happiness which the gods have never beheld."

TIRUVARUD—PAYEN.

"They who, inclining their mind to exalted wisdom, have attained a state of mental happiness, are at rest: say what besides is so.

"Those of mature understanding, who are no longer attached to works by which the three worlds are obtained, enjoy even in this, the happiness of the world to come.

"Although they possess knowledge, which extends to all things, they will here know only one thing.

"Reflecting on the unhappiness of the ignorant, their compassion swells like a flood."

NYANADICARAYER CAPPIAM.

"The instability of this mortal body is like a ship when sailing on the sea, or when overwhelmed by the boisterous rage of the winds; of all who have assumed a corporeal form, none have remained permanently on the earth, for the soul is disunited from the body, even as the bird which quits the egg, and soars singing to the sky.

"The eminent devotees, considering that wordly prosperity is transient, as a drop of dew falling from the tip of a blade of grass on the sand, as smoke rising from the fire into the sky, as the bubbles, formed when the rains falls abundantly from the clouds, or as the gay flowers on the trees aspiring to the heavens, have approached that which is not transient, and, having forsaken all, are freed from every taint of guilt.

"As the robber death follows incessantly the inhabitants of the earth, and entering, by means of disease, or of his own accord, on a sudden seizes and bears away their lives; the holy devotees, considering that the time of his coming is unknown, vigilant and fearless, are always prepared for him."

GENERAL RELIGIOUS CHARACTER OF THE HINDOOS.

THE description given in the preceding section is applicable to few, if to any, of the thousands of the people with whom the European, if he chooses, may hold daily communication. It is obvious to all conversant with the Hindoos generally, that they are either blind devotees, excluding all exercise of reason on the nature or propriety of their superstitious observances, which is probably the case with the majority of them; or scepticism takes the place of superstition, sincerity ceases to have any share in their constant attention to the numerous ceremonies they are bound to perform, and a heartless hypocrisy is induced upon a character already debased by natural corruption and ignorance of the truth. This latter remark applies especially to the Brahmans and others, whose superior education, or more vigorous natural powers, have emboldened them to think for themselves on the superstitions demanding their homage and observance.

As they have no notion of the infinite demerit of sin, and of eternal punishment, as its just consequence, it is no wonder they imagine its penalty may be easily avoided. I believe it was in the Bhagavat Purana I read a story, which was related to illustrate the efficacy of one of the names of Vishnu, in averting the consequences of sin. The story describes a man, who had been exceedingly wicked: he had one son, whom he called Narayana, a name of Vishnu. When he was about to die, *Yamagingiliergl*, or the angels of Yama, the Hindoo Pluto, waited around him to seize on his guilty soul, the moment it should quit his body, and to hurry it into the presence of their master to be sentenced, as his crimes had deserved, to one of the temporary hells, fabled in their mythology. The dying man, wishing to have his son near him at the moment of dissolution, called him several times, repeating his name, "Narayana, Narayana," when such was the efficacy of that name, though pronounced without any devotional intention, that the messengers of justice could not seize on his guilty soul, and he escaped the punishment his crimes had merited. These absurdities are regarded by many as truth. An old palankeen-bearer, who travelled with me several days on one journey, was accustomed to lie down at night, crying, "Rama, Rama," till he fell asleep; if he awoke during the night, he cried, "Rama, Rama;" and when he arose in the morning, he repeated the same words. It is not uncommon to meet with mendicants who, whilst they sit to receive the alms of passengers, incessantly repeat the names of the gods; in the course of one day uttering the same word many thousand times. Various trifling ceremonies, and especially washing according to the prescribed rules, or bathing in the Ganges, and other sacred rivers, are esteemed efficacious to the removal of moral pollution.

The doctrine of fate, as held by them, has a tendency to blunt their natural sense of accountableness, and prevents them from entertaining any influential apprehension of right and wrong: perhaps the notion that they are ruled by fate, is one cause why they evince so little shame or emotion of any kind, when detected in the perpetration of falsehood or fraud; and may, in part, account for their patient endurance of privation and suffering, whether arising from necessity or religious choice.

With such views, and with the vile examples of the gods before them, in their mythological histories and songs, it is no wonder that the "too superstitious" Hindoos are an immoral people, notwithstanding the beautiful precepts scattered in their books; and that appalling cruelties and vices are practised under the sanction of a religion, framed under the influence, and calculated to gratify the most corrupt propensities, of the human heart.

It may not be denied that morality, kindness, natural affection, and hospitality, in some measure, exist amongst the Hindoos; but it may be safely averred that none of these are owing to their religion,—a system which would influence the mind to close its vision against that "light which lighteth every man that cometh into the world," and which is favourable to truth and goodness, divine or human, only so far as such partial regard or acknowledgment may appear necessary to strengthen some parts of its system, and more effectually detain the minds of men in spiritual slavery and the trammels of superstition.

CONCLUDING OBSERVATIONS

ON

THE CHARACTER, THE PROBABLE ORIGIN, AND THE PRESENT INFLUENCE OF HINDOOISM.

On a review of the Hindoo system, the main principles of which have been thus partially exposed, and its more prominent features illustrated, by the light shed from the devotional works of its votaries and dupes, and by the opposing views of those who, though within the precincts of its sanctuary, have ventured to let in upon it some of the natural light of reason, we are led to inquire what proportion of truth it may contain, how that truth has become amalgamated with so much error, and what is the aspect of the whole system, in reference to Christianity, now introduced amongst the people by the labours of Missionaries.

The views thus afforded of the Hindoo system are deemed sufficient to demonstrate, that there has been no more truth admitted into its composition than was absolutely necessary to give it some degree of consistency, and maintain a connexion between its monstrous and disproportionate limbs, whilst it should receive the homage, and secure the mental and spiritual bondage, of the successive generations of a hundred millions of the human race.

The Hindoo system admits the being of a God, the necessary and rational foundation of any religious belief: having acknowledged this, it stops short, and denies to the supreme Author and End of all being, any interest or interference in the affairs of the world; and allows him neither the fear nor the love of man, neither reverence nor worship. Among the hundreds of the temples of India, there are none to his honour; among the thousands of its priests, there are none for his service; yet it is professed that no creature, except man, can attain to a knowledge of him and union with him: to man it is possible; but, in order to attain it, entire renunciation of all that is desirable and proper to humanity is enjoined, and is to be attained not by any gracious assistance, not in answer to prayer, but by the exercise of natural powers of the mind; on the accomplishment of this object, being and consciousness become extinct, and, to use their own figures, are like the bursting of a bubble on the water, or a particle of combustible matter floating in the air, when drawn with the flame of a lamp. Can any system be more unjust and derogatory to the divine character than this, or more calculated to increase the natural pride of man's heart, and, in affection and desire, remove him far from God?

Hindooism acknowledges a superior and invisible agency, in the government and continuance of the world; but it is not the agency of a gracious and superintending Providence,—the paternal care and tender mercies of God over the works of his own hands: the government of the world is taken out of the hands even of the fancied Creator, and committed to agency, at best, of a mixed character; storms, earthquakes, and general calamities are said to be *sami vileiatt*, "the Lord's play;" and endemic diseases, and family or personal misfortunes, are attributed to the interference of some inferior demon. This part of the system is so constructed as to produce and perpetuate a slavish superstition, without a particle of that consoling security and holy joy, resulting from the conviction that the "Lord God omnipotent reigneth."

It is remarkable that a system, entirely of heathen origin, should profess to record and believe several incarnations of a being worshipped as God. The Avatars, or incarnations of Vishnu, are ten in number, one of which is said to be yet to come; his votaries seem to have no difficulty in believing his identity, whether he is born of human parents, as Crishna, or starts in a moment from a stone pillar, as Narasingha, the Man-lion. The debaucheries of one incarnation, the cruelties of another, the frauds of a third, and the monstrous improbabilities of them all, appear to be received without difficulty. To afford a good example, to atone for transgression, or to redeem man from present and eternal misery, was no part of the object with which these incarnations are said to have been performed; and yet it may not be an improbable conjecture, that the idea of incarnation was borrowed from revealed truth, and that, perhaps, even before the coming of Christ. However, it should be borne in mind, that these incarnations are peculiarities of the Vaishnava system, which is said to be comparatively modern in its origin; and they may have been intended as counterfeits, to discredit or supersede the belief of the incarnation of God, in the person of our blessed Redeemer, the Lord Jesus Christ.

The existence of sin is generally admitted by the Hindoos, though with very imperfect views of its extreme turpitude and awful consequences. The removal of its guilt by bodily sufferings, certain forms of words and ceremonies, and the possibility of entire deliverance from it by abstraction, in which the mind requires no aid beyond its own energies, as believed by the Hindoos, might induce us to conclude, that the existence of sin had only been acknowledged in order to be made light of, or to give cause to ceremonies, and find employment for the ever-busy mind of man.

The belief of the liability of the human soul to a supernatural influence, both good and evil, exists amongst the Hindoos, as may have been observed by the attentive reader of the translated extracts already given. This doctrine, as propounded in revelation, has a most important bearing on the character, the dignity, and the interests of man: its effect, as held by the Hindoos, is to promote superstition, and consequent misery, and to give a considerable degree of popularity to the pretenders to magical power and skill.

A death unto sin, and a new birth unto righteousness, are insisted on by Christianity, as necessary to the happiness and safety of the soul; and the means are pointed out whereby this great change in the character and spiritual relations of man may be effectually wrought. The Hindoo also expects to be born again, and to be improved, perhaps, by the change; but it is after his death that he looks for this advantage, in the transmigration of his soul to another body, in which he hopes to have less of temporal suffering, and more ease and sensual enjoyment.

Another peculiarity of the Hindoo system already adverted to is, that it denies the distinct individuality and immortality of the soul. The Hindoos are not taught to desire eternal life, or even to hope for it; a temporary state of existence, more pleasurable than the present, either on earth or in the lower heaven, the sensual paradise of Devendren, is, in general, the utmost of their expectations and their wishes. Eternity of rewards to the righteous, and eternity of punishment to the wicked, are excluded from their systems of doctrine; and, in consequence, no motive is presented sufficient to correct the tendencies of corrupt nature, or efficiently to alarm and trouble the conscience. The whole is "cunningly devised," if not to deceive the understanding, to captivate the will and affections, to soothe the pride, and to gratify the corrupt inclinations of the human heart.

It would be an interesting, though a melancholy, task, to trace the gradual formation of this system, and the engrafting of its monstrous errors on the truths which it partially acknowledges : this, however, is not practicable ; it now stands before us in all its horrible disproportions, with the marks of remote antiquity about it; and it would be fruitless to attempt deciding which parts may be called its first formations, or its last additions. There are about it, especially in some of its less important ceremonies and enjoined observances, sufficient evidences of human contrivance ; but, when we contemplate the main features, and the whole of the system, we may justly suspect something more than mere human imagination and ingenuity.

The place it assigns to God; his exclusion from interest and interference in the affairs of men ; the incarnations of which it boasts ; the ease with which it professes sin may be removed, and its consequences averted; the perverted use it makes of the doctrine of supernatural influence on the mind; the ingenious invention of the transmigration of souls; the horrible doctrine of absorption, and the difficulties in the way of obtaining even that feigned deliverance from the evils of repeated births ; the concealment from the vulgar of the Vedas, the books esteemed most sacred; the character of its objects of worship; the immorality, cruelty, superstition, and degradation of both passions and intellect, produced and encouraged in the worshippers ; and the effectual manner in which this system is interwoven with all that is esteemed honourable and desirable in the world ;—all intimate to us, that as a scheme for the deception and spiritual thraldom of mankind, it has had the cunning assistance of an intelligence superior to man, and owes much of its substance and character to diabolical suggestion. We have no reason to suppose that the enemy of God and man has lost his ancient desire for divine honours; he is as truly worshipped, under various forms, by the idolatrous Hindoos, as by the devil-worshippers of Ceylon; we may therefore conclude, that what appears above human imagination and contrivance in the Hindoo system, and particularly those parts of it that aim at superseding and neutralizing the divine and saving truths of revelation, proceed from the father of lies, the old serpent, that still deceiveth the nations.

It may now appear almost superfluous to add any thing on the aspect of this system, in reference to Christianity, as at present attempting to be introduced in India, by the labours of Missionaries. It is essentially hostile. There are, however, one or two peculiarities which have not yet been mentioned. There is an extraordinary spirit of toleration towards all other systems of religion. The Hindoos do not wish or endeavour to make proselytes; they profess that, as their religion is good and sufficient for themselves, so the religion of others may be equally suitable for those amongst whom it is found. This, at first view, may seem an advantage, as it leaves no room for the fear of persecution; but, whatever it may be in this respect, it creates an indifference to truth, neutralizes the spirit of inquiry and research, and induces them, passively, to yield their minds to the dominion of error. We may regard it as no inconsiderable point gained, when the mind of a Hindoo is excited to sincere and earnest inquiry after religious truth.

Another obstacle presented by Hindooism to the progress of Christianity is, that the whole scheme of society is founded on the system: the distinctions of caste, so essential to its continuance, are guarded by established custom, by superstitious theories, and by the veneration attaching to antiquity. The whole of this frame must be shaken, before any part can be materially affected. The difficulty does not lie in the re-organization of the whole; but in producing an influence so powerful and so extended as to act at once and efficiently on all classes and portions of such a numerous people: the agency which breaks up the present system will effect a new order of things, without any convulsion, or requiring any additional energy. Let the present artificial adhesion of the different parts be dissolved, and nothing that is real in rank, or wealth, or character, will be lost: Christianity will maintain in full value whatever is estimable; but it has, perhaps, achieved no conquest of greater difficulty than that which is now contemplated, in the equal reduction of high and low caste to its renovating influence.

To be added to these, are the pride of learning and the prejudices of a deceitful philosophy, closely interwoven, as they are, with the prevailing superstition. These are difficulties Christianity had not to contend with in ancient Rome. Throughout the Roman world, it is said, that the priests had neither any sacred writings nor any determined faith; religion was distinct from morals and philosophy; amongst the Hindoos it is combined with both; and, though both are defective, they powerfully assist it in maintaining its ground, and will continue to do so, unless the correct systems which we possess be assisted in their promulgation by something more powerful than their own inherent truth and value. True learning and correct philosophy will probably follow, rather than precede, the general reception of Christianity in India.

Thus have I attempted to describe, however defectively, the character and position of that system with which the truth of God has already commenced a contest, by the diffusion of the sacred Scriptures, and the personal exertions of the Messengers of the churches; partly with a view to afford what information I possessed, to any who might wish to inquire into a subject in which the greatest interests of so many of our fellow-men and fellow-subjects are involved; but chiefly in the indulgence of an earnest hope, that these plain details will have the effect of stimulating Christian zeal to more active energy, and of promoting still wider and more powerful co-operation in the prosecution of the noble task, to which a considerable portion of the church has already addressed itself. It is true, that if the great work to be effected were not divine in its authority, its encouragements, and its influence, we might reasonably, on a view of the great difficulties to be encountered, shrink from exertion, and lay aside all expectation of success; but, having the command, the promise, and the prophetic declarations of the God of mercy and of truth, we are determined not to be weary in the prosecution of our benevolent designs, knowing that, "in due season we shall reap, if we faint not."

AN ACCOUNT

OF

THE VIOLENT METHODS ADOPTED BY THE CHURCH OF ROME

TO PROSELYTIZE THE SYRIAN CHRISTIANS IN MALAYALA, OR THE MOUNTAIN COUNTRY OF TRAVANCORE, IN SOUTH INDIA.*

THE very ancient churches of the Syrian Christians, as also all other eastern churches, were at no time subject to the Pope of Rome.

It was their practice never to wander from their native country. They also held that celibacy is not necessary for the clergy. On these accounts they have gradually increased; so that at this day, there are more than one thousand four hundred churches.

They call themselves Năsătmapilleigl; and their clergy Cassanars.† From early antiquity they have been accustomed to conduct divine service in the Syrian language. From the fourth century of the Christian era, it has been reported, that the Patriarch of the Hindoos had his residence in the city of Seleucia, (the capital of the Persian empire,) near to Babylon.‡ The Bishop of Antioch, in Syria, was formerly accustomed to consecrate him to his office.

* Translated from Walther's "Tamul Church History," Tranquebar, 1735.

† *Năsătmăpilleigl*, is a term compounded of three words, and means, "children of the lapsed soul." *Cassanar* is compounded of two words, and means "lords of the elephant." Human nature is often represented by the Hindoos, under the figure of a maddened elephant. The term "Cassanar" implies the mastery which the persons to whom it is applied are supposed to have over their passions.

‡ At the Council of Nice, A.D. 325, there was present Johannes, who signed himself as Bishop of Persia, and of the greater India. At the same Council it was decreed, Canon 33, "Let the See of Seleucia, which is one of the eastern cities, be honoured likewise, and have the title of *Catholicon;* and let the prelate thereof ordain Archbishops as the other Patriarchs do, that so the eastern Christians who live under Heathens may not be wronged by waiting the Patriarch of Antioch's leisure, or by going to him; but may have a way opened to them to

Since the destruction of Seleucia, the Bishop of (Seleucia or) Babylon has had his residence in Mosul, which is supposed to be ancient Nineveh. The Metrani, or Metropolitan of the Syrian Christians, is sent thence to this country. He has chief authority among those Christians, both as to secular and spiritual affairs.*

In 547, Cosmo, the Egyptian, wrote thus: "In Taprobane, or Ceylon, and in Malayala, there are churches of Christ. The Bishop of Calicut receives his appointment from Persia."

Their doctrines, in many particulars, agree with the doctrines of the Protestant church.

1. In the adminisration of the sacrament of the Lord's supper, they use leavened bread, and wine: and they do not teach that they are changed into the sacred body and blood of Christ.

2. They use no images, but only the sacred symbol of the cross.

3. They have only two orders of clergy: the Priests, and the Deacons, or Stewards of the church. These marry, if they choose, three or four times; and even marry widows.

4. Marriage with them is not a sacrament.

5. They know nothing of *sponsors in baptism*, or of *nyana-uda-piroppu*, which perhaps may be rendered, baptismal regeneration.

6. They know nothing of confirmation,

7. Of Auricular Confession, or of,

8. Purgatory.

In cases of severe sickness, they send for the Priest, and desire him to pray for them; but they are unacquainted with extreme unction.†

supply their own necessities. Neither will any injury be done to the Patriarch of Antioch thereby, seeing he has consented to its being thus, upon the Synod's having desired it of him."

* The word "Metrani" means one who has chief power; it is used indiscriminately to mean Bishop, Metropolitan, or Patriarch.

† Dr. Buchanan visited these churches in 1806; and I cannot resist the opportunity of enriching these pages with some extracts from the very interesting volume, to the publication of which, the Syrian Christians and the church generally are so greatly indebted.

"From the Palace of Travancore, I proceeded to Mavely-car, and thence to the hills at the bottom of the high Ghauts, which divide the Carnatic from Malayala. The face of the country in general, in the vicinity of the mountains, exhibits a varied scene of hill and dale, and winding streams; these streams fall from the mountains, and preserve the valleys in perpetual verdure. The woods produce pepper, cardamoms, and cassia, or common cinnamon; also frankincense, and

When the Portuguese Admiral, Vasco de Gama, with several ships, touched at the coast of Cochin, in 1502, the

other aromatic gums. What adds much to the grandeur of the scenery in this country is, that the adjacent mountains of Travancore are not barren, but are covered with forests of teak-wood, (the Indian oak,) producing, it is said, the largest timber in the world.

"The first view of the Christian churches in this sequestered region of Hindostan, connected with the idea of their tranquil duration for so many ages, cannot fail to excite pleasing emotions in the mind of the beholder. The form of the oldest buildings is not unlike that of some of the oldest parish churches in England, the style of building in both being of Saracenic origin: they have sloping roofs, pointed arch windows, and buttresses, supporting the walls. The beams of the roof being exposed to view, are ornamented; and the ceiling of the choir and altar is circular and fretted. In the cathedral churches, the shrines of the deceased Bishops are placed on each side of the altar. Most of the churches are built of a reddish stone, squared and polished at the quarry, and are of durable construction. The bells of the churches are cast in the foundries of the country; some of them are of large dimensions, and have inscriptions in Syriac and Malayalim. In approaching a town in the evening, I once heard the sound of bells among the hills; a circumstance which made me forget, for a moment, that I was in Hindostan, and reminded me of another country."

"I have now visited eight churches, and scarcely believe that I am in the land of the Hindoos; only that I now and then see a Hindoo temple on the banks of the river. I observe that the bells of most of the churches are within the building, and not in a tower; the reason, they said, was this: when a Hindoo temple happens to be near a church, the Hindoos do not like the bell to sound loud, for they say it frightens their god. I perceive that the Syrian Christians assimilate much to the Hindoos, in the practice of frequent ablutions for health and cleanliness, and in the use of vegetables and light food.

"I attended divine service on the Sunday: their Liturgy is that which was formerly used in the churches of the Patriarch of Antioch. During the prayers, there were intervals of silence; the Priests praying in a low voice, and every man praying for himself: these silent intervals add much to the solemnity and appearance of devotion. They use incense in the churches: it grows in the woods around them; and contributes much, they say, to health, and to the warmth and comfort of the church, during the cold and rainy season of the year. At the conclusion of the service a ceremony takes place, which pleased me much. The Priest (or Bishop, if he be present) comes forward, and all the people pass by him as they go out, receiving his benediction individually. If any man has been guilty of any immorality, he does not receive the blessing; and this, in their primitive and patriarchal state, is accounted a severe punishment. Instruction by preaching is little in use among them now; many of the old men lamented the decay of piety and religious knowledge, and spoke with pleasure of the record of ancient times. They have some ceremonies nearly allied to those of the Greek church. Here, as in all churches in a state of decline, there is too much formality in the worship; but they have the Bible, and a scriptural Liturgy; and these will save a church in the worst of times; these may preserve the spark

Syrian Christians sent ambassadors to him; saying, that as they had heard that he was the servant of a Christian King, they prayed him to take them under his protection. They also sent him the sceptre of their King, who had died only a few days before. He received them and their present, and formed a treaty with them: but the time came when they had reason to repent of this step; for the Portuguese used every means to bring them under the power of the Pope.

The first Priests who visited these Christians in 1545, were Franciscans; they saw that their cause would not prevail, without aid from the secular arm.

In 1546, the Franciscans established a seminary in Cranganore, or, as it is otherwise called, Nodungaloor; and taught the Latin language, and the ceremonies of the Romish Church, to the children of the Syrian Christians. But when the youths thus educated had been ordained Priests, the Syrian Christians regarded them as belonging to another people, and would not permit them to enter their churches.

In 1557, the Jesuits of Goa found that these Christians always persisted in asserting that they were not Latinists, but that they were of Syrian descent. Seeing that no other plan would succeed, they removed from the convent of San Paolo, in Goa, and established a seminary at Veippicottah, near Nodungaloor, in which they taught the doctrines of the Church of Rome, to the children of those Christians, in the Syriac language. In this undertaking they expended much money; they also had printing types of the Syriac language, prepared in Rome.

But those who were educated in this seminary did not venture to change any of the doctrines which they had received from their ancestors, but continued afterwards, as they had before been accustomed, to mention the name of the Bishop of Babylon, in the celebration of divine service in the church.

and life of religion, though the flame be out. And as there were but few copies of the Bible among the Syrians, (for every copy was transcribed with the pen,) it is highly probable, that if they had not enjoyed the advantage of the daily prayers, and daily portions of Scripture in their Liturgy, there would have been, in the revolution of ages, no vestige of Christianity left among them."

"In every church, and in many of the private houses, there are manuscripts in the Syriac language; and I have been successful in procuring some old and valuable copies of the Scriptures and other books, written in different ages and in different characters."—*Christian Researches.*

When the Jesuits found that this plan also was unsuccessful, they inveigled Mar Joseph, at that time the Metrani of those Christians, and forced him away to go to Rome.

The Metrani arrived in Portugal in 1558. He there made so favourable an impression on Queen Donna Catherina, to whom he had rendered some service, that she decided that it was unnecessary for him to go to Rome; and she dismissed him with great kindness, that he might return to India.

Meantime, after the abduction of Mar Joseph to Europe, a new Metrani, Mar Abraham, had arrived in India from Mosul, and had been joyfully received by the Syrian Christians. But afterwards, by the return of Mar Joseph, the people were divided into two parties. Mar Joseph appealed, concerning this matter, to the Viceroy of Goa, who wrote letters to Cochin, and caused Mar Abraham to be seized, and thrown into prison. He was afterwards put on board ship, to be sent to Europe. But the ship touching at a certain coast, (Mosambique, then belonging to the Portuguese,) he made his escape, and again reached Mosul. From that place, with a most persevering courage, he travelled overland to Rome.

There, in 1560, he engaged to conform to the Romish Church, and received consecration to the office of Metrani, from Pope Pius IV. He set out on his return to India; but on his arrival at Venice, it was discovered by the people of that city, that he had never been regularly ordained Priest: and by command of the Pope, whom he had deceived, he was made Priest with all the usual ceremonies.

During Mar Abraham's absence, Mar Joseph threw off the disguise, and taught the old doctrines which he had abjured when in Portugal, swearing that he would never teach them again. When this was known to Pope Pius V. he wrote to Goa in 1567, commanding that Mar Joseph should be deposed, imprisoned, and sent to Rome. He arrived there, and died within a few days afterwards.

When Mar Abraham reached Goa, with the power conferred on him by the Pope, the authorities of Goa did not acknowledge him; but said it was necessary for them to write to the Pope whom he had deceived, to give him better information. They placed Mar Abraham in a convent, from whence, however, he escaped, and was received with ecstasies of joy by the Syrian Christians, who had meantime endured great persecutions from the Portuguese, and were now instructed by him according to their ancient faith.

Intelligence of this reached Pope Gregory XIII., who addressed a letter to Mar Abraham in 1578, commanding him to attend a Council which should he held in Goa; and furnished him with a letter of safe conduct, engaging that no harm should happen to him.

He went, because it was impossible to escape from the Portuguese, whose authority was now paramount in India. He there took an oath that he would never again teach the old doctrine. He was obliged to promise that he would be obedient to the Romish Church; and that he would cause all the so-called heretical books written in the Syriac language, to be sent to Goa, that they might be burnt. He acknowledged his error, that when, on his return from Rome, he had a second time ordained his Priests, according to the form prescribed to him there, he had not used wine, but had administered an empty cup, with the bread: it was on this account decided that the ordination was void; he had, therefore, to ordain his Priests a third time, in the presence of certain Jesuits, who understood the Syriac language.

When Mar Abraham returned to his own people, with the exception that he ordained his Priests in the way which had been prescribed by the Council, he continued to do all things as he had done them before. Some days afterwards, he wrote a letter to his Patriarch in Mosul, informing him, that the Portuguese were continually beating at his head, as a hammer at an anvil, and that he had, therefore, been under the necessity of attending the Council in Goa. This epistle fell into the hands of the Portuguese.

At that time, a Syrian, whose name was Mar Simeon, came to Malayala. He professed to have been sent by the Patriarch of Mosul, to supersede Mar Abraham. He was immediately joined by a great number of the people, and assumed the office of Metrani, in the town of Nadaturutti. Great feuds, in consequence, arose between him and Mar Abraham. The Syrian churches were convulsed and divided. Mar Abraham complained to Goa, and the Portuguese afforded him their patronage and protection.

Mar Simeon yielded to the persuasion of certain Monks, and went first to Cochin, and then to Goa; from whence he was sent to Portugal and to Rome.

In 1685, Pope Sixtus V. decided that Mar Simeon was not a Metrani, and caused him to be sent to Portugal. From a convent in Lisbon, Mar Simeon wrote several letters to India, stating that he was the true Metrani. One of them fell into the hands of Menezes, Archbishop of Goa, in 1599, who immediately sent it to the chief Inquisitor in Lisbon. There is no doubt that, had Mar Simeon been then living, he would have been condemned to suffer death.

At that time Mar Abraham acted without disguise. In 1590, he was invited to attend a Council in Goa. He returned for answer, that "a cat, once bitten by a serpent, would be afraid at the mere sight of a piece of cord." *

Pope Clement VIII. having been made acquainted with all these circumstances, addressed a letter, on the 27th of January, 1595, to Alexis de Menezes, an Augustinian Monk, who was about to proceed to Goa as Archbishop, directing that if Mar Abraham was the guilty person he had been represented to be, he should depose him, and appoint some Romish Ecclesiastic in his place. This, Gouvea, one of his own order, has recorded in his Memoir of Menezes.

Whilst Menezes was Archbishop of Goa, he laboured more to reduce the Syrian Christians to the authority of the Pope, than in any other supposed duty of his office.

When Menezes arrived in India, he inquired into every circumstance relating to Mar Abraham; and, having ascertained that he had applied to Mosul for another Metrani, he gave the strictest orders that no Syrian, Persian, or Armenian Priest should enter India from any quarter, without his permission. All travellers, both going and returning, were therefore closely examined; and one, who was discovered, was sent back by the way he came.

On the 17th of December, 1597, a letter was addressed to Menezes, who was at that time absent from Goa, informing him that Mar Abraham was dead. He immediately conse-

* A reply which would be well understood by those to whom it was addressed. Some serpents, when at rest, have very much the appearance of a piece of cord. Father Martin, who is often quoted, says, "When I had been two days in Aoor, after assisting in the evening, with Father Bouchet, at the prayers and other pious exercises, usually offered up in the church, we entered the room where two of our Fathers, who were come to pay me a visit, were saying their breviary by the light of a small lamp. I then fancied I saw, in the middle of the room, a kind of rope, in the form of a horse's halter; whereupon I took it up in order to carry it to the lamp, and there examine whether it was good for any thing. But how great was my surprise, when I found that my supposed rope was a serpent, which was raising itself up in order to bite me. In my fright I shook it from me, and it was killed that instant. I wonder I did not perceive the motion of the serpent sooner; or, that it did not bite me the moment I put my fingers to it. But this would have cost me my life, the bite of the serpent in question being found mortal."

crated Francisco Roz, a Jesuit, as his successor. But after he had returned to Goa in the month of May, it was decided, in assembled Council, that the office should be conferred on the venerable Archdeacon George, whom Mar Abraham had appointed to succeed him, and who was much esteemed by the Syrian Christians. The above-mentioned Francisco Roz, and another of the same order, were therefore sent to help the Archdeacon, and to obtain his signature to a statement containing the doctrines peculiar to Rome. The Archdeacon replied, that he had no need of help; and he also desired a delay of four months before he should give his signature. Within that time he hoped that a new Metrani would arrive from Mosul. The Syrian Christians afterwards assembled a Council in Angamallee, their principal city, and caused it to be reported every where that they had sworn to continue steadfast in their ancient faith; and that they would not renounce it, even at the cost of life itself.

Towards the close of the year 1597, Archbishop Menezes wrote to announce that he himself was about to pay them a visit. The Archdeacon, with a view to prevent him, returned as answer, that if any one not a Jesuit were sent to him, he would give his signature. The Archbishop accordingly sent a Franciscan; and the Archdeacon wrote a statement, professing himself a Catholic; that he believed as the holy Church believed; and that he held that the Pope was the universal Pastor of the Church. But he omitted the word "Roman;" and the affair remained unsettled.

On the 27th of December, 1598, Archbishop Menezes set out from Goa; and on the 1st of February, 1599, he reached Cochin. He immediately summoned the Syrian Archdeacon to appear before him. The Archdeacon, with his Council, feared that the Portuguese would place some restrictions on the pepper trade, in which his Christians were engaged. They found also in their records, that it was not against their ecclesiastical law for a foreign Metrani to conduct divine service in their churches. Prepared by these considerations, he collected a force of three thousand men, and proceeded to Cochin. He and his Cassanars fell on their knees before the Archbishop, and kissed his hand; and were received by him with great favour.

PROCEEDINGS AT VEIPPICOTTAH.

The Archbishop desired the Archdeacon to accompany him to Veippicottah. He there delivered a sermon on John x. 1, to the effect that all Ministers who were not appointed by the Pope were "thieves and robbers." The Archbishop attended the daily morning and evening prayers of the Syrian Christians; but at first he was not aware, that, when they prayed for the Bishop of Babylon, they styled him the universal Pastor of the Church. When he was informed of this, he assembled the Jesuits, and the Archdeacon and his Cassanars. He pronounced, that the Pope was the only head of the church on earth; and declared, that the Bishop of Babylon was a heretic. He directed a denunciation to be read in Latin, and to be interpreted into Malayalim; and then commanded the Archdeacon and his Cassanars to sign it. When they hesitated to consent to this, the Archbishop, looking at the Archdeacon, said, in a threatening manner, "Sign it, Father; for 'now also the axe is laid to the root of the tree!'" The Archdeacon and his Cassanars said nothing in reply, but affixed their signatures.

When the Syrian Christians heard tidings of this event, they assembled in vast numbers, and offered the most determined opposition. The Archdeacon endeavoured to pacify them; but they declared they would not forsake their ancient faith, though it might cost them the loss of all things, and even of life itself. On this account the Portuguese themselves reproached the Archbishop. But he replied, "It is the Lord's business; he will direct;" and, quitting Veippicottah, he went to Paroor.

PAROOR.*

The inhabitants of that town were greatly incensed by what they had heard, and assembled in the church at which he had arrived, purposely to oppose his proceedings. When he prepared to administer confirmation to them, they cried out, "We do not want this ceremony, which the Portuguese have invented for the purpose of making us slaves." The

* Buchanan gives the following interesting description of Paroor:—"Not far from Cranganore is the town of Paroor, where there is an ancient Syrian church, which bears the name of the Apostle Thomas. It is supposed to be the oldest in Malabar, and is still used for divine service. I took a drawing of it. The tradition among the Syrians is, that the Apostle continued at this place for a time, before he went to preach at Mielapoor and St. Thomas's Mount, on the coast of Coromandel, where he was put to death. The fact is certainly of little consequence; but, I am satisfied, we have as good authority for believing that the Apostle Thomas died in India, as that the Apostle Peter died at Rome."

Archdeacon then went out, and brought in eight or ten children, whom he placed before the Archbishop, and desired him to confirm them.

THE NORTHERN DISTRICT.

The Archbishop then visited the five principal churches of the Syrian Christians to the north of Cochin. He preached a sermon, according to his practice, on two subjects; first, "the errors in doctrine held by the Syrian Christians;" and secondly, "the necessity of submitting to the authority of the Pope."

THE SOUTHERN DISTRICT.

Finding that he was ill received in those places, he returned to Cochin on March 1st, 1599; and, as the Christians of the south bordered more closely on the Portuguese, he proceeded to Pirkadu, south of Cochin, and administered confirmation without the consent of the Christians of that place. Thus at that time, and often subsequently, he violated his own written engagement, to which he had affixed his seal, not to interfere with the Syrians in their churches, until they should have held a General Synod.

The native King of Cochin, fearing that the Archbishop intended to make these Christians subject to the King of Portugal, imposed on them a tax, to be levied at certain periods; and commanded them to continue attached to the Archdeacon. The Archbishop then proceeded to Udiamper.

UDIAMPER.*

Udiamper, in former times, had been the residence of some of the Metranis of that country. The Archbishop caused it to be published, that as there had been no Metrani in that place for the space of two years, he would confer ordination; and sent a message desiring the Archdeacon to come to him.

The Archdeacon wrote in reply, that a Council must assemble in order to decide whether the Archbishop should bear sway amongst them; and that his present proposal was

* Udiamper is thus noticed by Buchanan: "In a tour to the interior, we first visited Udiamper, or, as the Portuguese writers call it, Diamper. This was formerly the residence of Beliarte, King of the Christians; and here is the Syrian church at which Archbishop Menezes, from Goa, convened the Synod of the Syrian Clergy in 1599, when he burned the Syriac and Chaldaic books. The Syrians report, that while the flames ascended, he went round the church in procession, chanting a song of triumph."—*Christian Researches.*

contrary to the agreement he had formerly entered into. The Archbishop answered, "I act by command of his Holiness the Pope; to whom all the churches in the world ought to yield obedience."

The Archdeacon then charged all his Christians, under pain of a curse, to have no intercourse with the Archbishop. When this direction was known in Udiamper, the inhabitants of that place said contemptuously to the Archbishop, "The confirmation you administer is unnecessary. Our children had their heads anointed with oil, after their baptism." But the Archbishop threatened them with the power of the Portuguese, as superior both to that of the Archdeacon and of the heathen Chiefs; and proceeded to confer ordination on thirty-seven persons, without requiring any qualification.

NADATURUTTI.

Before the last week in Lent, he came to the town of Nadaturutti. The next day he invited on board his vessel some of the most respectable Christians of the place, and won them over by a great show of kindness, and by large gifts of money. He procured the interest of Mapilleimattu and Mapilleimaney, two of the principal inhabitants, who proved of great service to him.

He celebrated Palm Sunday with great pomp; but the Cassanars and the Christians took no part in it.

On Holy Thursday, a Jesuit preached in the Malayalim language.

On the next day, Good Friday, the ceremony of worshipping the crucifix was conducted with much display. A Cassanar, who had been cursed by the Archbishop, happening to enter the church, he caused him to be expelled with great tumult. In the evening many of the Cassanars, and some other of the Chiefs, came to the Archbishop, renounced, by oath, the Patriarch of Babylon, and were received into the Romish Church. Thus the inhabitants of Nadaturutti were the first to submit to the Archbisbop. On this occasion he rejoiced greatly, and considered how he might displace Archdeacon George, and introduce Thomas Curia, his relative, into the office of Metrani.

On Saturday, he conferred Priests' orders on many persons who had before been rejected. Francisco Roz, the Jesuit, met him, and said, "A few months ago I celebrated mass in this place, and when I elevated the host, all the Christians covered their eyes, and would not look upon it. When I showed them the image of the holy Virgin, they said, 'We want not that abomination! We are Christians! We are not idolaters!' They also chastised one of their young men for mentioning the name of the Pope in his prayer."

The Archbishop celebrated the festival of Easter with great magnificence; and on that occasion, those of the northern district, who had hitherto been stoutly opposed to him, as well as those of the southern district, yielded obedience to the Romish Church.

After the service of the day, the Christians held a love-feast, called *nerka*, or "concord." This feast used to be celebrated with corn and prepared fruit, of which a double portion was allotted to their Pastors. (1 Tim. v. 17.) When the Archbishop was invited to join them, he said he was unable to attend, begged them to excuse him, and gave them his blessing. They then sent him plantain-fruit and honey-fritters as his portion.

The next day he proceeded to Nagupeli, near to Varandoor; and admitted many persons into the Romish Church by confirmation.

MOLANDURUTTI.

The same day, the Archbishop went for the second time to Molandurutti. But the King of Cochin had levied a new tax on the Christians; and had sent some of their chief men, bound as prisoners, to the Archdeacon. Therefore, not one of them joined the Archbishop, as they had done on the former occasion.

The Archbishop went again to Udiamper. In the course of an interview which he had there with the Prime Minister of the King of Cochin, he angrily struck his staff three times upon the ground, and sharply reprimanded both him and his master; threatening that the King of Portugal would be revenged. The Minister then assembled the Christians, and very strictly enjoined them to submit in all things to the Archbishop. By this threat of coercion, the Archbishop induced a great number to submit to him without delay.

The next day he administered confirmation to those Christians, and said to them, "I have cursed the Archdeacon, who has joined himself to heathen Chiefs in opposition to Christianity, and refuses to submit to his Holiness the Pope, Christ's Vicar upon earth. You must abandon him, and receive me as your head." To this the people appeared to assent. In the evening he visited the sick, and distributed alms to the poor; and appealed to them whether this was not conduct suitable to their Metrani.

When the Archdeacon heard that the Archbishop had succeeded in three principal places, he was greatly perplexed. He wrote an answer to a letter which the Archbishop had addressed to him some time before; prayed that his fault might be forgiven, and that he might be admitted into the Romish Church. The Archbishop was overjoyed at this, and wrote to him that he accepted his submission, on condition that he should give his signature, and swear to ten particulars, which he would specify.

He afterwards went to Cochin, and engaged the Governor of that place to use his influence with the King of Cochin, that he might assist him in reducing all the Syrian Christians to the power of the Pope; and then went to Nodungaloor, and, with the help of the Jesuits, wrote and arranged the particulars necessary for the Council, which was about to assemble.

When the Archdeacon saw that there was no protection for him, he went to meet the Archbishop in Veippicottah; and, falling at his feet, he said, "I have sinned against heaven, and in thy sight." He entreated him to forgive his fault. The Archbishop accepted his submission, and raised him to his feet. He afterwards made an agreement with him privately, as to the proceedings to be adopted at the approaching Council at Udiamper.

THE COUNCIL OF UDIAMPER.*

On the 20th of June, 1599, the Archdeacon and all the Cassanars, and the other Elders of the Syrian Christians, the Archbishop, the Governor of Cochin, many Romish Priests, and some chief persons among the Portuguese, assembled as a Council in Udiamper.

This Council met together nine times successively. Many of the sacred truths held by the Syrian Christians were perverted; and all the doctrines of the Council of Trent, as before described, were confirmed and adopted.

The holy Scriptures, in the Syriac language, were altered and corrupted in many passages, to make them agree with the Latin version.

It was determined, that the King of Portugal should receive

* For a most full account of the Council or Synod of Udiamper, and a translation into English of its Acts and Decrees, see the second volume of Hough's "History of Christianity in India."

those Christians under his protection; and that they in return should defend the holy Catholic faith. Thus were they reduced to a nominal conformity to the Romish Church; and, in reality, were brought into subjection to the King of Portugal. It was with reference to this proceeding that the King of Cochin called confirmation "the Portuguese mask."

Marriage was thenceforth forbidden to those Cassanars who yet remained unmarried, under penalty of a curse. It was also decreed, that the second marriages of those Cassanars who were already married, and the marriages of such as had been united to widows, were null and void. The case of such as were married for the first time the members of the Council determined to refer to the decision of his Holiness the Pope. It was also decreed at the same time, that married men were not eligible to discharge the functions of the Priest's office; but that those who would divorce their wives might continue in the priesthood. (Matt. v. 32.)

Whilst the Council thus proceeded, many of the Christians uttered the bitterest complaints of being forcibly separated from the Metrani, to whom they had so long been subject; but they complained in vain; for the Archbishop had taken an oath from full three parts of the Cassanars assembled in Council, at the time of their ordination.

At the close of the Council seventy-five Priests were appointed to seventy-five churches in the neighbourhood of Udiamper, according to the ceremonies of the Romish Church. Previous to this there had been no distinction among them, except the difference occasioned by age and seniority.

On the 26th of June, 1599, the Council closed. Its proceedings were attested by the Archbishop, by one hundred and fifty-three Cassanars, and by six hundred and sixty other persons.

The Archbishop had especially won over eight of the Cassanars; these and certain Jesuits introduced the rites of the Romish Church among those Christians.

Under the pretence that the baptism which the Cassanar of the place had administered according to the rites of his own Church, was void, Menezes privately re-baptized all the inhabitants. He visited the churches in other places for the same purpose; he took an oath from those Cassanars who had not attended the Council, and divorced them from the women whom they had married.

On the 3d of July, he observed the holy-day of St. Thomas. But he directed that Mar Sapor and Mar Pheroz, or Beroses, the Teachers who came from Babylon in the year 822, should be no longer numbered in the catalogue of saints.

ANGAMALEE.

He also proceeded to Molandurutti and to Angamalee, and reformed the churches in those places.*

* Buchanan gives the following interesting notice, headed,—

"*Angamalee, a Syrian town, containing three churches. January,* 1807.—I have penetrated once more inland to visit the Syrian churches. At the town of Cenotta, I was surprised to meet with Jews and Christians in the same street. The Jews led me first to their synagogue, and allowed me to take away some manuscripts for money. The Syrian Christians then conducted me to their ancient church. I afterwards sat down on an eminence above the town to contemplate this interesting spectacle; a Jewish synagogue and a Christian church, standing over against each other, exhibiting, as it were, during many revolving ages, the LAW and the GOSPEL to the view of the heathen people.

"Angamalee is one of the most remote of the Syrian towns in this direction, and is situated on a high land. This was once the residence of the Syrian Bishop. The inhabitants told me, that when Tippoo Sultan invaded Travancore, a detachment of his cavalry penetrated to Angamalee, where they expected to find great wealth, from its ancient fame. Being Mahometans, they expressed their abhorrence of the Christian religion by destroying one of the lesser churches, and stabling their horses in the great church. In this place I have found a good many valuable manuscripts. I had been led to suppose, from the statement of the Portuguese historians, that possibly all the Syrian manuscripts of the Bible had been burned by the Romish Church at the Synod of Diamper, in 1599; but this was not the case. The Inquisitors condemned many books to the flames; but they saved the Bible, being content to order that the Syriac Scriptures should be amended agreeably to the Vulgate of Rome. But many Bibles and other volumes were not produced at all. The Syriac version of the Scriptures was brought to India, according to the popular belief, before the year 325. Some of their present copies are certainly of ancient date. Though written on a strong thick paper, like that of some MSS. in the British Museum, commonly called Eastern paper, the ink has, in several places, eat through the material in the exact form of the letter. In other copies, where the ink had less of a corroding quality, it has fallen off, and left a dark vestige of the letter; faint, indeed, but not in general illegible.

"There is a volume which was deposited in one of the remote churches near the mountains, which merits a particular description. It contains the Old and New Testaments, engrossed on strong vellum, in large folio, having three columns in a page; and is written with beautiful accuracy. The character is Estrangelo Syriac; and the words of every book are *numbered*. But the volume has suffered injury from time or neglect. In certain places the ink has been totally obliterated from the page, and left the parchment in its state of natural whiteness; but the letters can, in general, be distinctly traced from the impress of the pen, or from the partial corrosion of the ink. I scarcely expected that the Syrian church would have parted with this manuscript. But the Bishop was pleased to

Angamalee had been the residence of the Metrani from the remotest antiquity. The inhabitants received the Archbishop with great honour, and spread cloths of silk over the way by which he approached. He continued there for a considerable time, and administered baptism to some native Malayalas. *He committed to the flames many of the ancient books written in Syriac, which he found in the Metrani's library*, and acted in the same way in other places.*

He determined that for the future the Metrani should have his residence in Kodungaloor, (Cranganore,) because, at that time there was a Portuguese fort there. From that place he proceeded to Tiruvankodu (Travancore).

When the Archbishop had visited the churches round that neighbourhood, he returned to Kaduturutti, the first-fruit of his labours; and conferred priests' orders on many Cassanars.

The Archbishop then heard that Philip II., King of Spain

present it to me, 'It will be safer in your hands than in our own,' alluding to the revolutions in Hindostan. 'And yet,' said he, 'we have kept it, as some think, for near a thousand years.' 'I wish,' said I, 'that England may be able to keep it a thousand years.' In looking over it, I found the very first proposed emendation of Dr. Kennicott, (Gen. iv. 8,) in this manuscript; and no doubt it is the right reading.'"

The Doctor adds, in a note, "Most of the manuscripts which I collected among the Syrian Christians, I have presented to the University of Cambridge; and they are now deposited in the public library of that University, together with the copper-plate *fac-similes* of the Christian and Jewish tablets."—*Christian Researches.*

In another place, he says, "The cathedral church of Angamalee is the largest of the Syrian edifices, and contains the tombs of Bishops and Archbishops for many centuries. As I approached the town in the evening, I heard the sullen roar of the great bell reverberating through the mountains. When the Romish Archbishop Menezes visited this place in 1599, the Christians strewed the way up the hill with flowers as he advanced. And yet he came to burn their ancient library and archives. As the flame ascended, the old Priests wept; but they were obliged to hide their tears, dreading the Inquisition at Goa. The Archbishop presented himself next day to the multitude, arrayed in his pontificals, resplendent with gold and precious stones. To this day they have a lively tradition of the splendour of his robes blazing in the sun, and forming a striking contrast with the plain white garments of their own primitive church."

* "If any thing can consign to perpetual infamy the name and progress of this barbarian, surely it must be the destruction of so many ancient and invaluable documents of the Christian church. It is indeed painful to follow a man thus carrying misery and destruction along with him, and dispensing them on the right hand and on the left, as his ambition or his ignorance might suggest; and, what is worse, for the propagation of a spiritual tyranny, which, it was hoped, would reach to the utmost boundaries of the earth."—*Professor Lee's History.*

and Portugal, had died during the year; and, it being necessary for him to return to Goa, he was obliged to desist from further visitation of the churches.

He assembled the Cassanars of the neighbourhood of Cochin, and the chief persons of the churches round about; and announced to them the appointment of the Archdeacon to act as Metrani, until the Pope should appoint some one else to the office. He also associated with him, as his helpers, Francisco Roz, and another Jesuit. Archbishop Menezes then set out for Goa, where he arrived on the 16th of November, 1599. He thus completed his journey, and his visitation of the Syrian churches, within the short space of eleven months.

Menezes continued in Goa three years, in the exercise of the authority of the deceased Viceroy. After his return to Europe he was made Viceroy of Portugal; he died in the city of Madrid. The Spaniard, Manuel de Faria, has thus written concerning him: "If this celebrated Prelate had not returned to Spain, he would certainly have been reckoned in the number of the Saints. Men generally suppose, that he lost that distinguished honour, because of the difficulty of discharging perfectly the duties of the high offices which he sought, or which were spontaneously conferred upon him."

In 1601, by command of Pope Clement VIII., the abovementioned Francisco Roz was appointed as the first Latin Bishop over the Syrian Christians. For more than a thousand years previous, they had been governed by Syrian Metranis only.

In 1605, Pope Paul V. removed the seat of the Metrani from Angamalee to Cranganore; and made the diocese subject to the Archbishop of Goa.* And thus, for about sixty years, the Jesuits governed the Syrian Churches. But as Vincent Maria, a German Carmelite Monk, has written, "Those Bishops oppressed them as though they had been slaves.

* Dr. Buchanan visited Cranganore on December 9th, 1807. He says, "This is that celebrated place of Christian antiquity where the Apostle Thomas is said to have landed, when he first arrived in India, from Aden, in Arabia. There was formerly a town and fort at Cranganore, the Portuguese having once thought of making it the emporium of their commerce in India; but both are now in ruins. There is, however, one substantial relic of its greatness. There is an Archbishop at Cranganore, and subject to him there are forty-five churches; many of which I entered. In some of them the worship is conducted with as much decorum as in the Romish churches of the west of Ireland."—*Christian Researches.*

Their dominion was intolerable, but it nevertheless continued for a long time."

More particularly Garcia, the last Bishop, who came to the see in 1654, held the Syrians in such contempt, and treated them so insolently, that they resorted to extreme measures. Twelve Cassanars conferred the office of Metrani on George Cambu, the successor of George the Archdeacon. By an old canon law in their book of church discipline, permission is given to adopt such a mode of proceeding in case of extremity. In like manner, from early antiquity, it has been the custom for the Patriarch of Alexandria to receive consecration from the Presbyters of the church.

When this affair came to the knowledge of Pope Alexander VII., he was of opinion that the schism had been occasioned by the mismanagement of the Jesuits. With the view of repairing the breach, he immediately dispatched four Carmelites to India. One of them was the aforesaid Vincent Maria, who wrote an account of the whole in the Italian language.*

In 1657, he and another arrived at Cannanore, and proceeded by land to Calicut. Previously to that, the Syrians had already addressed letters to the three Patriarchs of Babylon, Alexandria, and Antioch, requesting them to send a Metrani. The Patriarch of Alexandria, whose residence was at Cairo in Egypt, sent one, whose name was Abdallah.

When Abdallah landed at Surat, two Capuchin Monks of that place gave notice of his arrival to the Visitors of the Inquisition in Goa. He was apprehended at Mielapoor, and sent by the Jesuits to Cochin. When this fact was known to the Syrian Christians of that place, they rose, and sought means to rescue by force their newly-arrived Metrani. But the Portuguese of Cochin closed the gates of the fort, and

* "*Ill Viaggio all' Indie Orientali, del P. F. Vincenzo Maria, di S. Caterina da Siena. Fol. Roma*, 1673.

"A Voyage to the East Indies, performed by F. Vincent Maria, of St. Catherine of Siena, Procurator-General of the bare-footed Carmelites, and sent to India, by way of Turkey and Persia, by the Pope, together with F. Joseph of St. Mary, who also wrote an account of his travels. This author divides his work into five books. The first and last contain the journal, and an account of all the remarkable things he saw on his way going and returning. The second treats of the affairs of the Malabar Christians. The third and fourth, of the various natives of India, their manners, customs, wealth, government, religion, plants, animals, &c. The whole is a faithful, exact, and learned account of all things remarkable in those regions, and has scarcely ever been equalled."—*Churchill*.

suddenly sent Abdallah away to Goa, where he suffered death as a heretic, by sentence of the Inquisition.* The Syrians were justly indignant at this outrage, and chased away the Jesuits from every part of their country. They entered into a compact that they would be subject in all things to their own Archdeacon only, whom they acknowledged as chief.

The Carmelites, before mentioned, saw all this, and sought to set it aside. Canbu, the Archdeacon, requested them to consecrate him. They replied that they were not Bishops; that if he wished consecration, he must lay aside the office he had assumed, and humbly ask pardon for the offence of which he had been guilty.

Vincent Maria proceeded to Cochin, and requested the Governors of that place to afford him their assistance. He went afterwards to Cranganore, and the inhabitants of that place upbraided him with the murder of Abdallah. But others of that Church received him with honour, and declared that they only rejected the dominion of the Jesuits.

The Carmelites went to Mangattu; they assembled the Cassanars of the churches belonging to that district, and held a Council, at which those churches consented to submit to them, until another Metrani could come to them from Rome.

When the Carmelites returned to Cochin, they were informed by letter from Goa, that they must give up their Mission, and proceed elsewhere. But they pledged themselves not to exercise their office in any places belonging to the Portuguese; and continued to prosecute the object of their Mission. But the Jesuits greatly obstructed them. Garcia, the Jesuit Archbishop, wrote to the Carmelites to be attentive to his interests. They replied that they dili-

* A friend of mine, the Rev. John Hands, many years Missionary of the London Society, at the Bellary Station, which he had the honour to commence under circumstances of peculiar discouragement and difficulty, informed me that he had twice visited old Goa: once, in the year 1822, when the Inquisition was still standing, but closely shut up. He with much difficulty obtained admission, when he visited and examined the cells and dungeons, all of which, save one, he found empty and open. One was securely closed, in which, he was afterwards told, the instruments of torture, &c., were deposited. But at his second visit, in the year 1827, the vast pile of building described by Dellon and Buchanan, was hastening to ruin. There was no difficulty in obtaining access to it; but such was the extent of its dilapidation, that it was not considered safe to venture into some parts of it, and it was not without difficulty he discovered the passages leading down to the gloomy dungeons. So may every building perish, erected to the service of the mis-called *holy Inquisition!*

gently kept that object in view. He showed their letter to some of the Syrian Christians, and by this kind of expedient he induced many persons to secede from them.

COUNCIL OF RAPULIN.

In the year 1657, it was determined, with the consent of the Archdeacon, that a Council should assemble in the town of Rapulin. They met after Ascension-day, and the Archdeacon thus addressed the people: "It is not fit that our ancient Church, which has for so many hundred years conducted its own affairs independently of the Portuguese, should anew submit to the yoke which it has thrown off. We all know that the friendship of Archbishop Menezes was forced upon us. Other Churches of the East have not submitted to the Latin Church. Shall we alone submit? Perhaps they will say, that consecration to the office of Metrani conferred by Presbyters, is invalid. But do not the Cardinals of Rome consecrate the Pope himself?" By this address, he persuaded the people not to join the Carmelites, and retained them in his own interest.

Subsequently, however, that people again separated into two parties. On the 22d of July, many of the Cassanars fell prostrate before the Carmelites, acknowledged their sin of schism, and received absolution from them. The people of Mangattu, a district in which there was a principal church, refused to submit. But the Carmelites formed a treaty with the heathen Chief of that district, and awed the Christians into submission.

On September 8th, the representatives of twenty-four churches assembled in the town of Muttan, and held a Council. It was there decided that the consecration to the office of Metrani, which had been conferred on the Archdeacon, was no consecration. It seemed as though they were certain that the Archdeacon must yield to this decision. But when a letter was sent, warning him that if he submitted, he would meet with the same fate as Abdallah, there was again an end of the whole affair.

On the 23d of September, another Council assembled in a church near Cochin. The Jesuits directed that on that occasion, the Carmelites should publish a Bull, addressed to those Christians by the Pope, in which they were commanded again to yield obedience to the Jesuit Archbishop. But this direction was altogether disagreeable to the

Carmelites, and they only read the Bull which the Pope had committed to them. Joseph,* one of their number, received the office of Metrani : this did not meet with the approbation either of the Jesuit Archbishop, or of the Archdeacon.

The Carmelites finding that they did not succeed in any quarter, returned to Cochin, and again assembled a Council, on the first Sunday of our Lord's Advent ; and, taking leave of the forty-four Cassanars who had united with them, they embarked for Italy, on Christmas-day.

Hyacinth, one of the four Carmelites, returned to Malayala, on the 10th of March, 1658, by Portuguese vessels ; and for two years presided over those Syrian Christians, who still continued in communion with the Romish Church. He discharged the duties of his office, by aid from the heathen Chiefs. He died at an advanced age, on the 8th of February, 1660.

In 1659, Garcia, the Jesuit Archbishop, died in Cranganore. On the 16th of December, 1659, the office of Metrani, which the fore-mentioned Joseph, the Carmelite, had received in India, was confirmed to him in the city of Rome.

When he was setting out on his journey from Rome, on the 7th of February, 1660, Cardinal Barberini, wrote, and sent to this Metrani of the Syrian Christians, the Bull of plenary indulgence, which Pope Paul V. had issued in 1607. It was of small importance that the Bull was out of date ; according to that Bull, any one who has performed certain ceremonies, attended certain masses, and made certain gifts, may obtain forgiveness of sins, for sixty, or a hundred, or two hundred, or three hundred days ; or for three or seven years.

Towards the end of April, 1661, he arrived in India, and

* "*Prima Speditione all' Indie Orientali dell P. F. Gioseppe di Santa Maria,*" 4to, *Roma*, 1668.

"This author was sent by Pope Alexander VII., to the Malabar Christians of St. Thomas ; he was a bare-footed Carmelite, and has in this book left us a most curious production. He gives a very particular account of the places and people he saw, birds, beasts, and other animals ; and of the philosophy of the Brahmans, their secrets, and of all the other Malabars, as also of the infinite number of their gods. Hence he proceeds further to treat of the vast empire of the Mogul, of the pearl-fishery, of the Sabeans about Bassora, who pretend they received their religion from St. John the Baptist ; and concludes with the errors of the Jacobites, Nestorians, Greeks, Armenians, and other eastern sects."—*Churchill.*

was received at Cochin with great honour. The Jesuits in that place, and the Archdeacon, were much afraid of him. He sent two Carmelites to Cranganore, and commanded them to prepare the great church in that place for his reception.

On the 22d of August, he made his first visitation to the church in Muttān; and on the 26th, to the churches in Pirkādu, with great pomp.

Afterwards the Archdeacon came to Molandurutti: he and the Italian Metrani sent certain persons to the town of Tiruppuvanattār: and when the Brahman Ministers of the Queen of Cochin had assembled, they held a Council for a whole month. But the pride and cruelty of the Italian Carmelite Metrani were the cause of an entire separation among those Christians. The Metrani himself, in the History which he composed, wrote as follows: "All the devices which Luther, and Calvin, and other heretics invented, were resorted to in that assembly; and the force of arms was necessary in order to raise the fallen truth."

A Magistrate of the Cochin country then raised a corps of one hundred men, and surrounded the church which the Archdeacon occupied in Molandurutti. The commander of the Portuguese also came from Cochin with great force. One night the Archdeacon made his escape, and the Italian Metrani has recorded, that he was much grieved at the escape of a man who was fit prey for the Inquisition; but that his rage was somewhat appeased by the circumstance, that although they could not burn his body, they had committed some of his pillaged property to the flames.

The Dutch turned these disturbances to their own advantage. In January, 1662, they seized upon Cranganore, and the Syrian Christians joined neither them nor the Portuguese; but waited to see whether they should ever be delivered from their power. It appeared as though the blood of Abdallah, and other martyrs, cried aloud to heaven for vengeance.

When the Dutch took possession of Cochin, in 1663, Joseph, the Italian Metrani, was under the necessity of leaving, together with the Portuguese. He therefore transferred the office of Metrani to the Cassanar, Alexander Canpu, and introduced him to the Governor. On that account the Governor treated him with much respect, and greatly strengthened the interests of the Dutch, by means of the disunion between him and the Archdeacon.

In 1664, Baldæus, the Dutch Minister, who had been the

instrument of great spiritual benefit to the Christians of Ceylon,* addressed a letter to the Archdeacon, inviting him to meet him for the purpose of a friendly conference, on religious subjects. But he refused, alleging as a reason, that he was held in contempt; while his enemy Alexander Canpu was treated by the Dutch in Cochin with great honour.

On the 24th of January, 1664, the Italian Metrani, Joseph, embarked on his voyage from Goa; and arrived in Rome, on the 6th of May, 1665.

Subsequently to these events, the Portuguese Jesuit Superior in Ambalkattu, the Bishop of Cochin in Mampalli, and the Italian Carmelite Bishop, in Verapoli, have conducted the affairs of the Church of Rome in those quarters.†

* For an account of Baldæus and his labours, see above under the head of Ceylon.

† In December, 1806, Dr. Buchanan visited Verapoli, and gives the following information concerning it: "This is the residence of Bishop Raymondo, the Pope's Apostolical Vicar, in Malabar. There is a college here for the sacerdotal office, in which the students, from ten to twenty in number, are instructed in the Latin and Syriac languages. At Pulingunna there is another college, in which the Syriac alone is taught. Here I counted twelve students. The Apostolic Vicar superintends sixty-four churches; exclusive of the forty-five governed by the Archbishop of Cranganore, and exclusive of the large diocesses of the Bishops of Cochin, and of Quilon, whose churches extend to Cape Comorin, and are visible from the sea. The view of this assemblage of Christian congregations excited in my mind mingled sensations of pleasure and regret; of pleasure, to think that so many of the Hindoos have been rescued from the idolatry of Brahma, and its criminal worship; and of regret, when I reflected that there was not to be found among the whole body one copy of the Holy Bible.

"The Apostolical Vicar is an Italian, and corresponds with the Society *de propagandâ Fide*. He is a man of liberal manners, and gave me free access to the archives of Verapoli, which are upwards of two centuries old. In the library I found many volumes marked, *Liber hereticus prohibitus*. Almost every step I take in Christian India, I meet with a memento of the Inquisition. The Apostolical Vicar, however, does not acknowledge its authority, but places himself under British protection." Referring to the Doctor's intention to visit Goa, he said, "I do not know what you might do under the protection of a British force; but I should not like" (smiling, and pressing his capacious sides) "to trust *my* body in their hands."

"We then had some conversation on the subject of giving the Scriptures to the Roman Catholics. I visited the Bishop two or three times afterwards: at our last interview he said, 'I have been thinking of the good gift you are meditating for the native Christians; but, believe me, the Inquisition will endeavour to counteract your purposes by every means in their power.' I afterwards conversed with an intelligent native Priest, who was well acquainted with the state and character of the Christians, and asked him, whether he thought they would be happy

In 1676, the Archdeacon Thomas Canpu died; and Carmelites were afterwards sent from Rome, who were directed to appoint some one to succeed Alexander Canpu, in the office of Metrani. His namesake, Mar Thomas Canpu, afterwards became his successor.

In 1708, a Syrian Metrani, whose name was Mar Gabriel, arrived from Elias, the Patriarch of Mosul, to preside over the Christians of the northern district; and took charge of the twenty-five churches of Pallipoor.

In 1709, the above-mentioned Mar Thomas Canpu, the Metrani of those in the South, who had formerly joined the Romish Church, in a letter addressed to Ignatius, the Patriarch of Antioch, complained that Mar Gabriel asserted, that there were two natures and two persons in Christ; and requested him to send another Metrani to decide the difference which existed between them. (See the section which treats on the Nestorian controversy.) Moreover, there was this difference also,—that Mar Thomas celebrated the Eucharist with *amira*, leavened bread; and Mar Gabriel with *patira*, or unleavened bread.

It is believed that John, who came from Jerusalem, introduced that practice of the Greek church into the twenty-two churches, under the care of Mar Thomas; namely, the Armenian Mar Thomas Cana, in the fourth century of the Christian era; and Seren Perumāl, who rebuilt Calicut in the year 907,. and was afterwards King of Cranganore, gave a royal charter* to those Christians, constituting those in the

to obtain the Scriptures. '*Yes*,' answered he, '*those who have heard of them!*' I asked if he had got a Bible himself. 'No,' he said; 'but he had seen one at Goa.'"

* "There are ancient documents in Malabar, not less interesting than the Syrian manuscripts: certain tablets of brass, on which were engraved rights of nobility, and other privileges granted by a prince of a former age; the Christian tablets are six in number. They are composed of a mixed metal; the engraving on the largest plate is thirteen inches long, by about four broad. They are closely written; four of them on both sides of the plate, making, in all, eleven pages. On the plate reputed to be the oldest, there is writing perspicuously engraved in *nail-headed* or triangular-headed letters, resembling the Persepolitan or Babylonish. On the same plate, there is writing in another character, which is supposed to have no affinity with any existing character in Hindostan. The grant on this plate appears to have been witnessed by four Jews of rank, whose names are distinctly engraved in an old Hebrew character, resembling the alphabet called the Palmyrene; and to each name is prefixed the title of *Magen*, or chief, as the Jews translate it. It may be doubted whether there exists in the world any documents of

south district, Kulastripilleigl, or *children of the high caste woman;* and the Christian natives in the north district, Streepilleigl, or *children of the woman;* and thus a difference of caste obtained amongst them at an early period.

In 1711, the Christians in Malayala were found to be about one hundred thousand.

On the 6th of January, 1728, Mar Thomas returned an answer to a letter which had been addressed to him from Tranquebar, in 1727: in which he complained that one half of his people had joined the Fathers of San Paolo, (the Jesuits,) and the Carmelites.

He died in the same year, and they placed in his office his son-in-law, who bore the same name.

In 1730, another Metrani arrived in Surat from Babylon, to supply the place of Mar Gabriel, who had died that year. On that occasion, the Jesuit Superior, who was otherwise at enmity, and the Carmelite Bishop united, and prevented his coming.

May the Lord protect and save those our brethren, and restore them to their former prosperity!

so great length, which are of equal antiquity, and in such faultless preservation, as the Christian tablets of Malabar. As no person can be found in this country, who is able to translate the Christian Tablets, I have directed an engraver at Cochin, to execute on copper-plates a *facsimile* of the whole, for the purpose of transmitting copies to the learned Societies in Asia and Europe. The Christian and Jewish plates together make fourteen pages. A copy was sent in the first instance to the Pundits of the Shanskrit College, at Trichuir, by direction of the Rajah of Cochin: but they could not read the character."—*Christian Researches.*

THE END.